Shojo Beat

Märchen ✦ Prince

Volume 2

Story & Art by Matsuri Hino

Contents

MeruPuri: Märchen Prince

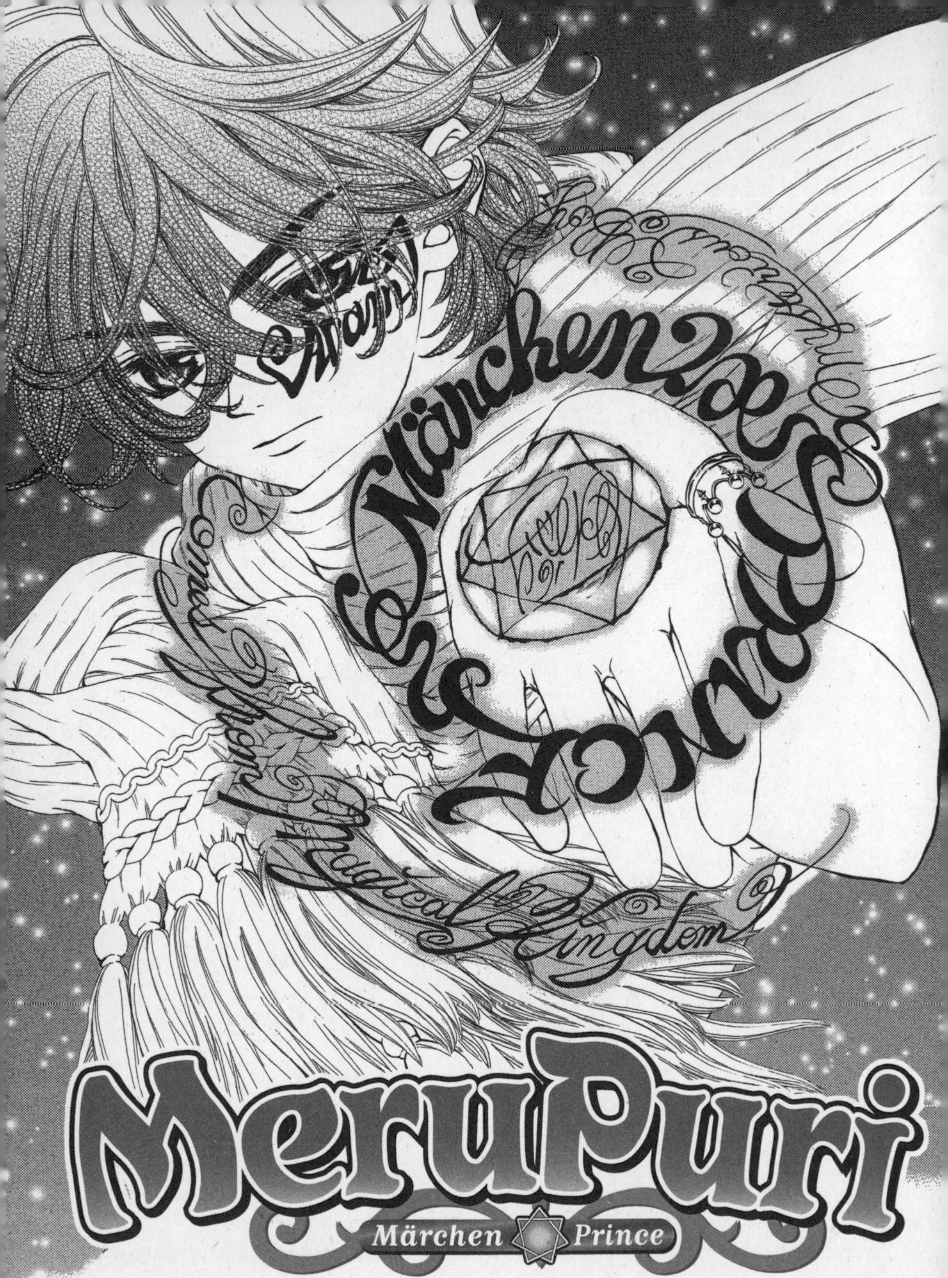

MeruPuri

Märchen Prince

CHAPTER 6

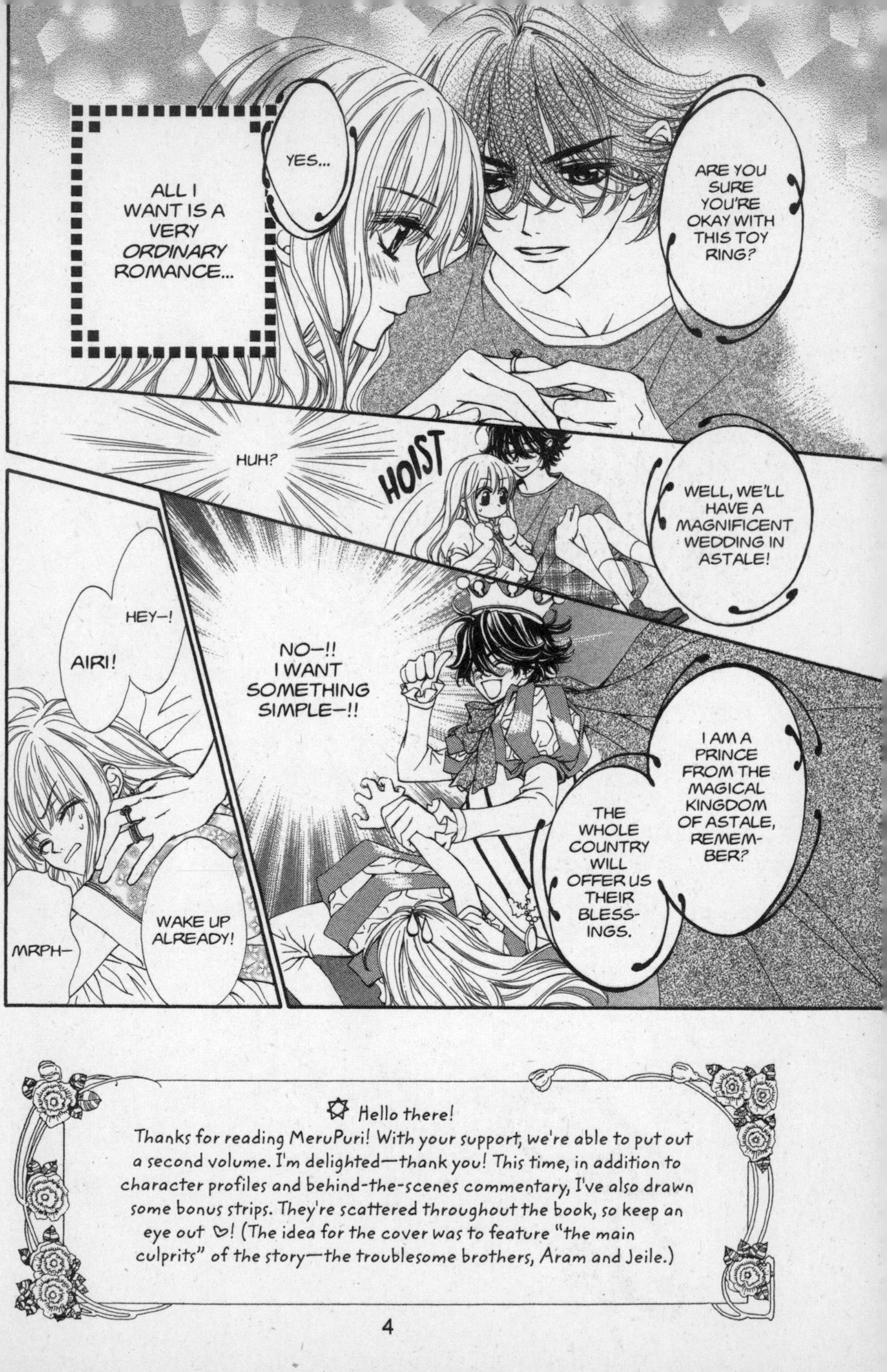
ARE YOU SURE YOU'RE OKAY WITH THIS TOY RING?
YES...
ALL I WANT IS A VERY ORDINARY ROMANCE...
WELL, WE'LL HAVE A MAGNIFICENT WEDDING IN ASTALE!
HOIST
HUH?
I AM A PRINCE FROM THE MAGICAL KINGDOM OF ASTALE, REMEMBER?
THE WHOLE COUNTRY WILL OFFER US THEIR BLESSINGS.
NO-!! I WANT SOMETHING SIMPLE-!!
HEY-!
AIRI!
WAKE UP ALREADY!
MRPH-

✡ Hello there!

Thanks for reading MeruPuri! With your support, we're able to put out a second volume. I'm delighted—thank you! This time, in addition to character profiles and behind-the-scenes commentary, I've also drawn some bonus strips. They're scattered throughout the book, so keep an eye out ♡! (The idea for the cover was to feature "the main culprits" of the story—the troublesome brothers, Aram and Jeile.)

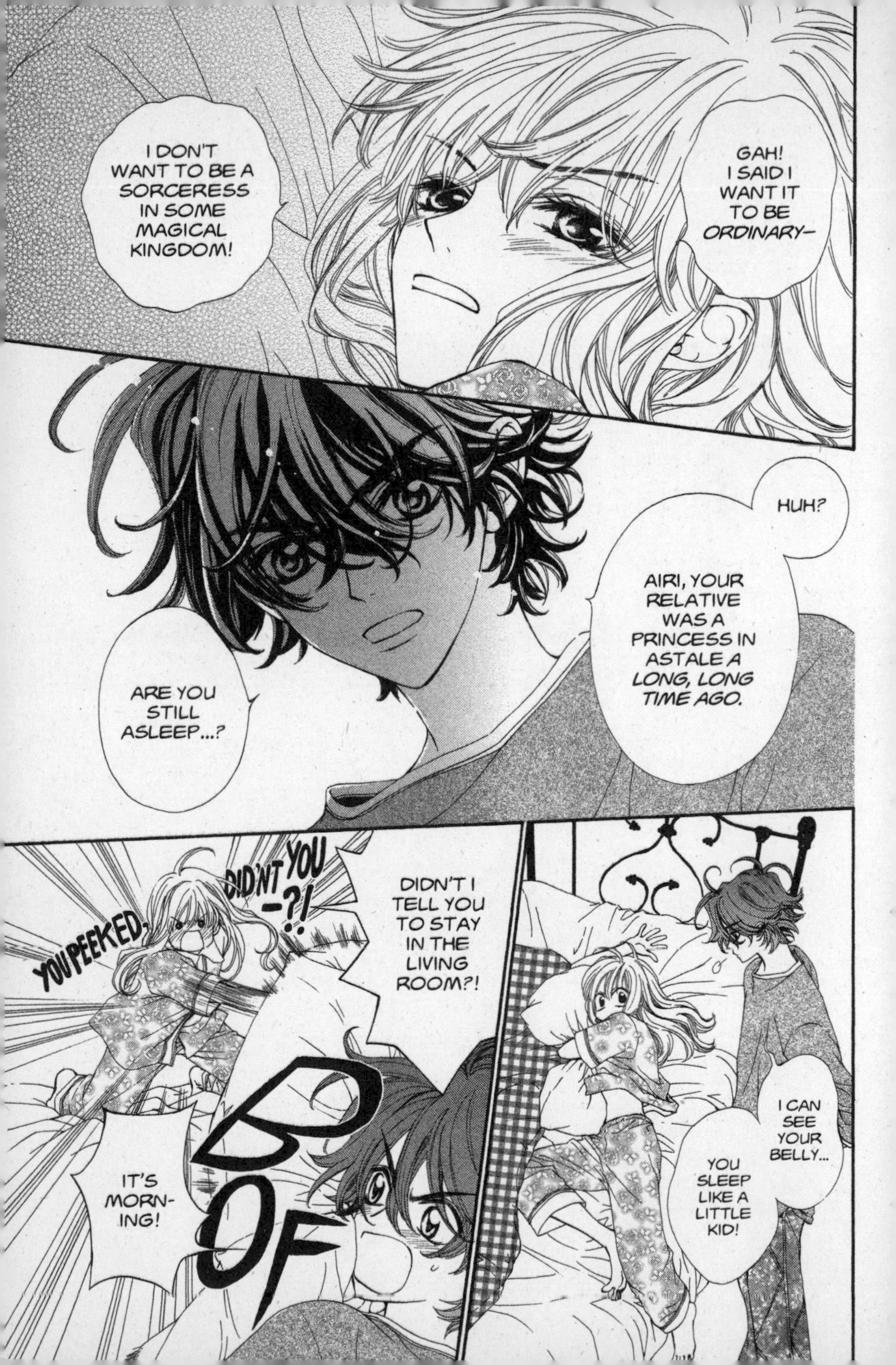
GAH! I SAID I WANT IT TO BE *ORDINARY*–
I DON'T WANT TO BE A SORCERESS IN SOME MAGICAL KINGDOM!
HUH?
AIRI, YOUR RELATIVE WAS A PRINCESS IN ASTALE A *LONG, LONG TIME AGO.*
ARE YOU STILL ASLEEP...?
I CAN SEE YOUR BELLY...
YOU SLEEP LIKE A LITTLE KID!
DIDN'T I TELL YOU TO STAY IN THE LIVING ROOM?!
DIDN'T YOU –?!
YOU PEEKED.
BOF
IT'S MORN-ING!

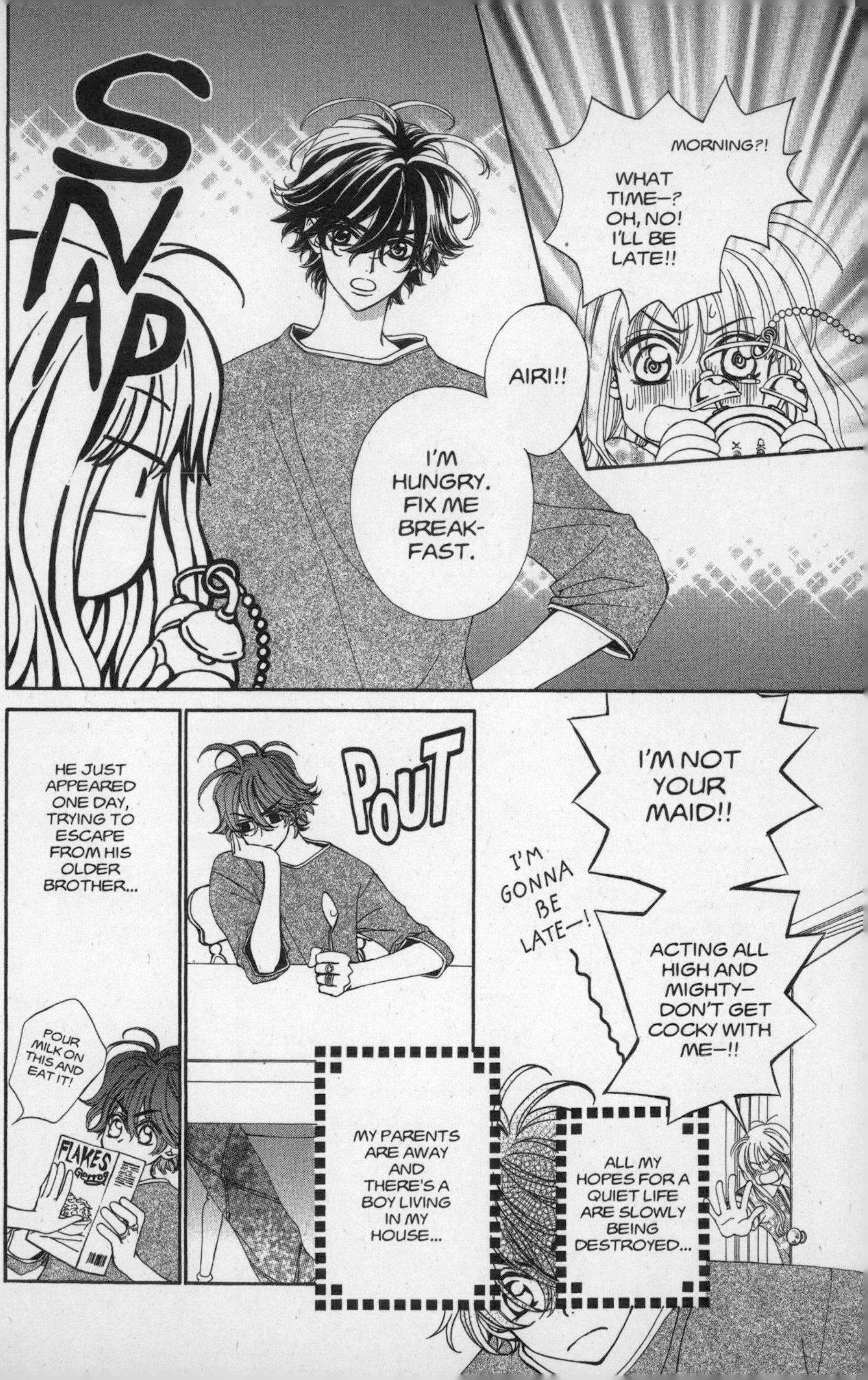
MORNING?!
WHAT TIME—? OH, NO! I'LL BE LATE!!
SNAP
AIRI!!
I'M HUNGRY. FIX ME BREAK-FAST.
I'M NOT YOUR MAID!!
I'M GONNA BE LATE—!
ACTING ALL HIGH AND MIGHTY— DON'T GET COCKY WITH ME—!!
POUT
HE JUST APPEARED ONE DAY, TRYING TO ESCAPE FROM HIS OLDER BROTHER...
ALL MY HOPES FOR A QUIET LIFE ARE SLOWLY BEING DESTROYED...
MY PARENTS ARE AWAY AND THERE'S A BOY LIVING IN MY HOUSE...
POUR MILK ON THIS AND EAT IT!
FLAKES

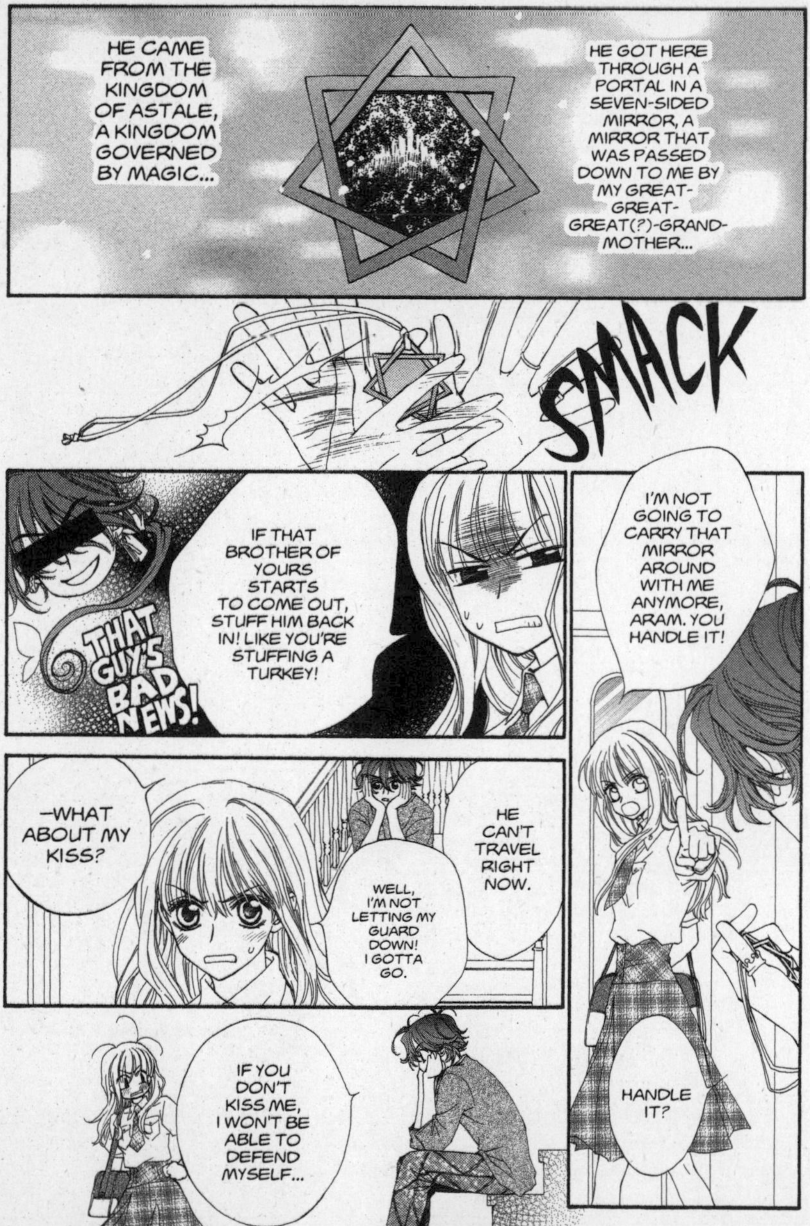
HE GOT HERE THROUGH A PORTAL IN A SEVEN-SIDED MIRROR, A MIRROR THAT WAS PASSED DOWN TO ME BY MY GREAT-GREAT-GREAT(?)-GRANDMOTHER...
HE CAME FROM THE KINGDOM OF ASTALE, A KINGDOM GOVERNED BY MAGIC...
SMACK
I'M NOT GOING TO CARRY THAT MIRROR AROUND WITH ME ANYMORE, ARAM. YOU HANDLE IT!
HANDLE IT?
IF THAT BROTHER OF YOURS STARTS TO COME OUT, STUFF HIM BACK IN! LIKE YOU'RE STUFFING A TURKEY!
THAT GUY'S BAD NEWS!
HE CAN'T TRAVEL RIGHT NOW.
WELL, I'M NOT LETTING MY GUARD DOWN! I GOTTA GO.
—WHAT ABOUT MY KISS?
IF YOU DON'T KISS ME, I WON'T BE ABLE TO DEFEND MYSELF...

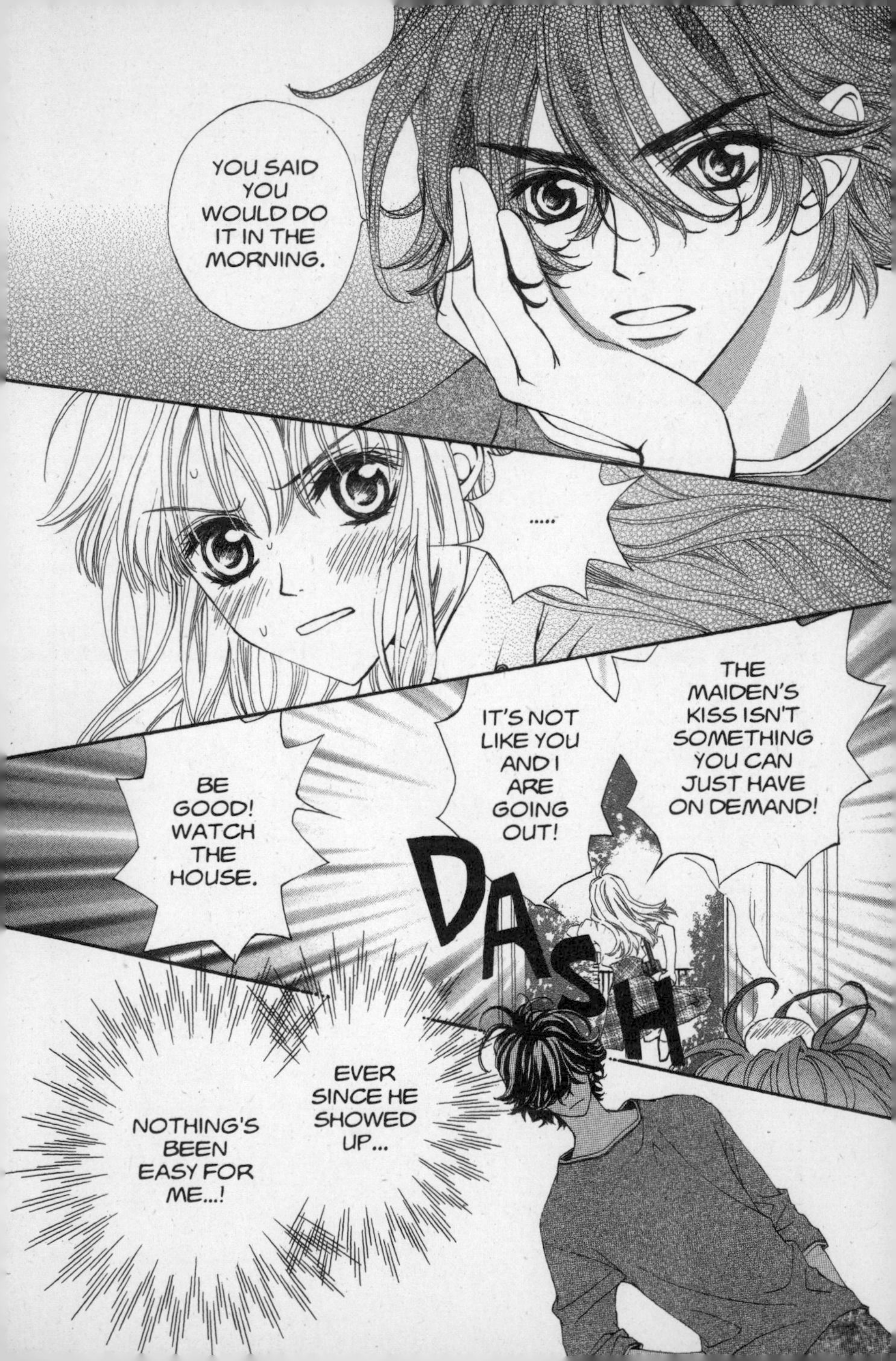
YOU SAID YOU WOULD DO IT IN THE MORNING.
.....
THE MAIDEN'S KISS ISN'T SOMETHING YOU CAN JUST HAVE ON DEMAND!
IT'S NOT LIKE YOU AND I ARE GOING OUT!
BE GOOD! WATCH THE HOUSE.
DASH
EVER SINCE HE SHOWED UP...
NOTHING'S BEEN EASY FOR ME...!

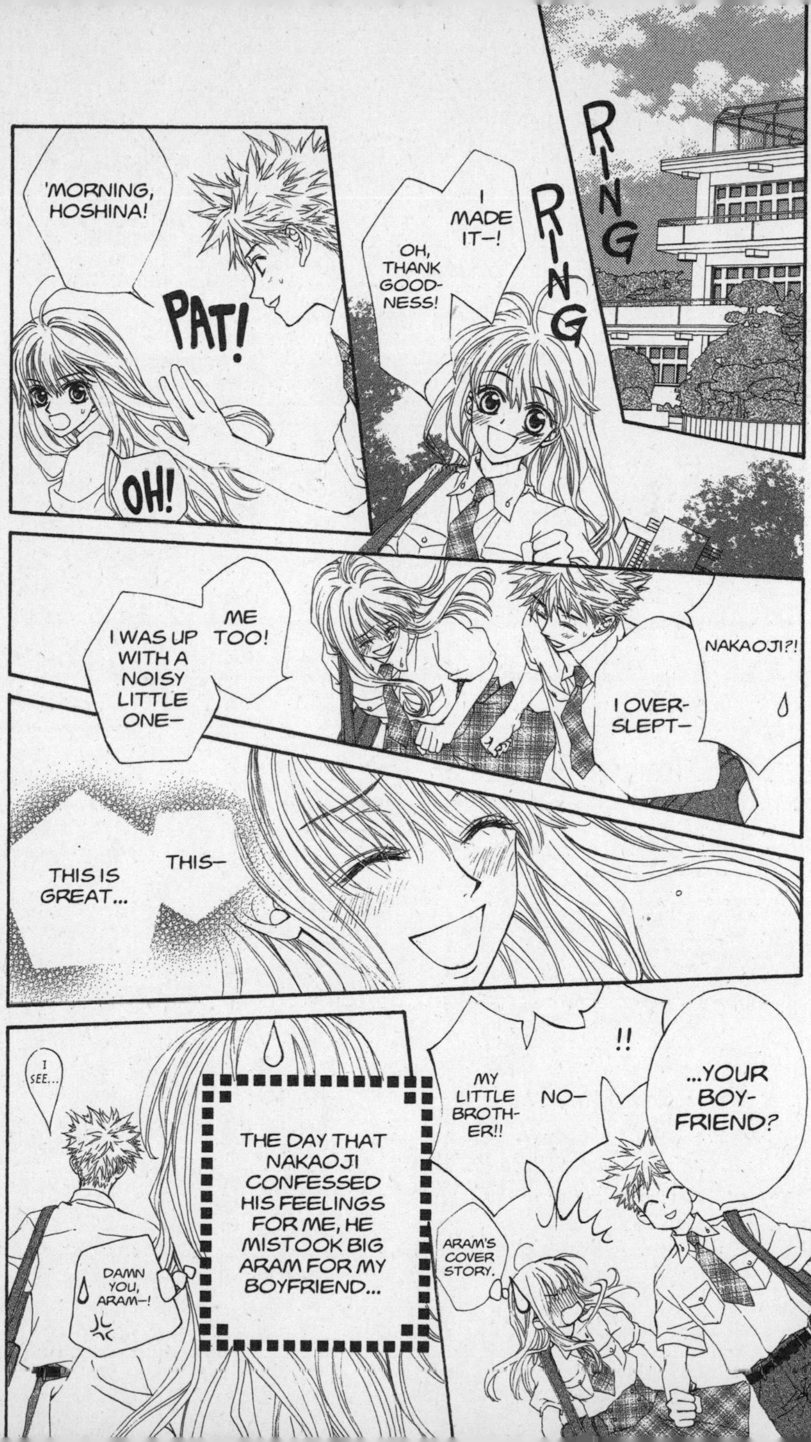
RING RING
I MADE IT—!
OH, THANK GOOD-NESS!
'MORNING, HOSHINA!
PAT!
OH!
NAKAOJI?!
I OVER-SLEPT—
ME TOO!
I WAS UP WITH A NOISY LITTLE ONE—
THIS—
THIS IS GREAT...
...YOUR BOY-FRIEND?
!!
NO—
MY LITTLE BROTH-ER!!
ARAM'S COVER STORY.
THE DAY THAT NAKAOJI CONFESSED HIS FEELINGS FOR ME, HE MISTOOK BIG ARAM FOR MY BOYFRIEND...
I SEE...
DAMN YOU, ARAM—!

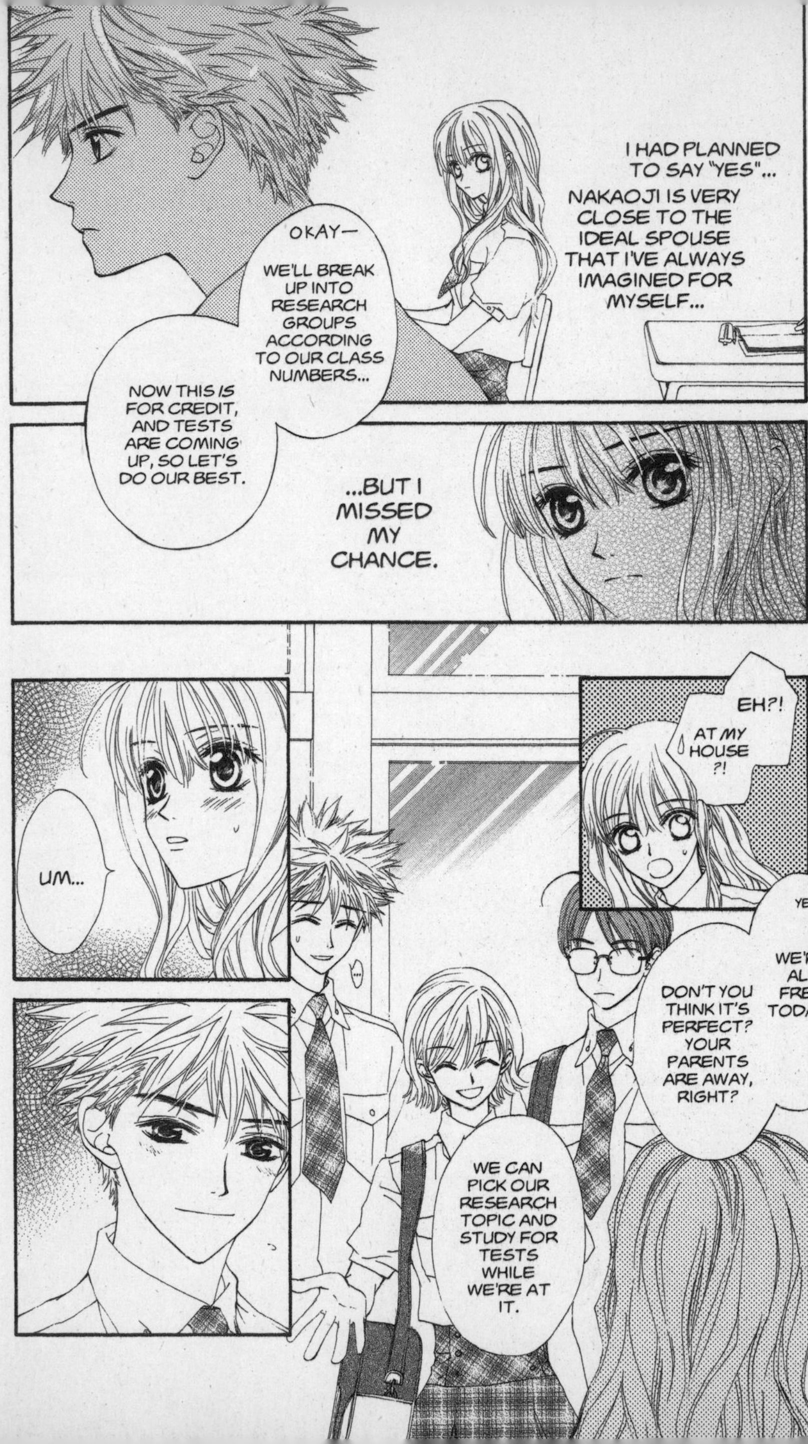
I HAD PLANNED TO SAY "YES"...
NAKAOJI IS VERY CLOSE TO THE IDEAL SPOUSE THAT I'VE ALWAYS IMAGINED FOR MYSELF...
OKAY—
WE'LL BREAK UP INTO RESEARCH GROUPS ACCORDING TO OUR CLASS NUMBERS...
NOW THIS IS FOR CREDIT, AND TESTS ARE COMING UP, SO LET'S DO OUR BEST.
...BUT I MISSED MY CHANCE.
EH?!
AT MY HOUSE ?!
UM...
YEP
WE'RE ALL FREE TODAY...
DON'T YOU THINK IT'S PERFECT? YOUR PARENTS ARE AWAY, RIGHT?
...
WE CAN PICK OUR RESEARCH TOPIC AND STUDY FOR TESTS WHILE WE'RE AT IT.

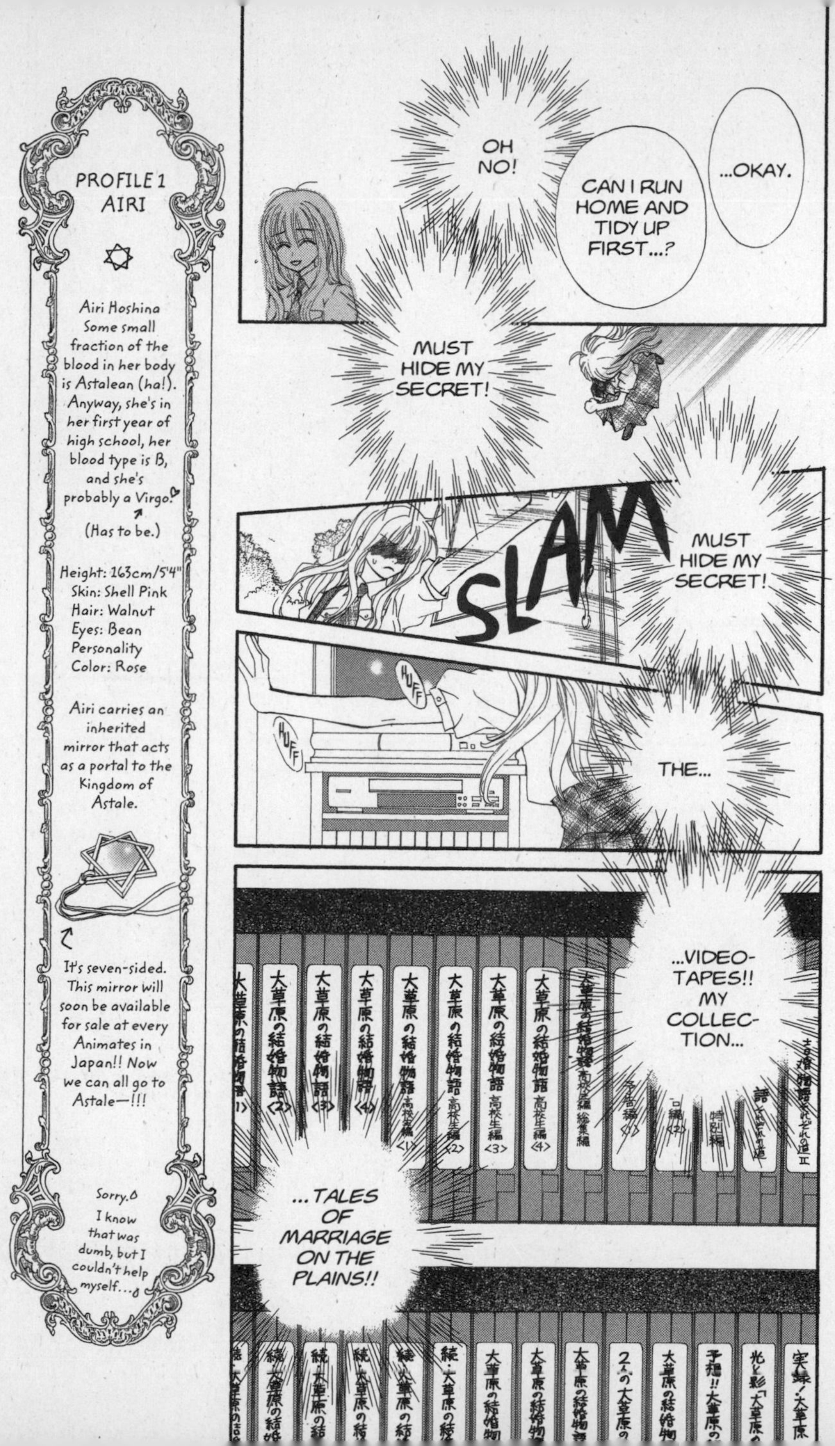
...OKAY.
CAN I RUN HOME AND TIDY UP FIRST...?
OH NO!
MUST HIDE MY SECRET!
SLAM
MUST HIDE MY SECRET!
HUFF
HUFF
THE...
...VIDEO-TAPES!! MY COLLECTION...
...TALES OF MARRIAGE ON THE PLAINS!!

PROFILE 1
AIRI

Airi Hoshina
Some small fraction of the blood in her body is Astalean (ha!). Anyway, she's in her first year of high school, her blood type is B, and she's probably a Virgo.♡
(Has to be.)

Height: 163cm/5'4"
Skin: Shell Pink
Hair: Walnut
Eyes: Bean
Personality Color: Rose

Airi carries an inherited mirror that acts as a portal to the Kingdom of Astale.

It's seven-sided. This mirror will soon be available for sale at every Animates in Japan!! Now we can all go to Astale—!!!

Sorry. I know that was dumb, but I couldn't help myself...

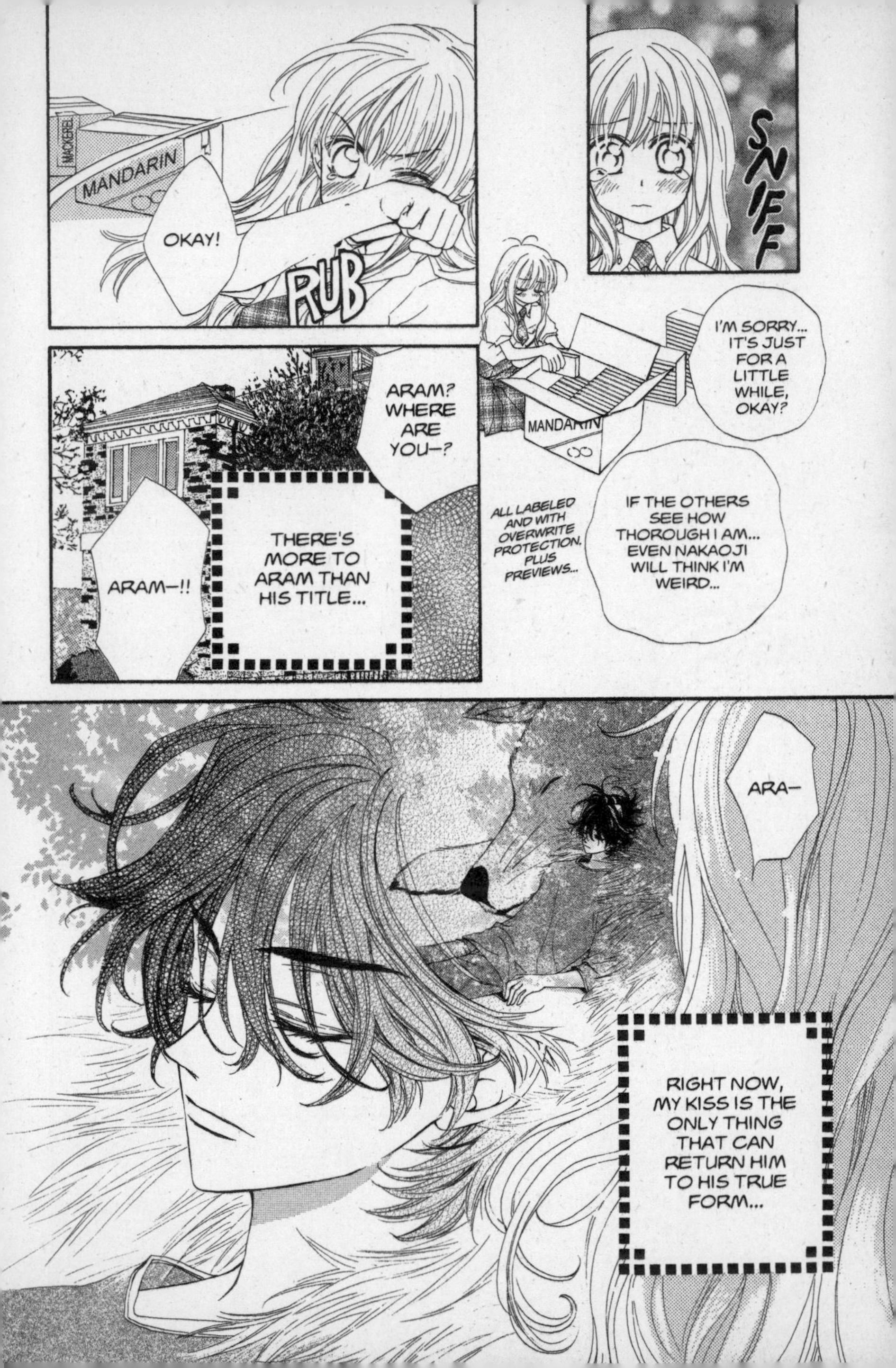
SNIFF
MACKEREL
MANDARIN
OKAY!
RUB
I'M SORRY... IT'S JUST FOR A LITTLE WHILE, OKAY?
MANDARIN
IF THE OTHERS SEE HOW THOROUGH I AM... EVEN NAKAOJI WILL THINK I'M WEIRD...
ALL LABELED AND WITH OVERWRITE PROTECTION, PLUS PREVIEWS...
ARAM? WHERE ARE YOU-?
THERE'S MORE TO ARAM THAN HIS TITLE...
ARAM-!!
ARA-
RIGHT NOW, MY KISS IS THE ONLY THING THAT CAN RETURN HIM TO HIS TRUE FORM...

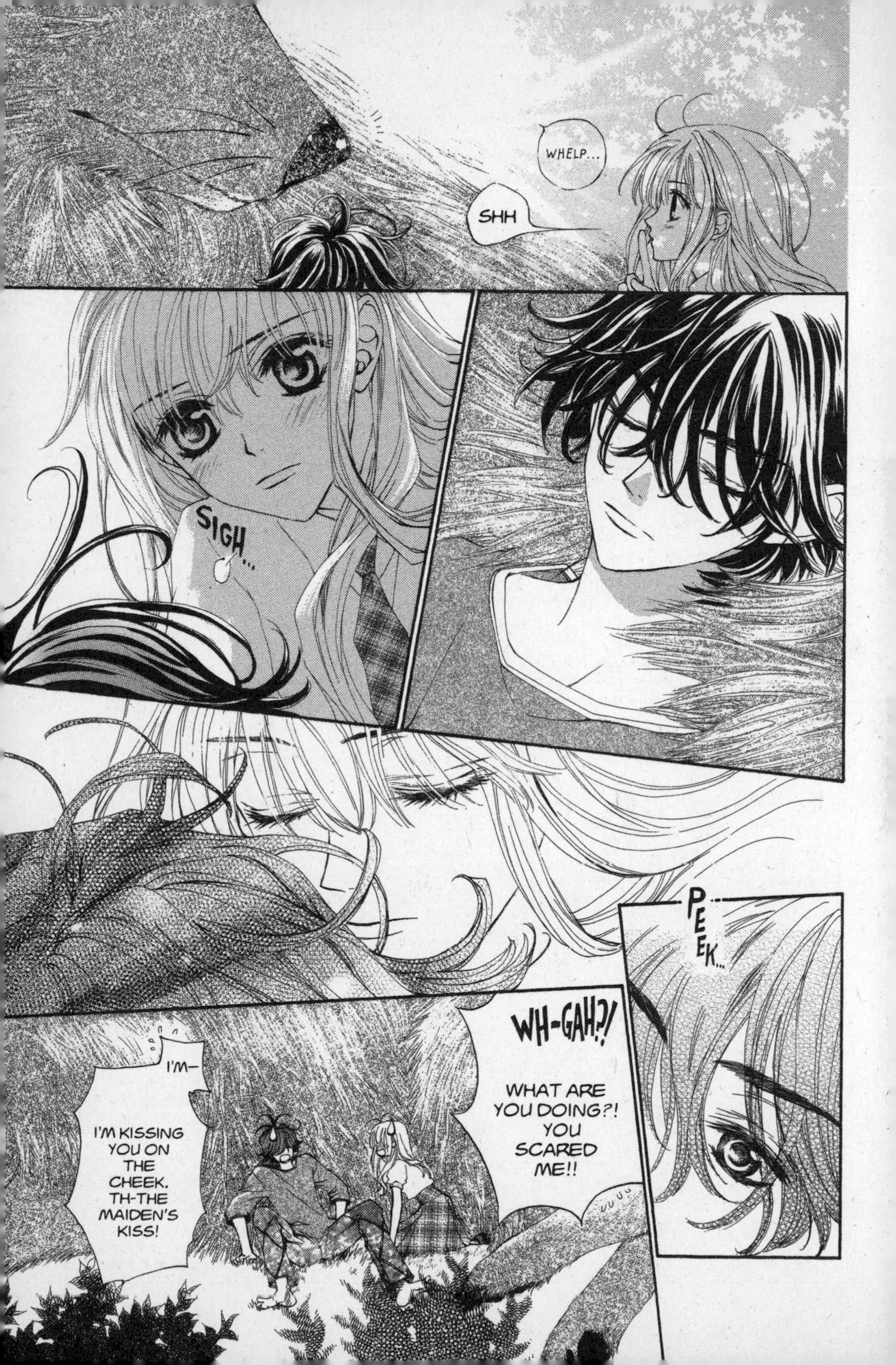
WHELP...
SHH
SIGH...
PEEK...
WH-GAH?!
WHAT ARE YOU DOING?! YOU SCARED ME!!
I'M—
I'M KISSING YOU ON THE CHEEK. TH-THE MAIDEN'S KISS!

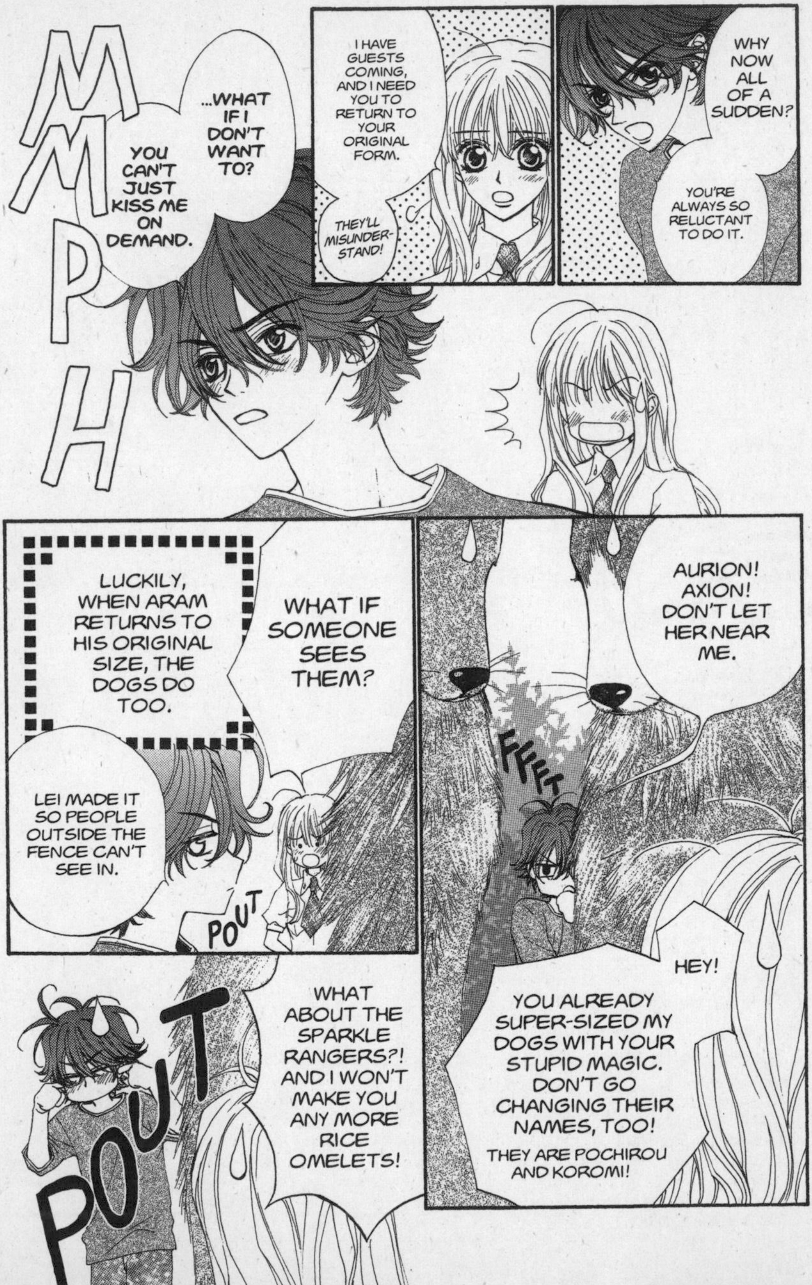
WHY NOW ALL OF A SUDDEN?
YOU'RE ALWAYS SO RELUCTANT TO DO IT.
I HAVE GUESTS COMING, AND I NEED YOU TO RETURN TO YOUR ORIGINAL FORM.
THEY'LL MISUNDER-STAND!
...WHAT IF I DON'T WANT TO?
YOU CAN'T JUST KISS ME ON DEMAND.
MMPH
AURION! AXION! DON'T LET HER NEAR ME.
FFFFT
HEY!
YOU ALREADY SUPER-SIZED MY DOGS WITH YOUR STUPID MAGIC. DON'T GO CHANGING THEIR NAMES, TOO!
THEY ARE POCHIROU AND KOROMI!
LUCKILY, WHEN ARAM RETURNS TO HIS ORIGINAL SIZE, THE DOGS DO TOO.
WHAT IF SOMEONE SEES THEM?
LEI MADE IT SO PEOPLE OUTSIDE THE FENCE CAN'T SEE IN.
POUT
WHAT ABOUT THE SPARKLE RANGERS?! AND I WON'T MAKE YOU ANY MORE RICE OMELETS!
POUT

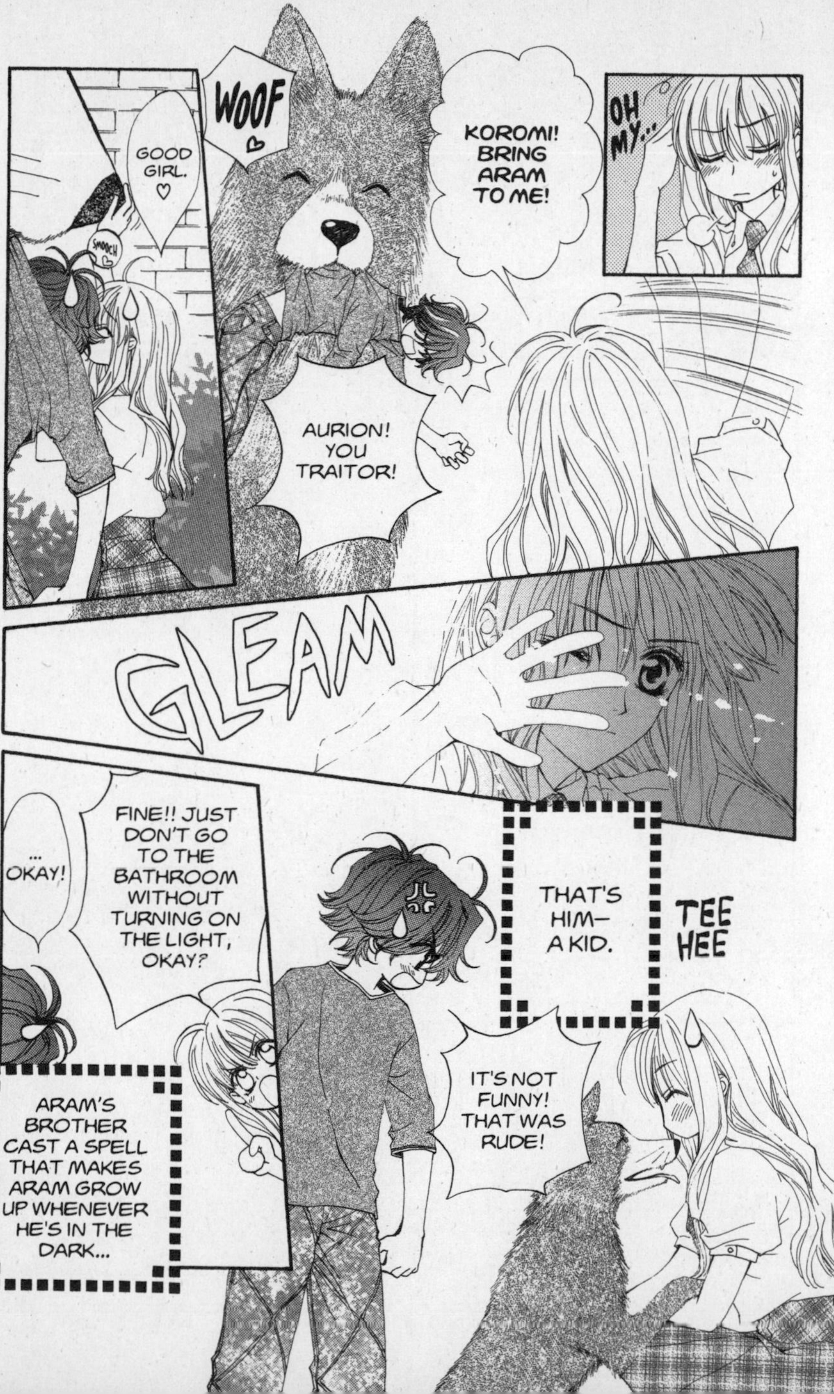
OH MY...
KOROMI! BRING ARAM TO ME!
WOOF ♡
AURION! YOU TRAITOR!
GOOD GIRL. ♡
SMOOCH ♡
GLEAM
THAT'S HIM— A KID.
TEE HEE
IT'S NOT FUNNY! THAT WAS RUDE!
FINE!! JUST DON'T GO TO THE BATHROOM WITHOUT TURNING ON THE LIGHT, OKAY?
...OKAY!
ARAM'S BROTHER CAST A SPELL THAT MAKES ARAM GROW UP WHENEVER HE'S IN THE DARK...

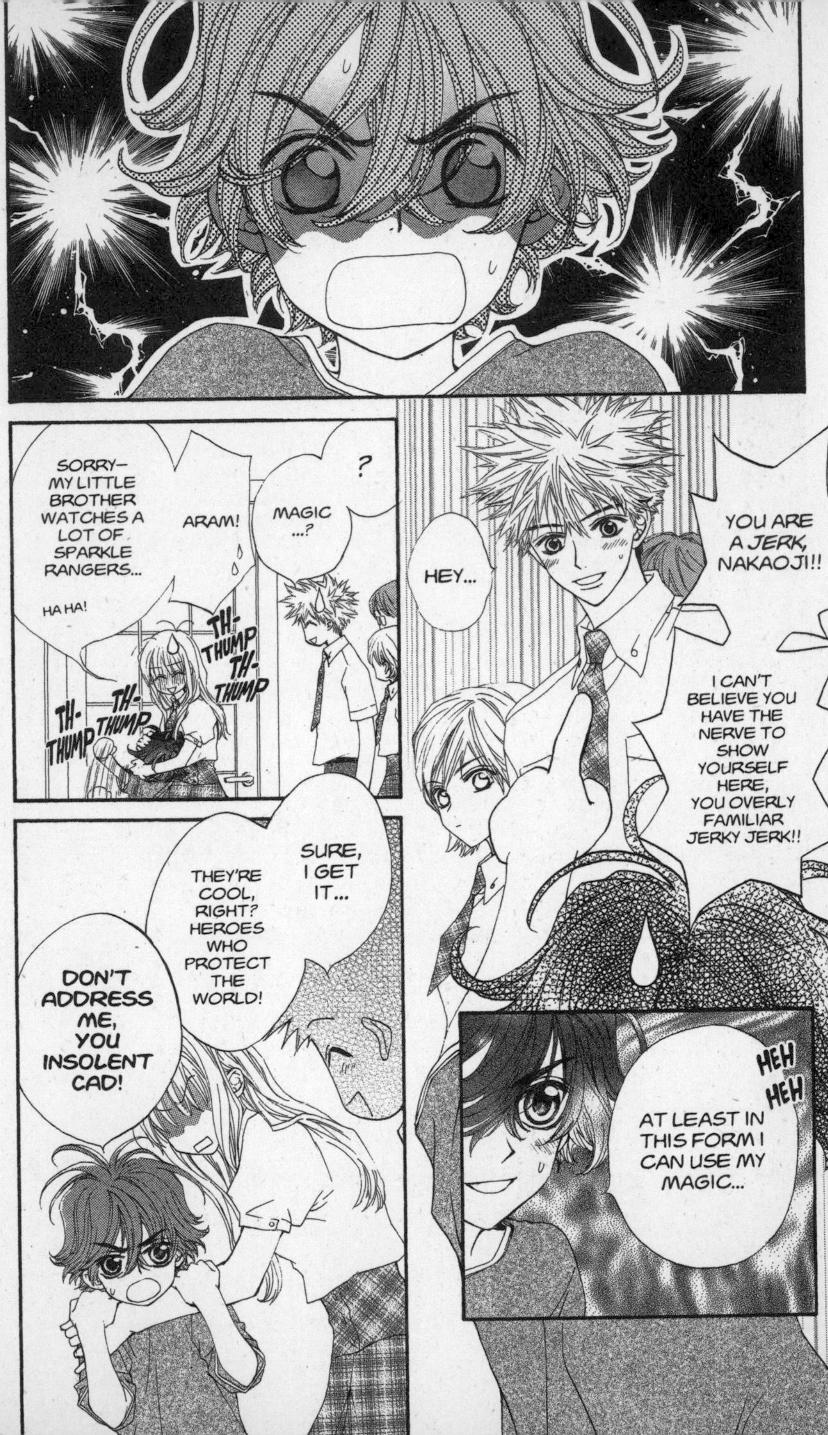
YOU ARE A JERK, NAKAOJI!!
HEY...
I CAN'T BELIEVE YOU HAVE THE NERVE TO SHOW YOURSELF HERE, YOU OVERLY FAMILIAR JERKY JERK!!
HEH HEH
AT LEAST IN THIS FORM I CAN USE MY MAGIC...
?
MAGIC ...?
ARAM!
SORRY— MY LITTLE BROTHER WATCHES A LOT OF SPARKLE RANGERS...
HA HA!
TH-THUMP TH-THUMP
TH-THUMP TH-THUMP
SURE, I GET IT...
THEY'RE COOL, RIGHT? HEROES WHO PROTECT THE WORLD!
DON'T ADDRESS ME, YOU INSOLENT CAD!

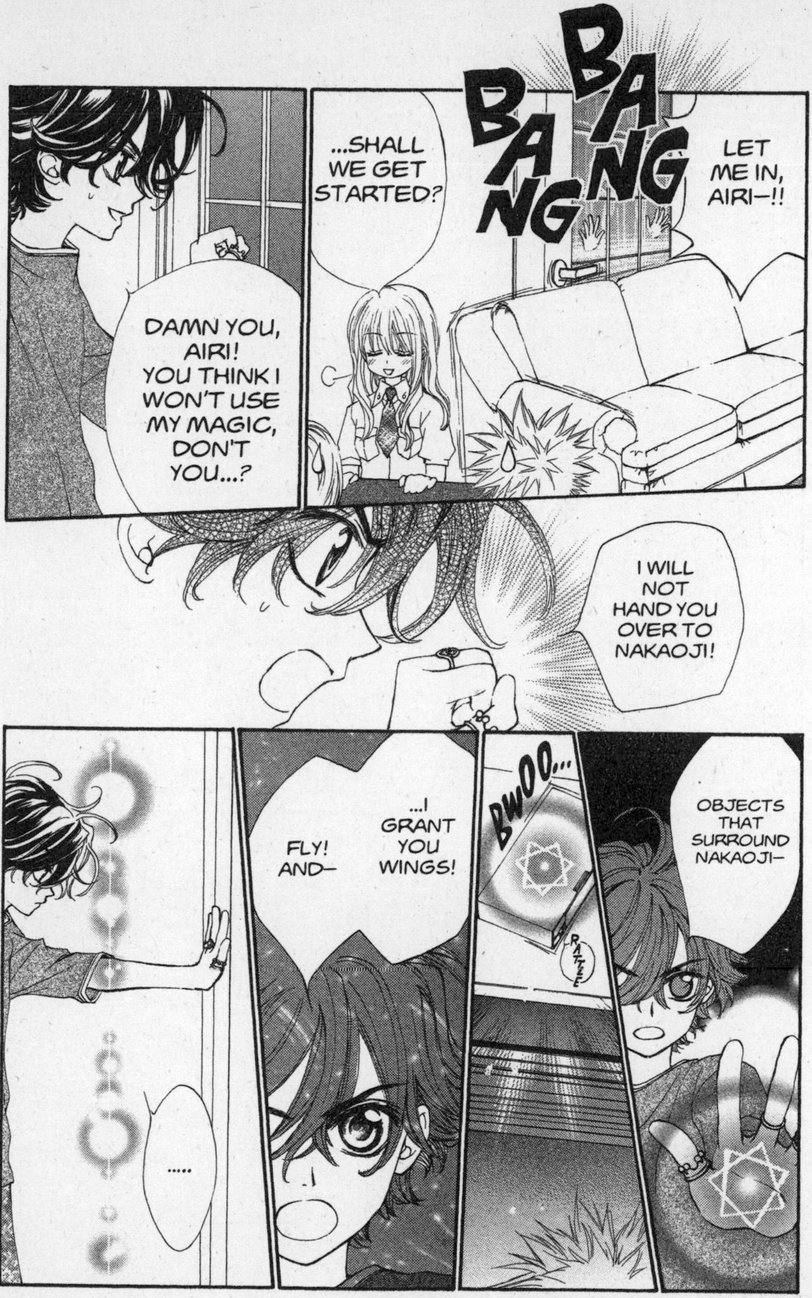
BANG BANG
LET ME IN, AIRI—!!
...SHALL WE GET STARTED?
DAMN YOU, AIRI! YOU THINK I WON'T USE MY MAGIC, DON'T YOU...?
I WILL NOT HAND YOU OVER TO NAKAOJI!
OBJECTS THAT SURROUND NAKAOJI—
BWOO...
RATTLE
FLY! AND—
...I GRANT YOU WINGS!
......

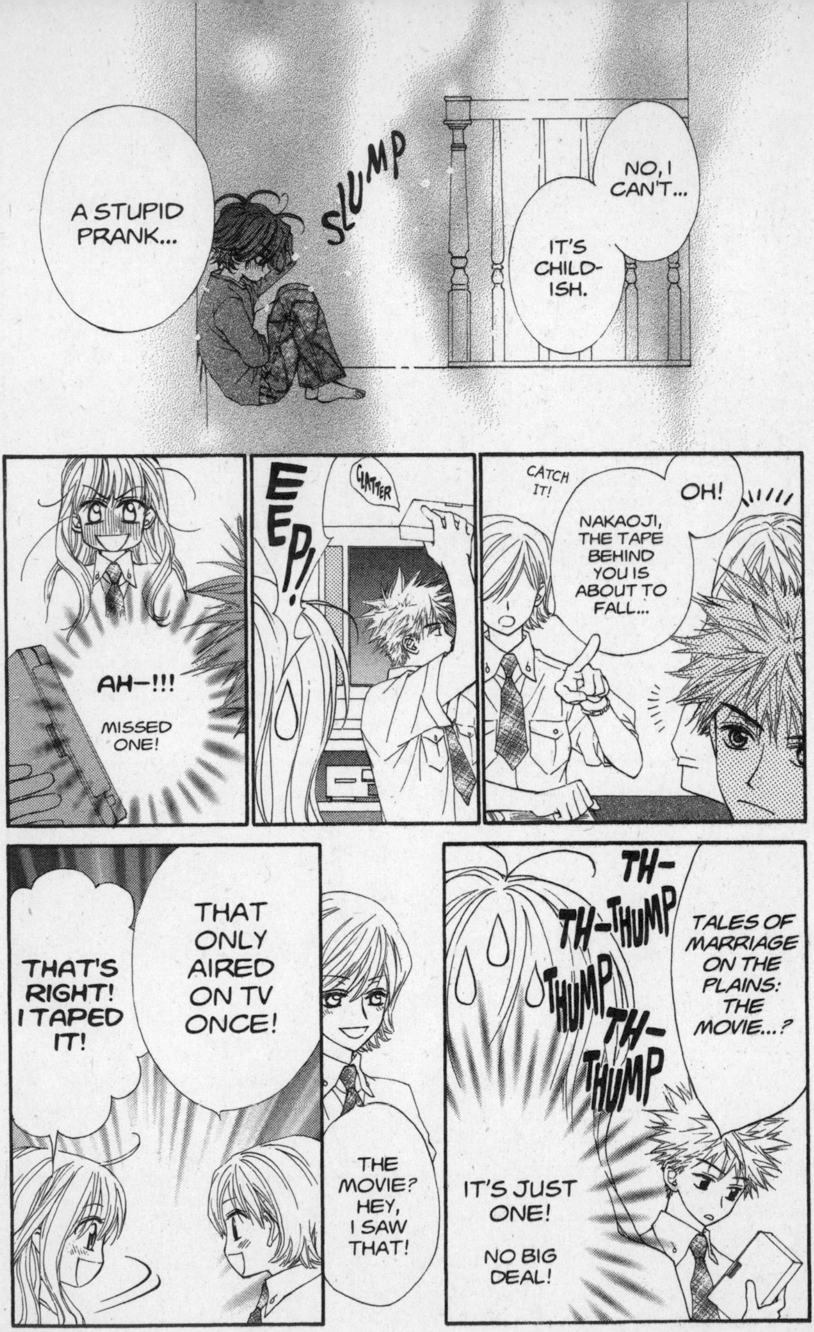
NO, I CAN'T...
IT'S CHILD-ISH.
SLUMP
A STUPID PRANK...
OH!
NAKAOJI, THE TAPE BEHIND YOU IS ABOUT TO FALL...
CATCH IT!
CLATTER
EEP!
AH—!!!
MISSED ONE!
TALES OF MARRIAGE ON THE PLAINS: THE MOVIE...?
TH-TH-THUMP
THUMP TH-THUMP
IT'S JUST ONE!
NO BIG DEAL!
THAT ONLY AIRED ON TV ONCE!
THAT'S RIGHT! I TAPED IT!
THE MOVIE? HEY, I SAW THAT!

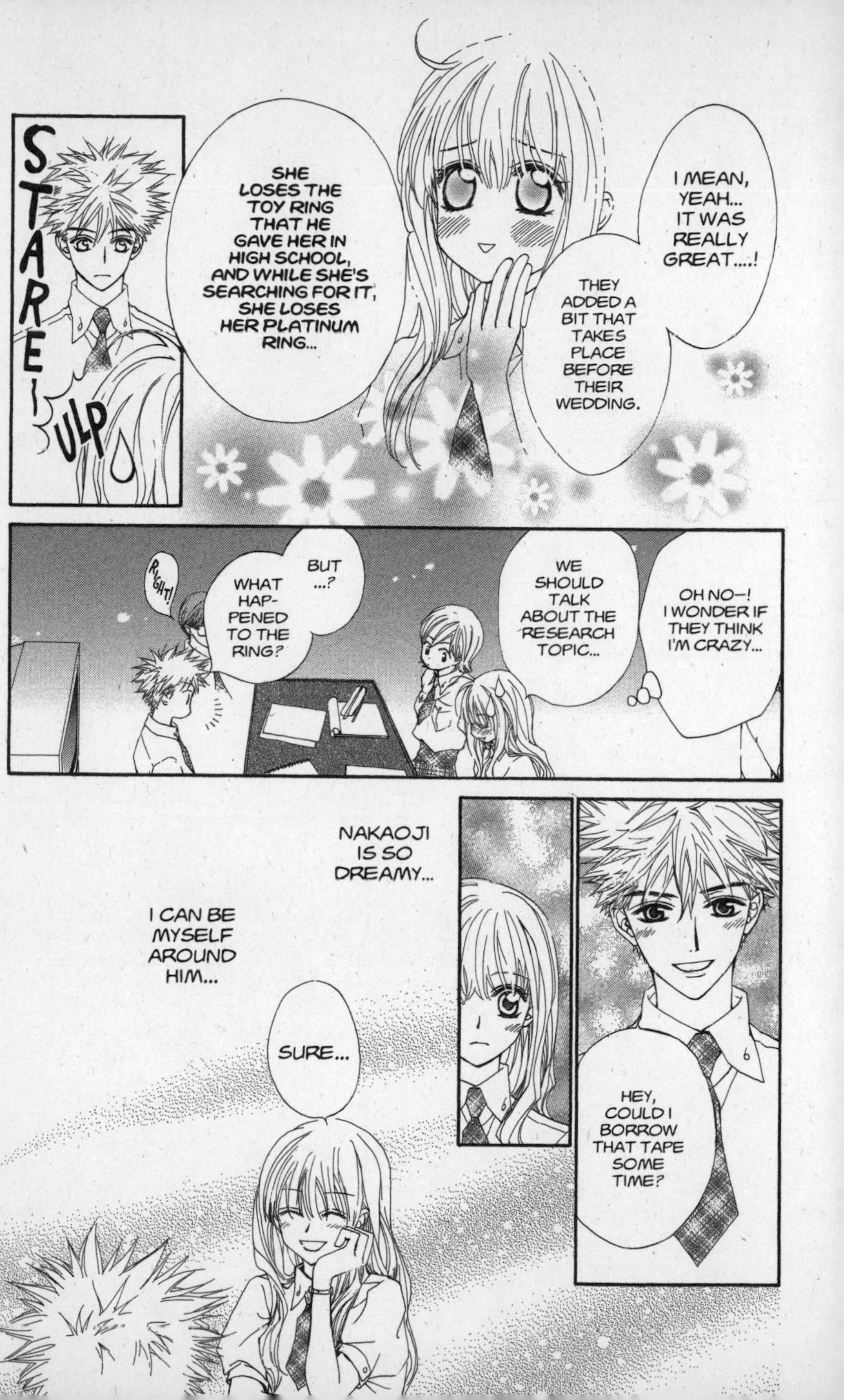
I MEAN, YEAH... IT WAS REALLY GREAT....!
THEY ADDED A BIT THAT TAKES PLACE BEFORE THEIR WEDDING.
SHE LOSES THE TOY RING THAT HE GAVE HER IN HIGH SCHOOL, AND WHILE SHE'S SEARCHING FOR IT, SHE LOSES HER PLATINUM RING...
STARE~
ULP
OH NO—! I WONDER IF THEY THINK I'M CRAZY...
WE SHOULD TALK ABOUT THE RESEARCH TOPIC...
BUT ...? WHAT HAP-PENED TO THE RING?
RIGHT!
HEY, COULD I BORROW THAT TAPE SOME TIME?
SURE...
NAKAOJI IS SO DREAMY...
I CAN BE MYSELF AROUND HIM...

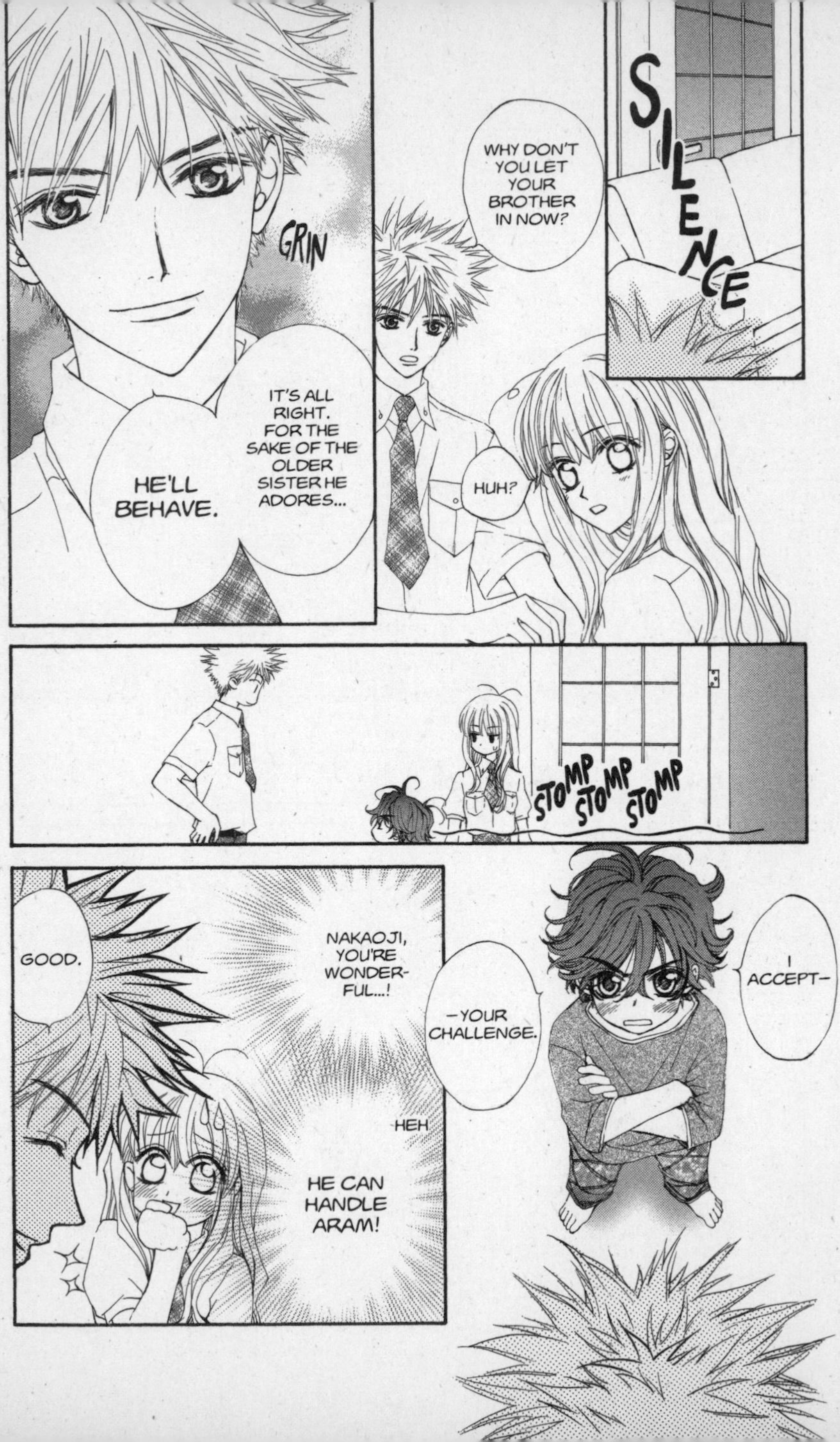
SILENCE
WHY DON'T YOU LET YOUR BROTHER IN NOW?
HUH?
GRIN
IT'S ALL RIGHT. FOR THE SAKE OF THE OLDER SISTER HE ADORES...
HE'LL BEHAVE.
STOMP STOMP STOMP
I ACCEPT–
–YOUR CHALLENGE.
NAKAOJI, YOU'RE WONDERFUL...!
GOOD.
HEH
HE CAN HANDLE ARAM!

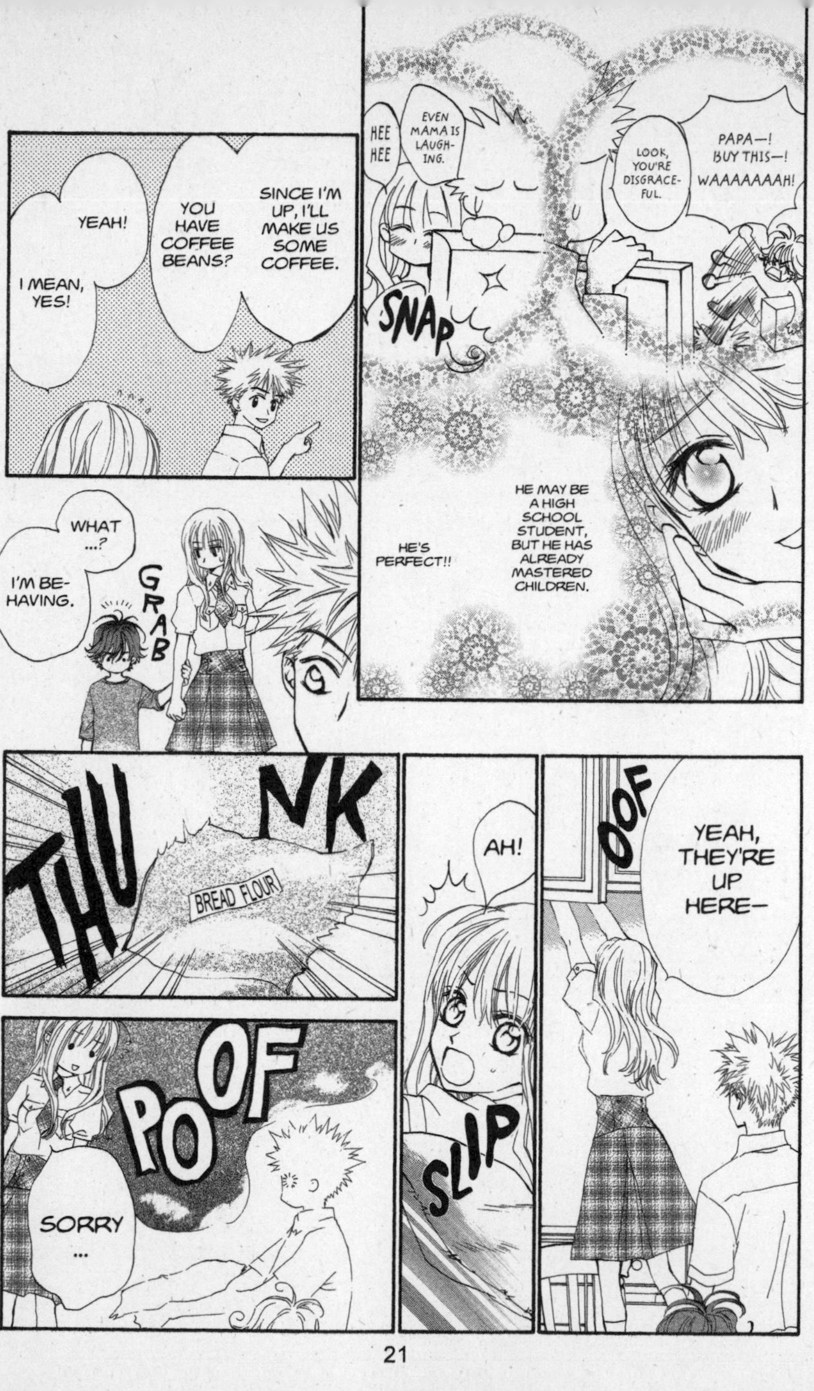
PAPA—! BUY THIS—!
WAAAAAAAH!
LOOK, YOU'RE DISGRACE-FUL.
EVEN MAMA IS LAUGH-ING.
HEE HEE
SNAP
HE MAY BE A HIGH SCHOOL STUDENT, BUT HE HAS ALREADY MASTERED CHILDREN.
HE'S PERFECT!!
SINCE I'M UP, I'LL MAKE US SOME COFFEE.
YOU HAVE COFFEE BEANS?
YEAH!
I MEAN, YES!
GRAB
WHAT ...?
I'M BE-HAVING.
YEAH, THEY'RE UP HERE—
OOF
AH!
SLIP
THUNK
BREAD FLOUR
POOF
SORRY ...

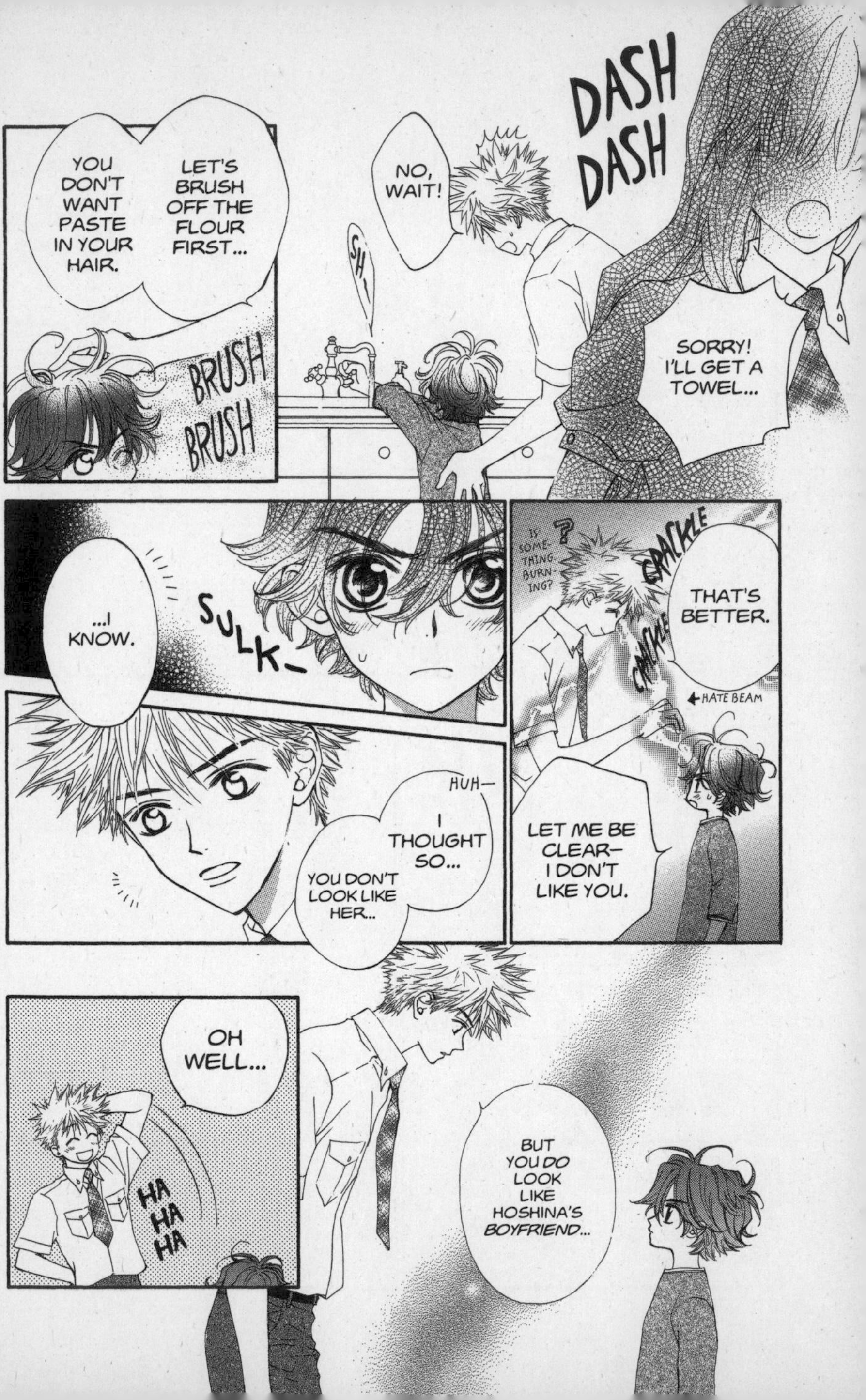
DASH DASH
SORRY! I'LL GET A TOWEL...
NO, WAIT!
SH
LET'S BRUSH OFF THE FLOUR FIRST...
YOU DON'T WANT PASTE IN YOUR HAIR.
BRUSH BRUSH
IS SOMETHING BURNING?
CRACKLE CRACKLE
THAT'S BETTER.
HATE BEAM
LET ME BE CLEAR— I DON'T LIKE YOU.
SULK
...I KNOW.
HUH—
I THOUGHT SO...
YOU DON'T LOOK LIKE HER...
BUT YOU DO LOOK LIKE HOSHINA'S *BOYFRIEND*...
OH WELL...
HA HA HA

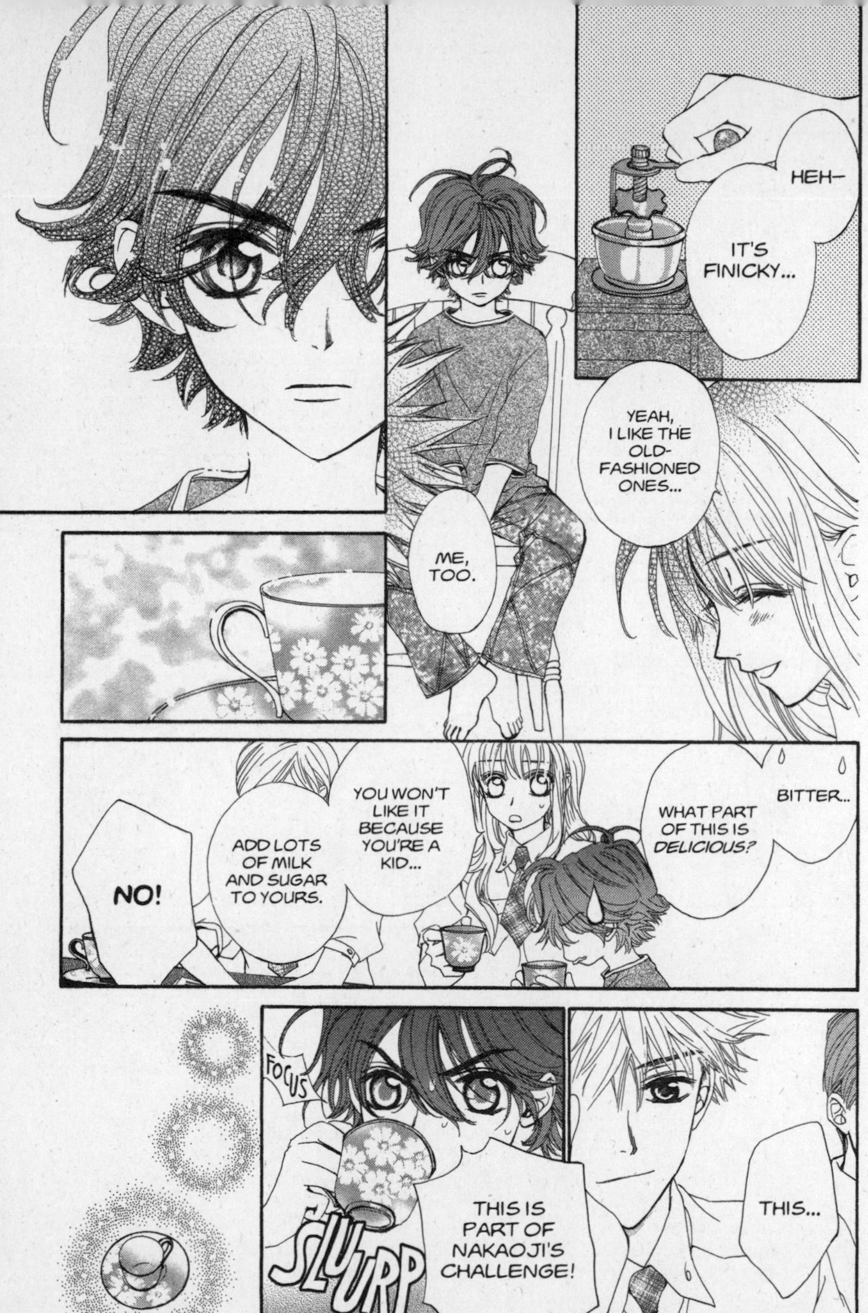
HEH—
IT'S FINICKY...
YEAH, I LIKE THE OLD-FASHIONED ONES...
ME, TOO.
BITTER...
WHAT PART OF THIS IS *DELICIOUS?*
YOU WON'T LIKE IT BECAUSE YOU'RE A KID...
ADD LOTS OF MILK AND SUGAR TO YOURS.
NO!
THIS...
THIS IS PART OF NAKAOJI'S CHALLENGE!
FOCUS
SLUURP

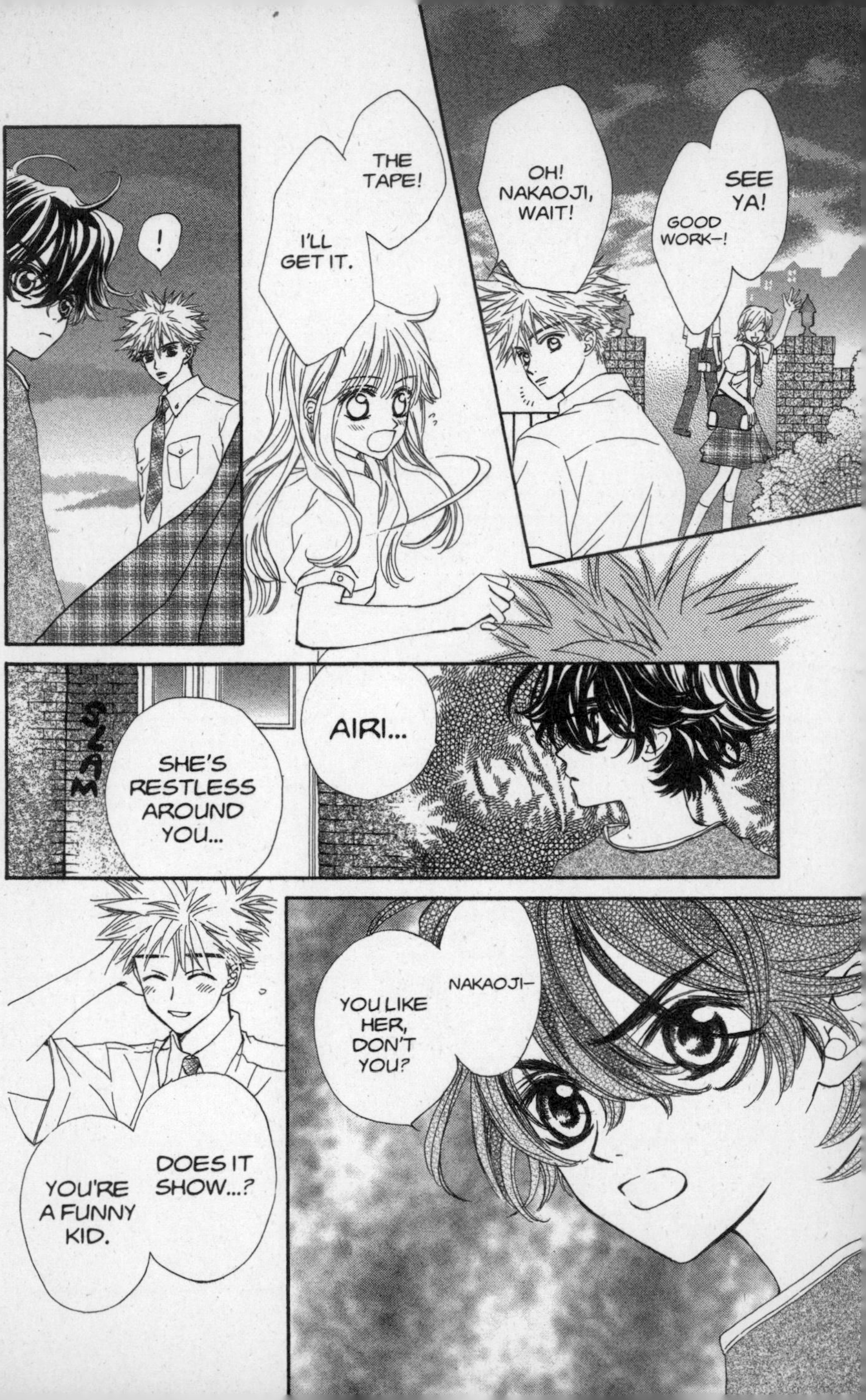
SEE YA! GOOD WORK–!
OH! NAKAOJI, WAIT!
THE TAPE! I'LL GET IT.
!
AIRI...
SHE'S RESTLESS AROUND YOU...
SLAM
NAKAOJI– YOU LIKE HER, DON'T YOU?
DOES IT SHOW...? YOU'RE A FUNNY KID.

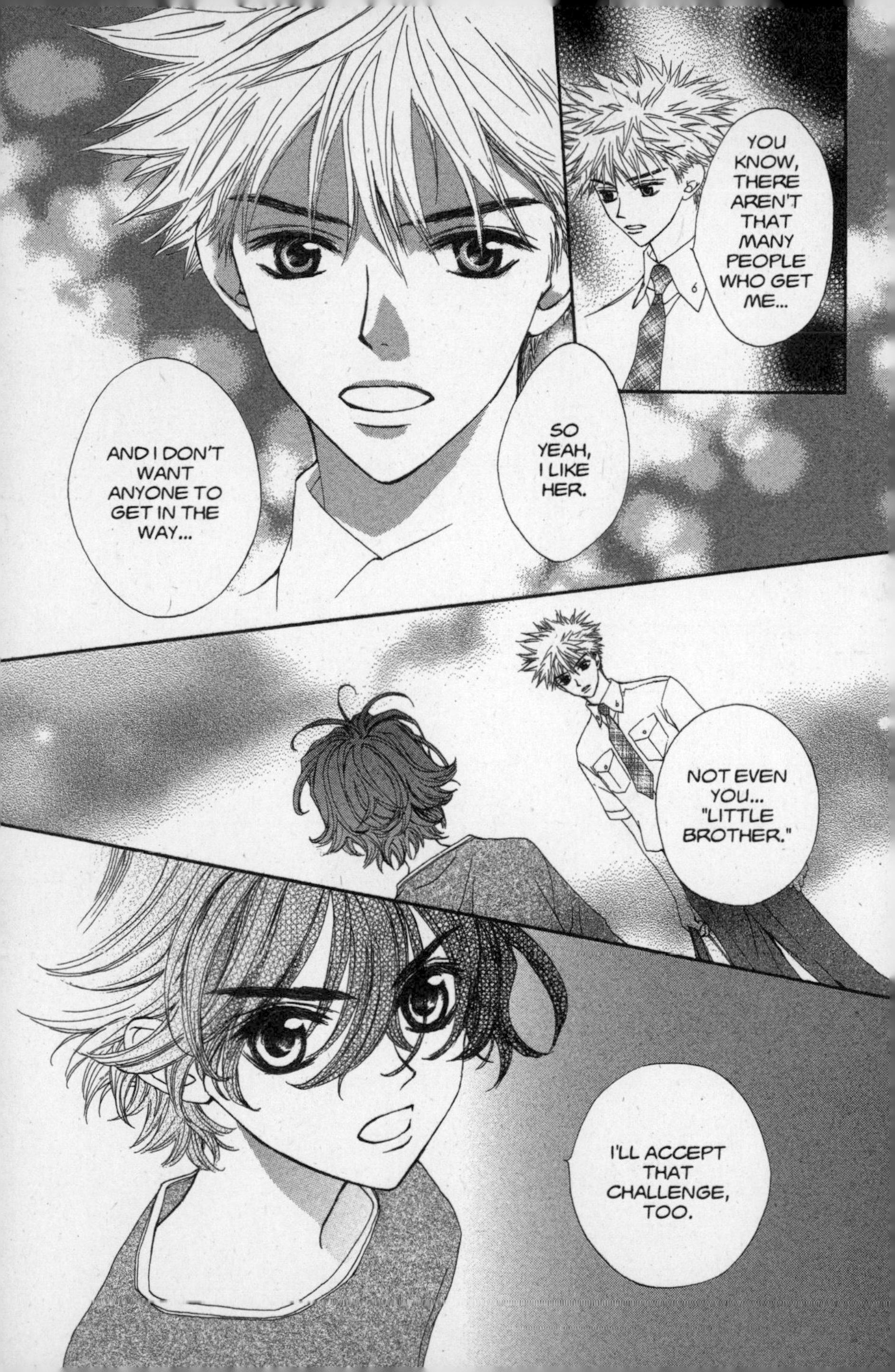
YOU KNOW, THERE AREN'T THAT MANY PEOPLE WHO GET ME...
SO YEAH, I LIKE HER.
AND I DON'T WANT ANYONE TO GET IN THE WAY...
NOT EVEN YOU... "LITTLE BROTHER."
I'LL ACCEPT THAT CHALLENGE, TOO.

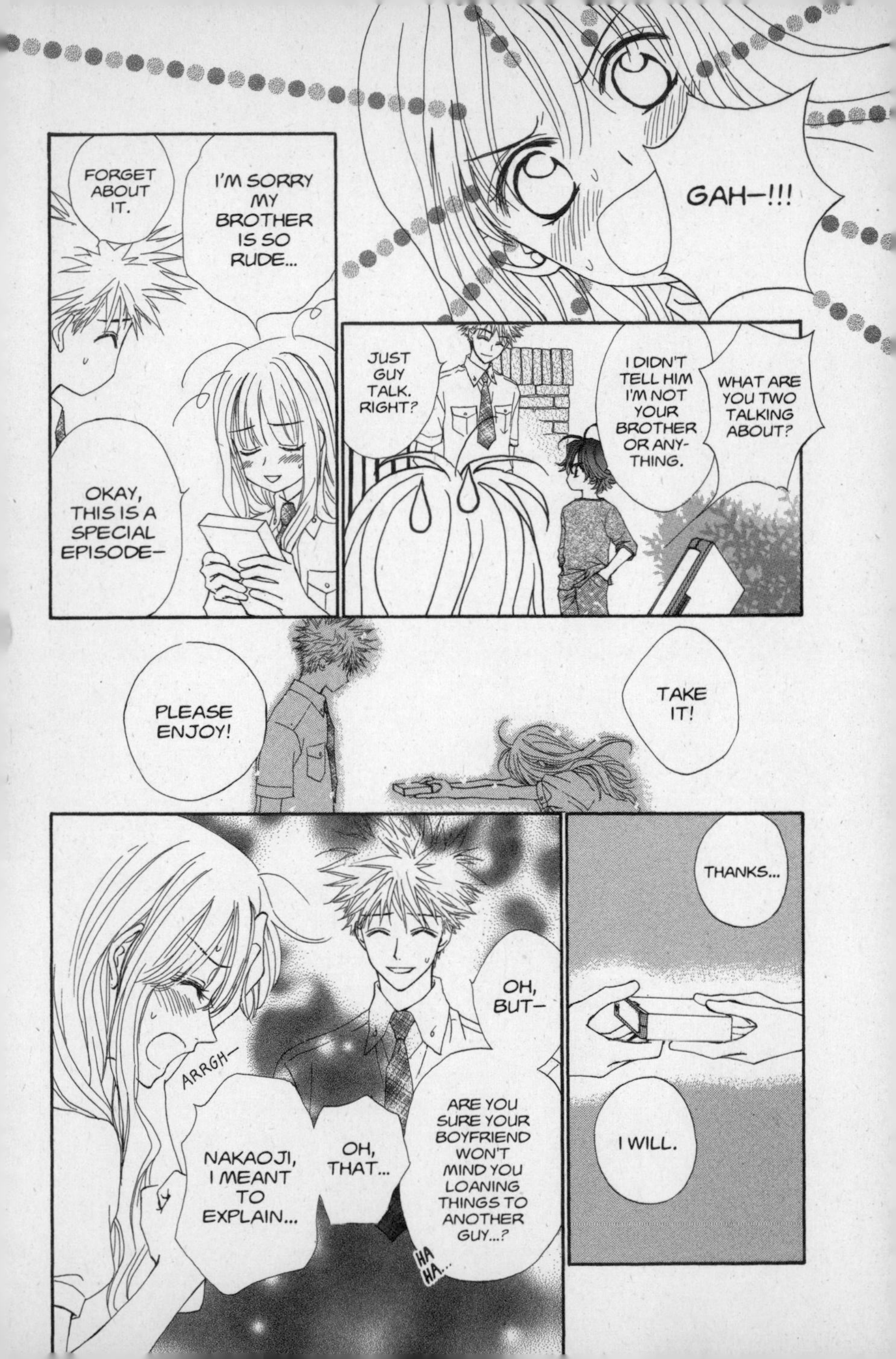
GAH–!!!
WHAT ARE YOU TWO TALKING ABOUT?
I DIDN'T TELL HIM I'M NOT YOUR BROTHER OR ANY-THING.
JUST GUY TALK. RIGHT?
I'M SORRY MY BROTHER IS SO RUDE...
FORGET ABOUT IT.
OKAY, THIS IS A SPECIAL EPISODE–
TAKE IT!
PLEASE ENJOY!
THANKS...
I WILL.
OH, BUT–
ARE YOU SURE YOUR BOYFRIEND WON'T MIND YOU LOANING THINGS TO ANOTHER GUY...?
HA HA...
OH, THAT...
ARRGH–
NAKAOJI, I MEANT TO EXPLAIN...

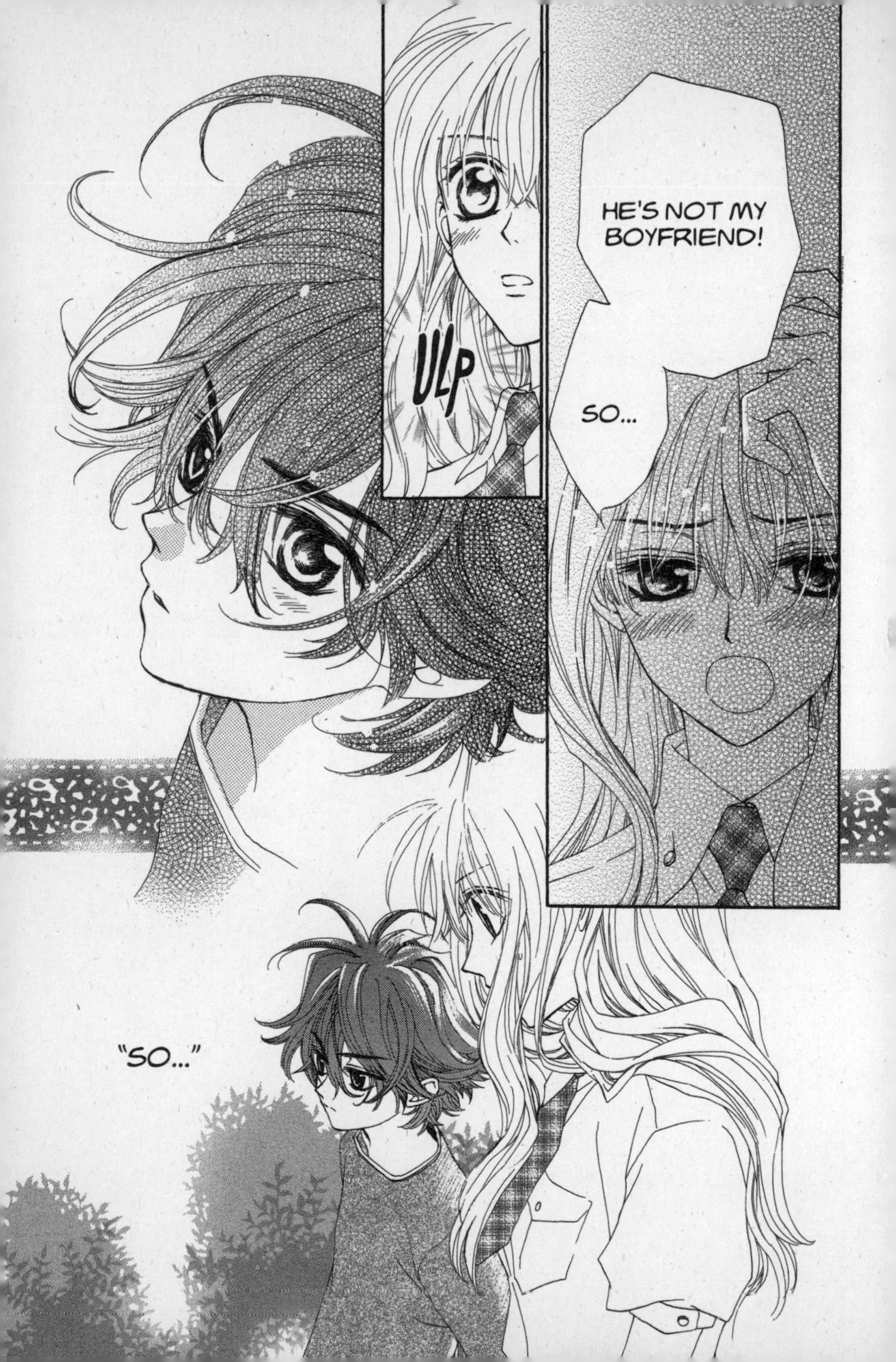
HE'S NOT MY BOYFRIEND!
SO...
ULP
"SO..."

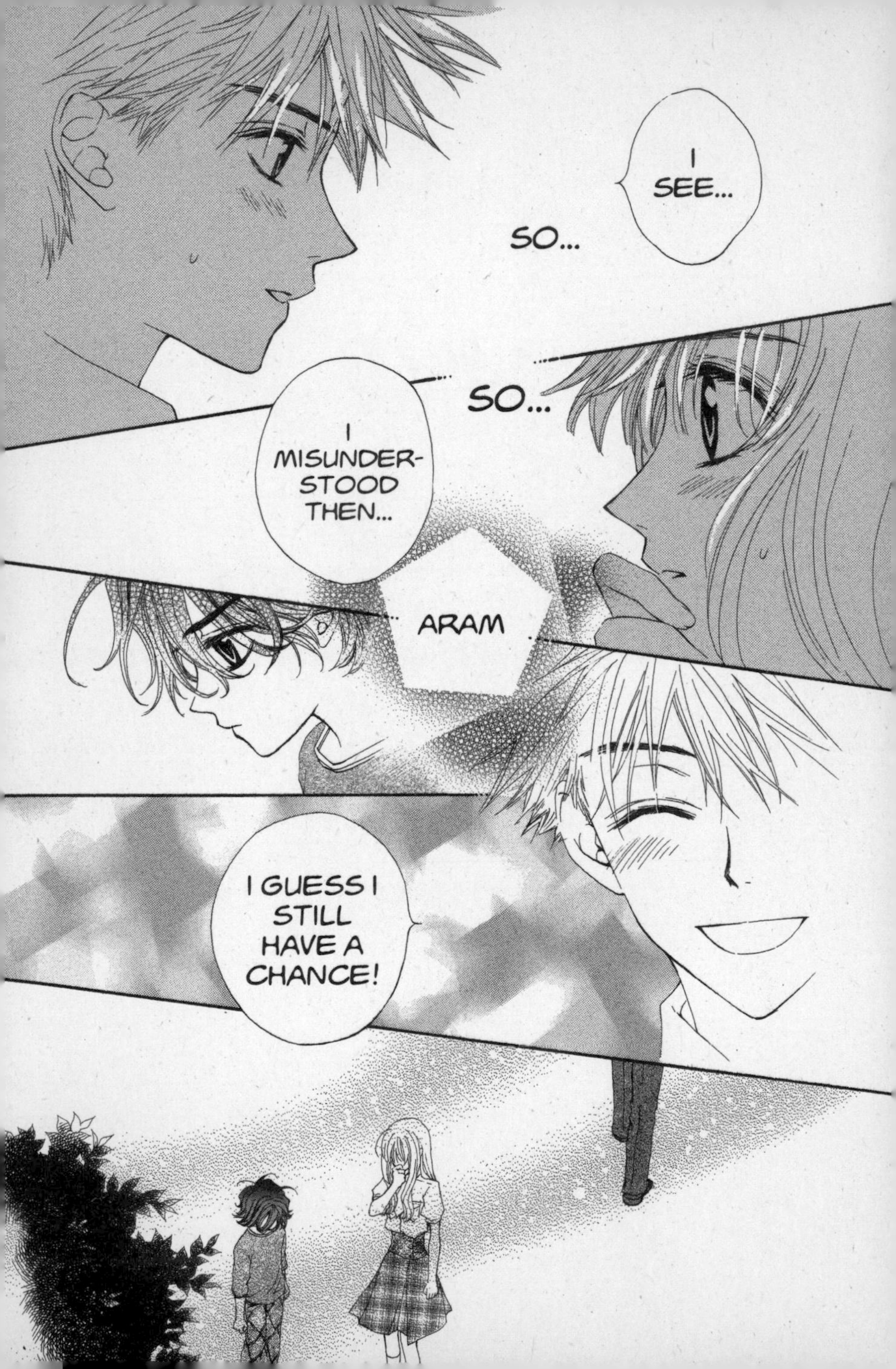
I SEE...
SO...
SO...
I MISUNDERSTOOD THEN...
ARAM
I GUESS I STILL HAVE A CHANCE!

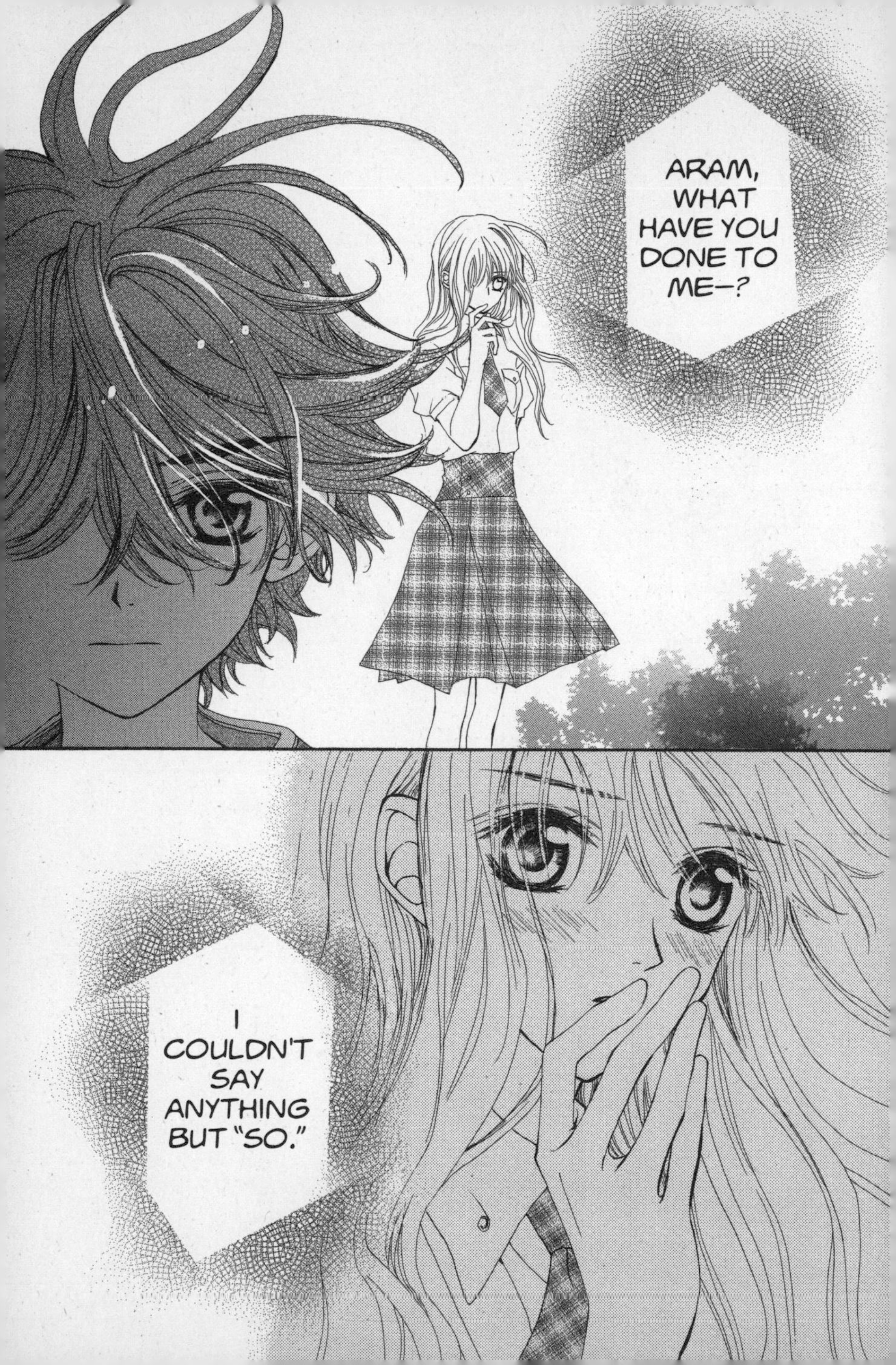
ARAM, WHAT HAVE YOU DONE TO ME--?
I COULDN'T SAY ANYTHING BUT "SO."

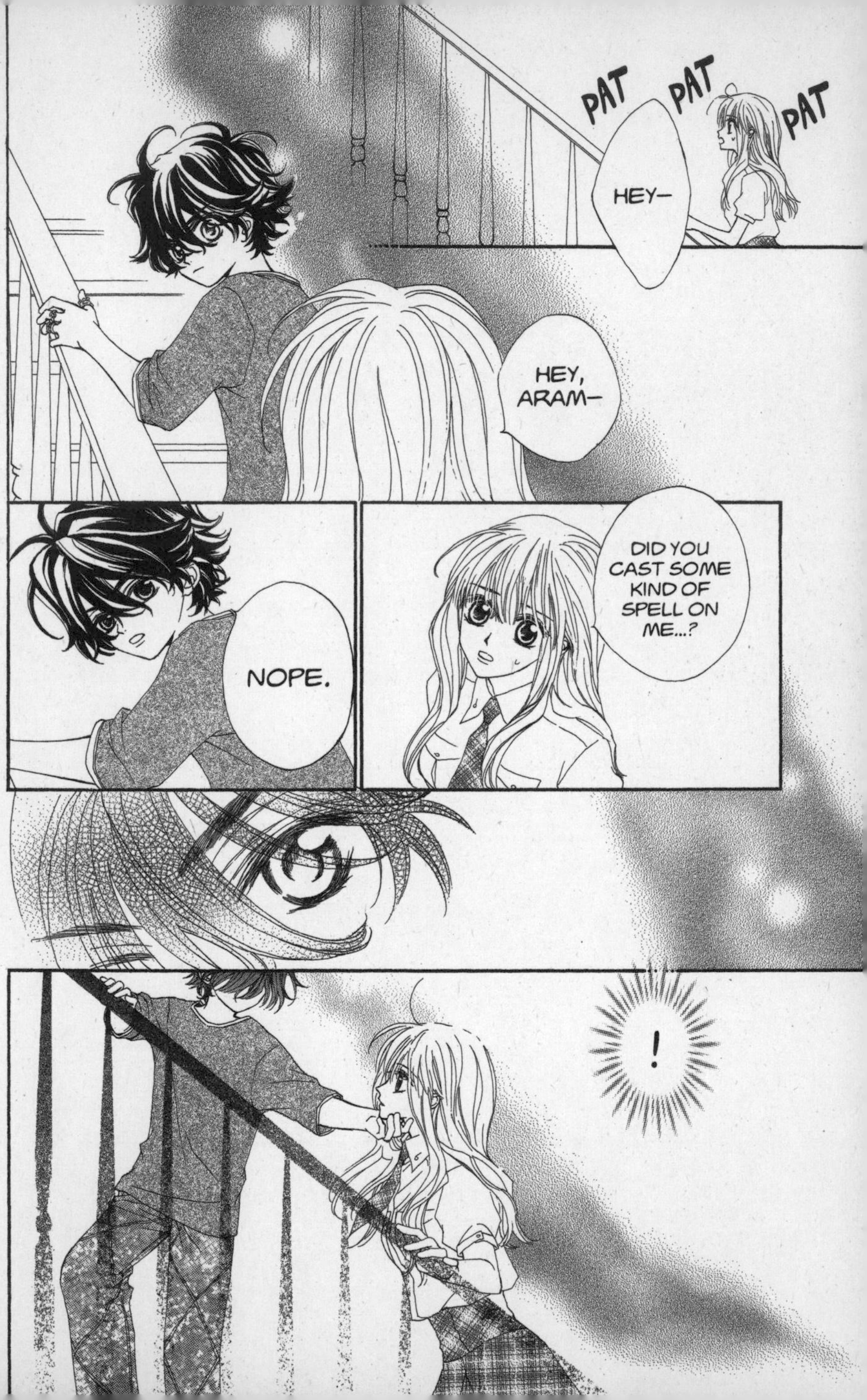
PAT PAT PAT
HEY—
HEY, ARAM—
DID YOU CAST SOME KIND OF SPELL ON ME...?
NOPE.
!

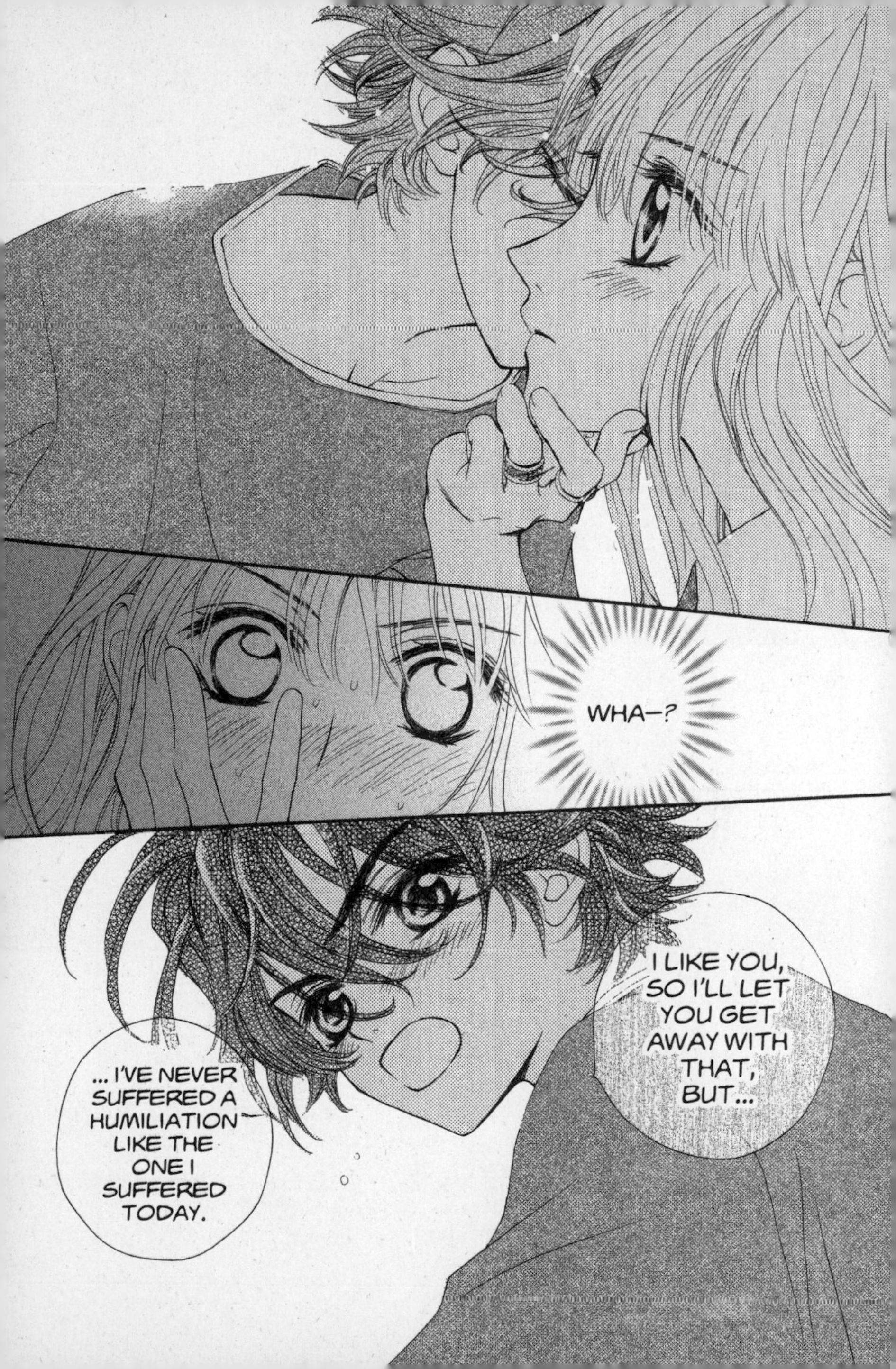
WHA-?
I LIKE YOU, SO I'LL LET YOU GET AWAY WITH THAT, BUT...
... I'VE NEVER SUFFERED A HUMILIATION LIKE THE ONE I SUFFERED TODAY.

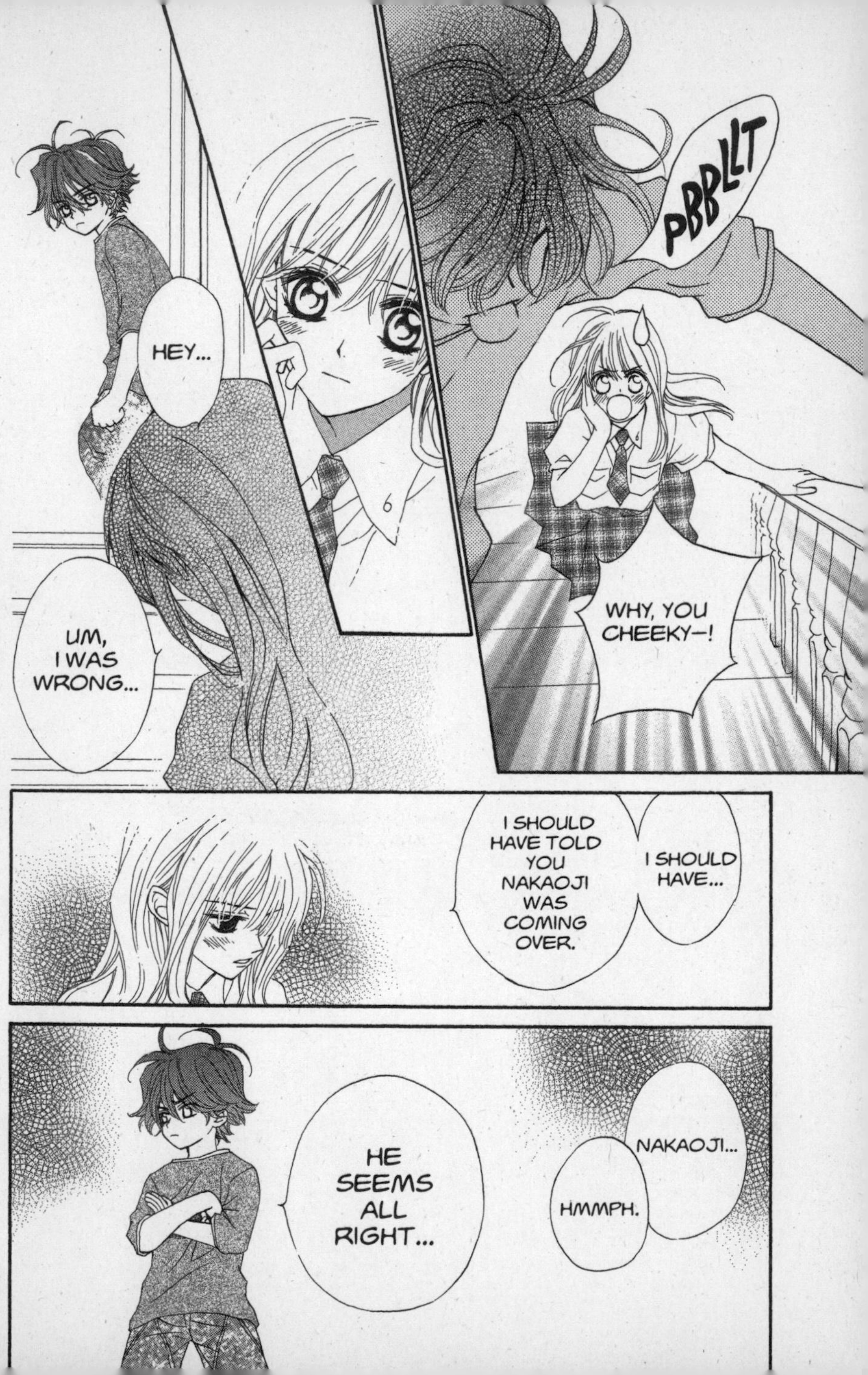
PBBLLT
WHY, YOU CHEEKY—!
HEY...
UM, I WAS WRONG...
I SHOULD HAVE...
I SHOULD HAVE TOLD YOU NAKAOJI WAS COMING OVER.
NAKAOJI...
HMMPH.
HE SEEMS ALL RIGHT...

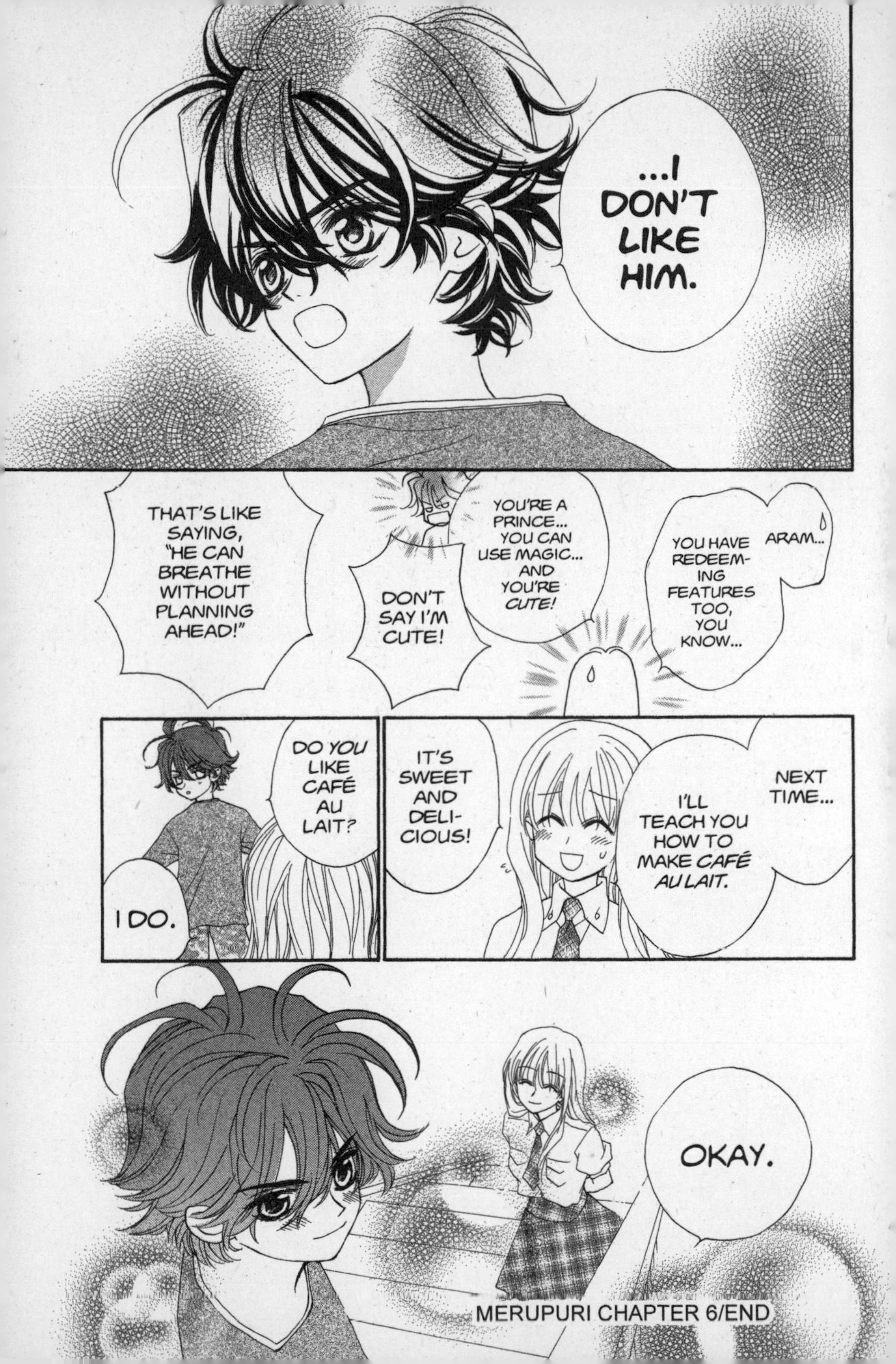
...I DON'T LIKE HIM.
ARAM...
YOU HAVE REDEEMING FEATURES TOO, YOU KNOW...
YOU'RE A PRINCE... YOU CAN USE MAGIC... AND YOU'RE *CUTE!*
DON'T SAY I'M CUTE!
THAT'S LIKE SAYING, "HE CAN BREATHE WITHOUT PLANNING AHEAD!"
NEXT TIME...
I'LL TEACH YOU HOW TO MAKE *CAFÉ AU LAIT.*
IT'S SWEET AND DELICIOUS!
DO *YOU* LIKE CAFÉ AU LAIT?
I DO.
OKAY.
MERUPURI CHAPTER 6/END

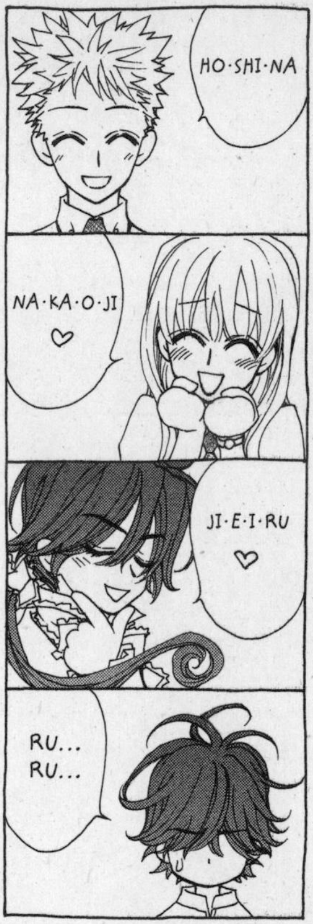
HO·SHI·NA
NA·KA·O·JI ♡
JI·E·I·RU ♡
RU...
RU...

Bonus Manga 1 Shiritori!

"Shiritori" is a Japanese word game in which a player starts with a word and the next player has to say a word that starts with the last syllable of the previous word. The game ends when a player cannot think of an appropriate word, or if a word ends with an "n" sound. "N" is the last syllable in the Japanese alphabet, and no words start with an "n" sound.

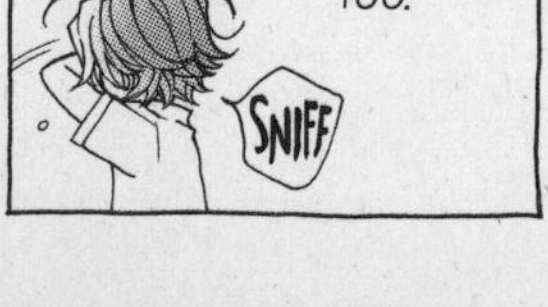
I WANT TO PLAY SHIRITORI WITH OUR NAMES, TOO.
RUB
SNIFF

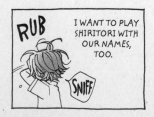

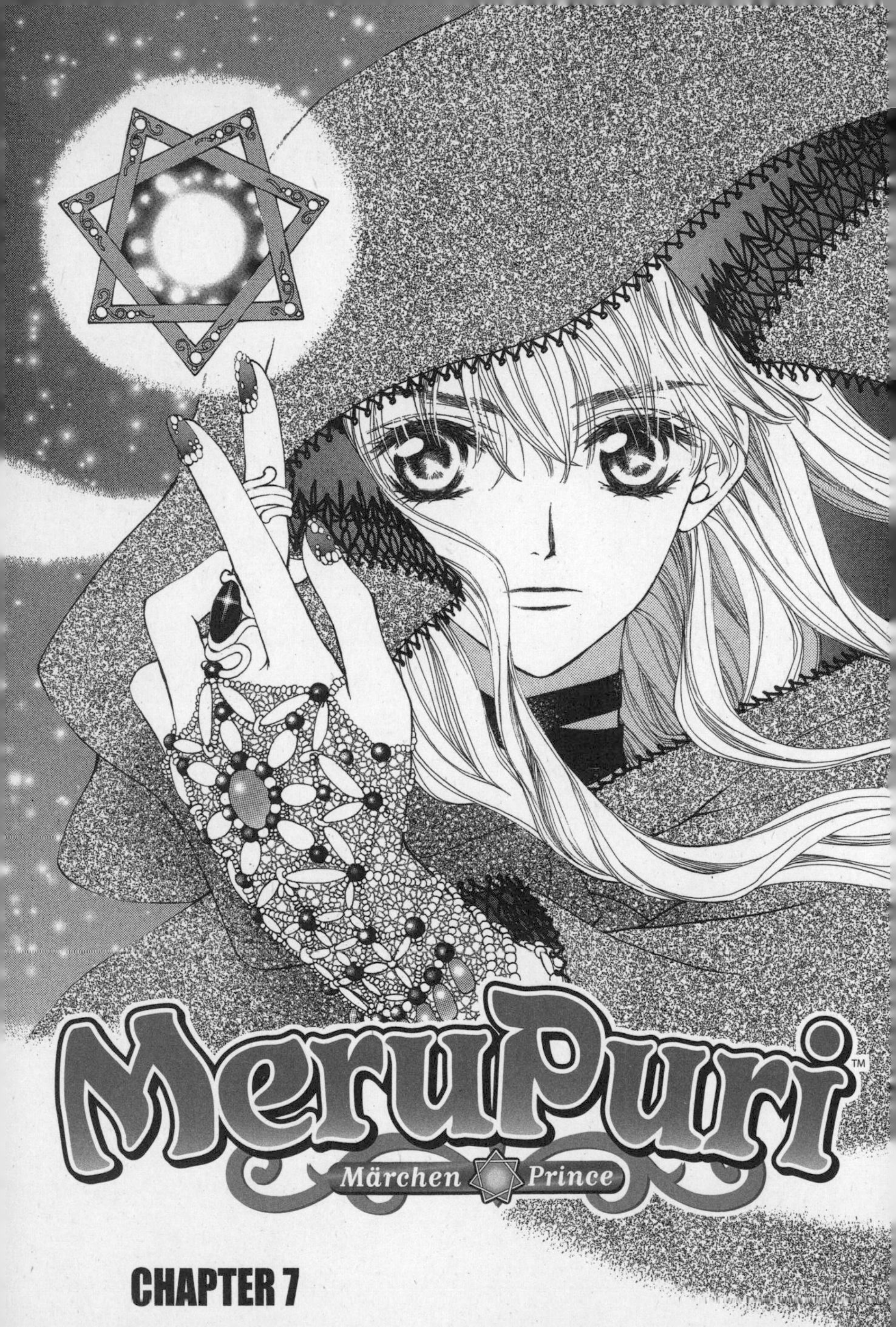

MeruPuri™

Märchen Prince

CHAPTER 7

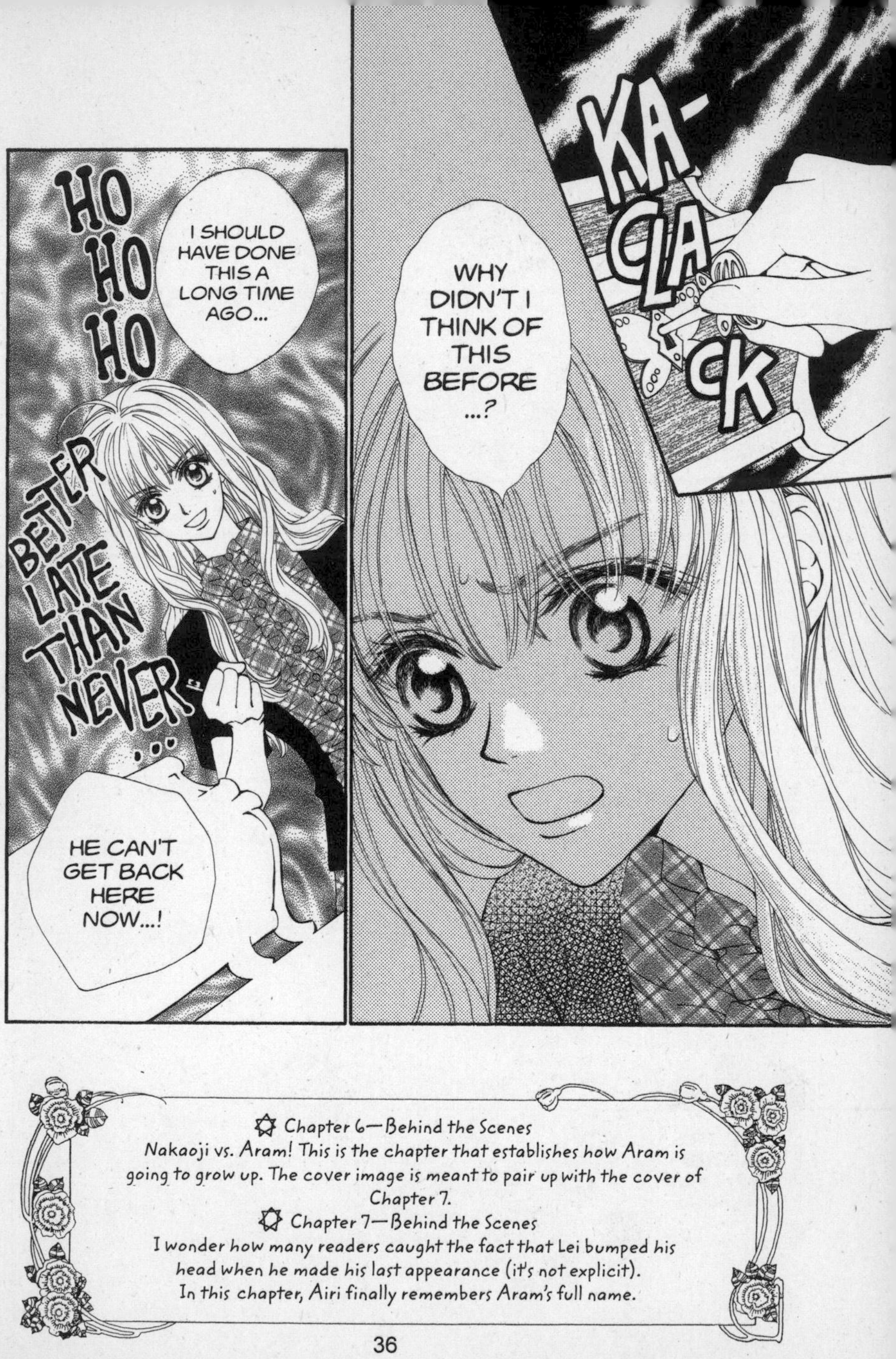
KA-CLACK
WHY DIDN'T I THINK OF THIS BEFORE ...?
HO HO HO
I SHOULD HAVE DONE THIS A LONG TIME AGO...
BETTER LATE THAN NEVER...
HE CAN'T GET BACK HERE NOW...!

✡ Chapter 6—Behind the Scenes

Nakaoji vs. Aram! This is the chapter that establishes how Aram is going to grow up. The cover image is meant to pair up with the cover of Chapter 7.

✡ Chapter 7—Behind the Scenes

I wonder how many readers caught the fact that Lei bumped his head when he made his last appearance (it's not explicit). In this chapter, Airi finally remembers Aram's full name.

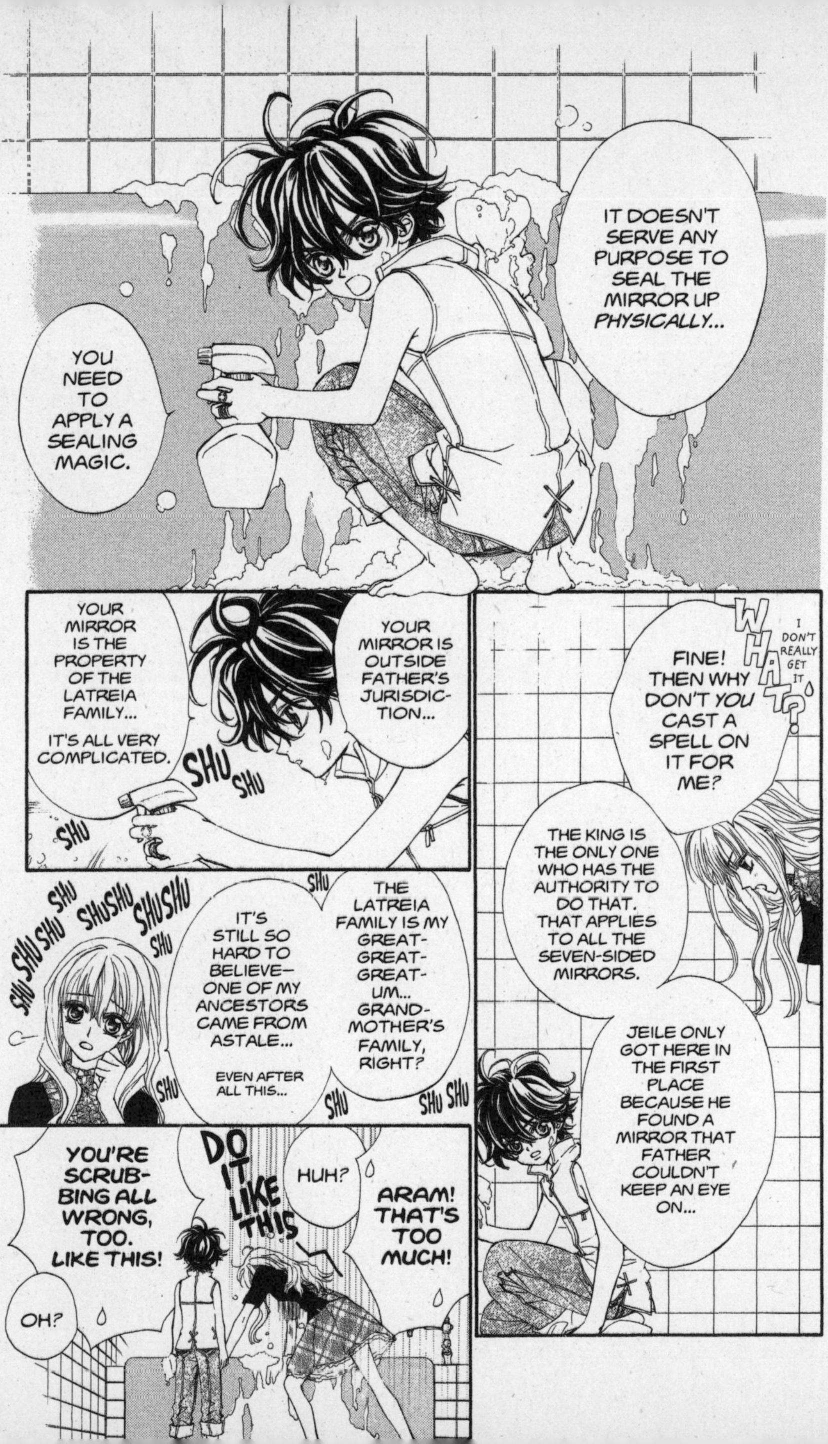

IT DOESN'T SERVE ANY PURPOSE TO SEAL THE MIRROR UP *PHYSICALLY*...
YOU NEED TO APPLY A SEALING MAGIC.
FINE! THEN WHY DON'T *YOU* CAST A SPELL ON IT FOR ME?
WHAT?!
I DON'T REALLY GET IT
THE KING IS THE ONLY ONE WHO HAS THE AUTHORITY TO DO THAT. THAT APPLIES TO ALL THE SEVEN-SIDED MIRRORS.
JEILE ONLY GOT HERE IN THE FIRST PLACE BECAUSE HE FOUND A MIRROR THAT FATHER COULDN'T KEEP AN EYE ON...
YOUR MIRROR IS OUTSIDE FATHER'S JURISDICTION...
YOUR MIRROR IS THE PROPERTY OF THE LATREIA FAMILY...
IT'S ALL VERY COMPLICATED.
SHU SHU
SHU
SHU
THE LATREIA FAMILY IS MY GREAT-GREAT-GREAT-UM... GRAND-MOTHER'S FAMILY, RIGHT?
IT'S STILL SO HARD TO BELIEVE—ONE OF MY ANCESTORS CAME FROM ASTALE...
EVEN AFTER ALL THIS...
SHU SHU SHU SHU SHUSHU SHUSHU SHU
SHU
SHU
SHU SHU
ARAM! THAT'S TOO MUCH!
HUH?
DO IT LIKE THIS
YOU'RE SCRUB-BING ALL WRONG, TOO. LIKE THIS!
OH?

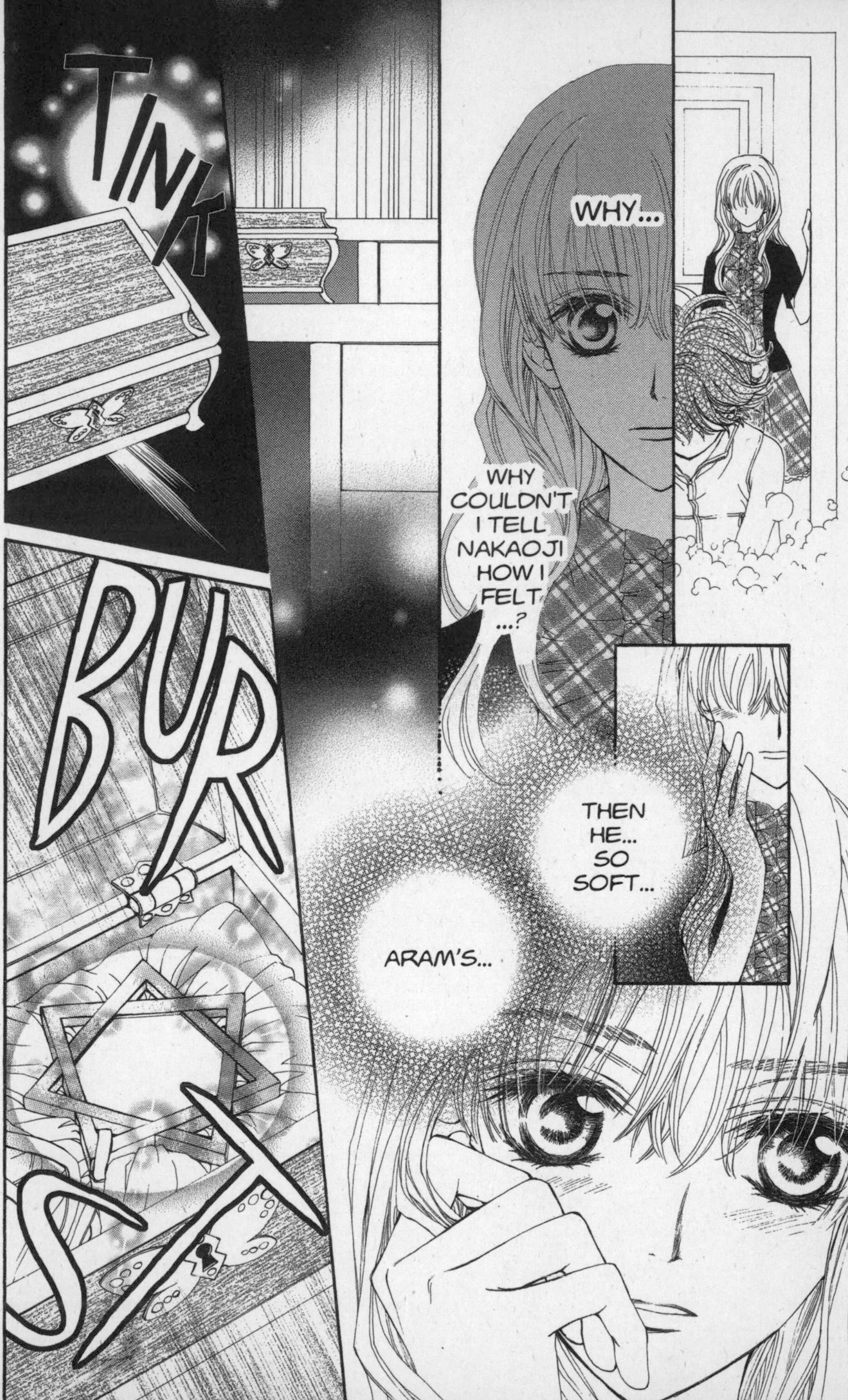
WHY...
WHY COULDN'T I TELL NAKAOJI HOW I FELT ...?
THEN HE... SO SOFT...
ARAM'S...
TINK
BURST

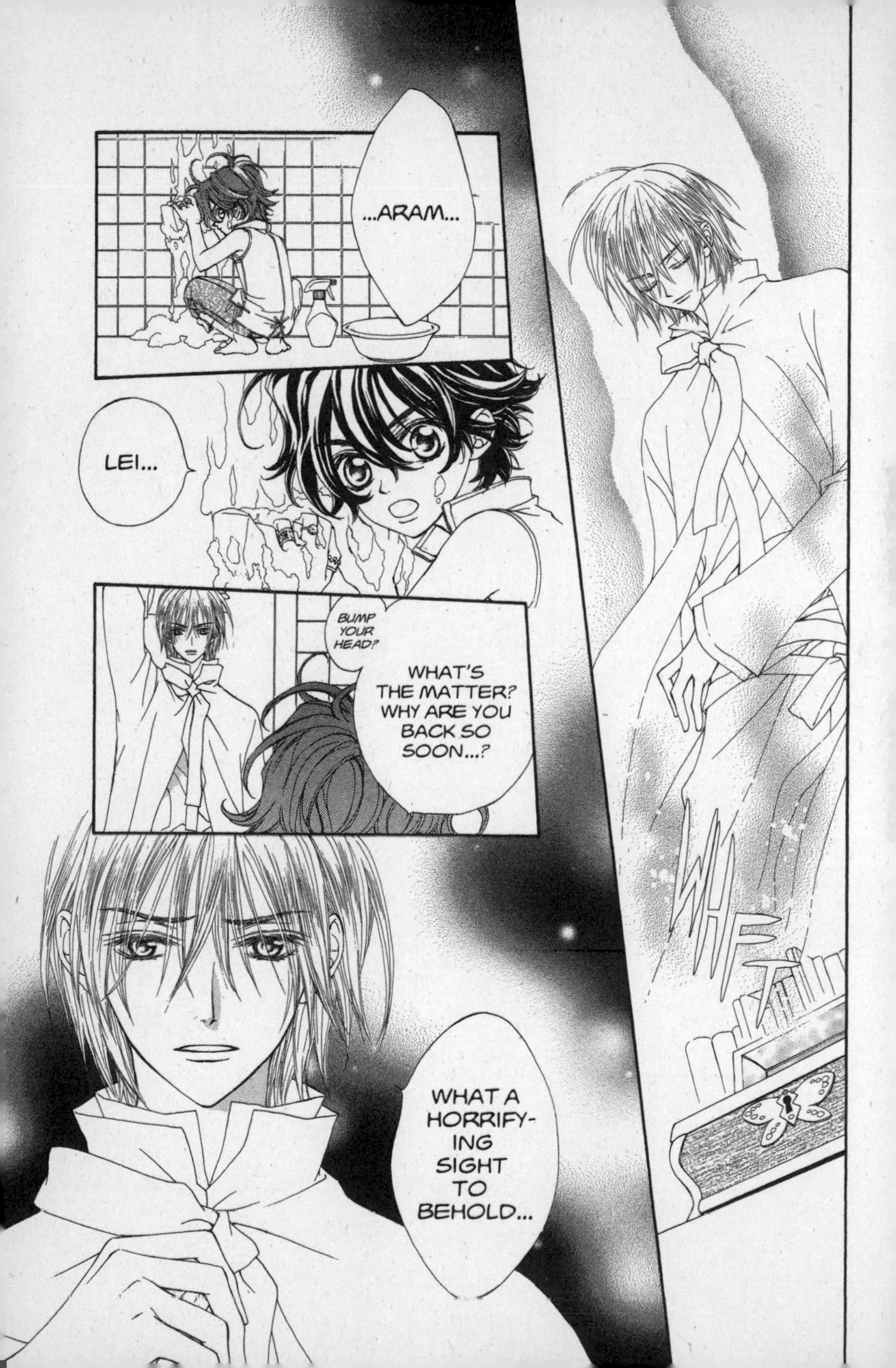
WHFT
...ARAM...
LEI...
WHAT'S THE MATTER? WHY ARE YOU BACK SO SOON...?
BUMP YOUR HEAD?
WHAT A HORRIFY-ING SIGHT TO BEHOLD...

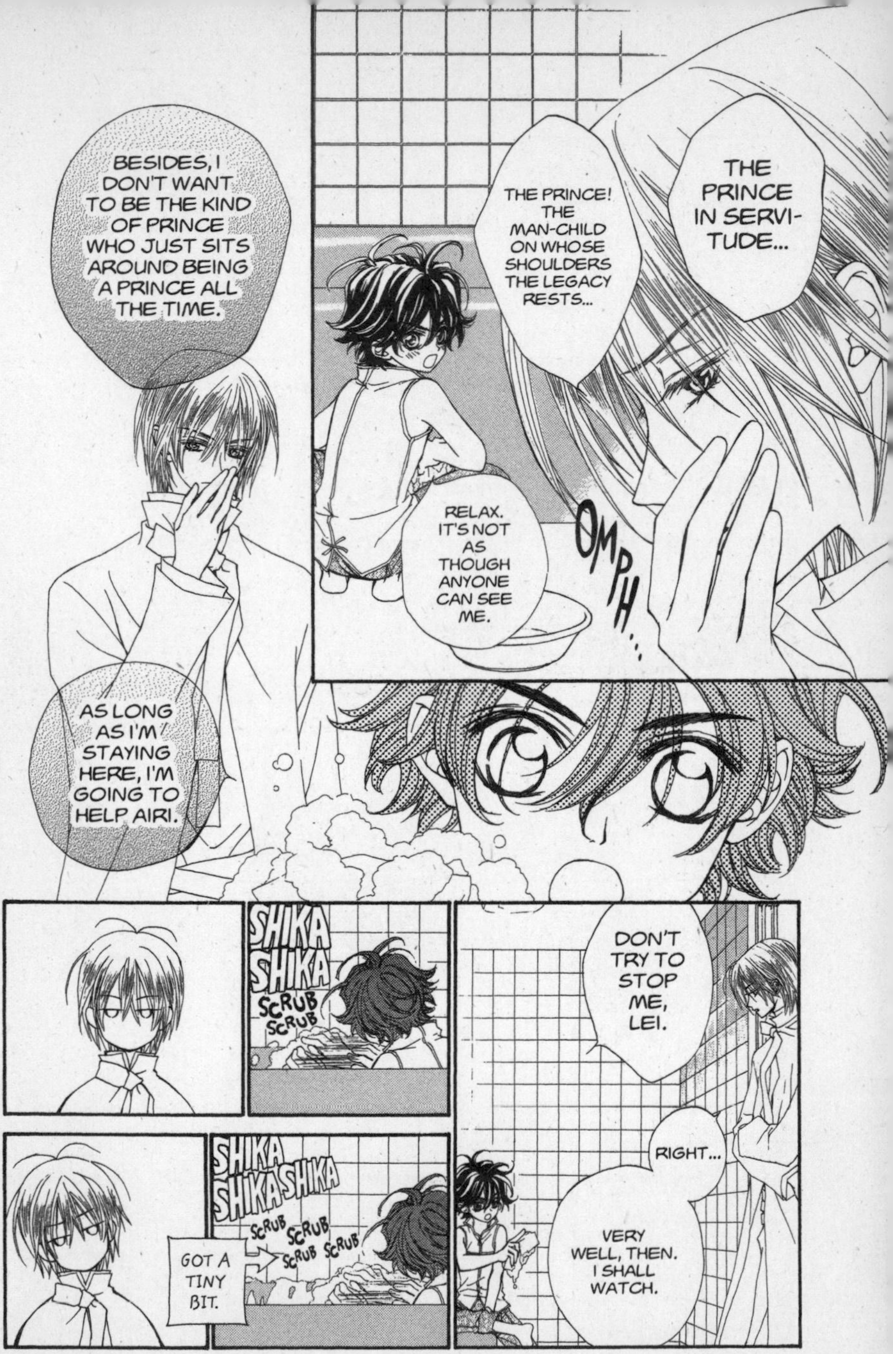
THE PRINCE IN SERVITUDE...
THE PRINCE! THE MAN-CHILD ON WHOSE SHOULDERS THE LEGACY RESTS...
OMPH...
RELAX. IT'S NOT AS THOUGH ANYONE CAN SEE ME.
BESIDES, I DON'T WANT TO BE THE KIND OF PRINCE WHO JUST SITS AROUND BEING A PRINCE ALL THE TIME.
AS LONG AS I'M STAYING HERE, I'M GOING TO HELP AIRI.
DON'T TRY TO STOP ME, LEI.
RIGHT...
VERY WELL, THEN. I SHALL WATCH.
SHIKA SHIKA
SCRUB SCRUB
SHIKA SHIKA SHIKA
SCRUB SCRUB SCRUB SCRUB
GOT A TINY BIT.

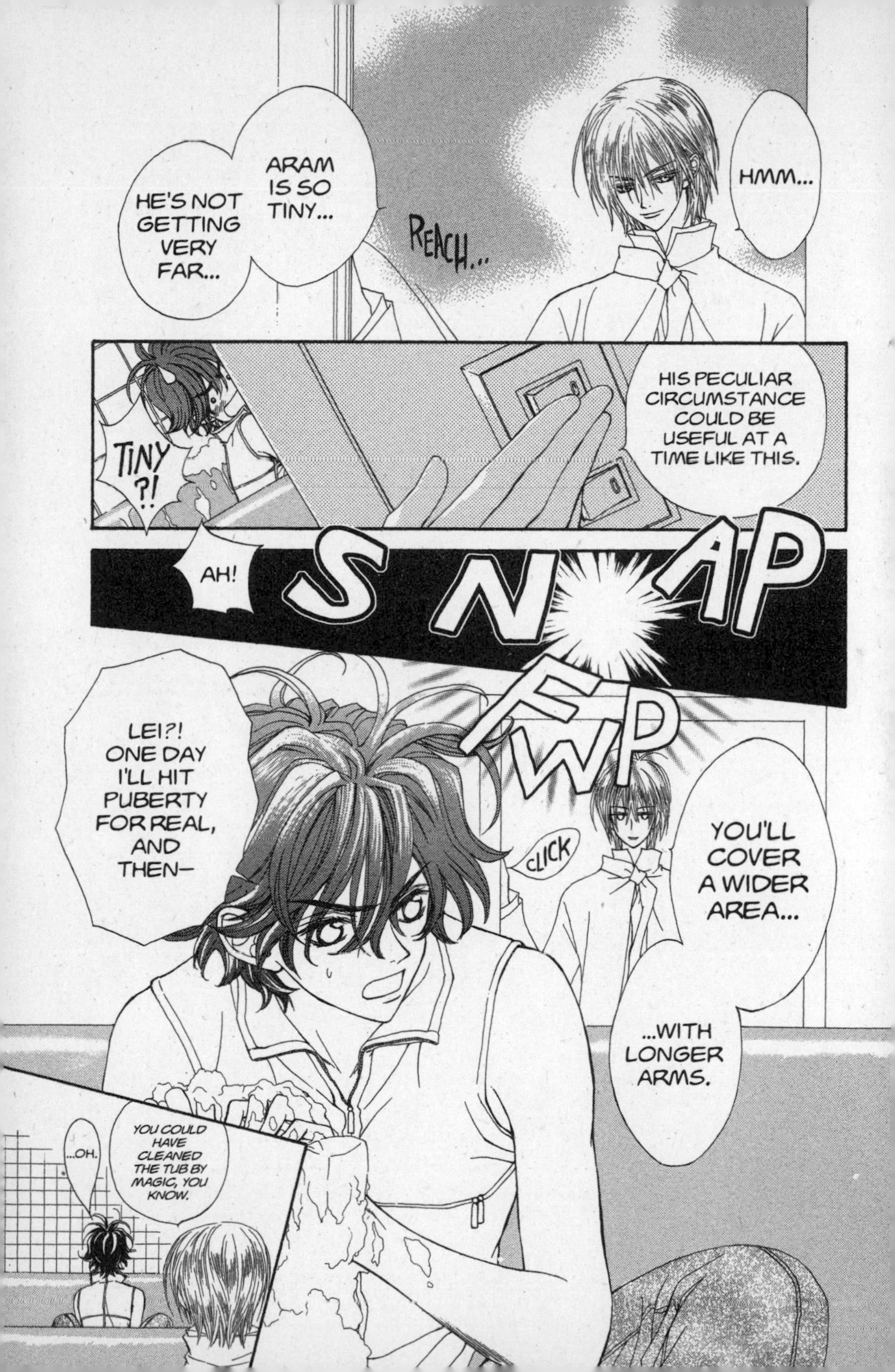
HMM...
ARAM IS SO TINY...
REACH...
HE'S NOT GETTING VERY FAR...
HIS PECULIAR CIRCUMSTANCE COULD BE USEFUL AT A TIME LIKE THIS.
TINY?!
SNAP
AH!
FWP
YOU'LL COVER A WIDER AREA...
CLICK
LEI?! ONE DAY I'LL HIT PUBERTY FOR REAL, AND THEN–
...WITH LONGER ARMS.
YOU COULD HAVE CLEANED THE TUB BY MAGIC, YOU KNOW.
...OH.

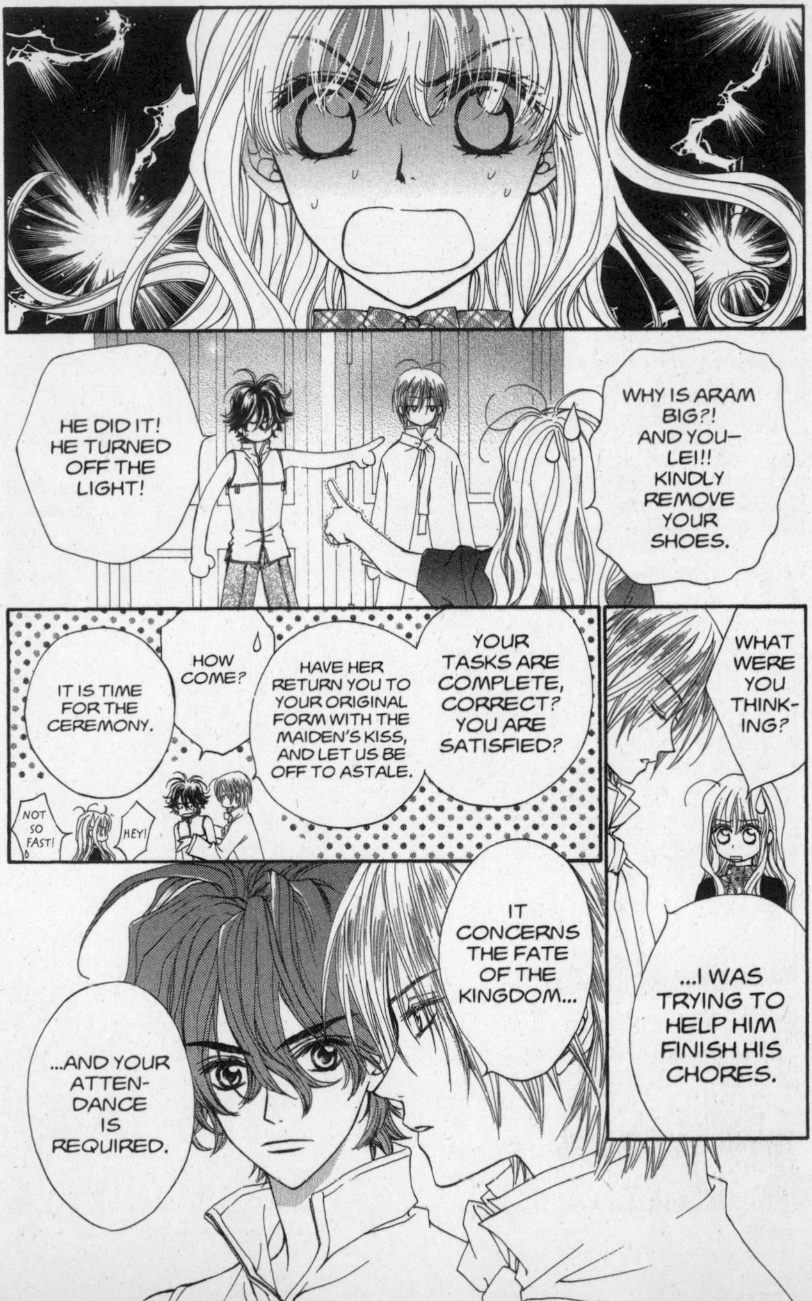
WHY IS ARAM BIG?! AND YOU— LEI!! KINDLY REMOVE YOUR SHOES.
HE DID IT! HE TURNED OFF THE LIGHT!
WHAT WERE YOU THINKING?
...I WAS TRYING TO HELP HIM FINISH HIS CHORES.
YOUR TASKS ARE COMPLETE, CORRECT? YOU ARE SATISFIED?
HAVE HER RETURN YOU TO YOUR ORIGINAL FORM WITH THE MAIDEN'S KISS, AND LET US BE OFF TO ASTALE.
HOW COME?
IT IS TIME FOR THE CEREMONY.
HEY!
NOT SO FAST!
IT CONCERNS THE FATE OF THE KINGDOM...
...AND YOUR ATTENDANCE IS REQUIRED.

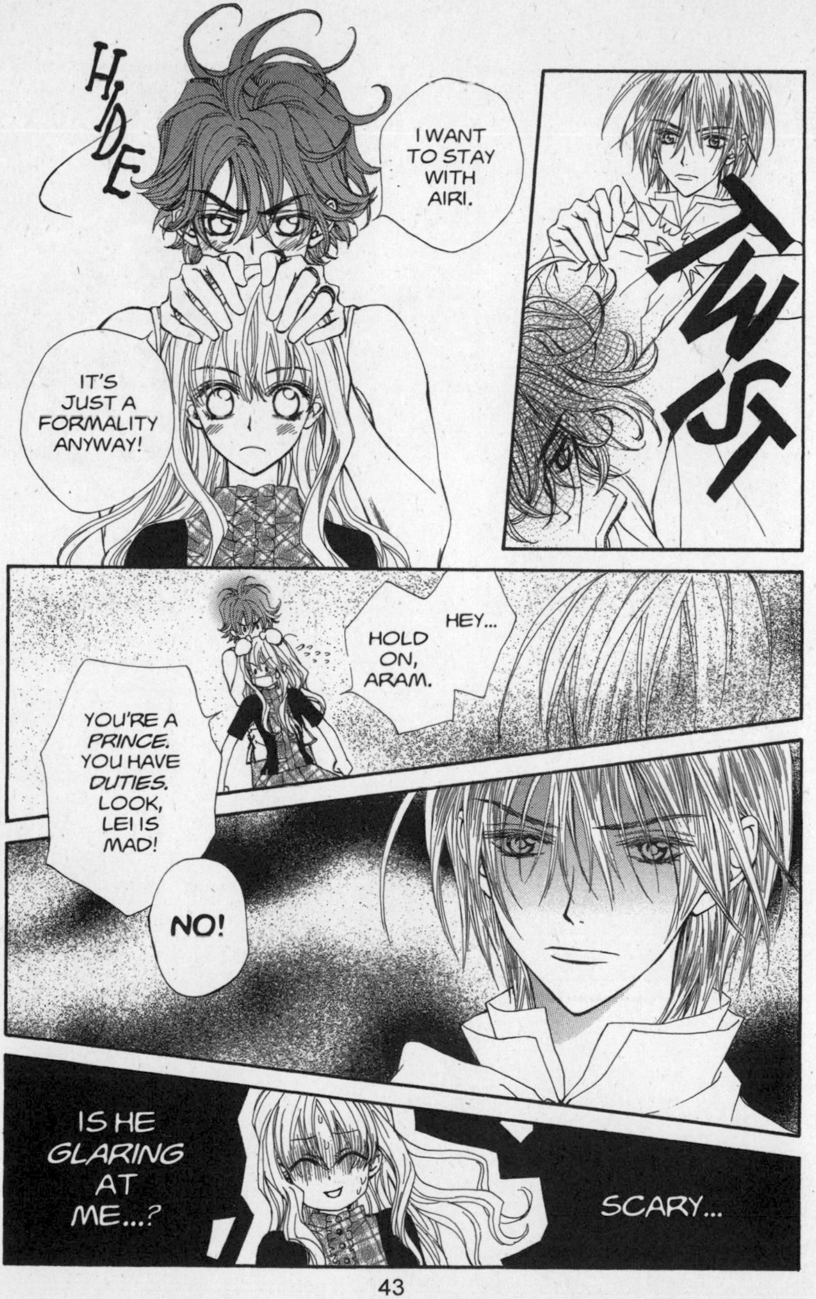
TWIST
HIDE
I WANT TO STAY WITH AIRI.
IT'S JUST A FORMALITY ANYWAY!
HEY... HOLD ON, ARAM.
YOU'RE A *PRINCE.* YOU HAVE *DUTIES.* LOOK, LEI IS MAD!
NO!
SCARY...
IS HE GLARING AT ME...?

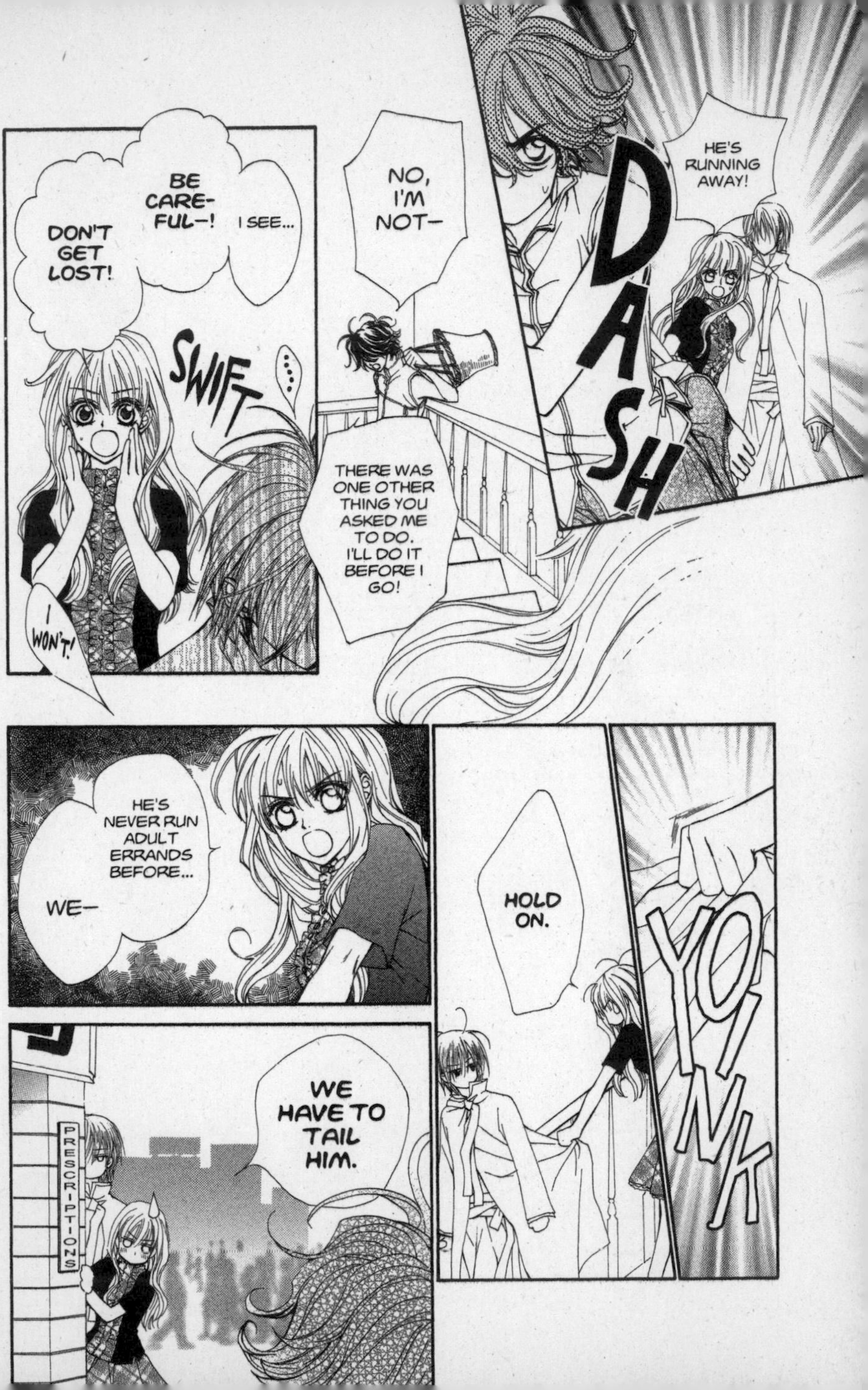
DASH
HE'S RUNNING AWAY!
NO, I'M NOT-
THERE WAS ONE OTHER THING YOU ASKED ME TO DO. I'LL DO IT BEFORE I GO!
I SEE...
BE CAREFUL-!
DON'T GET LOST!
SWIFT
...
I WON'T!
YOINK
HOLD ON.
HE'S NEVER RUN ADULT ERRANDS BEFORE...
WE-
PRESCRIPTIONS
WE HAVE TO TAIL HIM.

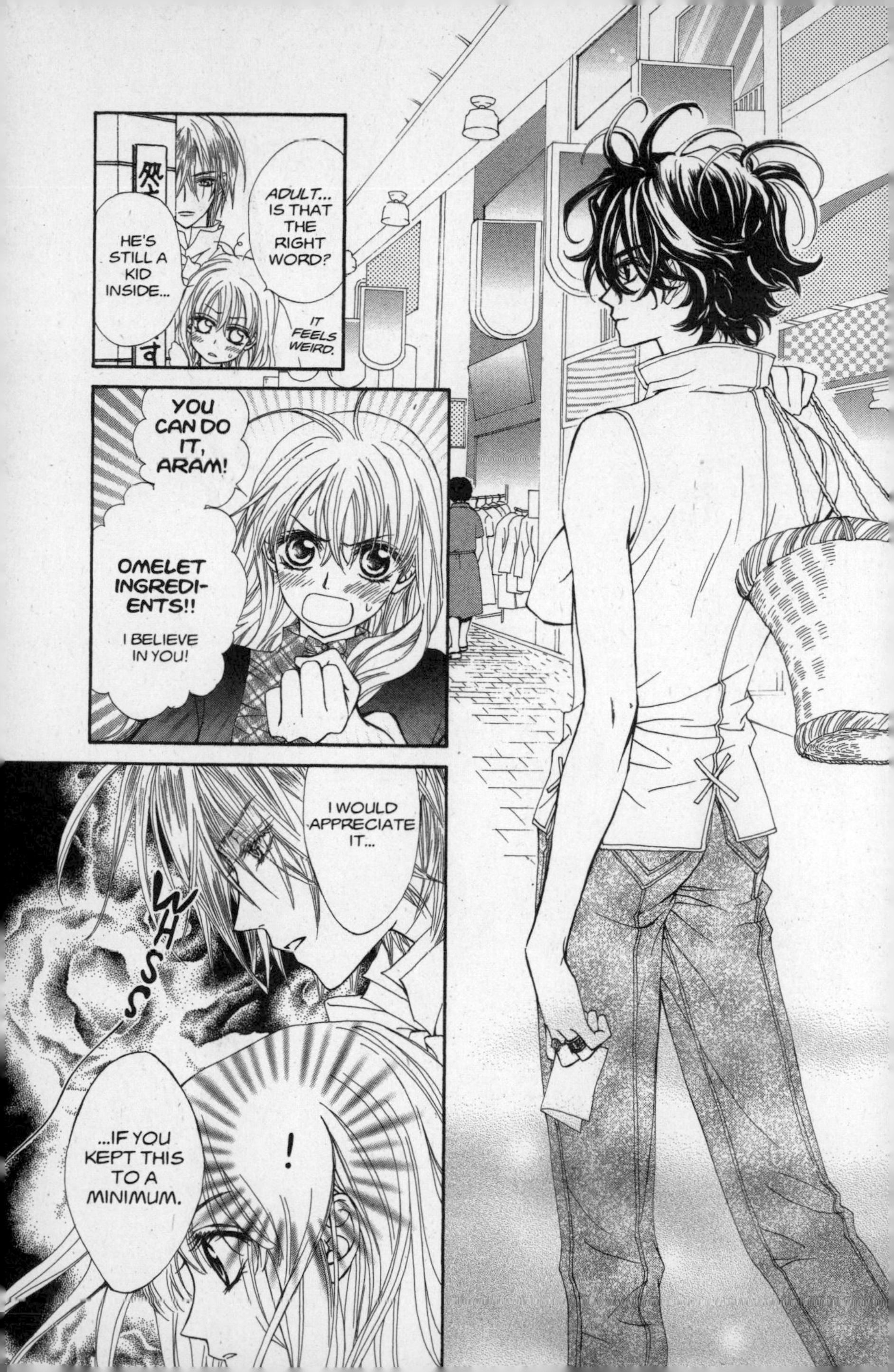
ADULT... IS THAT THE RIGHT WORD?
HE'S STILL A KID INSIDE...
IT FEELS WEIRD.
YOU CAN DO IT, ARAM!
OMELET INGREDIENTS!!
I BELIEVE IN YOU!
I WOULD APPRECIATE IT...
WHSS
!
...IF YOU KEPT THIS TO A MINIMUM.

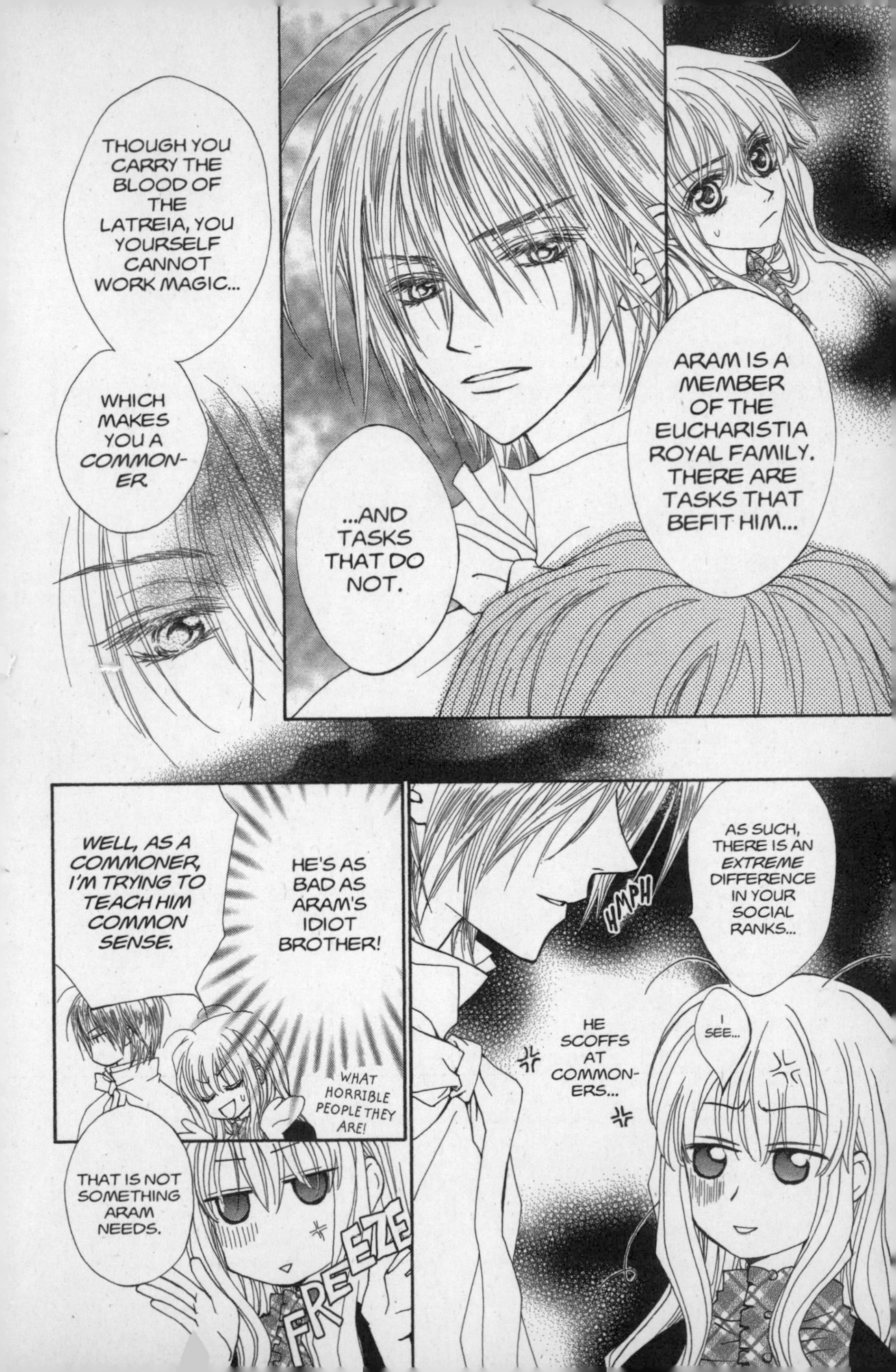
ARAM IS A MEMBER OF THE EUCHARISTIA ROYAL FAMILY. THERE ARE TASKS THAT BEFIT HIM...
...AND TASKS THAT DO NOT.
THOUGH YOU CARRY THE BLOOD OF THE LATREIA, YOU YOURSELF CANNOT WORK MAGIC...
WHICH MAKES YOU A COMMONER.
AS SUCH, THERE IS AN *EXTREME* DIFFERENCE IN YOUR SOCIAL RANKS...
HMPH
HE SCOFFS AT COMMONERS...
I SEE...
HE'S AS BAD AS ARAM'S IDIOT BROTHER!
WELL, AS A COMMONER, I'M TRYING TO TEACH HIM COMMON SENSE.
WHAT HORRIBLE PEOPLE THEY ARE!
THAT IS NOT SOMETHING ARAM NEEDS.
FREEZE

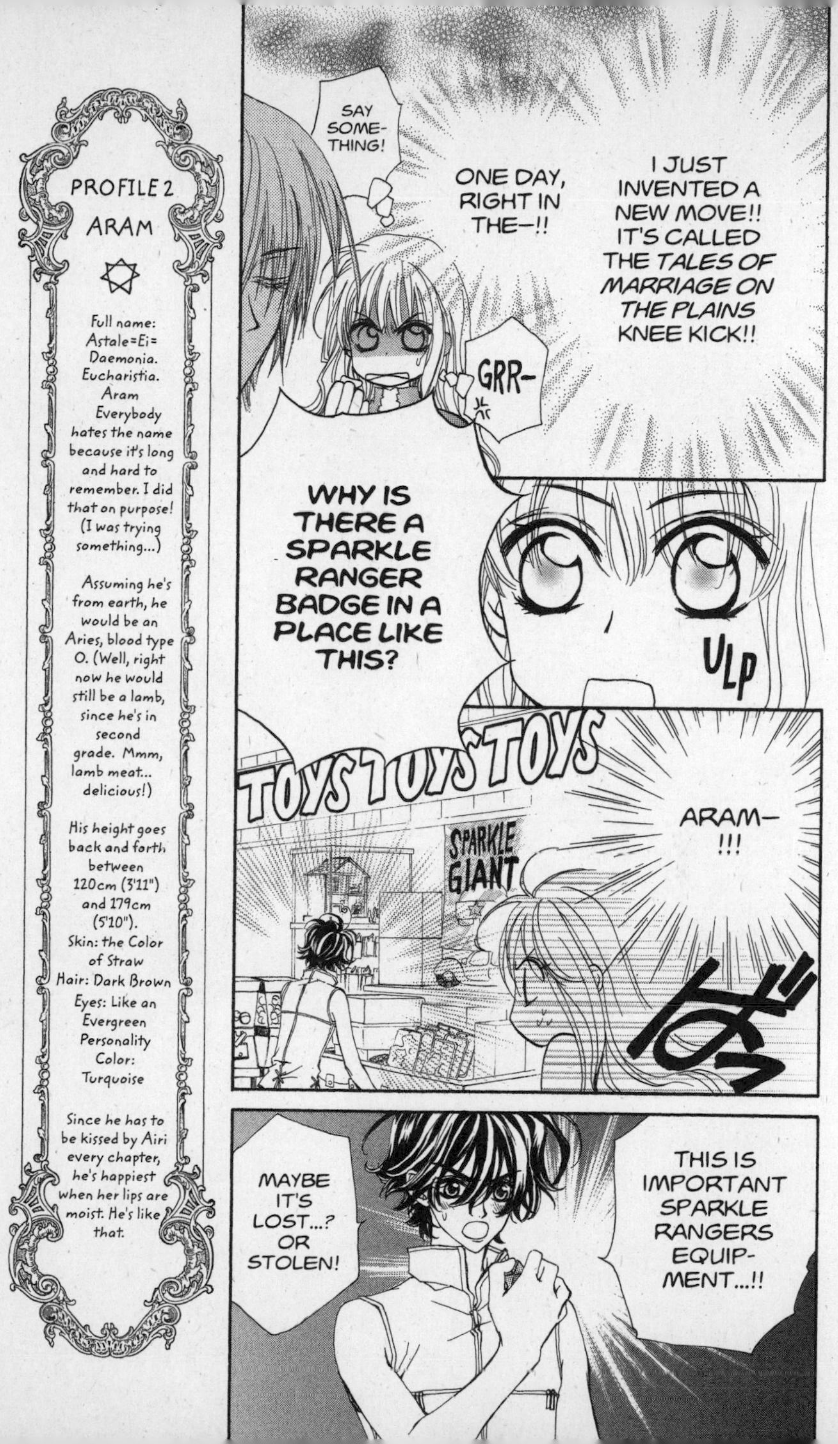
I JUST INVENTED A NEW MOVE!! IT'S CALLED THE *TALES OF MARRIAGE ON THE PLAINS* KNEE KICK!!
ONE DAY, RIGHT IN THE--!!
SAY SOME-THING!
GRR-
ULP
WHY IS THERE A SPARKLE RANGER BADGE IN A PLACE LIKE THIS?
ARAM- !!!
TOYS TOYS TOYS
SPARKLE GIANT
THIS IS IMPORTANT SPARKLE RANGERS EQUIP-MENT...!!
MAYBE IT'S LOST...? OR STOLEN!

PROFILE 2

ARAM

Full name: Astale=Ei= Daemonia. Eucharistia. Aram Everybody hates the name because it's long and hard to remember. I did that on purpose! (I was trying something...)

Assuming he's from earth, he would be an Aries, blood type O. (Well, right now he would still be a lamb, since he's in second grade. Mmm, lamb meat... delicious!)

His height goes back and forth between 120cm (3'11") and 179cm (5'10").
Skin: the Color of Straw
Hair: Dark Brown
Eyes: Like an Evergreen
Personality Color: Turquoise

Since he has to be kissed by Airi every chapter, he's happiest when her lips are moist. He's like that.

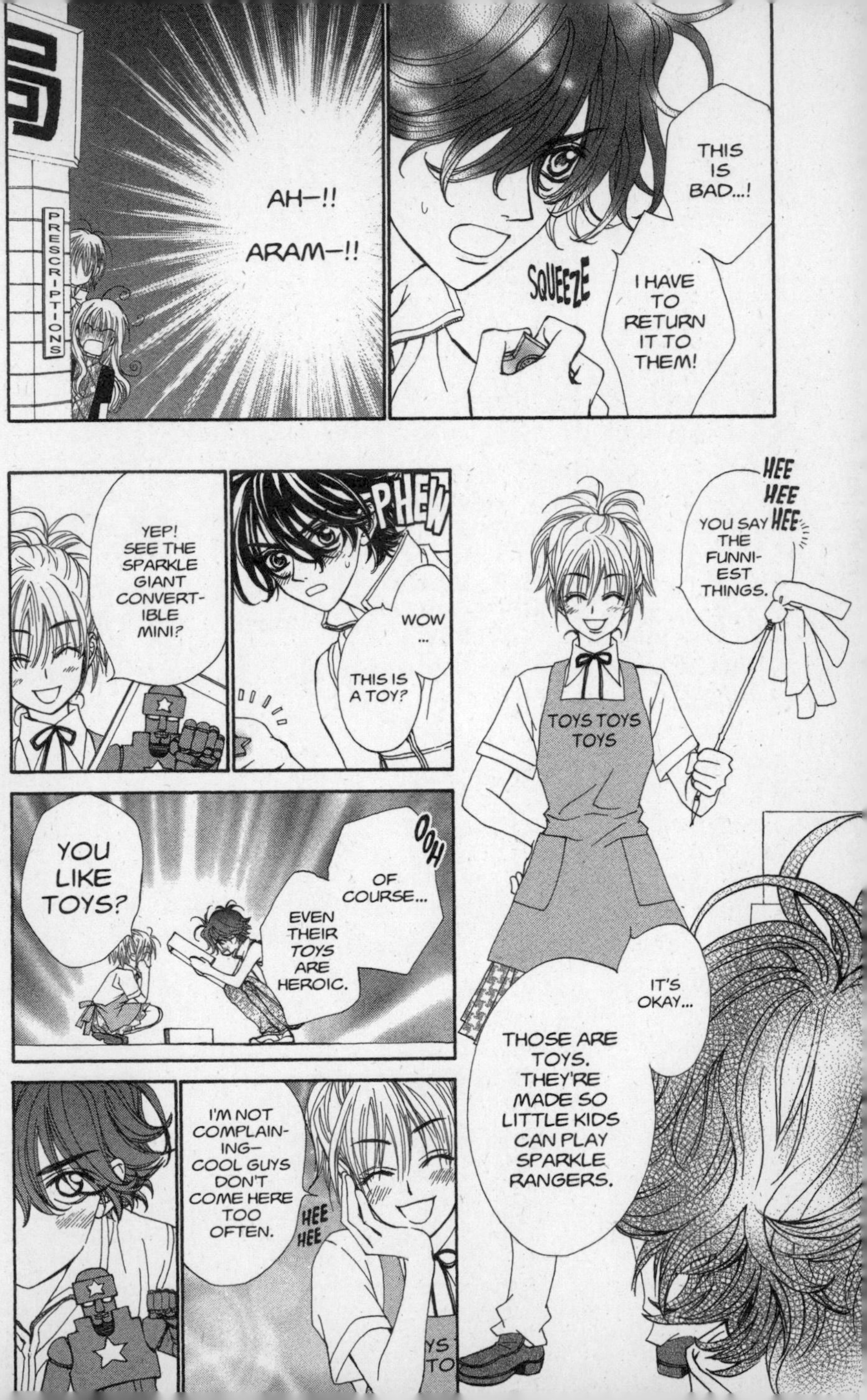

THIS IS BAD...!
SQUEEZE
I HAVE TO RETURN IT TO THEM!
AH—!!
ARAM—!!
PRESCRIPTIONS
HEE HEE HEE
YOU SAY THE FUNNIEST THINGS.
TOYS TOYS TOYS
IT'S OKAY...
THOSE ARE TOYS. THEY'RE MADE SO LITTLE KIDS CAN PLAY SPARKLE RANGERS.
PHEW
WOW ...
THIS IS A TOY?
YEP! SEE THE SPARKLE GIANT CONVERTIBLE MINI?
OOH
OF COURSE...
EVEN THEIR TOYS ARE HEROIC.
YOU LIKE TOYS?
I'M NOT COMPLAINING—COOL GUYS DON'T COME HERE TOO OFTEN.
HEE HEE

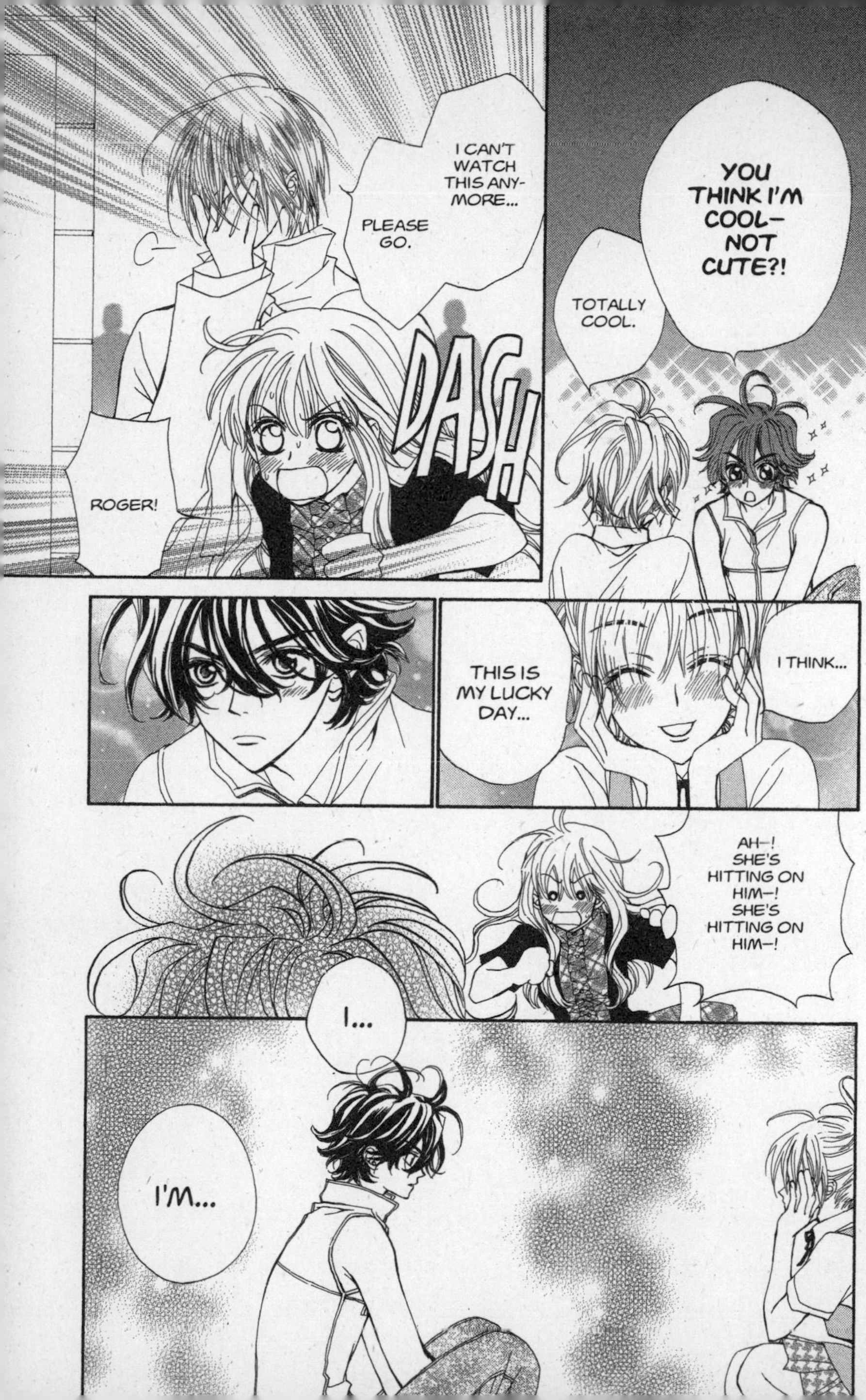
YOU THINK I'M COOL—NOT CUTE?!
TOTALLY COOL.
I CAN'T WATCH THIS ANYMORE...
PLEASE GO.
DASH
ROGER!
I THINK...
THIS IS MY LUCKY DAY...
AH—! SHE'S HITTING ON HIM—! SHE'S HITTING ON HIM—!
I...
I'M...

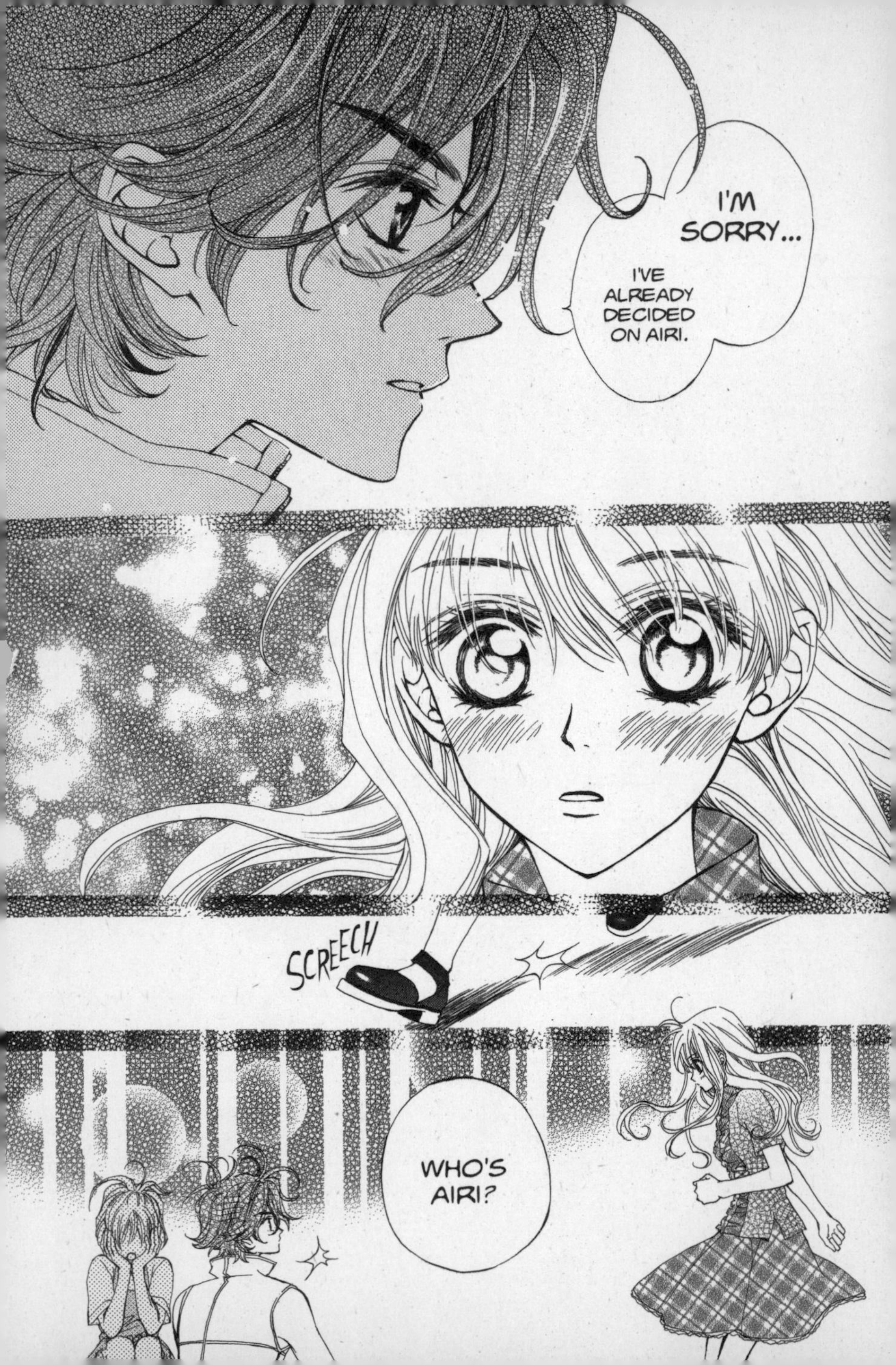
I'M SORRY...
I'VE ALREADY DECIDED ON AIRI.
SCREECH
WHO'S AIRI?

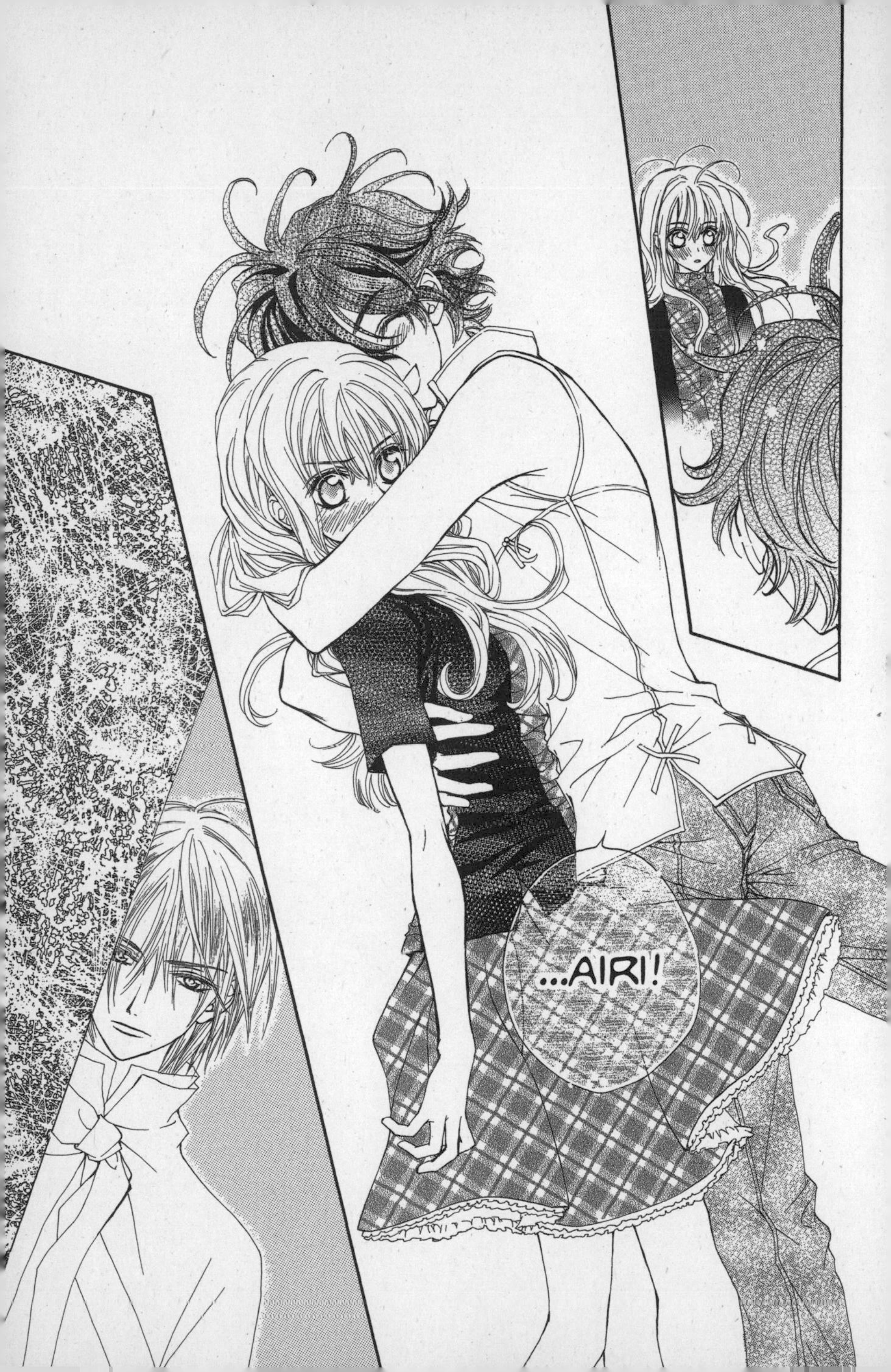
...AIRI!

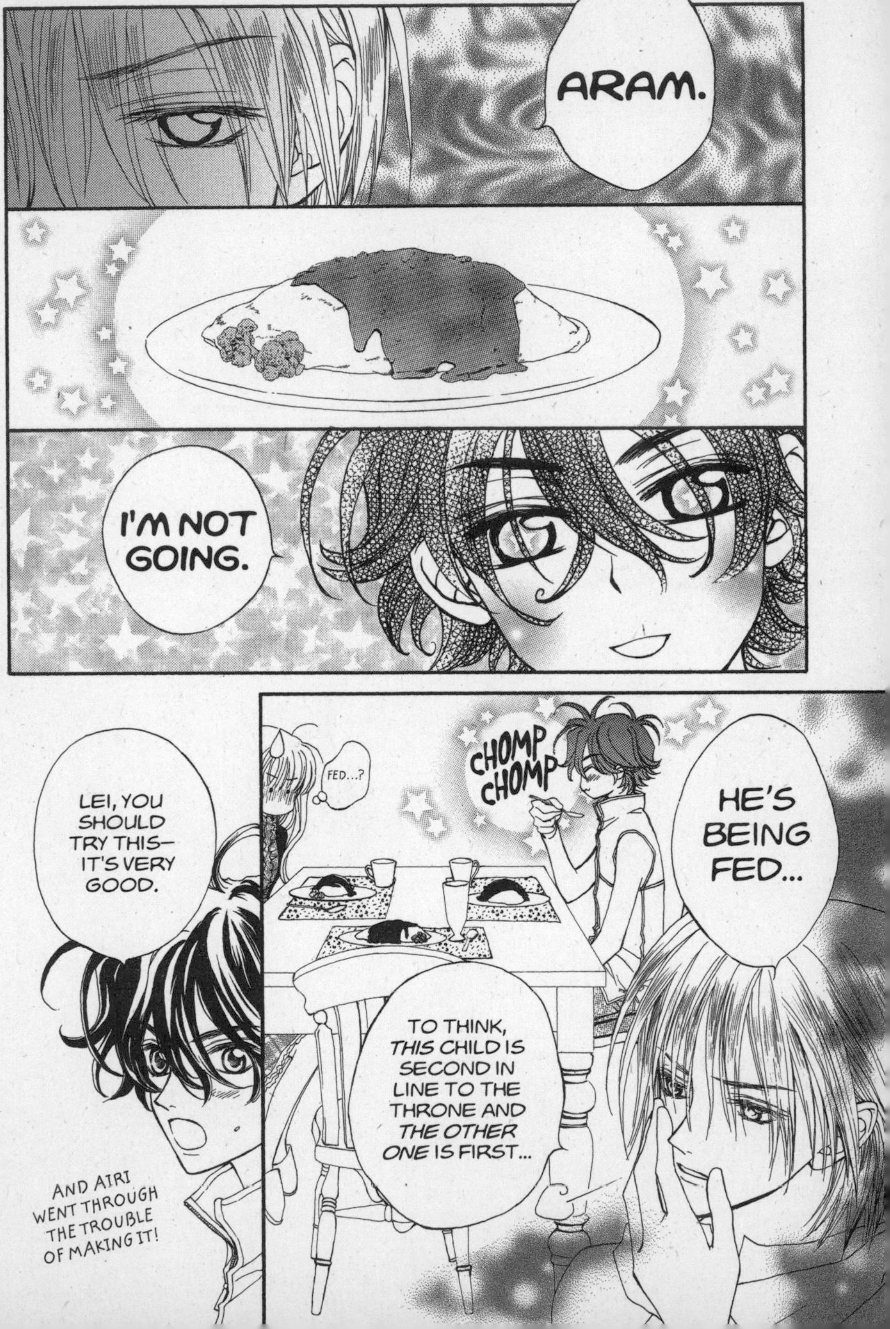
ARAM.
I'M NOT GOING.
HE'S BEING FED...
CHOMP CHOMP
FED...?
TO THINK, *THIS CHILD* IS SECOND IN LINE TO THE THRONE AND *THE OTHER ONE* IS FIRST...
LEI, YOU SHOULD TRY THIS— IT'S VERY GOOD.
AND AIRI WENT THROUGH THE TROUBLE OF MAKING IT!

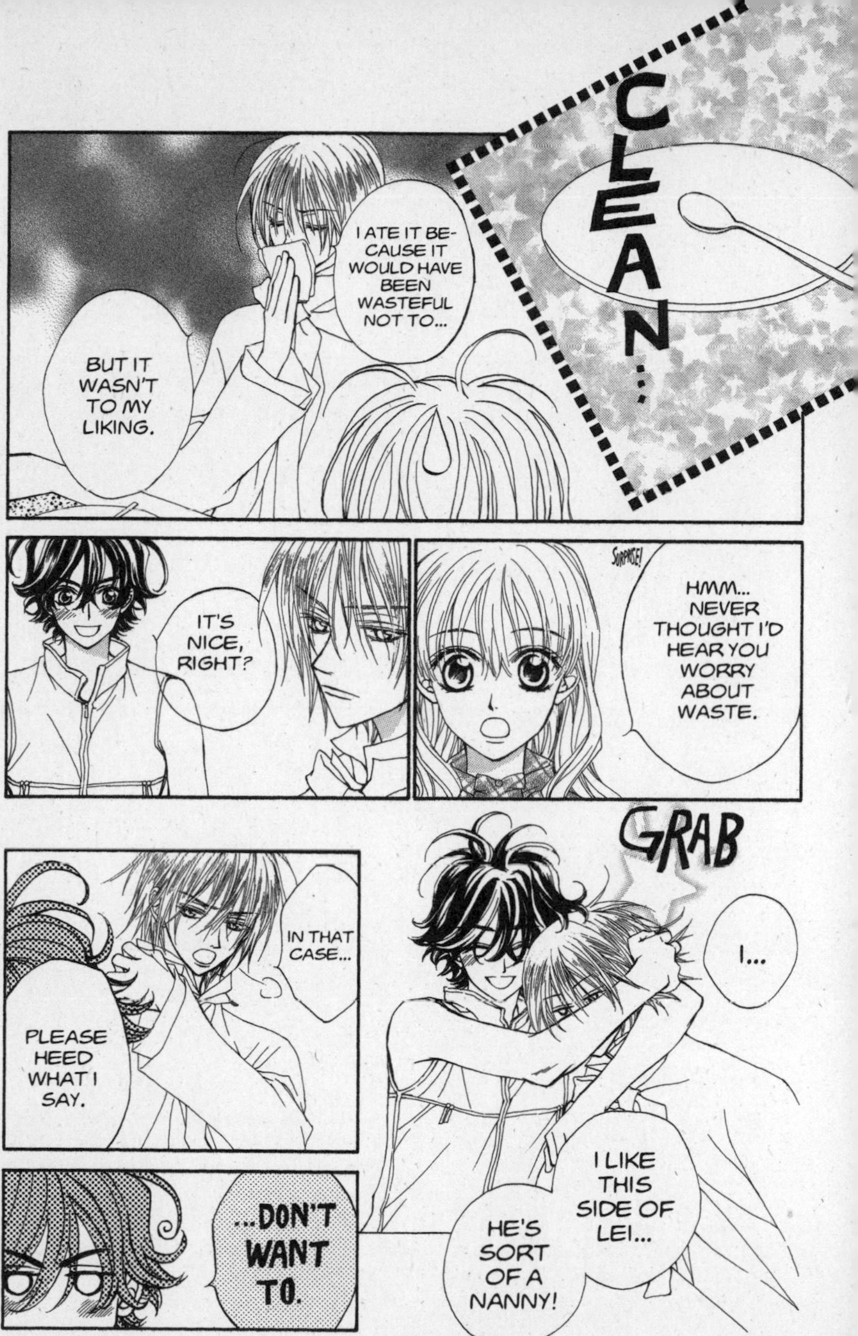
CLEAN...
I ATE IT BE-CAUSE IT WOULD HAVE BEEN WASTEFUL NOT TO...
BUT IT WASN'T TO MY LIKING.
SURPRISE!
HMM... NEVER THOUGHT I'D HEAR YOU WORRY ABOUT WASTE.
IT'S NICE, RIGHT?
GRAB
I...
I LIKE THIS SIDE OF LEI...
HE'S SORT OF A NANNY!
IN THAT CASE...
PLEASE HEED WHAT I SAY.
...DON'T WANT TO.

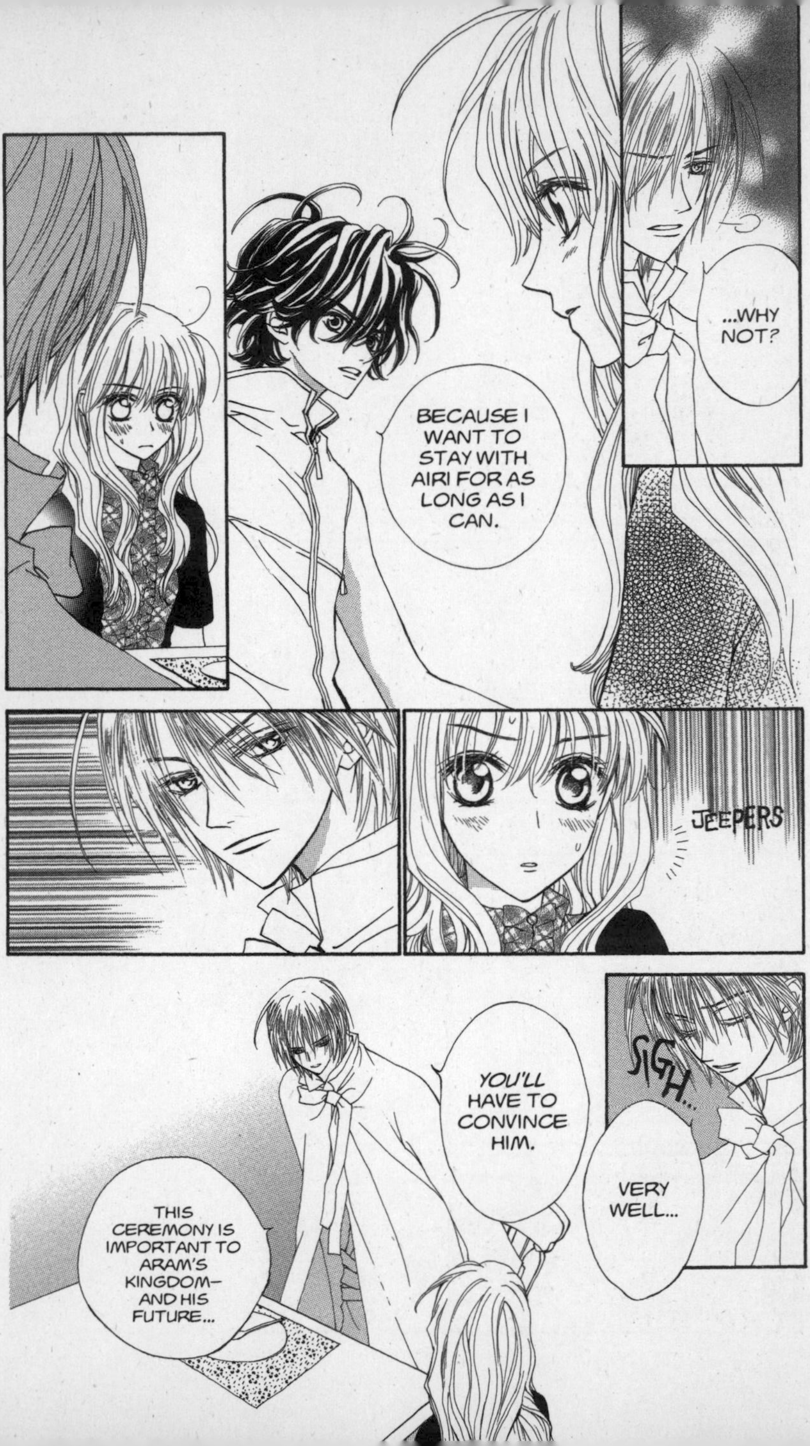
...WHY NOT?
BECAUSE I WANT TO STAY WITH AIRI FOR AS LONG AS I CAN.
JEEPERS
SIGH...
VERY WELL...
YOU'LL HAVE TO CONVINCE HIM.
THIS CEREMONY IS IMPORTANT TO ARAM'S KINGDOM—AND HIS FUTURE...

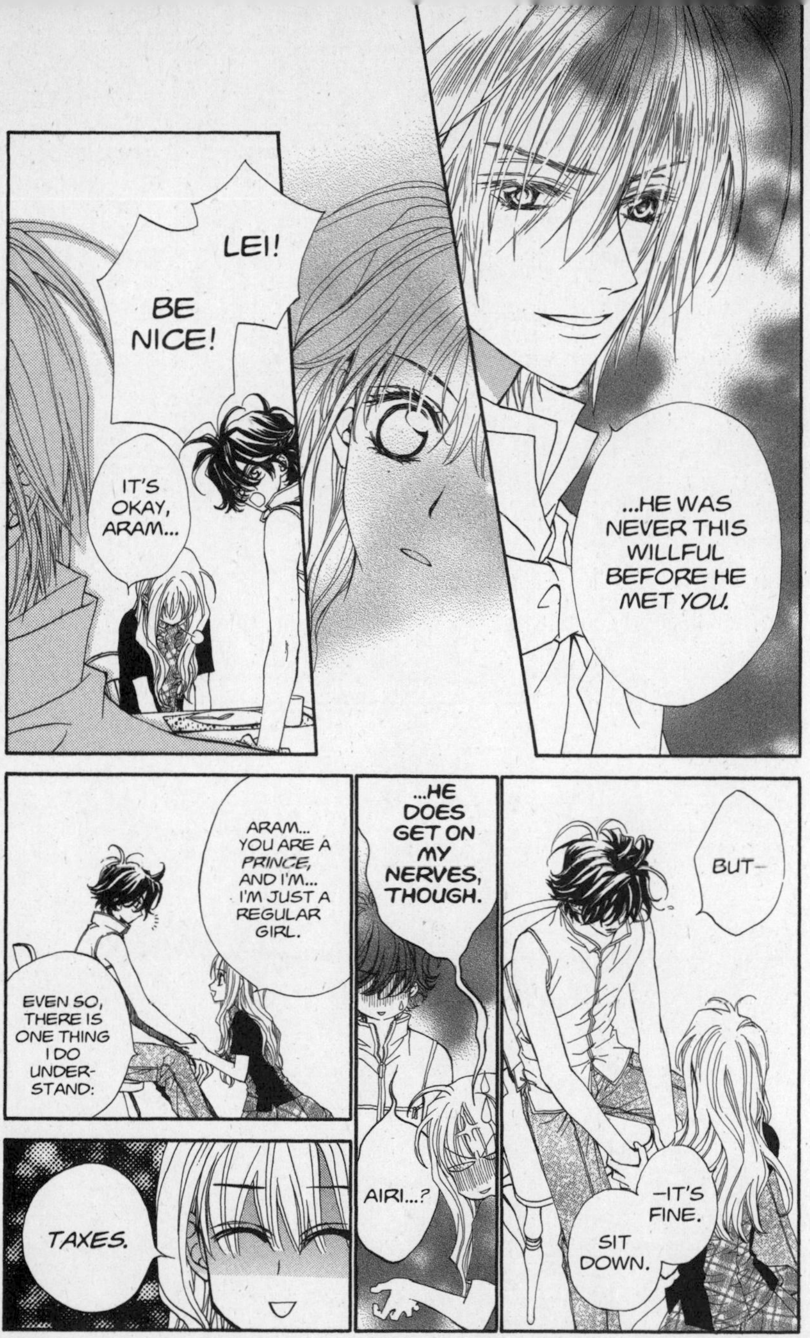
...HE WAS NEVER THIS WILLFUL BEFORE HE MET *YOU.*
LEI! BE NICE!
IT'S OKAY, ARAM...
BUT–
–IT'S FINE. SIT DOWN.
...HE DOES GET ON MY NERVES, THOUGH.
AIRI...?
ARAM... YOU ARE A *PRINCE,* AND I'M... I'M JUST A REGULAR GIRL.
EVEN SO, THERE IS ONE THING I DO UNDER-STAND:
TAXES.

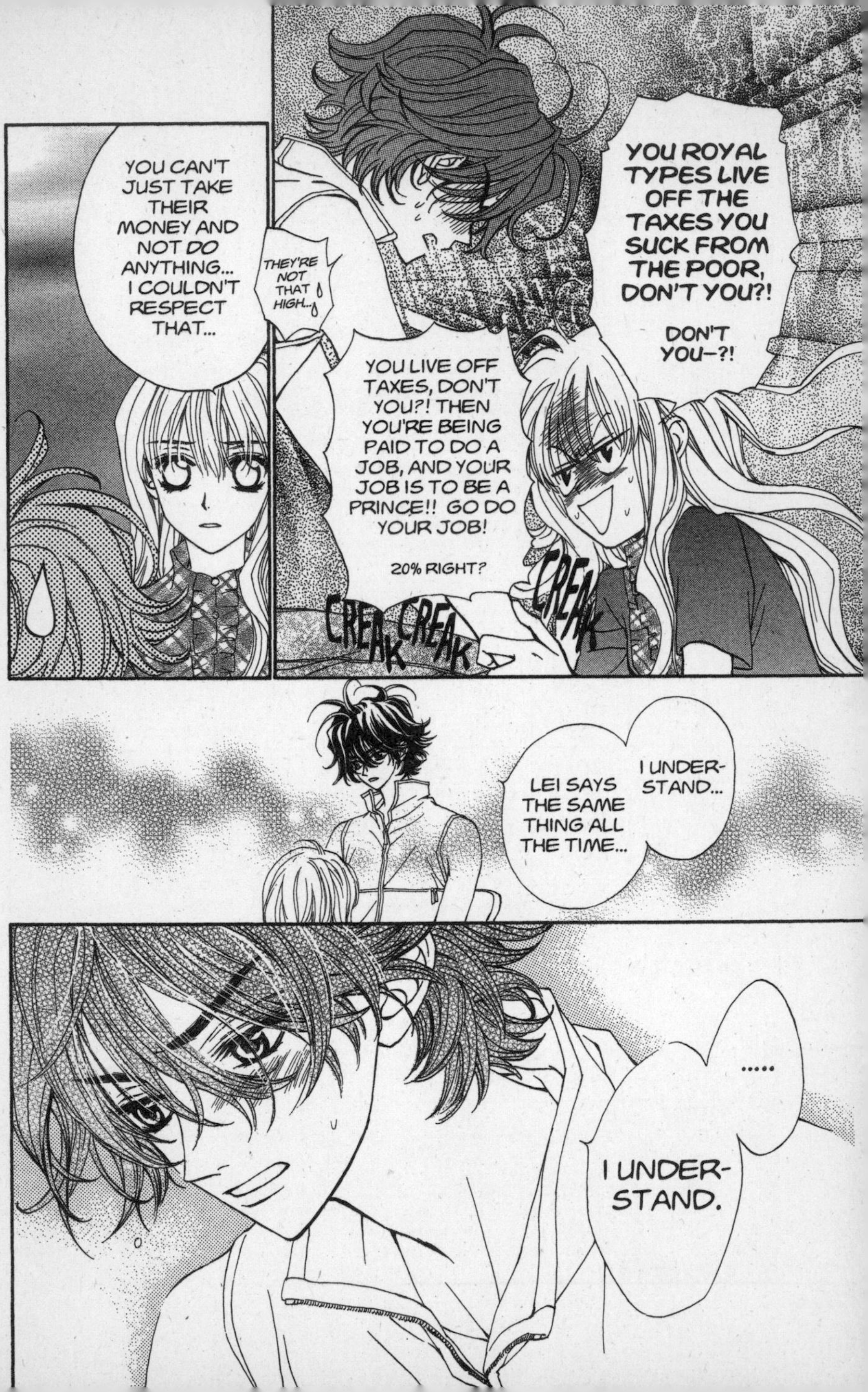
YOU ROYAL TYPES LIVE OFF THE TAXES YOU SUCK FROM THE POOR, DON'T YOU?!
DON'T YOU-?!
THEY'RE NOT THAT HIGH...
YOU LIVE OFF TAXES, DON'T YOU?! THEN YOU'RE BEING PAID TO DO A JOB, AND YOUR JOB IS TO BE A PRINCE!! GO DO YOUR JOB!
20% RIGHT?
CREAK
CREAK CREAK
YOU CAN'T JUST TAKE THEIR MONEY AND NOT DO ANYTHING... I COULDN'T RESPECT THAT...
I UNDER-STAND...
LEI SAYS THE SAME THING ALL THE TIME...
.....
I UNDER-STAND.

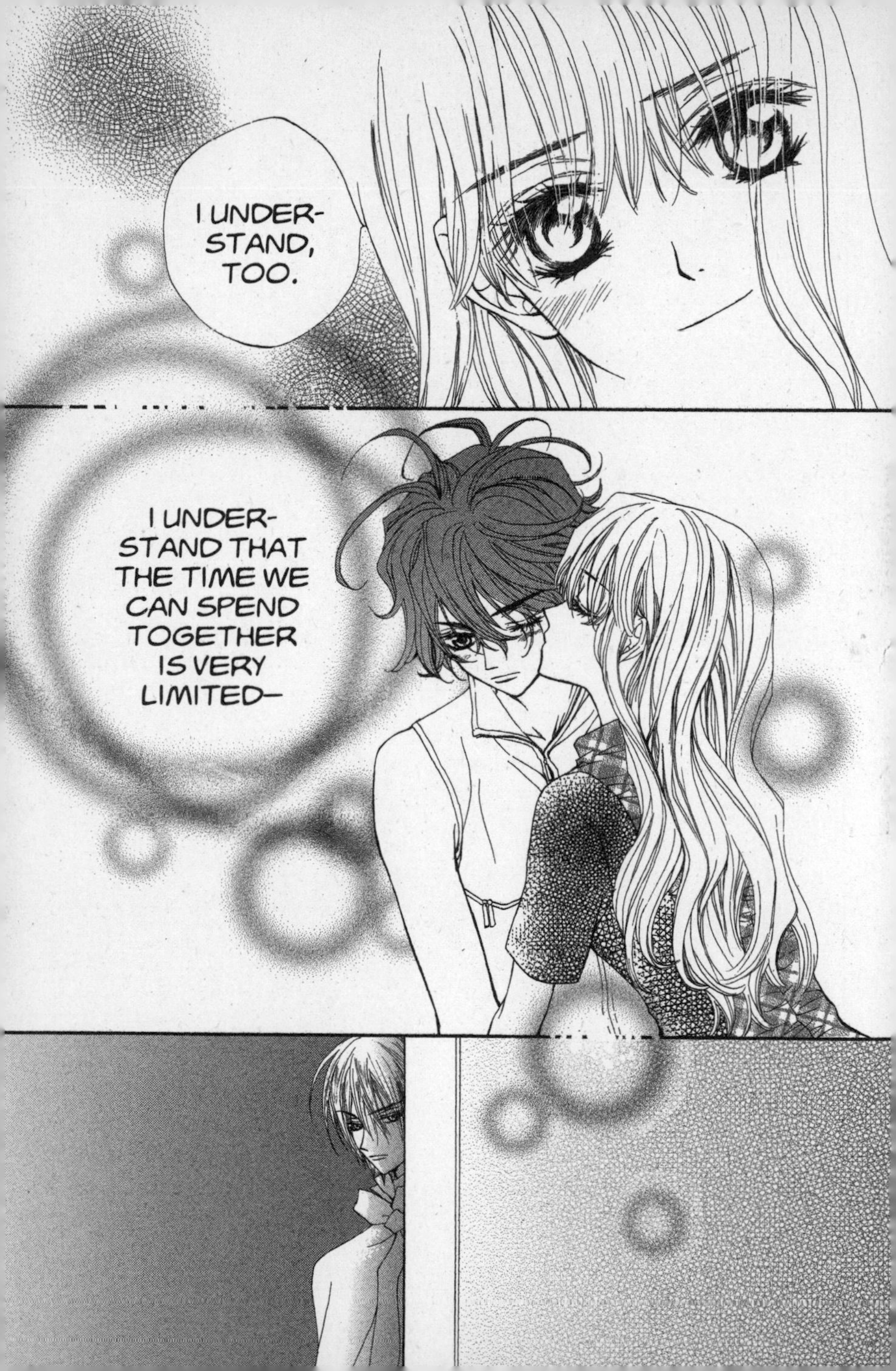
I UNDERSTAND, TOO.
I UNDERSTAND THAT THE TIME WE CAN SPEND TOGETHER IS VERY LIMITED–

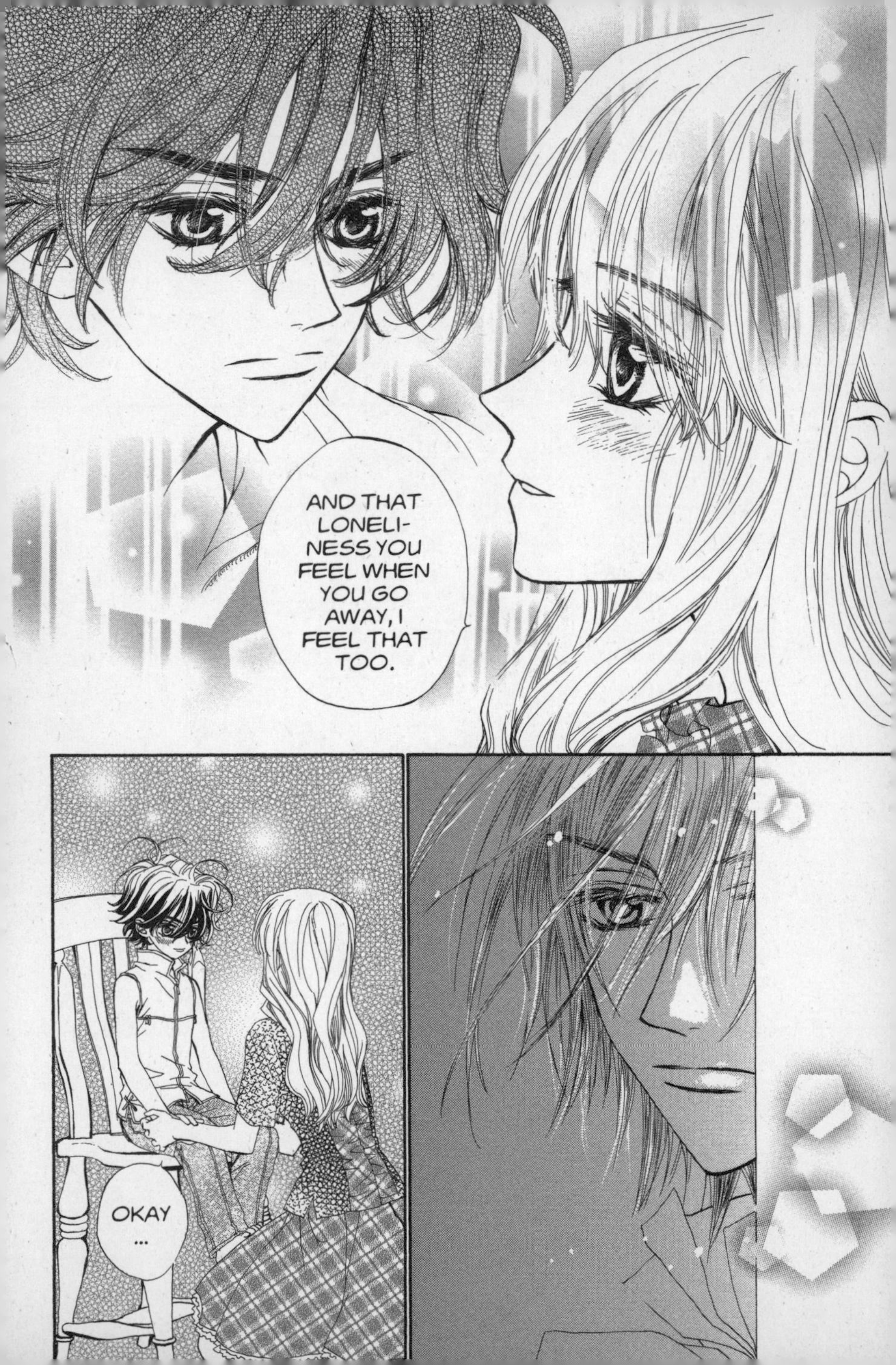
AND THAT LONELI-NESS YOU FEEL WHEN YOU GO AWAY, I FEEL THAT TOO.
OKAY ...

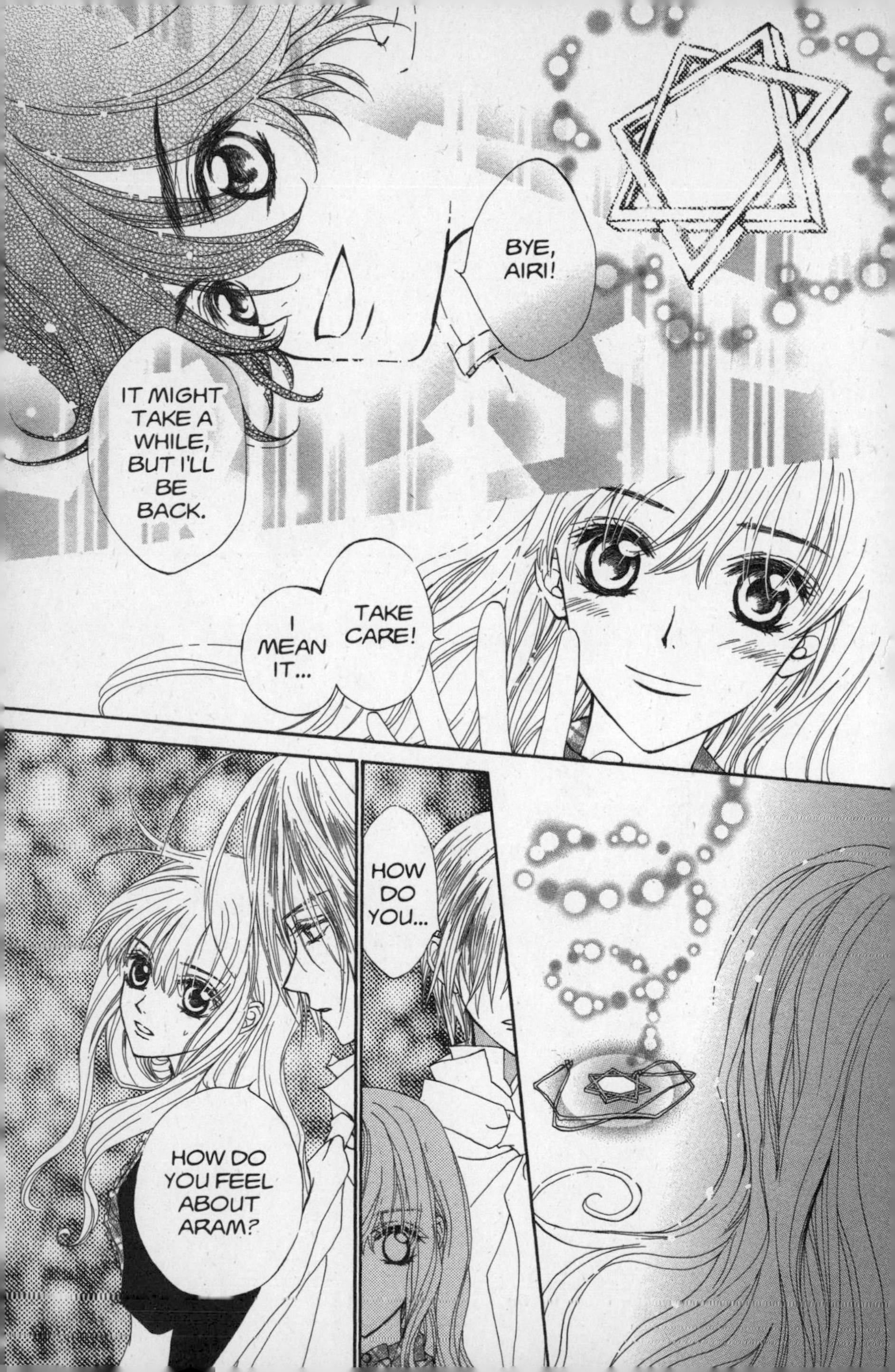
BYE, AIRI!
IT MIGHT TAKE A WHILE, BUT I'LL BE BACK.
TAKE CARE!
I MEAN IT...
HOW DO YOU...
HOW DO YOU FEEL ABOUT ARAM?

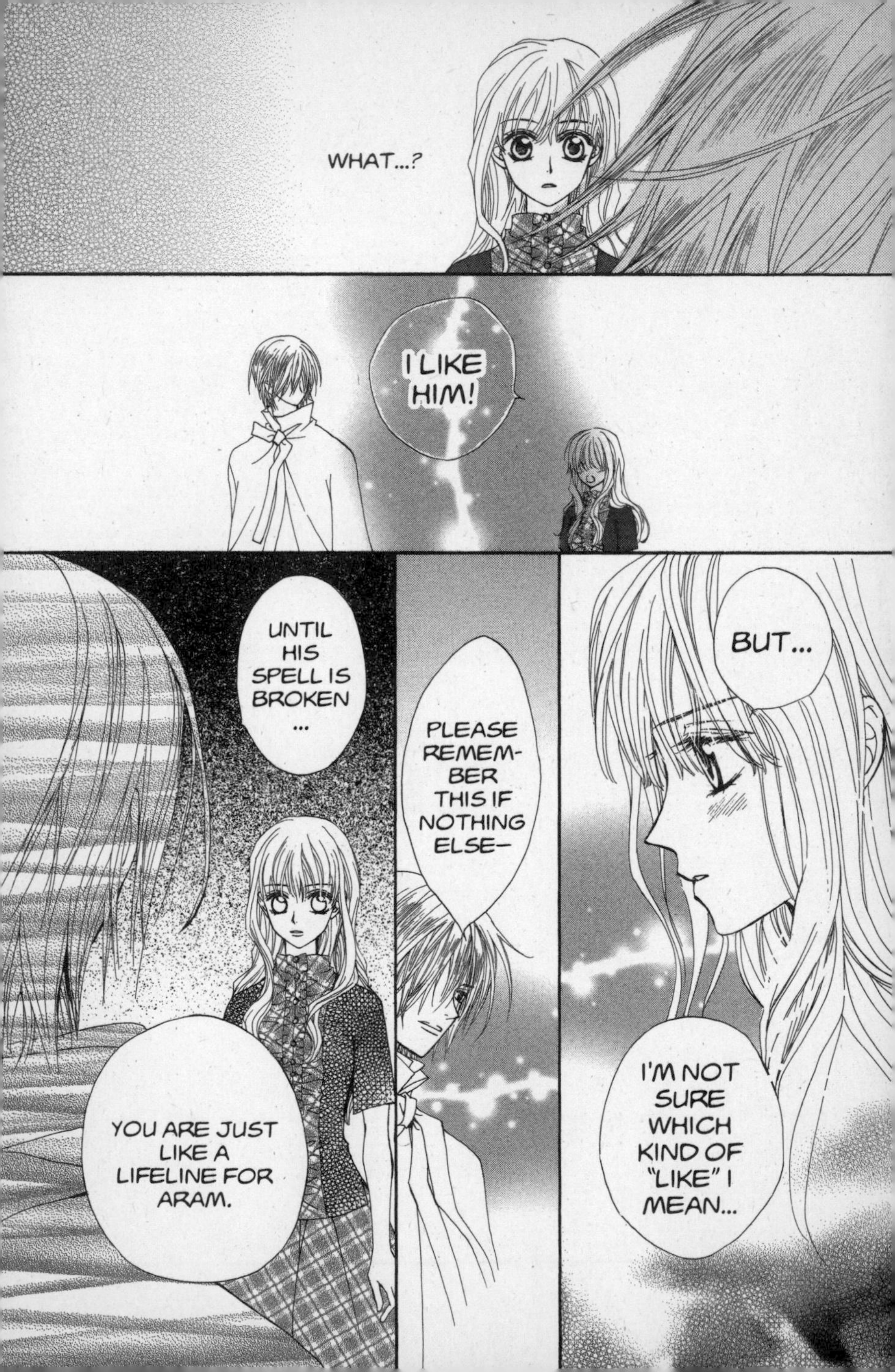
WHAT...?
I LIKE HIM!
BUT...
I'M NOT SURE WHICH KIND OF "LIKE" I MEAN...
PLEASE REMEMBER THIS IF NOTHING ELSE—
UNTIL HIS SPELL IS BROKEN...
YOU ARE JUST LIKE A LIFELINE FOR ARAM.

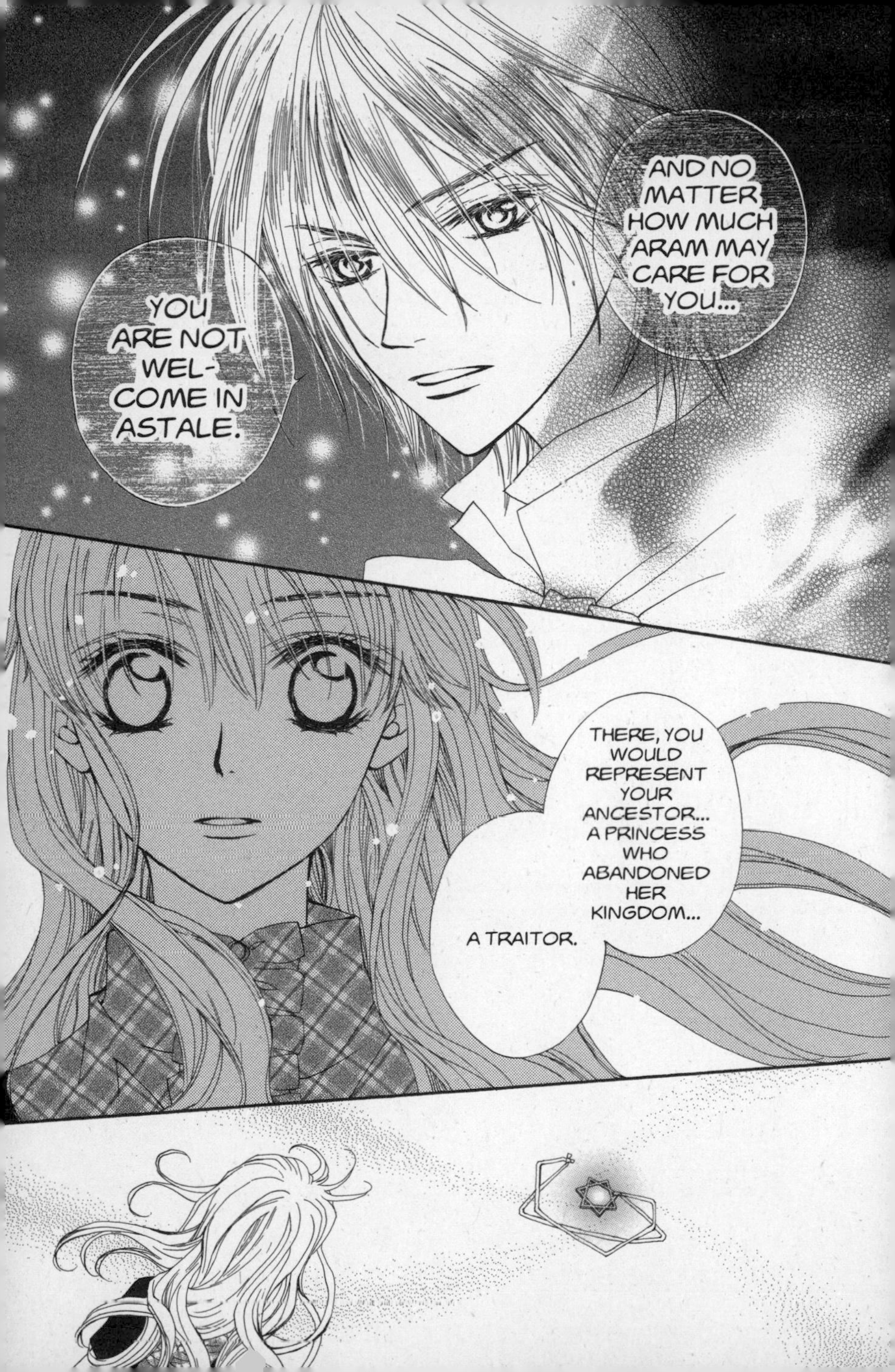
AND NO MATTER HOW MUCH ARAM MAY CARE FOR YOU...
YOU ARE NOT WEL-COME IN ASTALE.
THERE, YOU WOULD REPRESENT YOUR ANCESTOR... A PRINCESS WHO ABANDONED HER KINGDOM...
A TRAITOR.

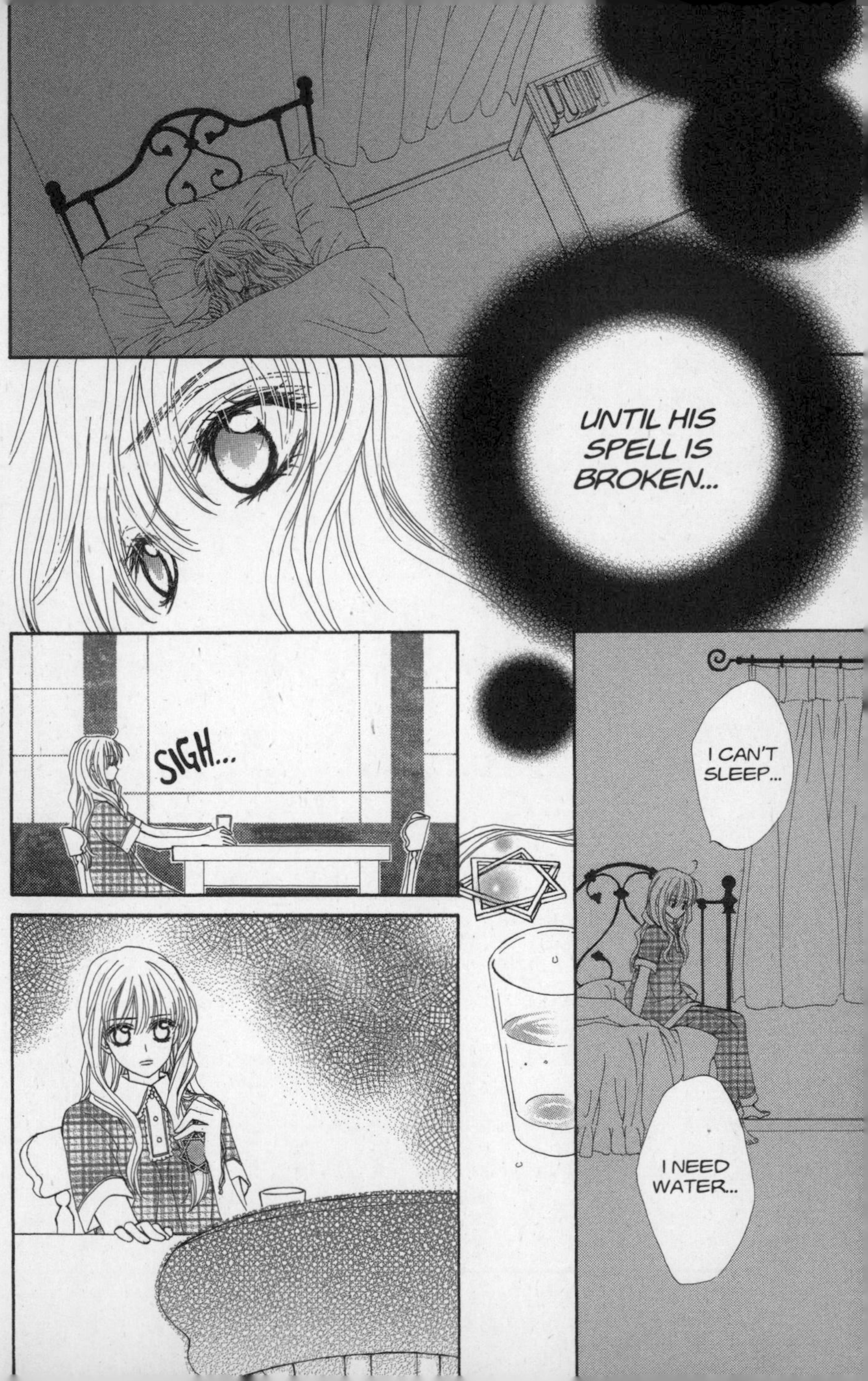
UNTIL HIS SPELL IS BROKEN...
I CAN'T SLEEP...
I NEED WATER...
SIGH...

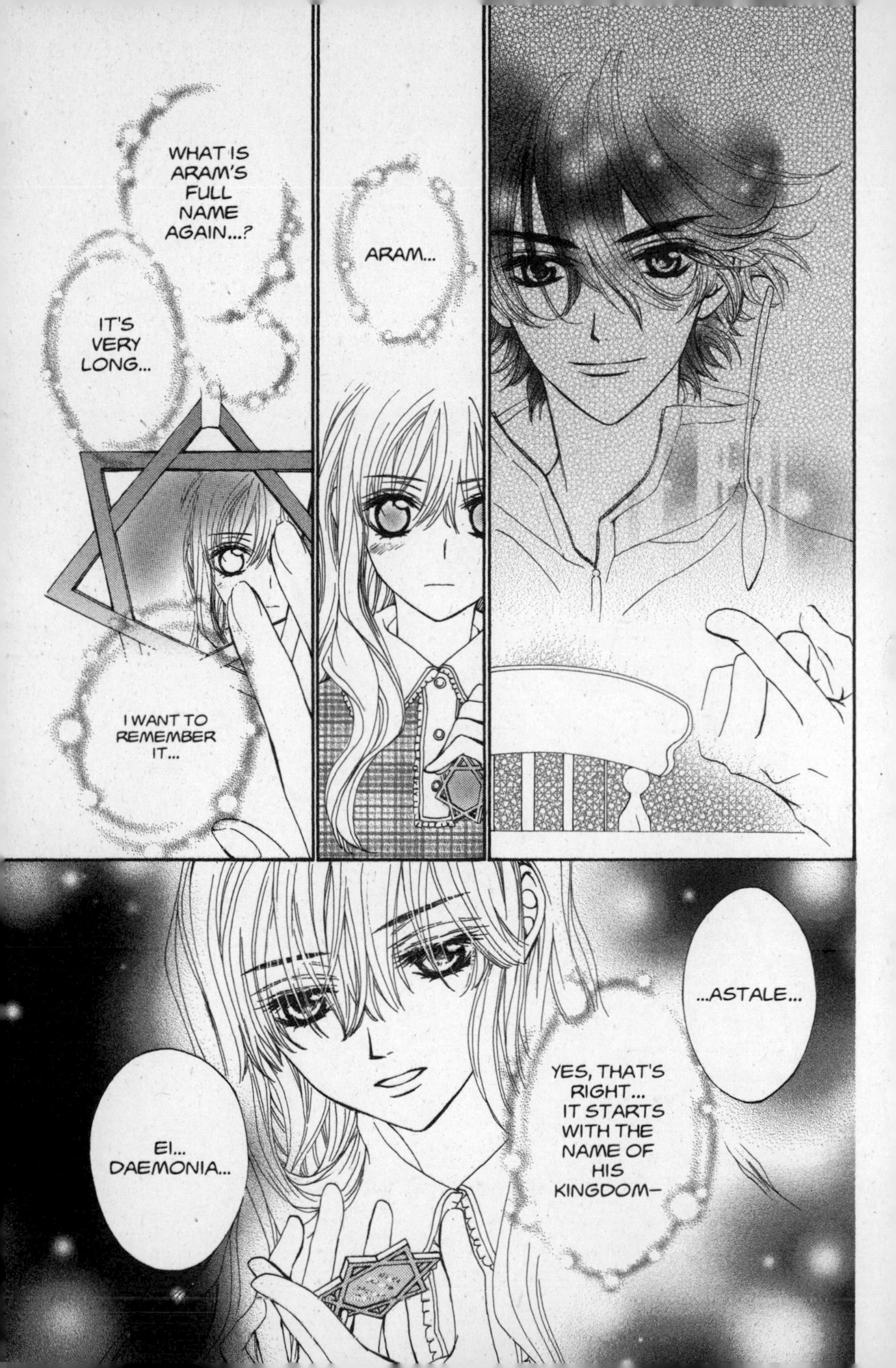
ARAM...
WHAT IS ARAM'S FULL NAME AGAIN...?
IT'S VERY LONG...
I WANT TO REMEMBER IT...
...ASTALE...
YES, THAT'S RIGHT... IT STARTS WITH THE NAME OF HIS KINGDOM—
EI... DAEMONIA...

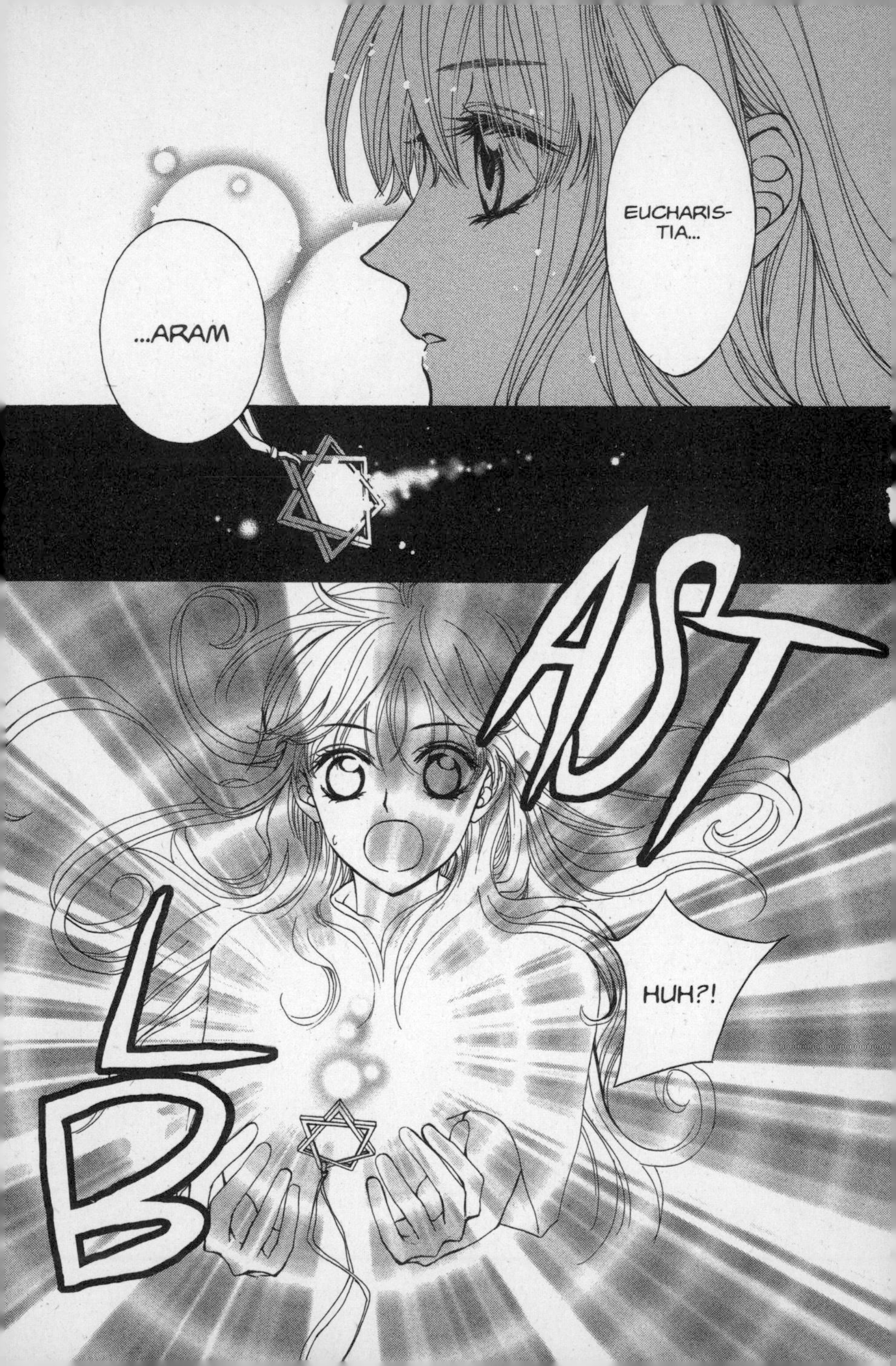
EUCHARIS-
TIA...
...ARAM
BLAST
HUH?!

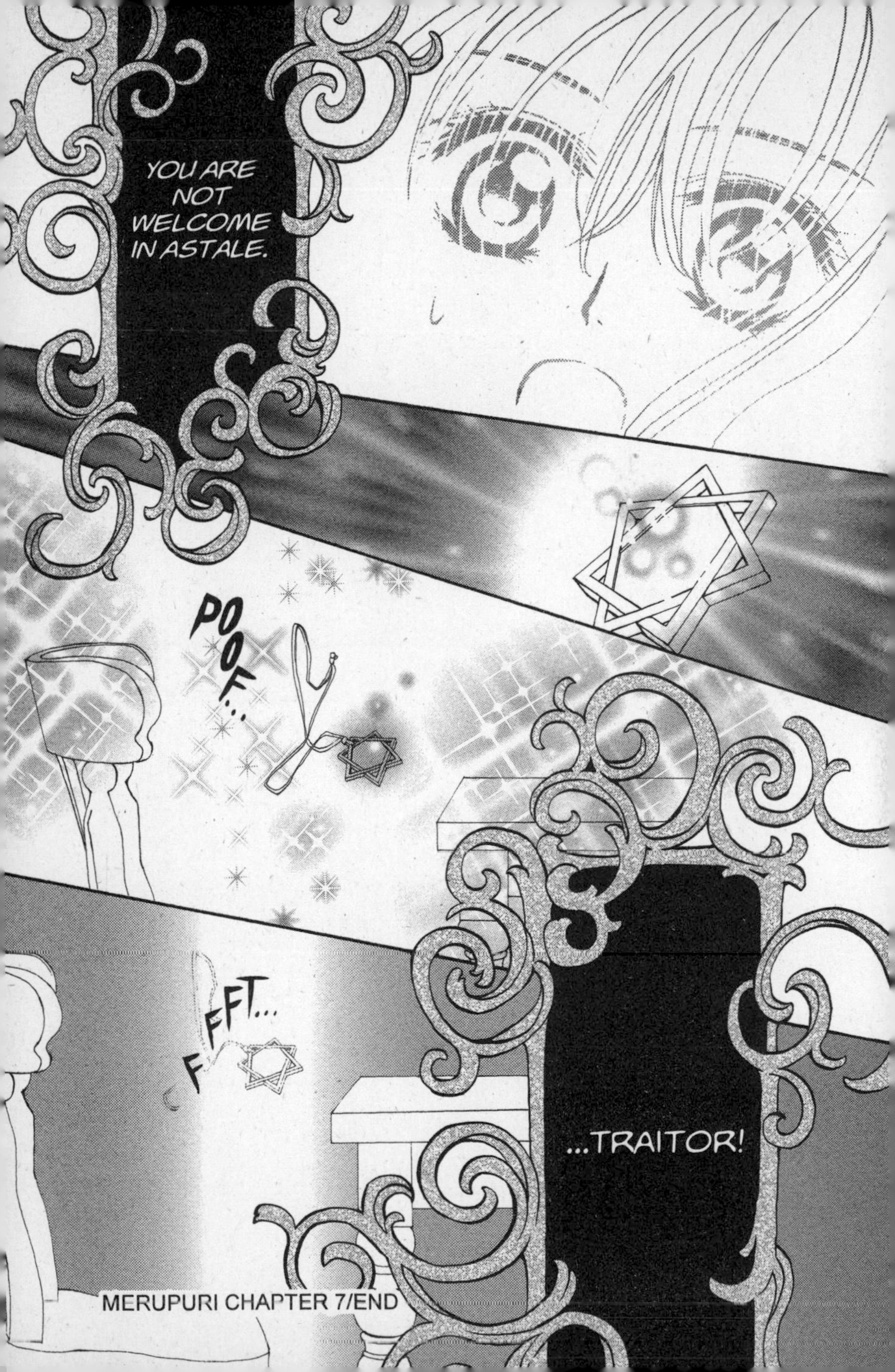
YOU ARE NOT WELCOME IN ASTALE.
POOF...
...TRAITOR!
FFFT...
MERUPURI CHAPTER 7/END

BONUS MANGA 2 BOY VS. MOSQUITO

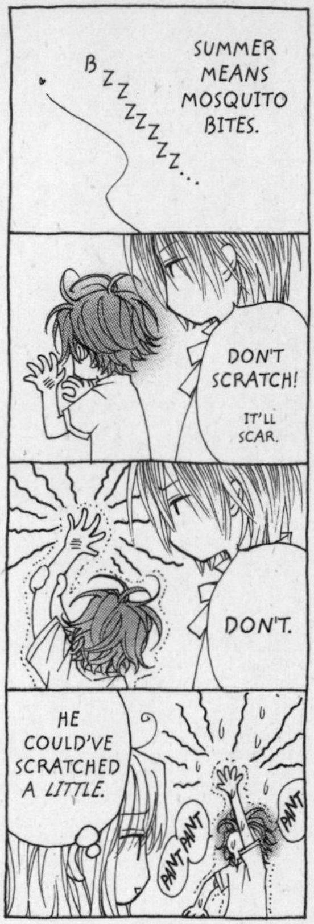
SUMMER MEANS MOSQUITO BITES.
BZZZZZZZ...
DON'T SCRATCH!
IT'LL SCAR.
DON'T.
HE COULD'VE SCRATCHED A *LITTLE*.
PANT
PANT PANT

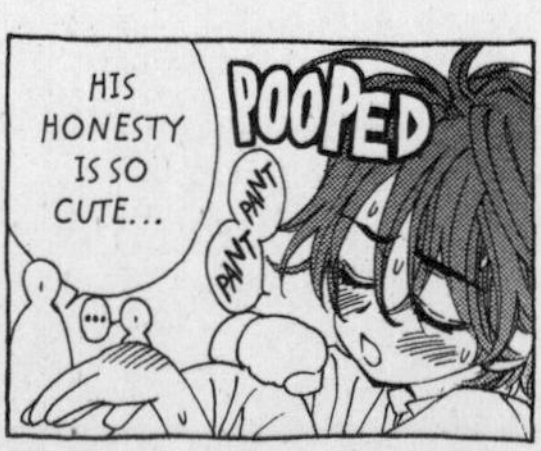
HIS HONESTY IS SO CUTE...
POOPED
PANT PANT
...

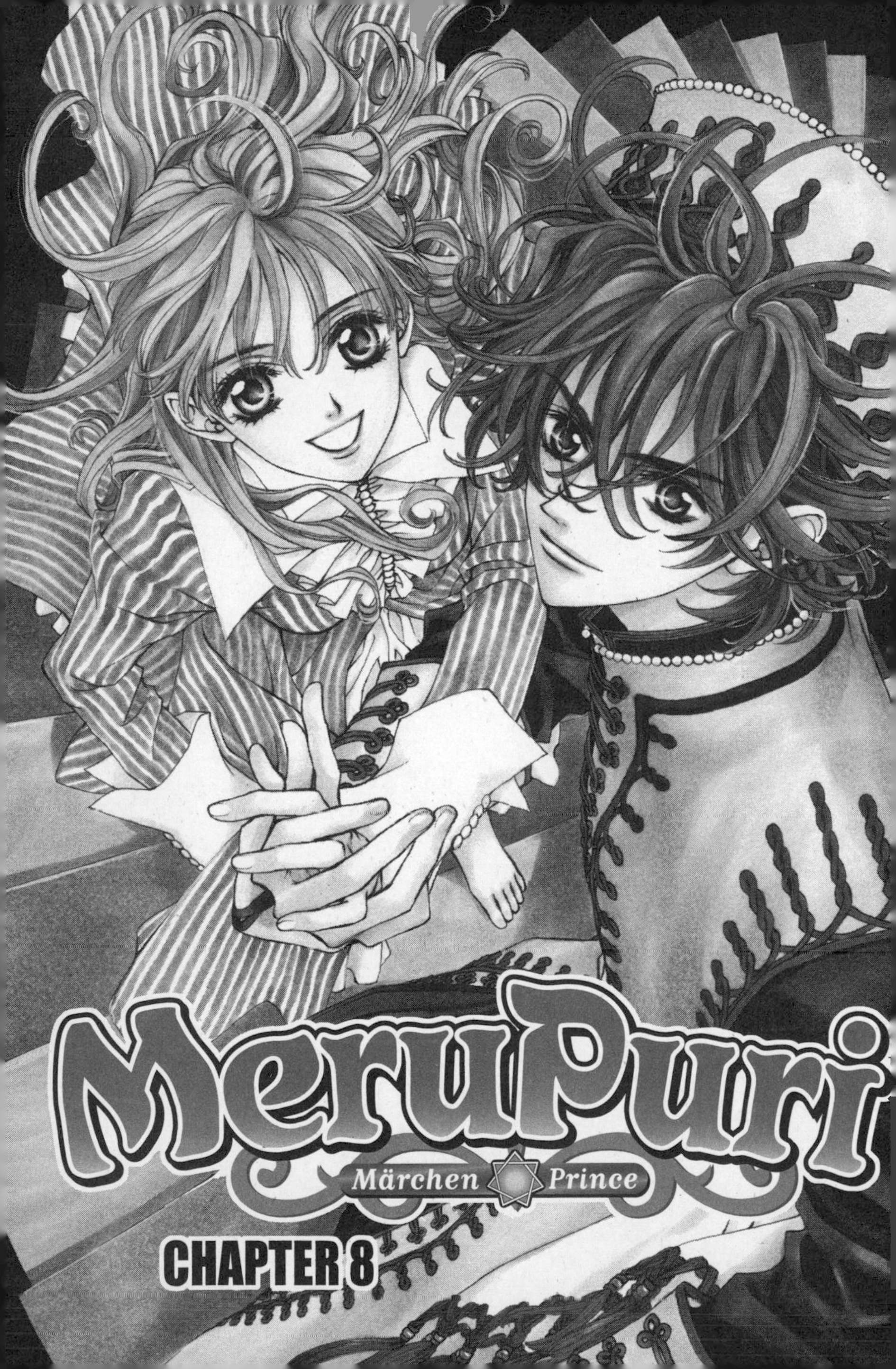
MeruPuri
Märchen Prince
CHAPTER 8

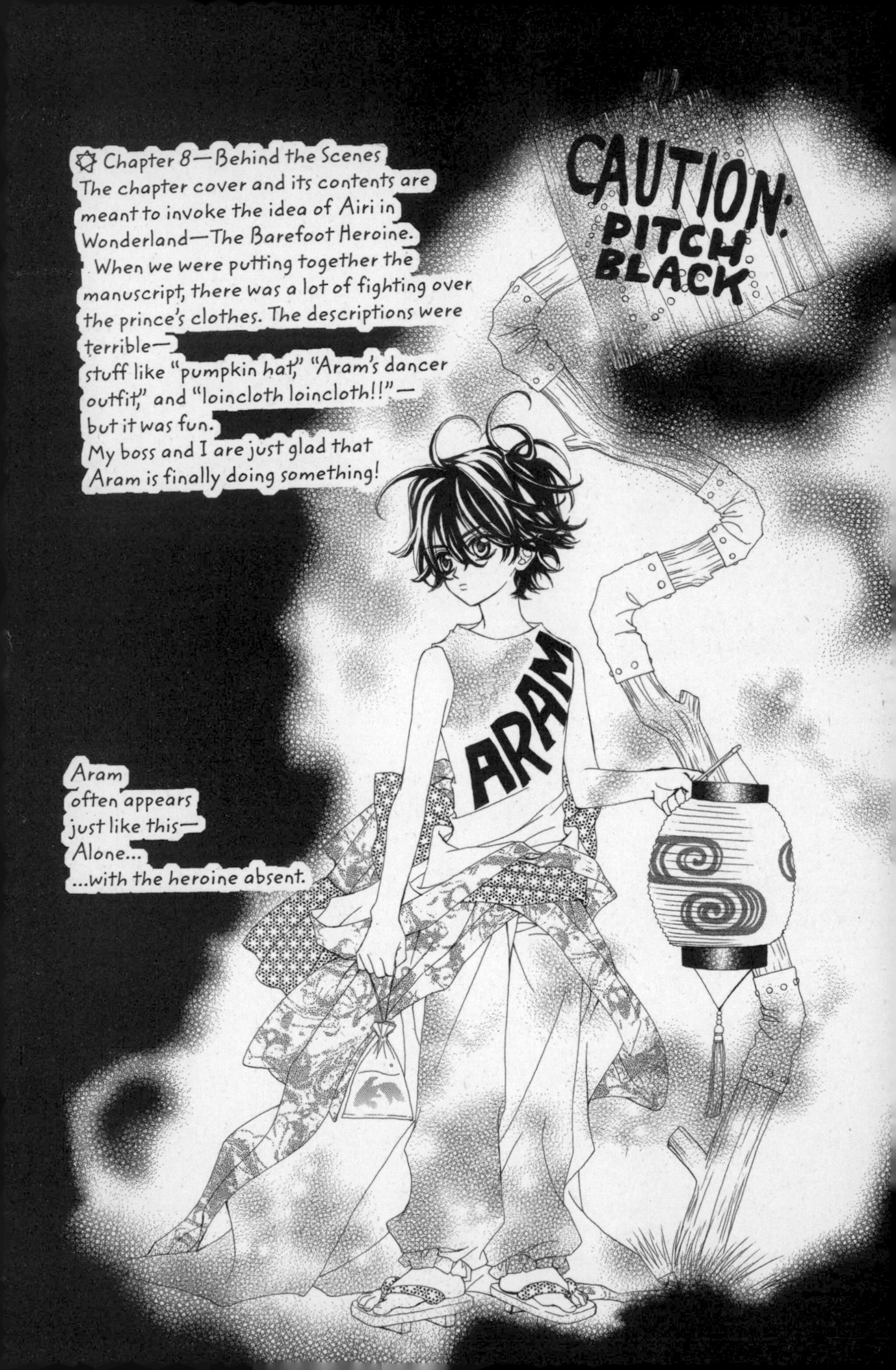
✡ Chapter 8—Behind the Scenes
The chapter cover and its contents are meant to invoke the idea of Airi in Wonderland—The Barefoot Heroine.
When we were putting together the manuscript, there was a lot of fighting over the prince's clothes. The descriptions were terrible—
stuff like "pumpkin hat," "Aram's dancer outfit," and "loincloth loincloth!!"—
but it was fun.
My boss and I are just glad that Aram is finally doing something!
CAUTION: PITCH BLACK
ARAM
Aram often appears just like this—
Alone...
...with the heroine absent.

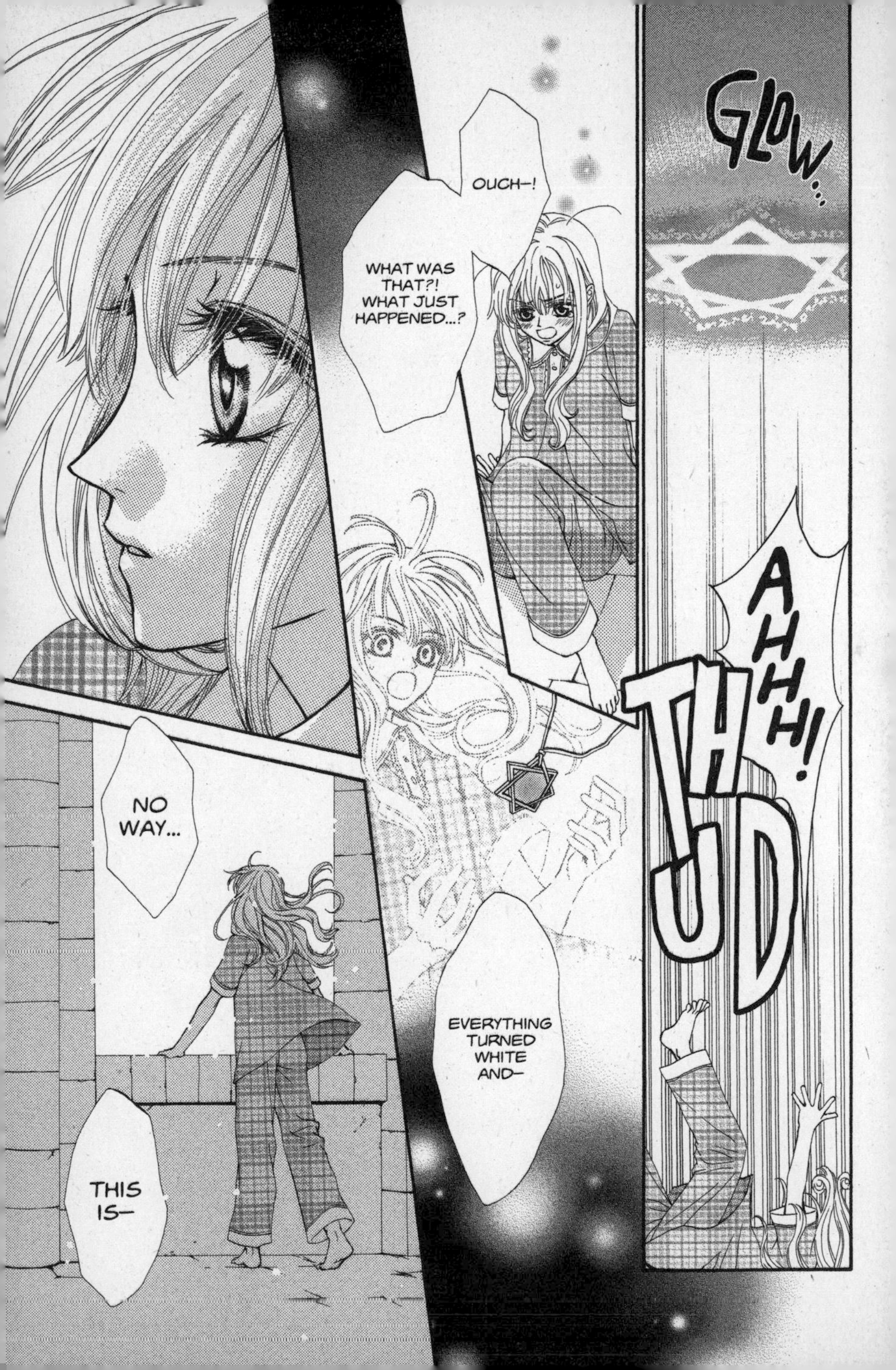
GLOW...
AHHH!
THUD
OUCH-!
WHAT WAS THAT?! WHAT JUST HAPPENED...?
EVERYTHING TURNED WHITE AND—
NO WAY...
THIS IS—

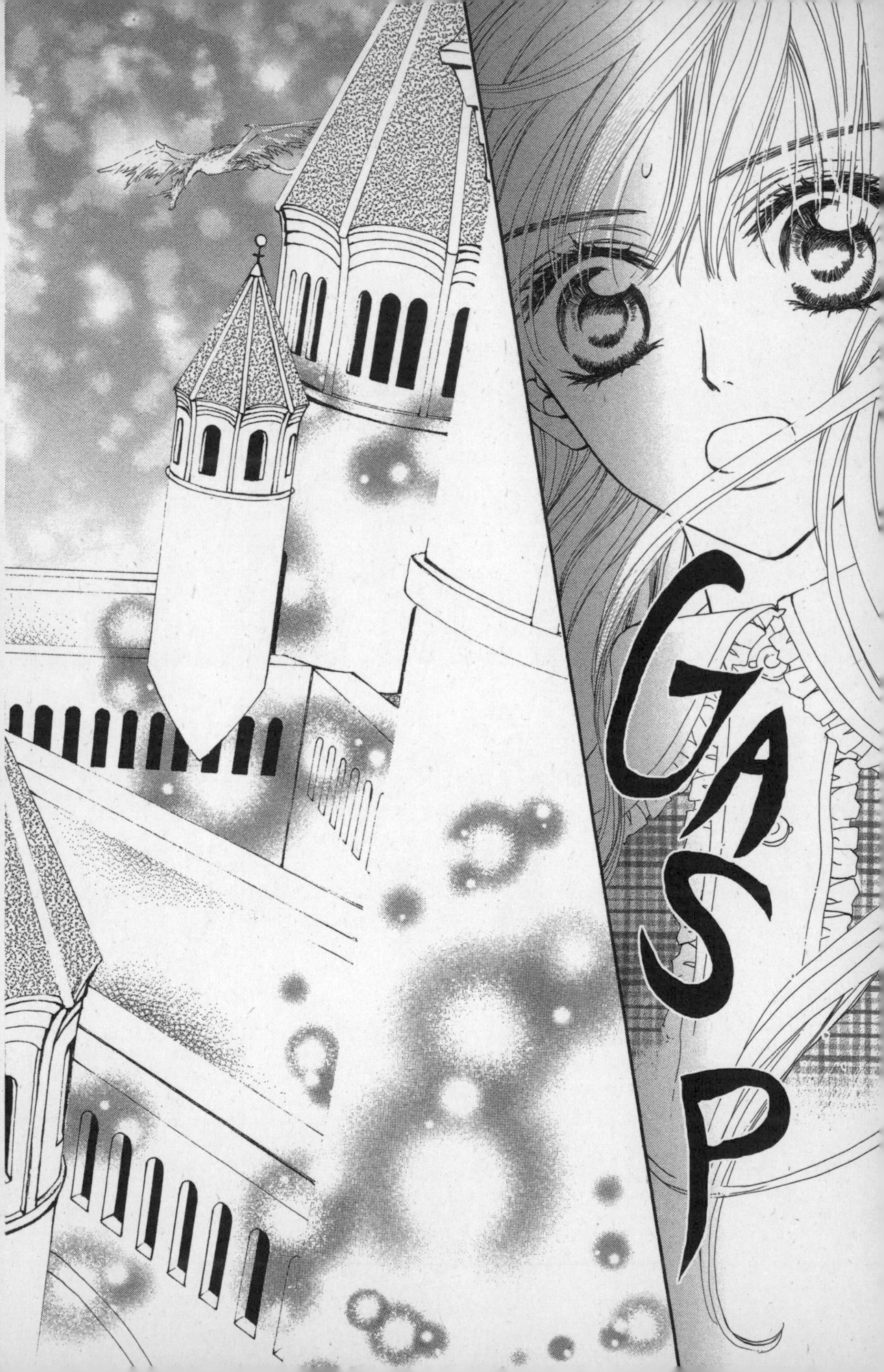
GASP

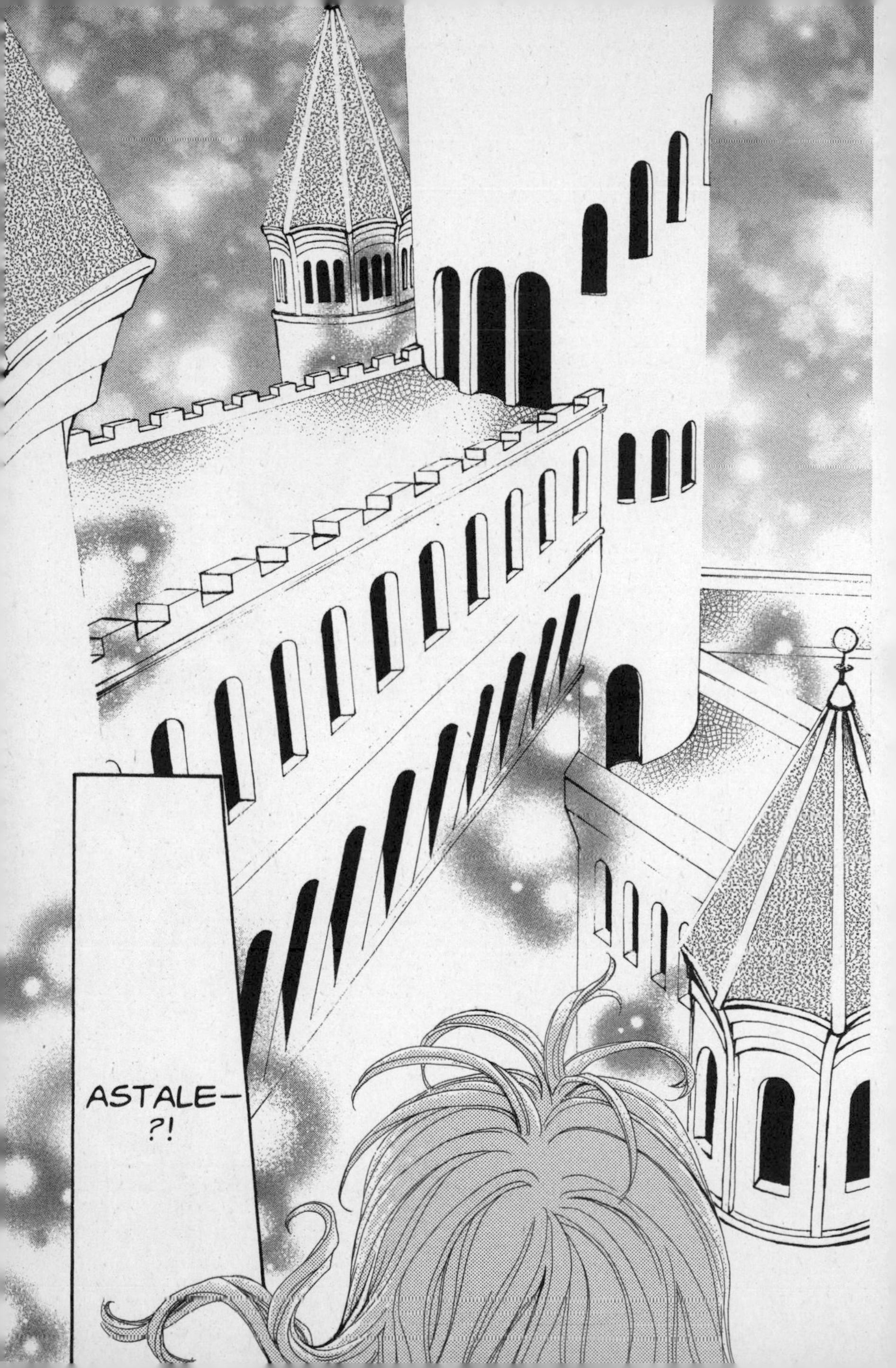
ASTALE—
?!

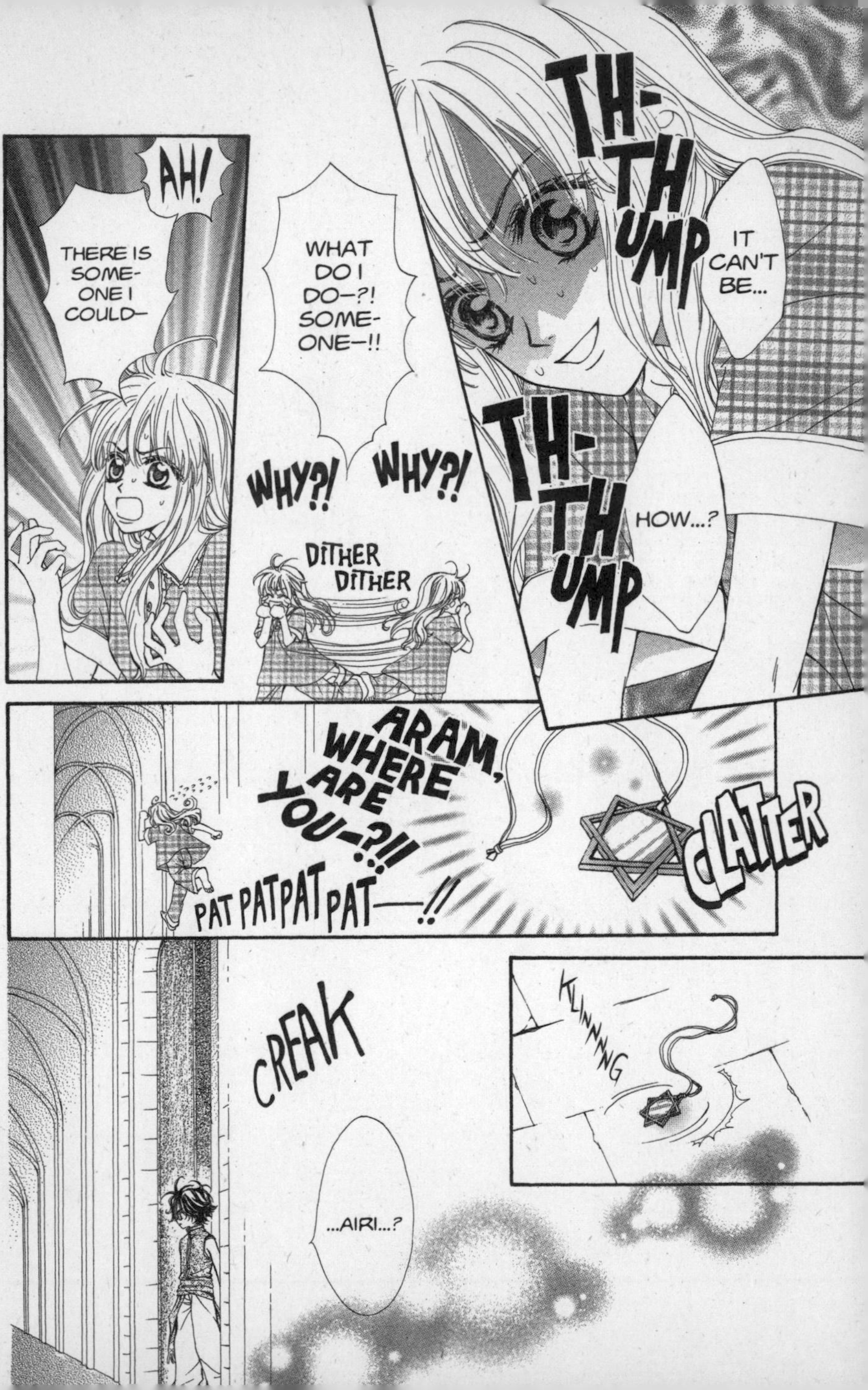
TH-THUMP
IT CAN'T BE...
TH-THUMP
HOW...?
WHAT DO I DO—?! SOME-ONE—!!
WHY?!
WHY?!
DITHER DITHER
AH!
THERE IS SOME-ONE I COULD—
ARAM, WHERE ARE YOU—?!!
CLATTER
PAT PATPAT PAT——!!
KLINNNNG
CREAK
...AIRI...?

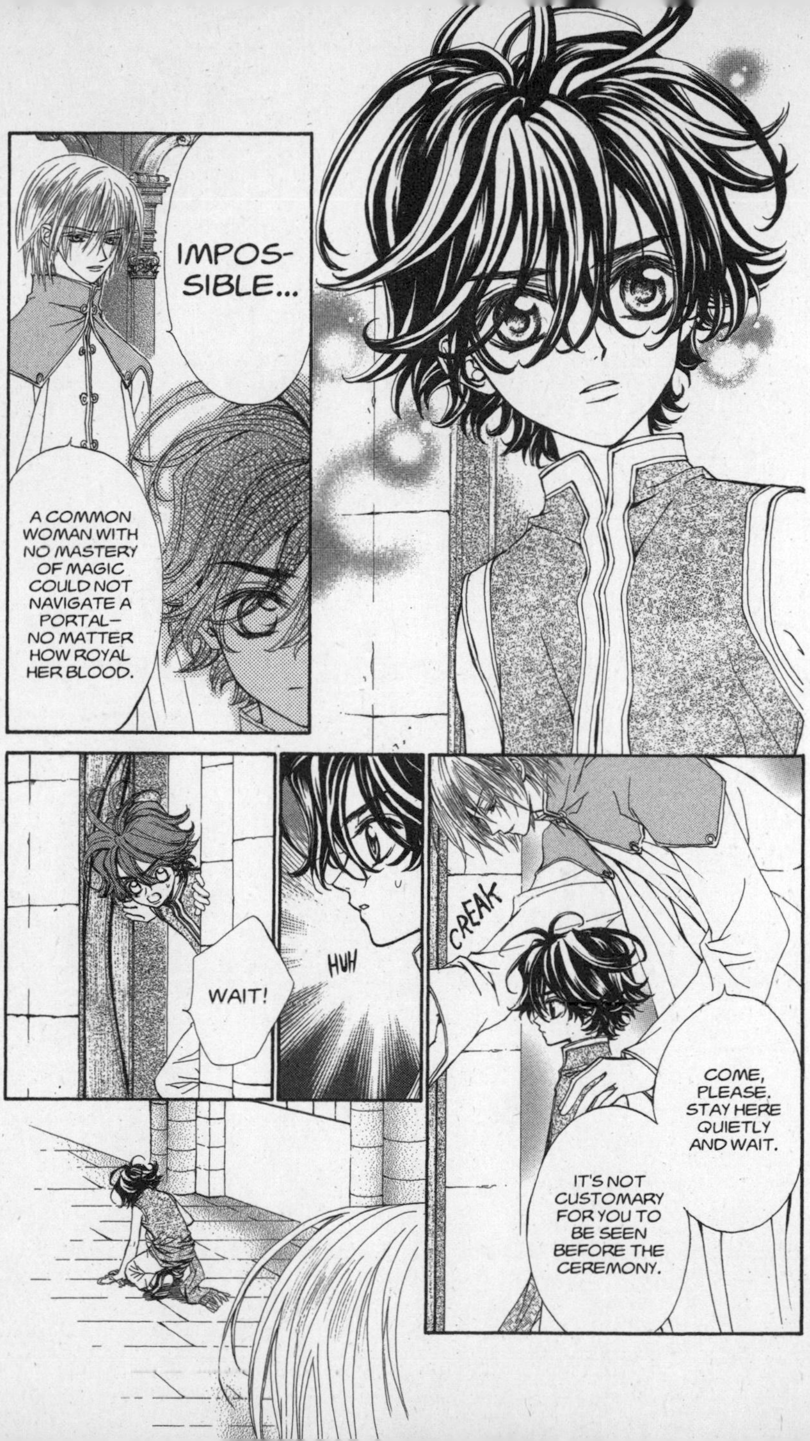
IMPOSSIBLE...
A COMMON WOMAN WITH NO MASTERY OF MAGIC COULD NOT NAVIGATE A PORTAL—NO MATTER HOW ROYAL HER BLOOD.
CREAK
COME, PLEASE. STAY HERE QUIETLY AND WAIT.
IT'S NOT CUSTOMARY FOR YOU TO BE SEEN BEFORE THE CEREMONY.
HUH
WAIT!

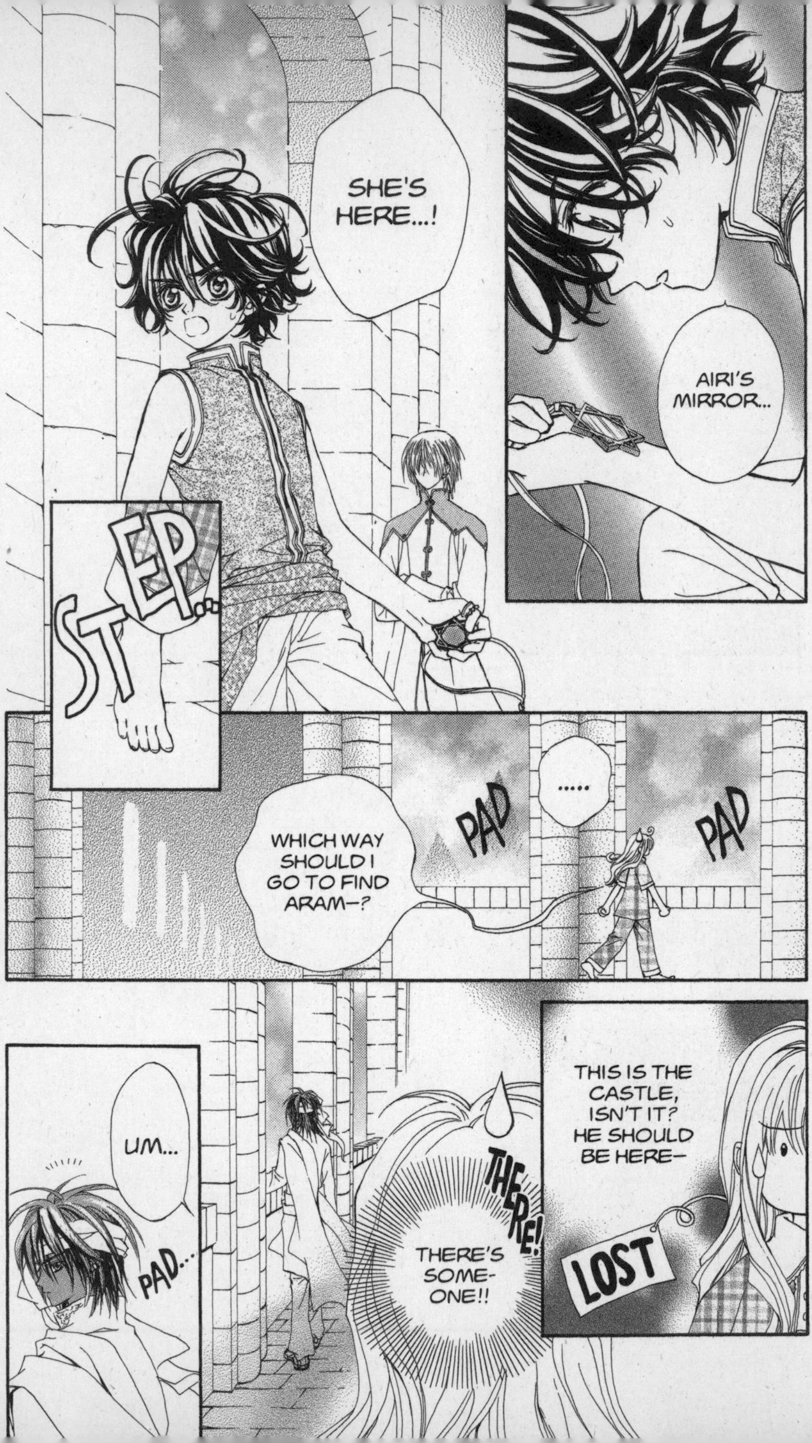
AIRI'S MIRROR...
SHE'S HERE...!
STEP...
......
PAD
PAD
WHICH WAY SHOULD I GO TO FIND ARAM--?
THIS IS THE CASTLE, ISN'T IT? HE SHOULD BE HERE--
LOST
THERE!
THERE'S SOME-ONE!!
UM...
PAD...

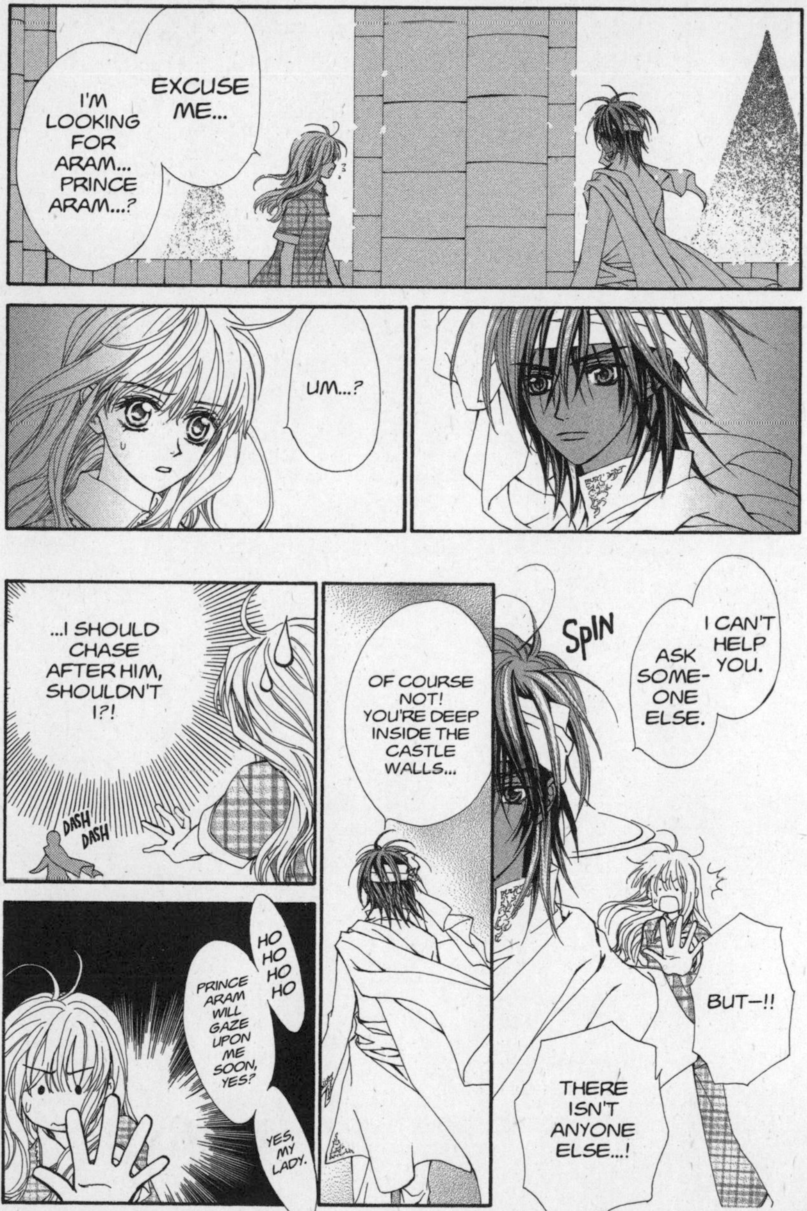
EXCUSE ME...
I'M LOOKING FOR ARAM... PRINCE ARAM...?
UM...?
SPIN
I CAN'T HELP YOU.
ASK SOME-ONE ELSE.
OF COURSE NOT! YOU'RE DEEP INSIDE THE CASTLE WALLS...
BUT—!!
THERE ISN'T ANYONE ELSE...!
...I SHOULD CHASE AFTER HIM, SHOULDN'T I?!
DASH DASH
HO HO HO HO
PRINCE ARAM WILL GAZE UPON ME SOON, YES?
YES, MY LADY.

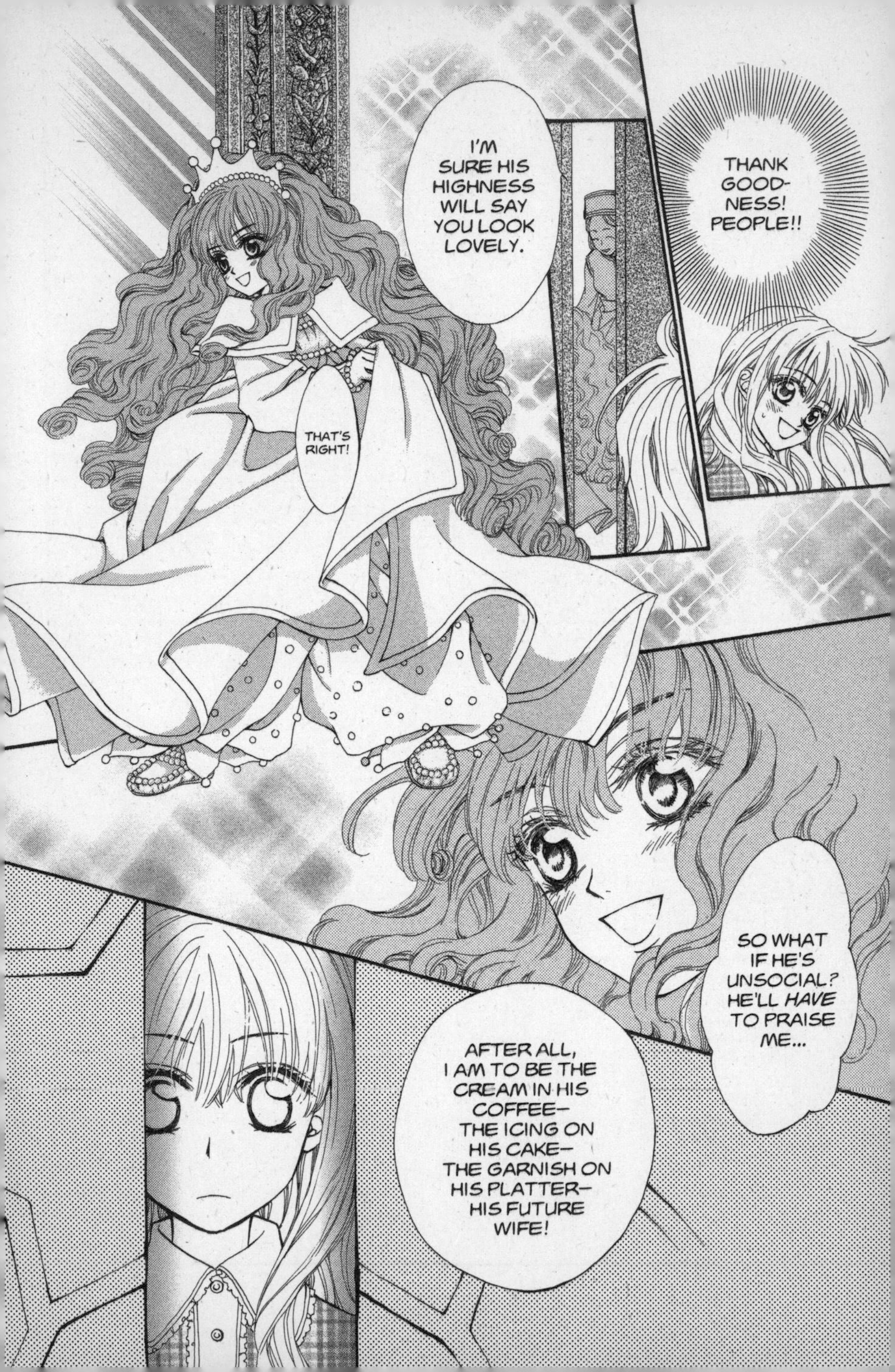
THANK GOOD-NESS! PEOPLE!!
I'M SURE HIS HIGHNESS WILL SAY YOU LOOK LOVELY.
THAT'S RIGHT!
SO WHAT IF HE'S UNSOCIAL? HE'LL *HAVE* TO PRAISE ME...
AFTER ALL, I AM TO BE THE CREAM IN HIS COFFEE— THE ICING ON HIS CAKE— THE GARNISH ON HIS PLATTER— HIS FUTURE WIFE!

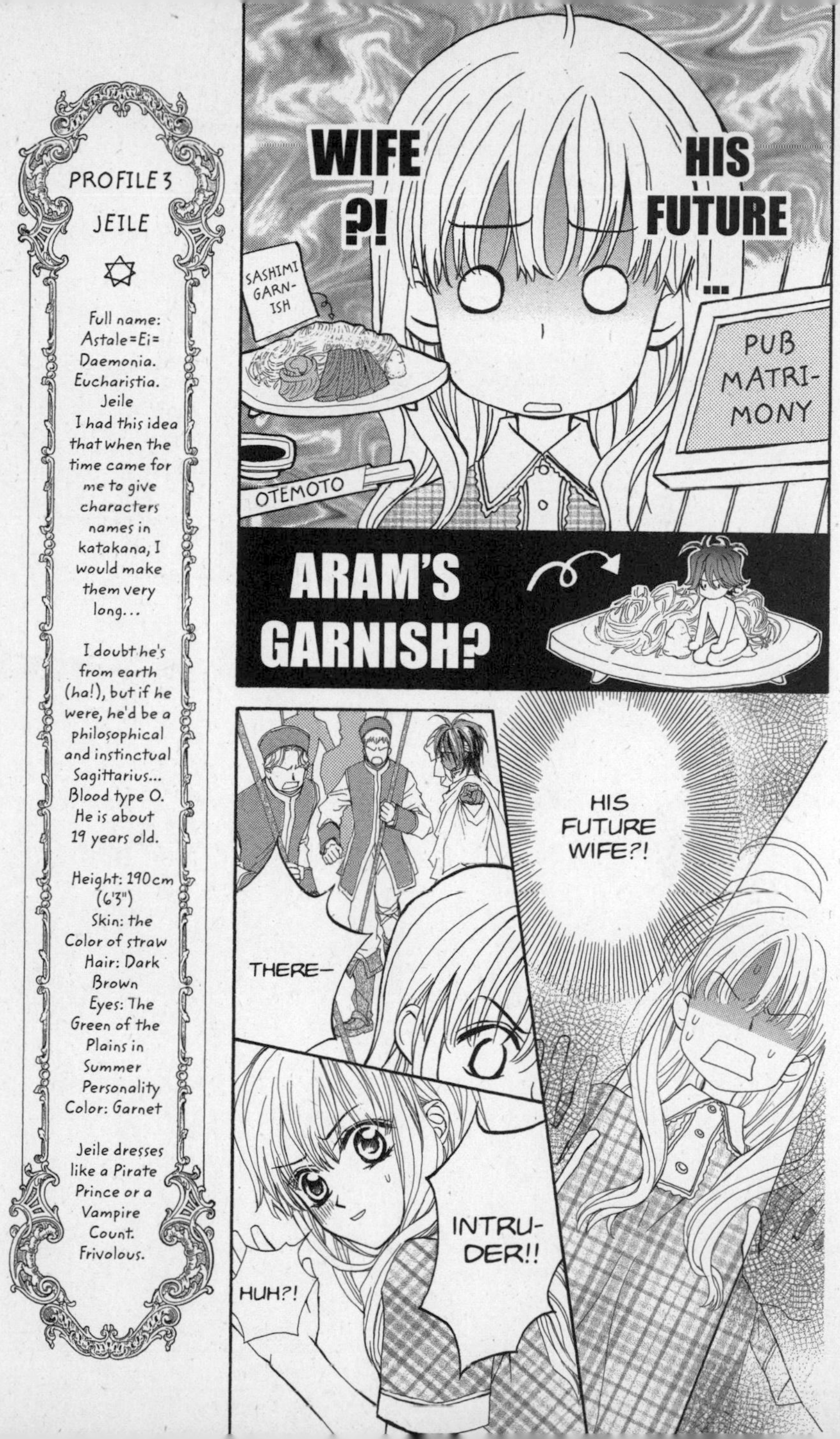
HIS FUTURE ...
WIFE ?!
SASHIMI GARNISH
PUB MATRIMONY
OTEMOTO
ARAM'S GARNISH?
HIS FUTURE WIFE?!
THERE—
INTRUDER!!
HUH?!

PROFILE 3

JEILE

Full name: Astale=Ei=Daemonia. Eucharistia. Jeile

I had this idea that when the time came for me to give characters names in katakana, I would make them very long...

I doubt he's from earth (ha!), but if he were, he'd be a philosophical and instinctual Sagittarius... Blood type O. He is about 19 years old.

Height: 190cm (6'3")
Skin: the Color of straw
Hair: Dark Brown
Eyes: The Green of the Plains in Summer
Personality Color: Garnet

Jeile dresses like a Pirate Prince or a Vampire Count. Frivolous.

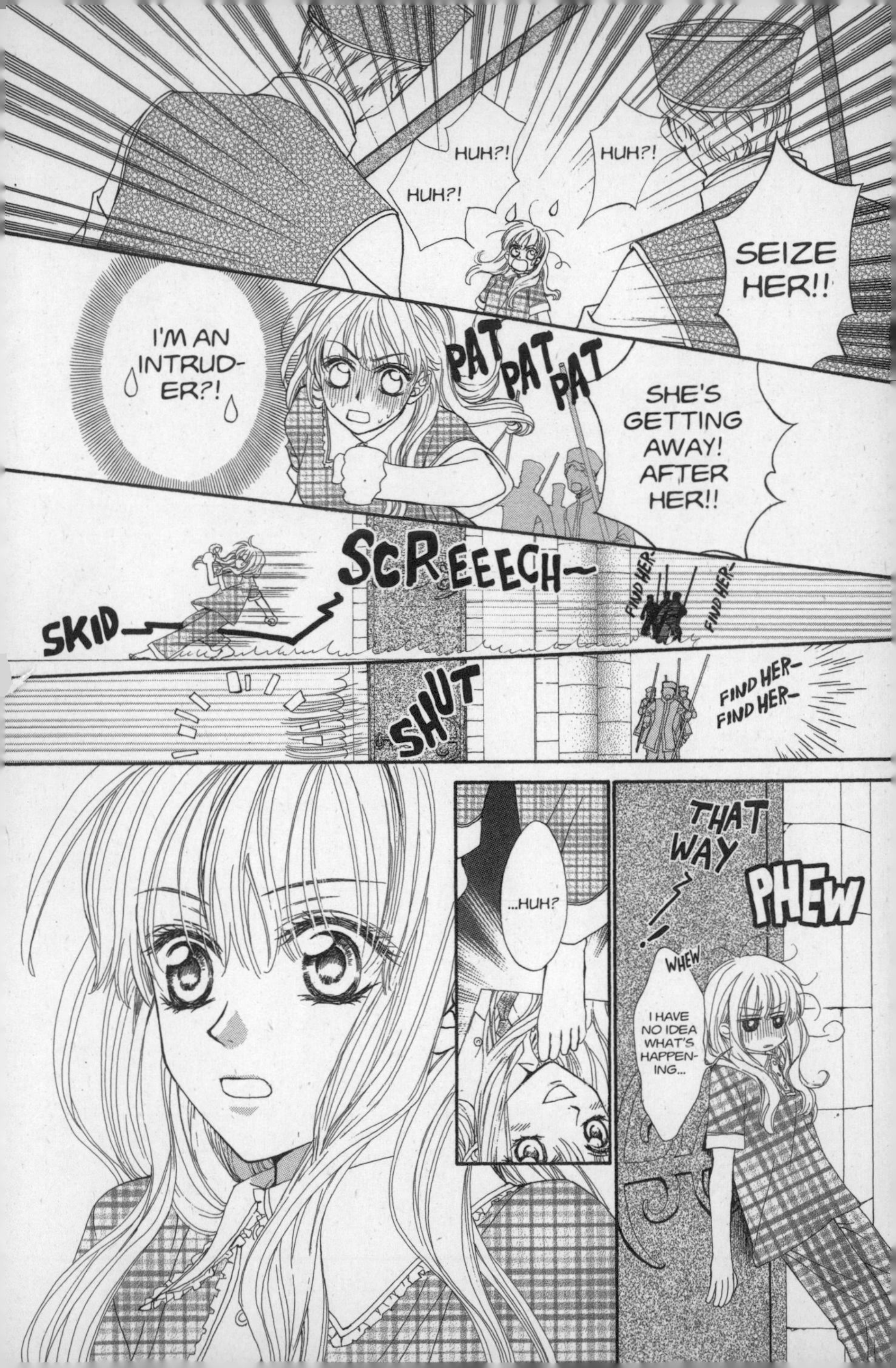
HUH?!
HUH?!
HUH?!
SEIZE HER!!
SHE'S GETTING AWAY! AFTER HER!!
PAT PAT PAT
I'M AN INTRUD-ER?!
FIND HER- FIND HER-
SCREEECH-
SKID-
FIND HER- FIND HER-
SHUT
THAT WAY
PHEW
WHEW
I HAVE NO IDEA WHAT'S HAPPEN-ING...
...HUH?

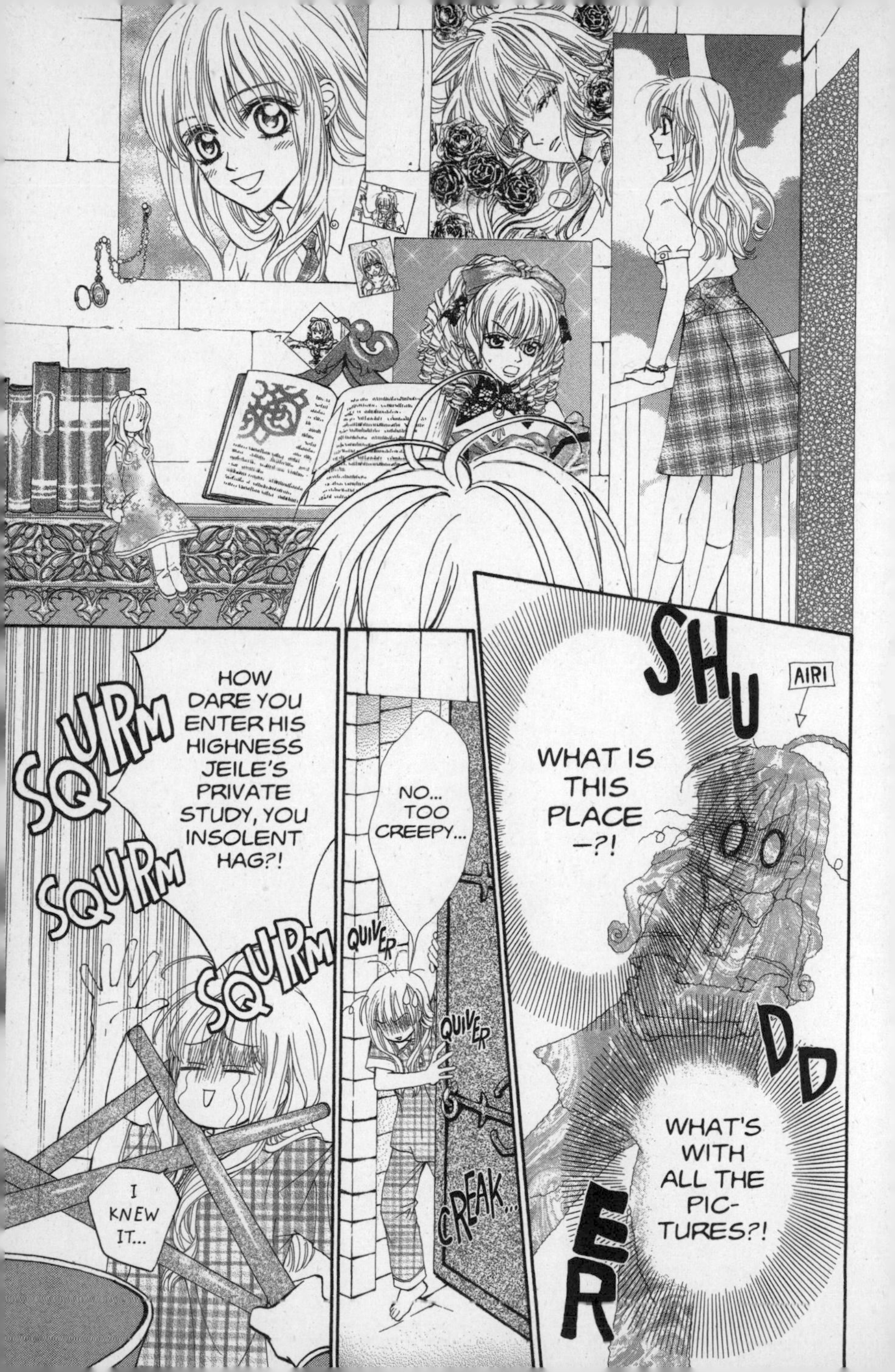
SHUDDER
AIRI
WHAT IS THIS PLACE —?!
WHAT'S WITH ALL THE PIC-TURES?!
NO... TOO CREEPY...
QUIVER—
QUIVER
CREAK...
HOW DARE YOU ENTER HIS HIGHNESS JEILE'S PRIVATE STUDY, YOU INSOLENT HAG?!
SQUIRM
SQUIRM
SQUIRM
I KNEW IT...

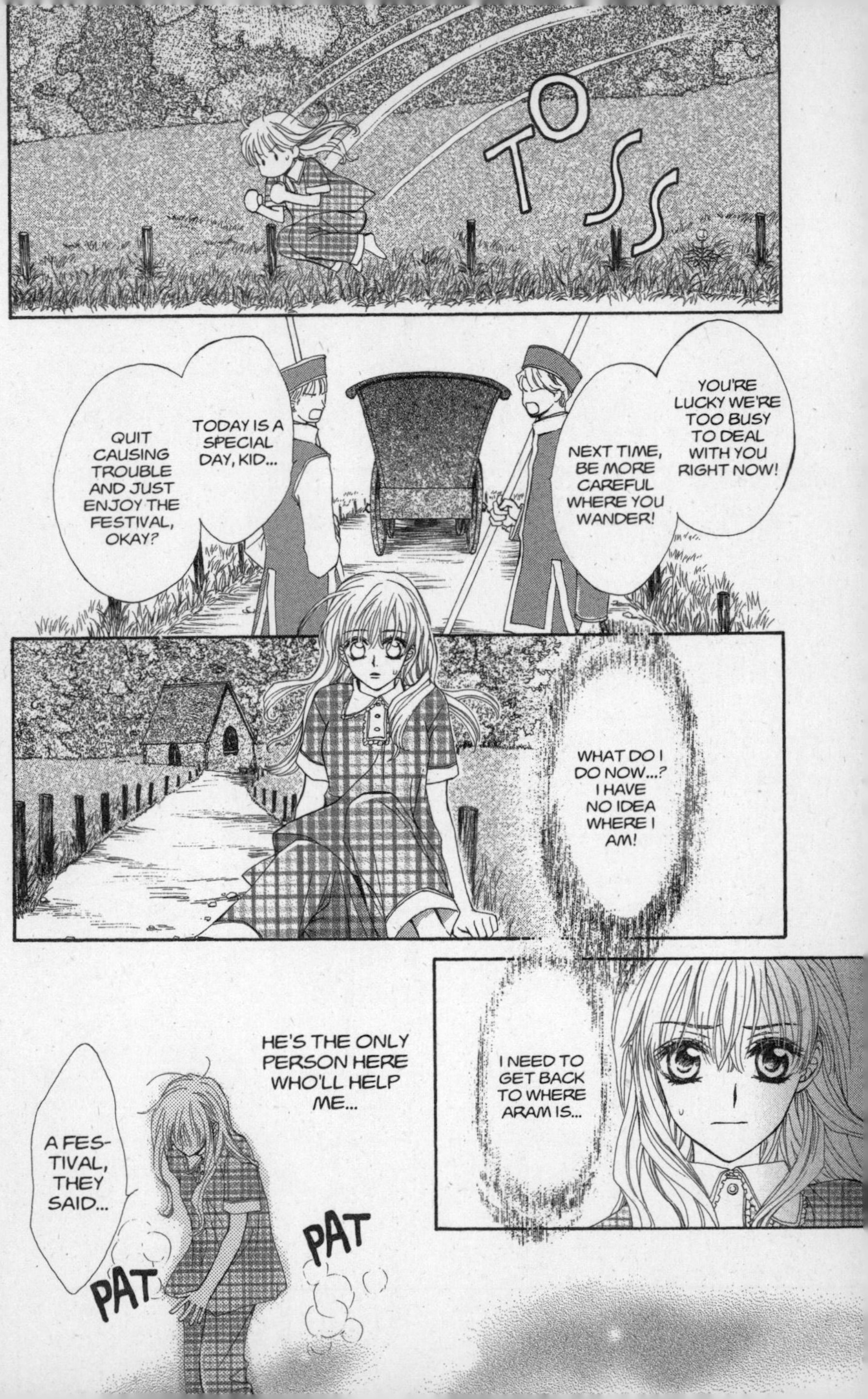
TOSS
YOU'RE LUCKY WE'RE TOO BUSY TO DEAL WITH YOU RIGHT NOW!
NEXT TIME, BE MORE CAREFUL WHERE YOU WANDER!
TODAY IS A SPECIAL DAY, KID...
QUIT CAUSING TROUBLE AND JUST ENJOY THE FESTIVAL, OKAY?
WHAT DO I DO NOW...? I HAVE NO IDEA WHERE I AM!
I NEED TO GET BACK TO WHERE ARAM IS...
HE'S THE ONLY PERSON HERE WHO'LL HELP ME...
PAT
A FES-TIVAL, THEY SAID...
PAT

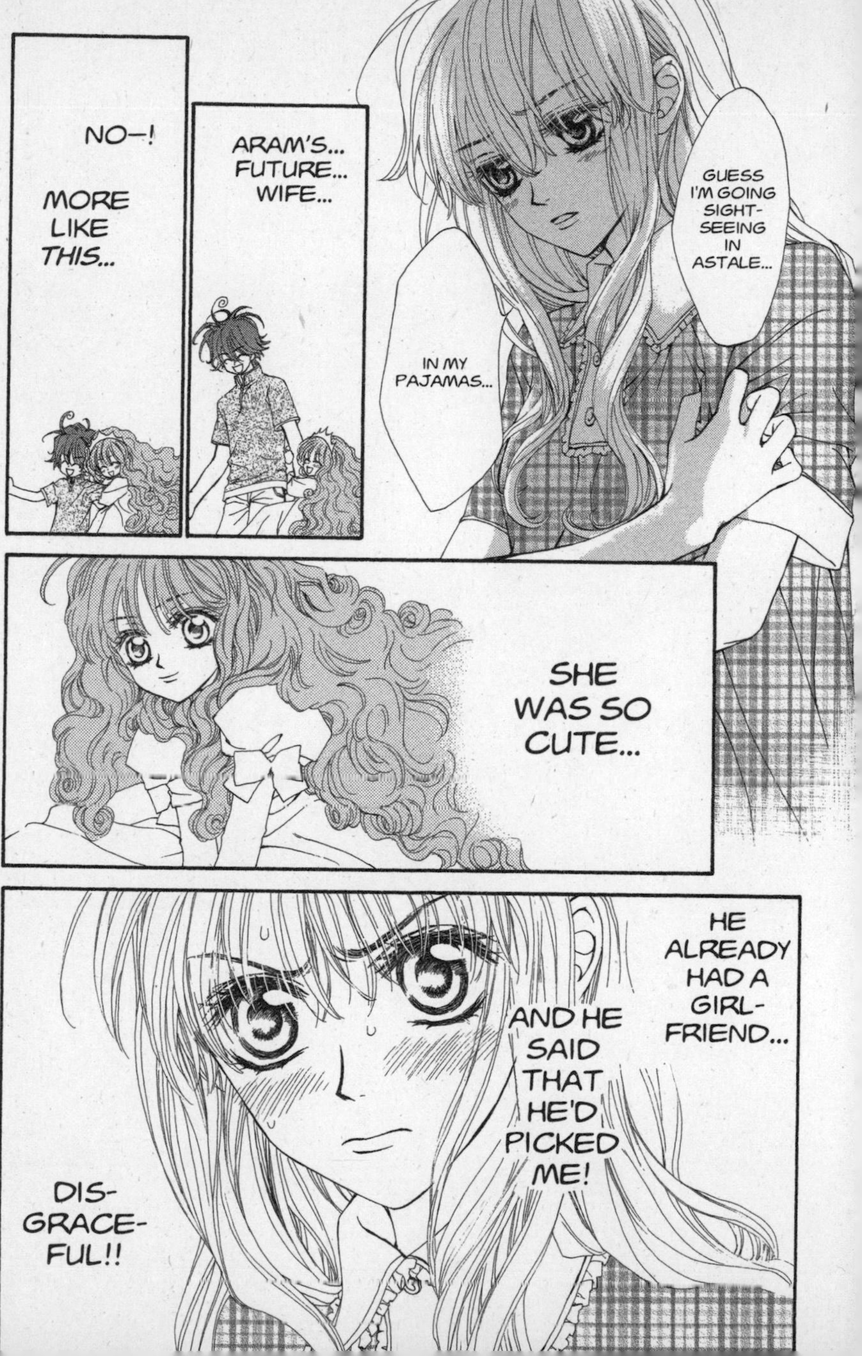
GUESS I'M GOING SIGHT-SEEING IN ASTALE...
IN MY PAJAMAS...
ARAM'S... FUTURE... WIFE...
NO—!
MORE LIKE THIS...
SHE WAS SO CUTE...
HE ALREADY HAD A GIRL-FRIEND...
AND HE SAID THAT HE'D PICKED ME!
DIS-GRACE-FUL!!

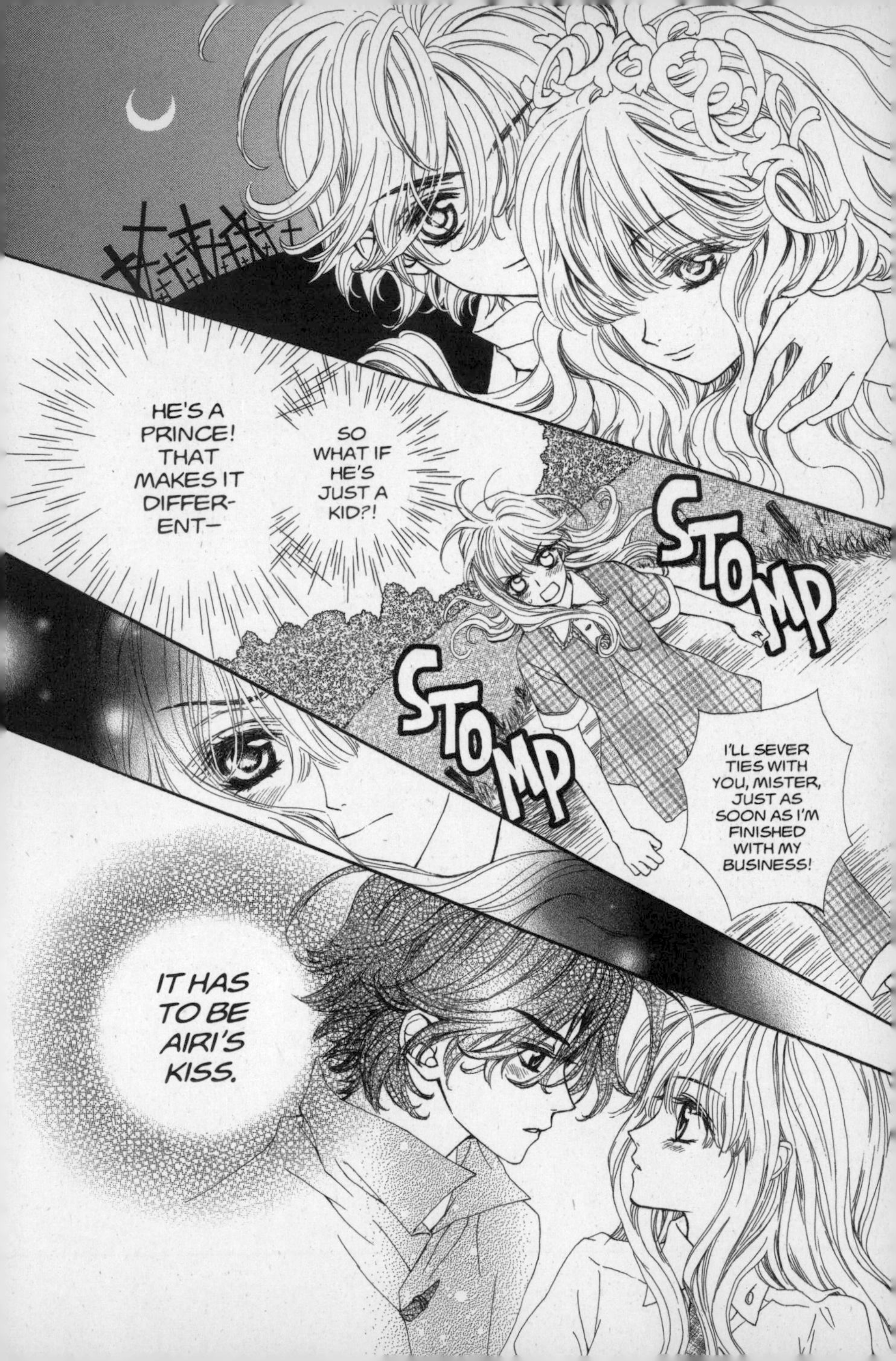
STOMP
STOMP
I'LL SEVER TIES WITH YOU, MISTER, JUST AS SOON AS I'M FINISHED WITH MY BUSINESS!
SO WHAT IF HE'S JUST A KID?!
HE'S A PRINCE! THAT MAKES IT DIFFER-ENT—
IT HAS TO BE AIRI'S KISS.

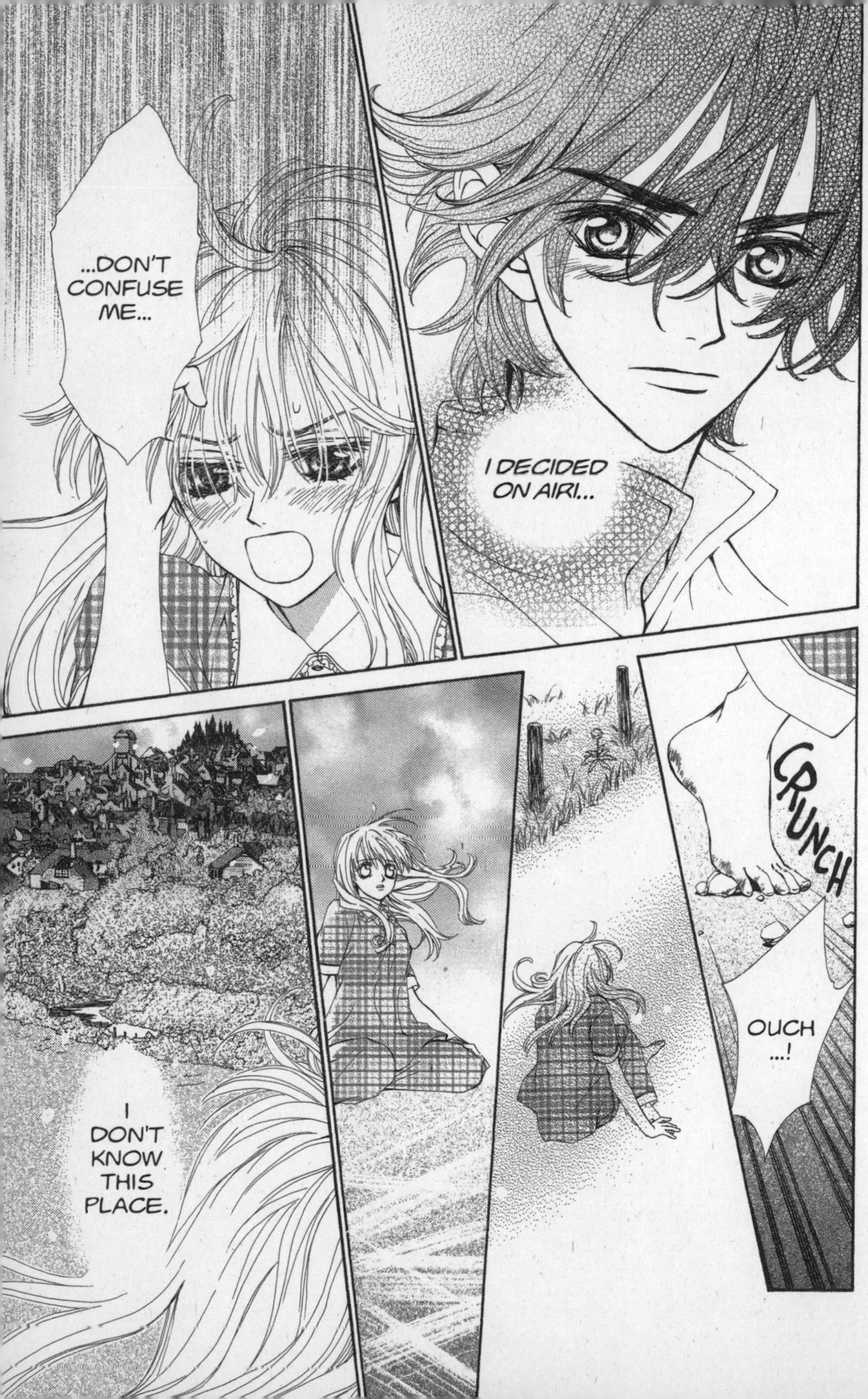
I DECIDED ON AIRI...
...DON'T CONFUSE ME...
CRUNCH
OUCH ...!
I DON'T KNOW THIS PLACE.

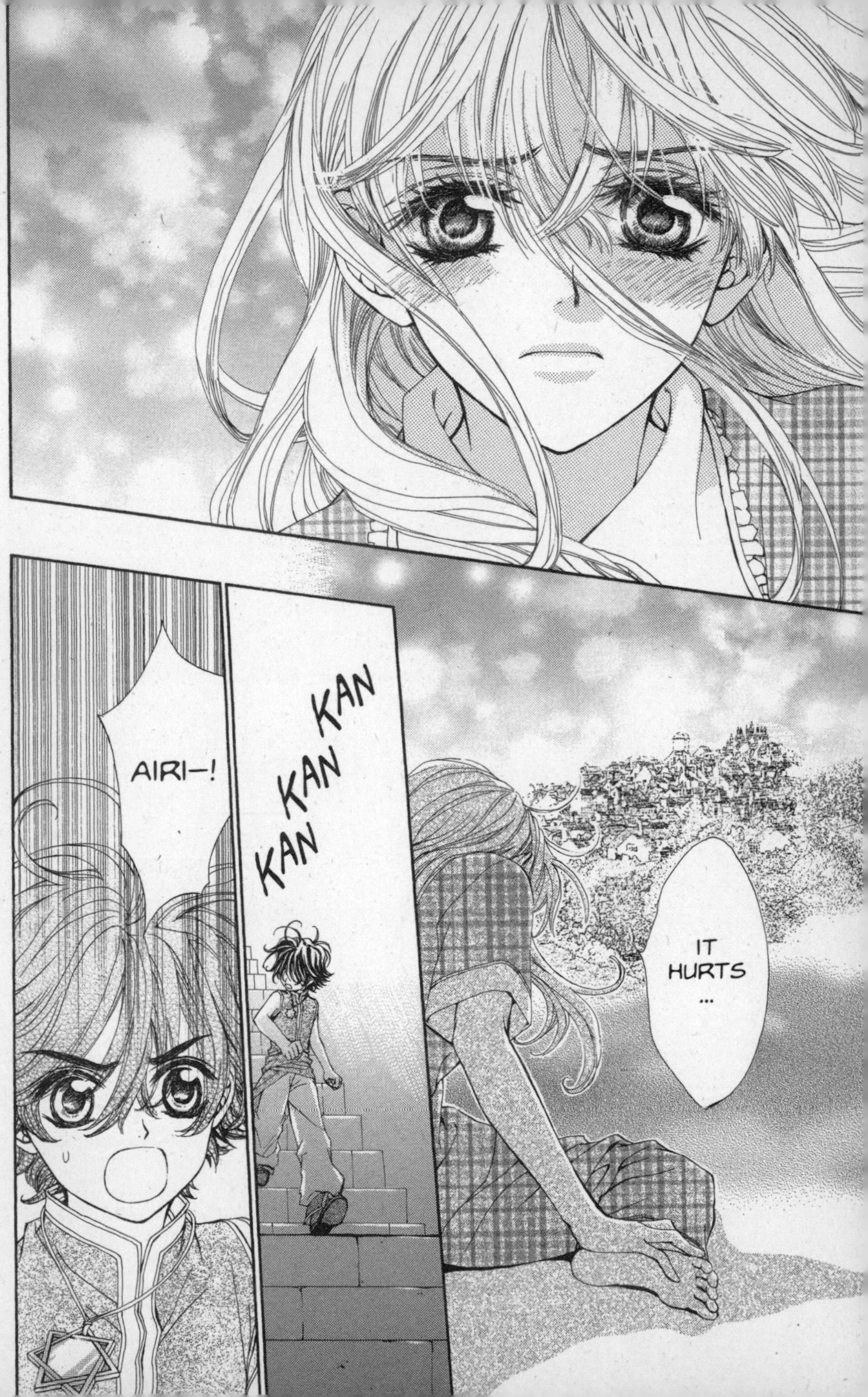
IT HURTS ...
KAN KAN KAN
AIRI—!

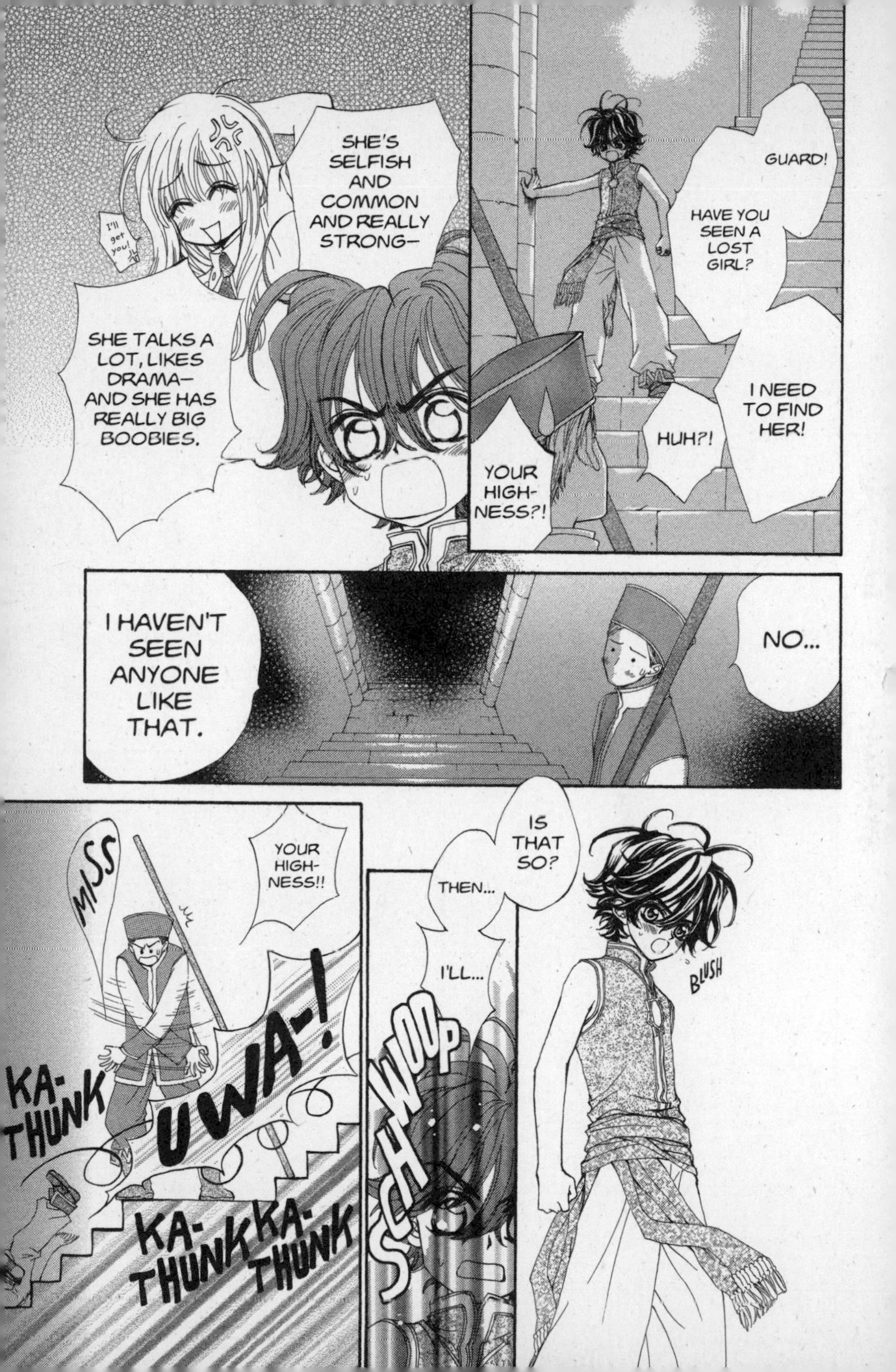
GUARD!
HAVE YOU SEEN A LOST GIRL?
I NEED TO FIND HER!
HUH?!
YOUR HIGHNESS?!
SHE'S SELFISH AND COMMON AND REALLY STRONG—
SHE TALKS A LOT, LIKES DRAMA— AND SHE HAS REALLY BIG BOOBIES.
I'll get you!
NO...
I HAVEN'T SEEN ANYONE LIKE THAT.
IS THAT SO?
BLUSH
THEN...
I'LL...
SCHWOOP
YOUR HIGHNESS!!
MISS
UWA-!
KA-THUNK
KA-THUNK KA-THUNK

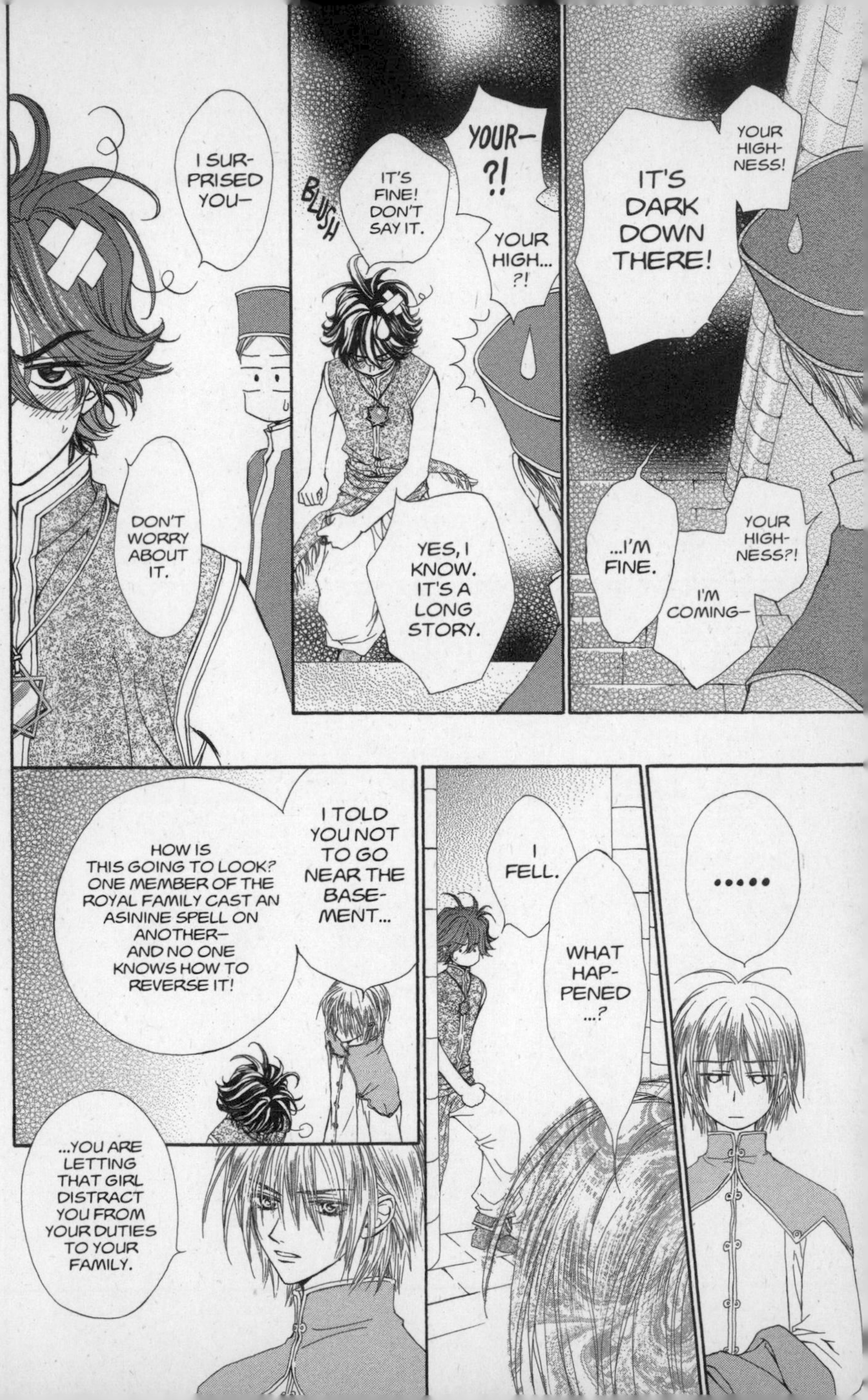
YOUR HIGHNESS!
IT'S DARK DOWN THERE!
YOUR HIGHNESS?!
I'M COMING—
...I'M FINE.
YOUR— ?!
YOUR HIGH... ?!
IT'S FINE! DON'T SAY IT.
BLUSH
YES, I KNOW. IT'S A LONG STORY.
I SURPRISED YOU—
DON'T WORRY ABOUT IT.
.....
I FELL.
WHAT HAPPENED ...?
I TOLD YOU NOT TO GO NEAR THE BASEMENT...
HOW IS THIS GOING TO LOOK? ONE MEMBER OF THE ROYAL FAMILY CAST AN ASININE SPELL ON ANOTHER— AND NO ONE KNOWS HOW TO REVERSE IT!
...YOU ARE LETTING THAT GIRL DISTRACT YOU FROM YOUR DUTIES TO YOUR FAMILY.

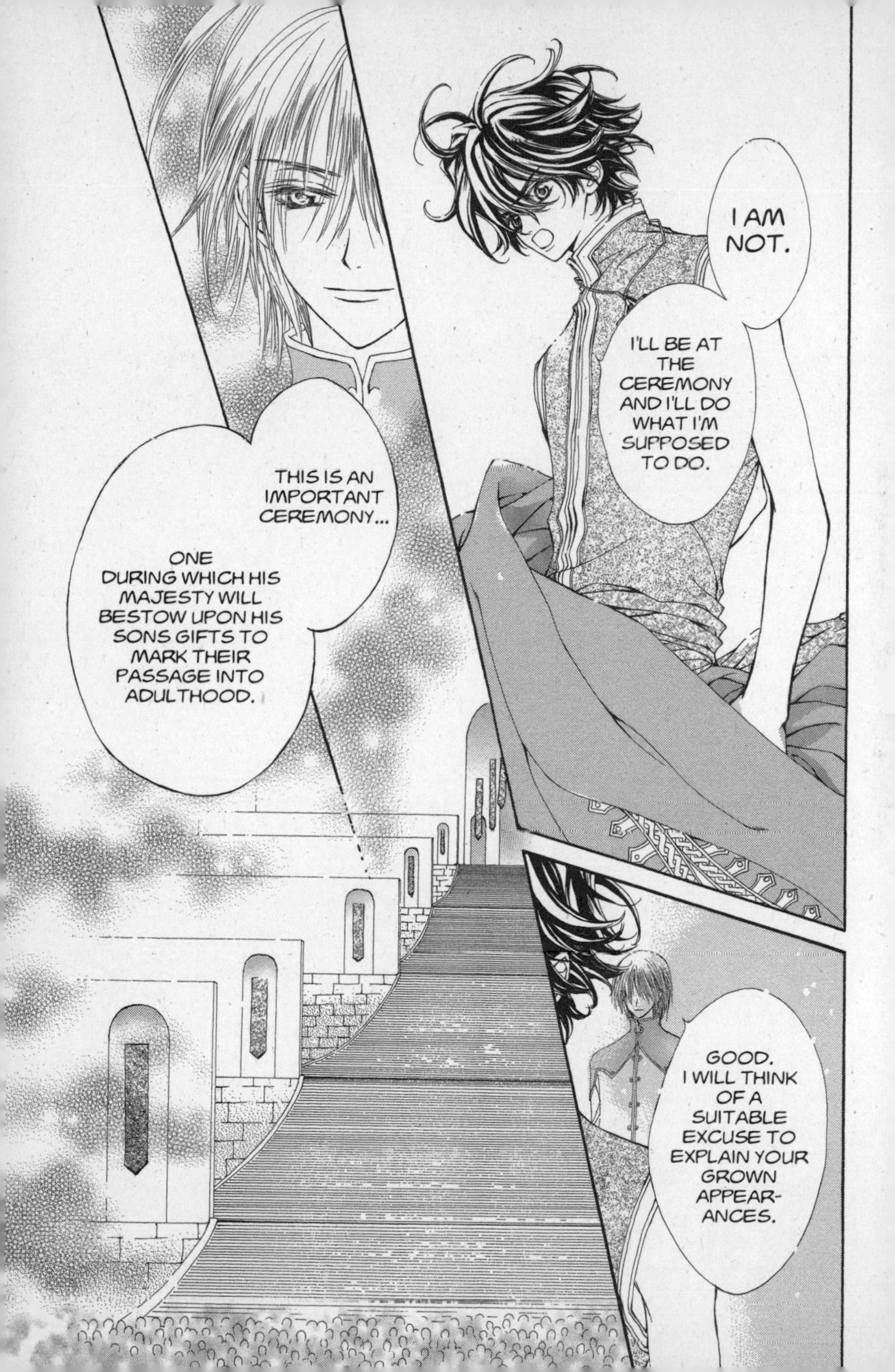
I AM NOT.
I'LL BE AT THE CEREMONY AND I'LL DO WHAT I'M SUPPOSED TO DO.
THIS IS AN IMPORTANT CEREMONY...
ONE DURING WHICH HIS MAJESTY WILL BESTOW UPON HIS SONS GIFTS TO MARK THEIR PASSAGE INTO ADULTHOOD.
GOOD. I WILL THINK OF A SUITABLE EXCUSE TO EXPLAIN YOUR GROWN APPEARANCES.

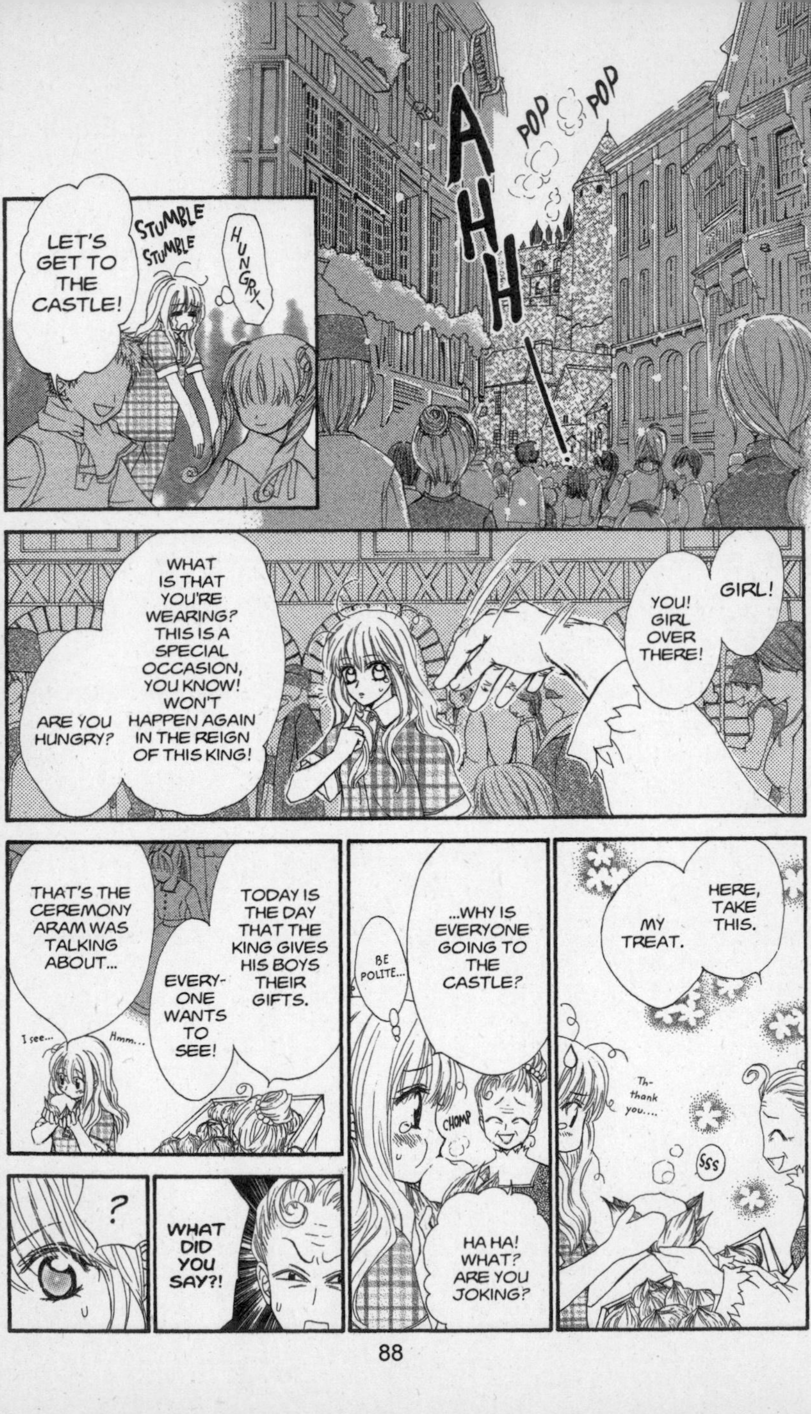
AHH!
POP POP
STUMBLE STUMBLE
HUNGRY...
LET'S GET TO THE CASTLE!
GIRL!
YOU! GIRL OVER THERE!
WHAT IS THAT YOU'RE WEARING? THIS IS A SPECIAL OCCASION, YOU KNOW! WON'T HAPPEN AGAIN IN THE REIGN OF THIS KING!
ARE YOU HUNGRY?
HERE, TAKE THIS.
MY TREAT.
Th-thank you....
SSS
...WHY IS EVERYONE GOING TO THE CASTLE?
BE POLITE...
CHOMP
HA HA! WHAT? ARE YOU JOKING?
TODAY IS THE DAY THAT THE KING GIVES HIS BOYS THEIR GIFTS.
EVERY-ONE WANTS TO SEE!
THAT'S THE CEREMONY ARAM WAS TALKING ABOUT...
Hmm...
I see...
WHAT DID YOU SAY?!
?

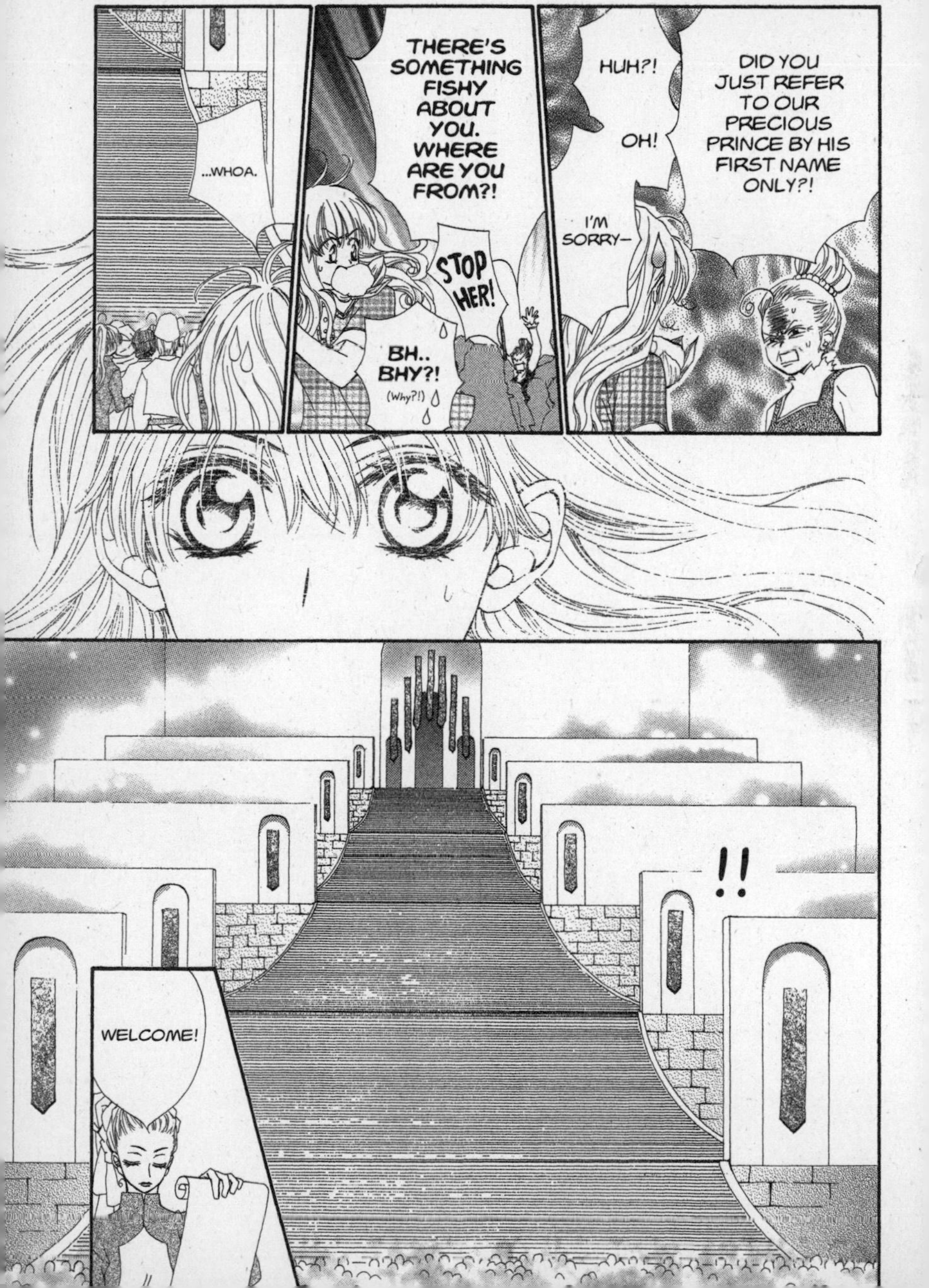
DID YOU JUST REFER TO OUR PRECIOUS PRINCE BY HIS FIRST NAME ONLY?!
HUH?!
OH!
I'M SORRY–
THERE'S SOMETHING FISHY ABOUT YOU. WHERE ARE YOU FROM?!
STOP HER!
BH.. BHY?!
(Why?!)
...WHOA.
!!
WELCOME!

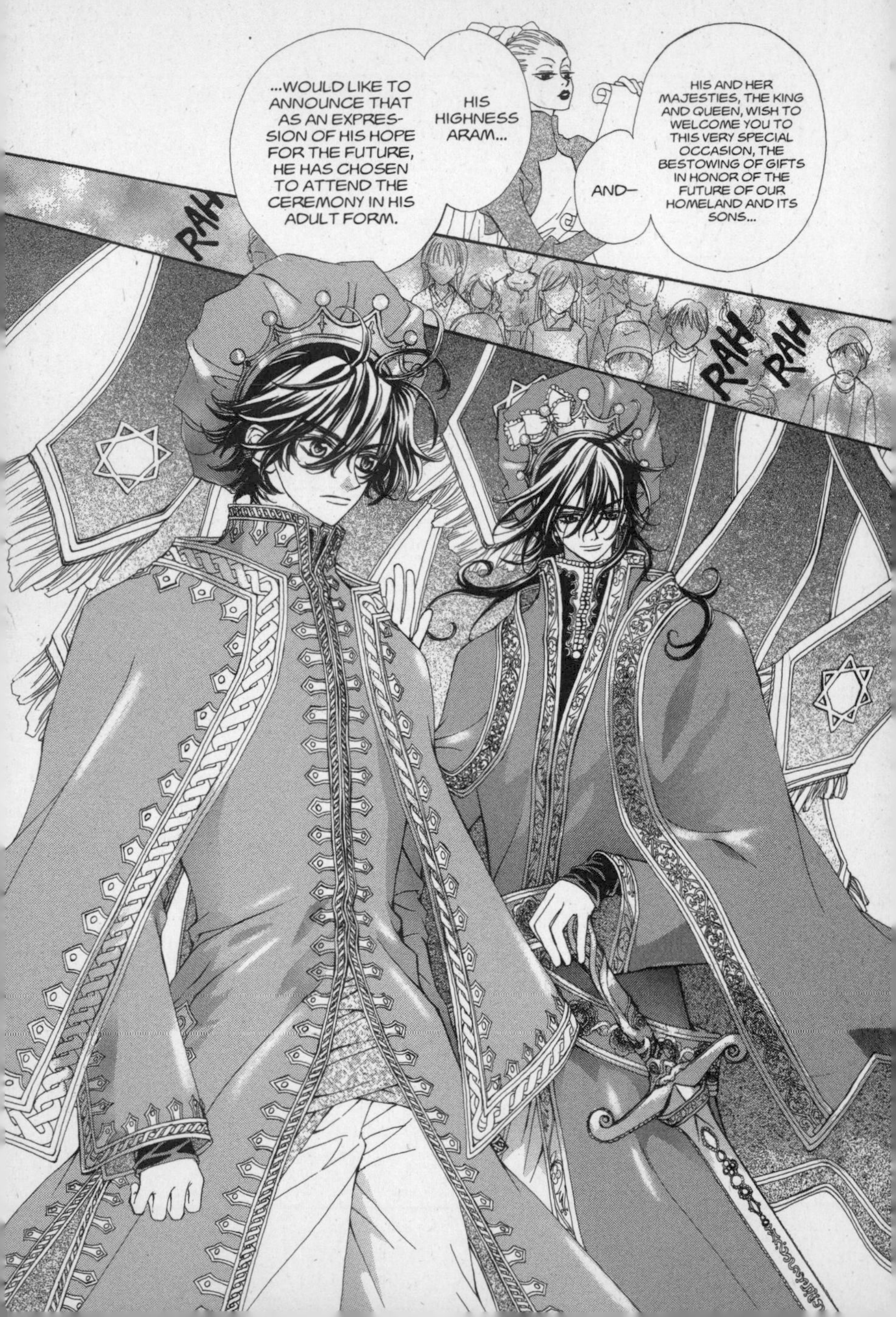
HIS AND HER MAJESTIES, THE KING AND QUEEN, WISH TO WELCOME YOU TO THIS VERY SPECIAL OCCASION, THE BESTOWING OF GIFTS IN HONOR OF THE FUTURE OF OUR HOMELAND AND ITS SONS...
AND—
HIS HIGHNESS ARAM...
...WOULD LIKE TO ANNOUNCE THAT AS AN EXPRESSION OF HIS HOPE FOR THE FUTURE, HE HAS CHOSEN TO ATTEND THE CEREMONY IN HIS ADULT FORM.
RAH
RAH
RAH

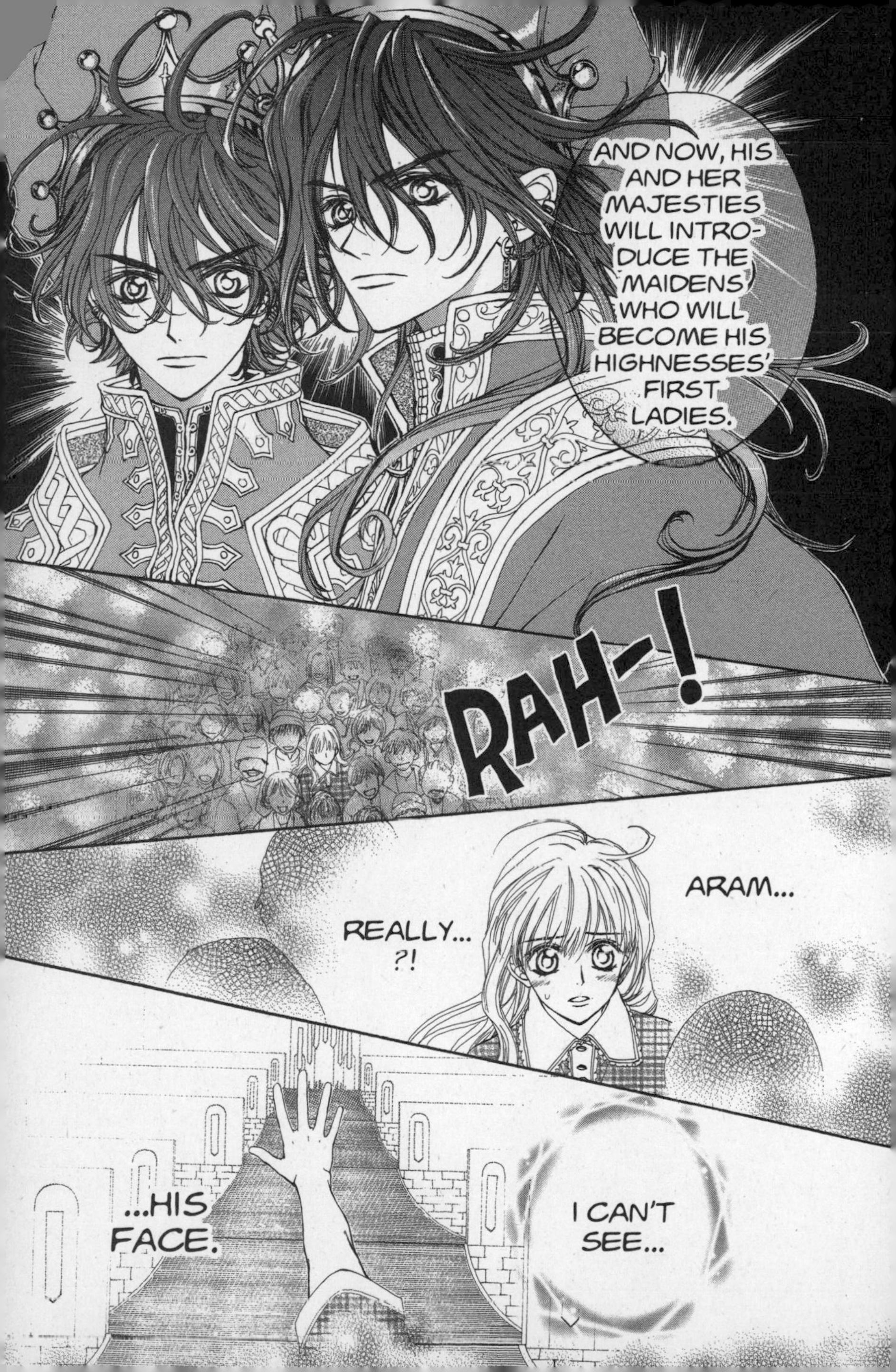
AND NOW, HIS AND HER MAJESTIES WILL INTRODUCE THE MAIDENS WHO WILL BECOME HIS HIGHNESSES' FIRST LADIES.
RAH-!
ARAM...
REALLY... ?!
I CAN'T SEE...
...HIS FACE.

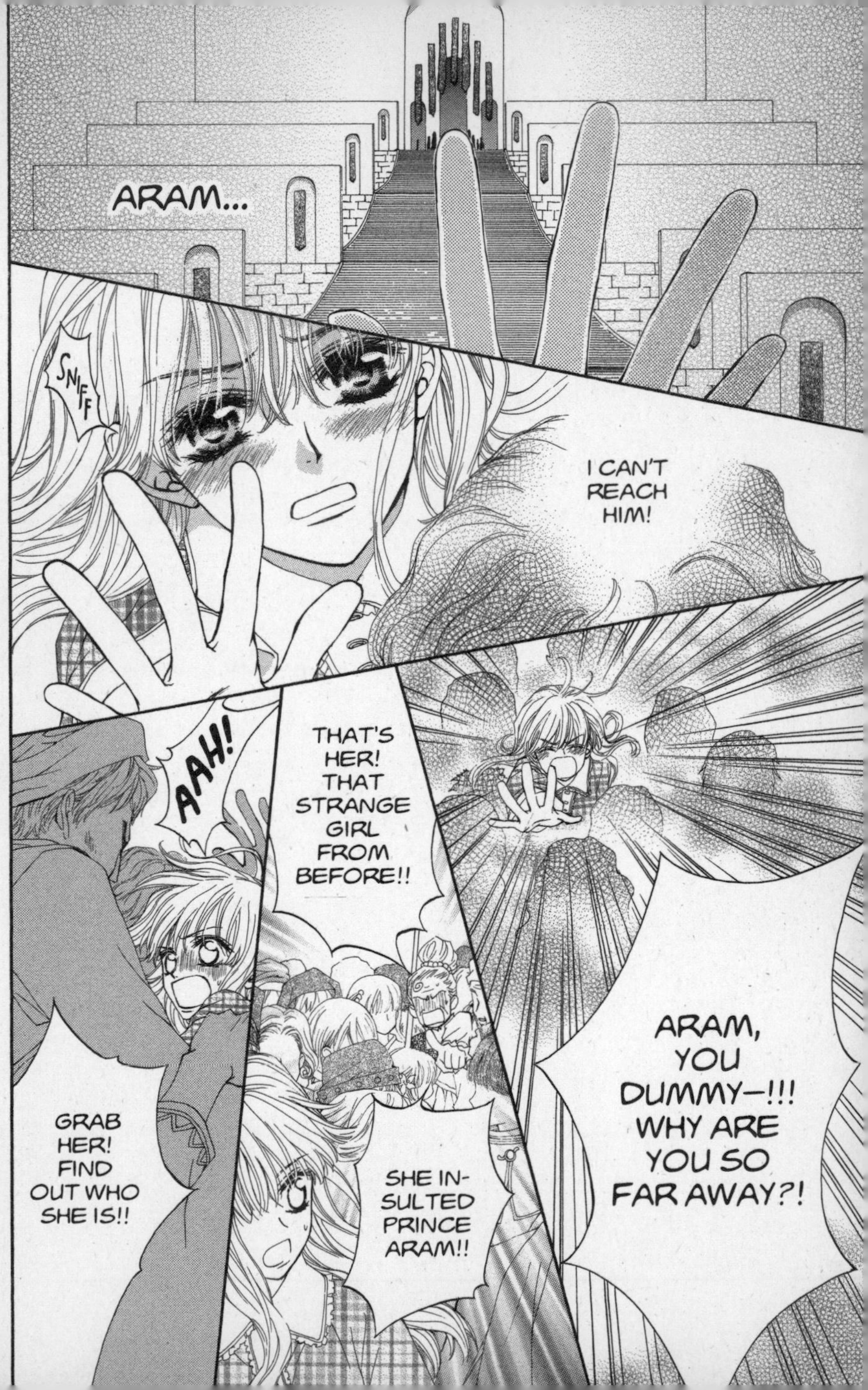
ARAM...
I CAN'T REACH HIM!
SNIFF
ARAM, YOU DUMMY—!!! WHY ARE YOU SO FAR AWAY?!
THAT'S HER! THAT STRANGE GIRL FROM BEFORE!!
SHE IN-SULTED PRINCE ARAM!!
AAH!
GRAB HER! FIND OUT WHO SHE IS!!

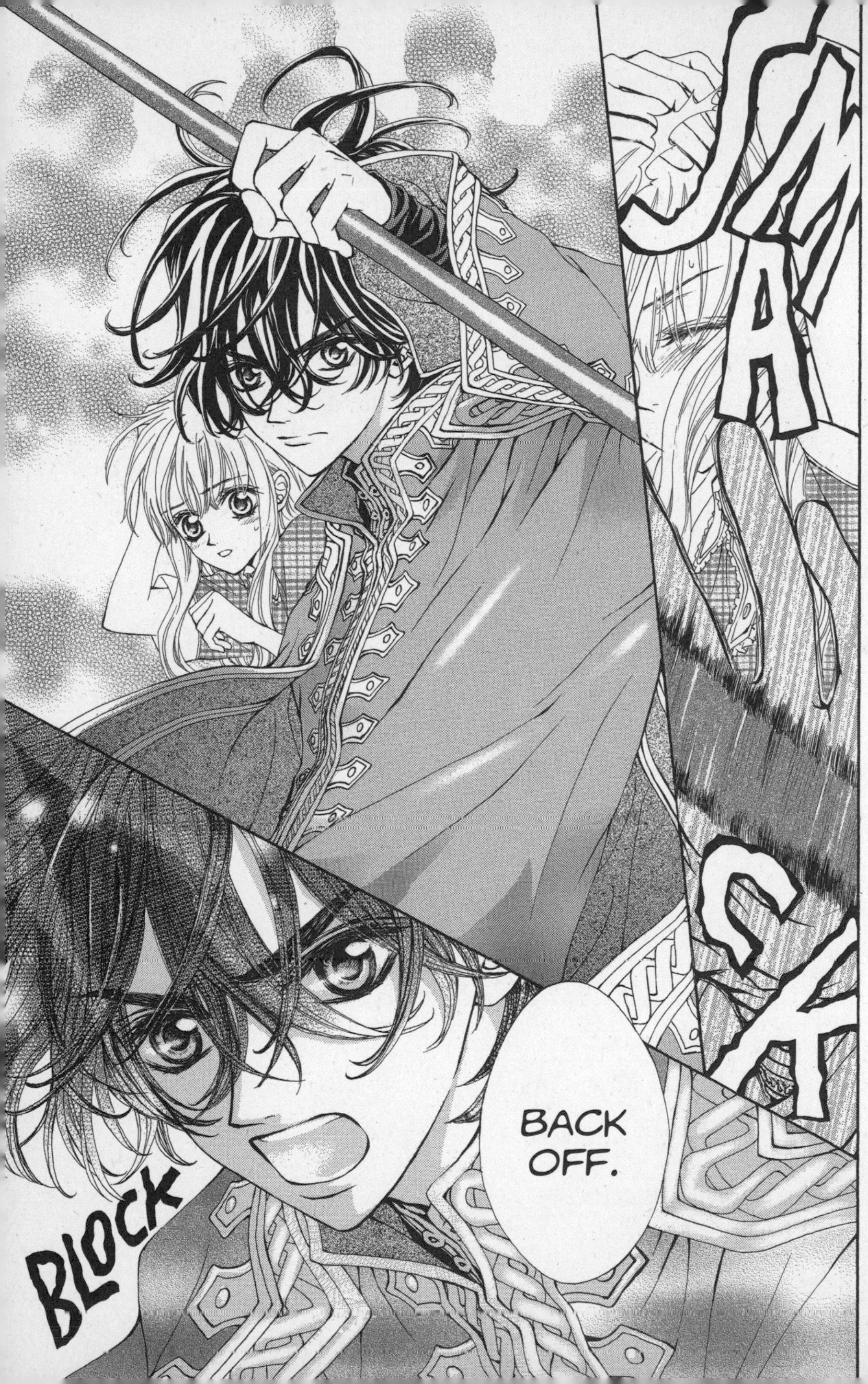
BACK OFF.
BLOCK

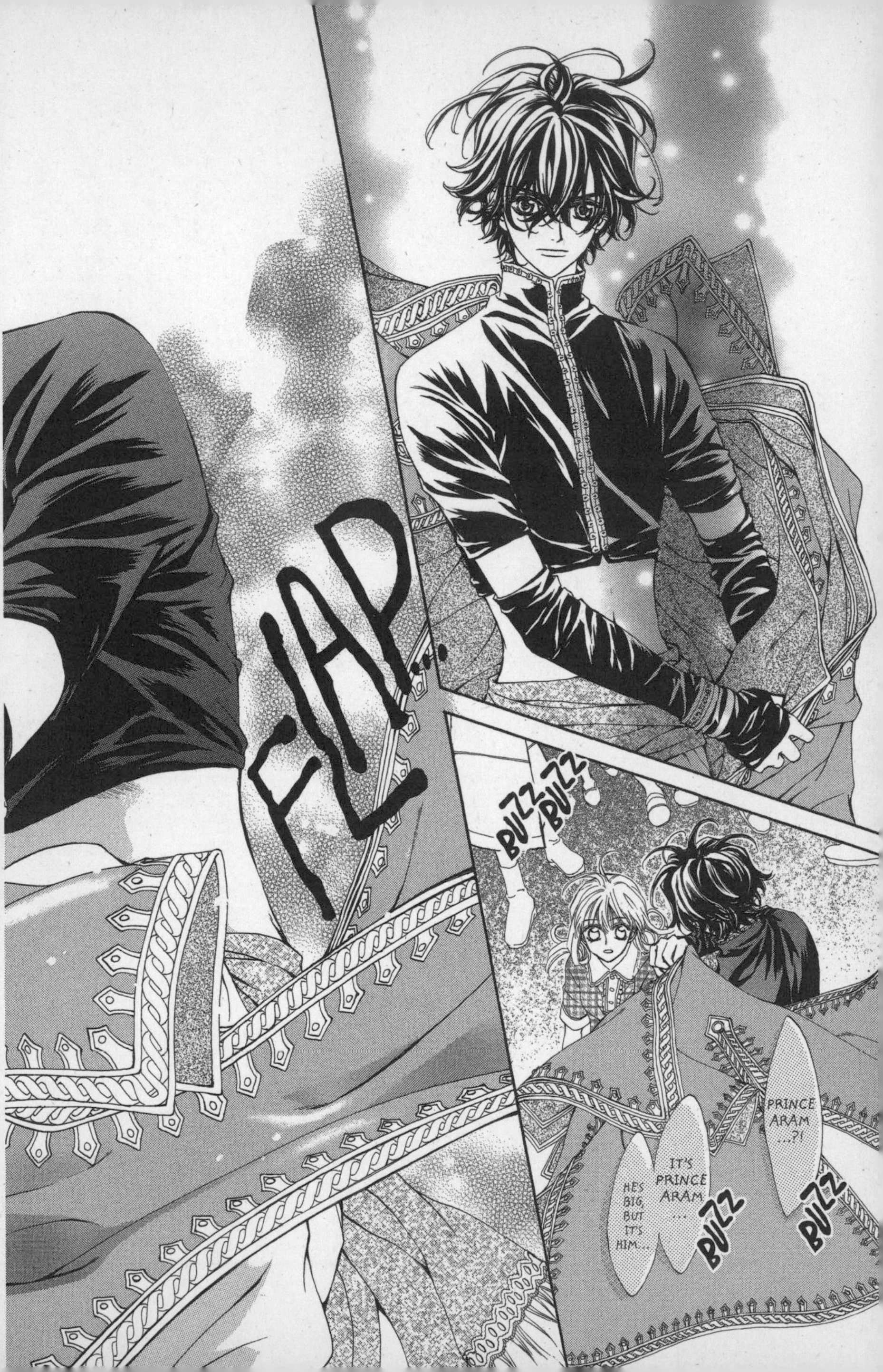
BUZZ BUZZ
PRINCE ARAM ...?!
IT'S PRINCE ARAM ...
HE'S BIG, BUT IT'S HIM...
BUZZ
BUZZ
FLAP...

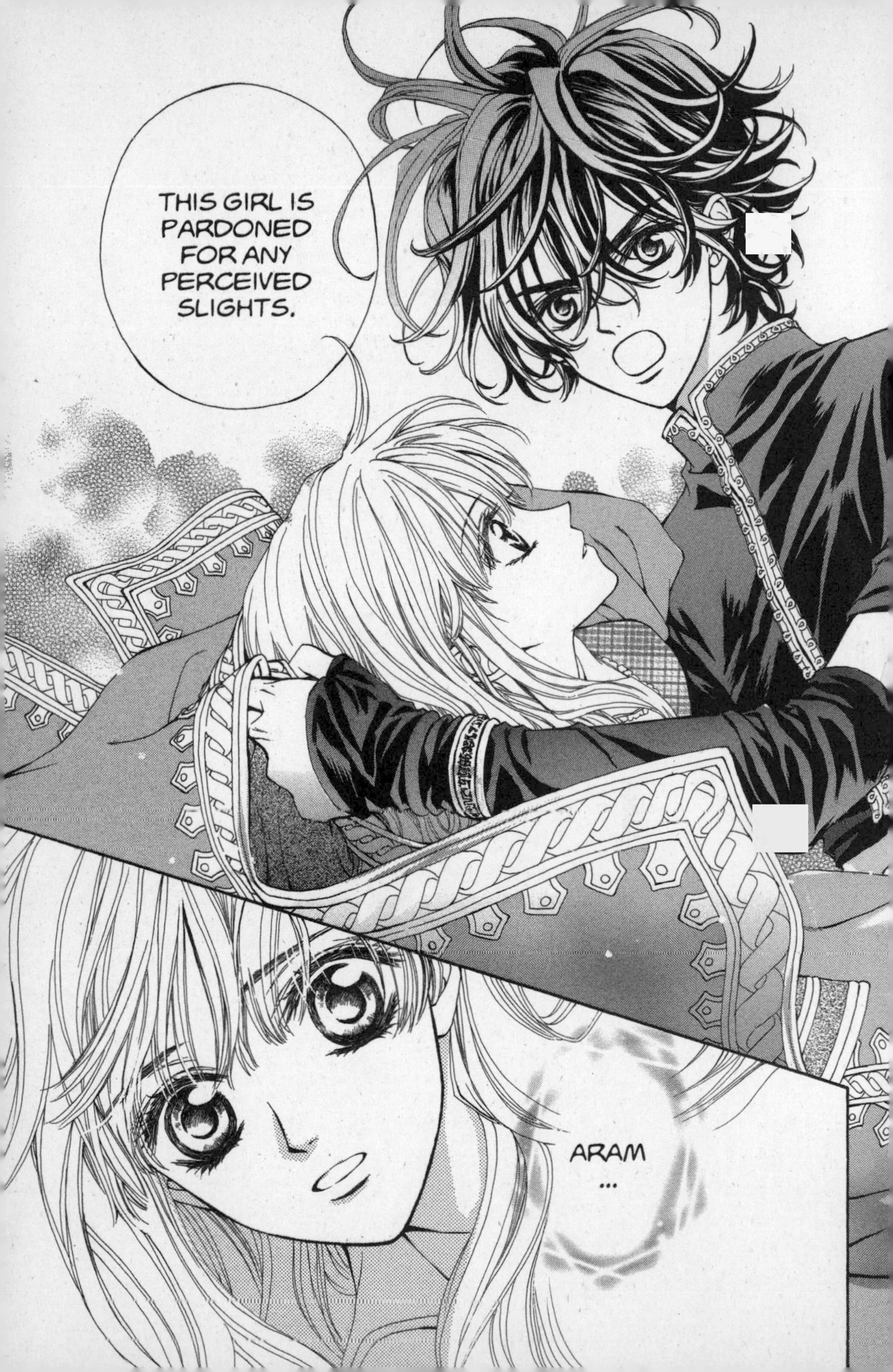
THIS GIRL IS PARDONED FOR ANY PERCEIVED SLIGHTS.
ARAM ...

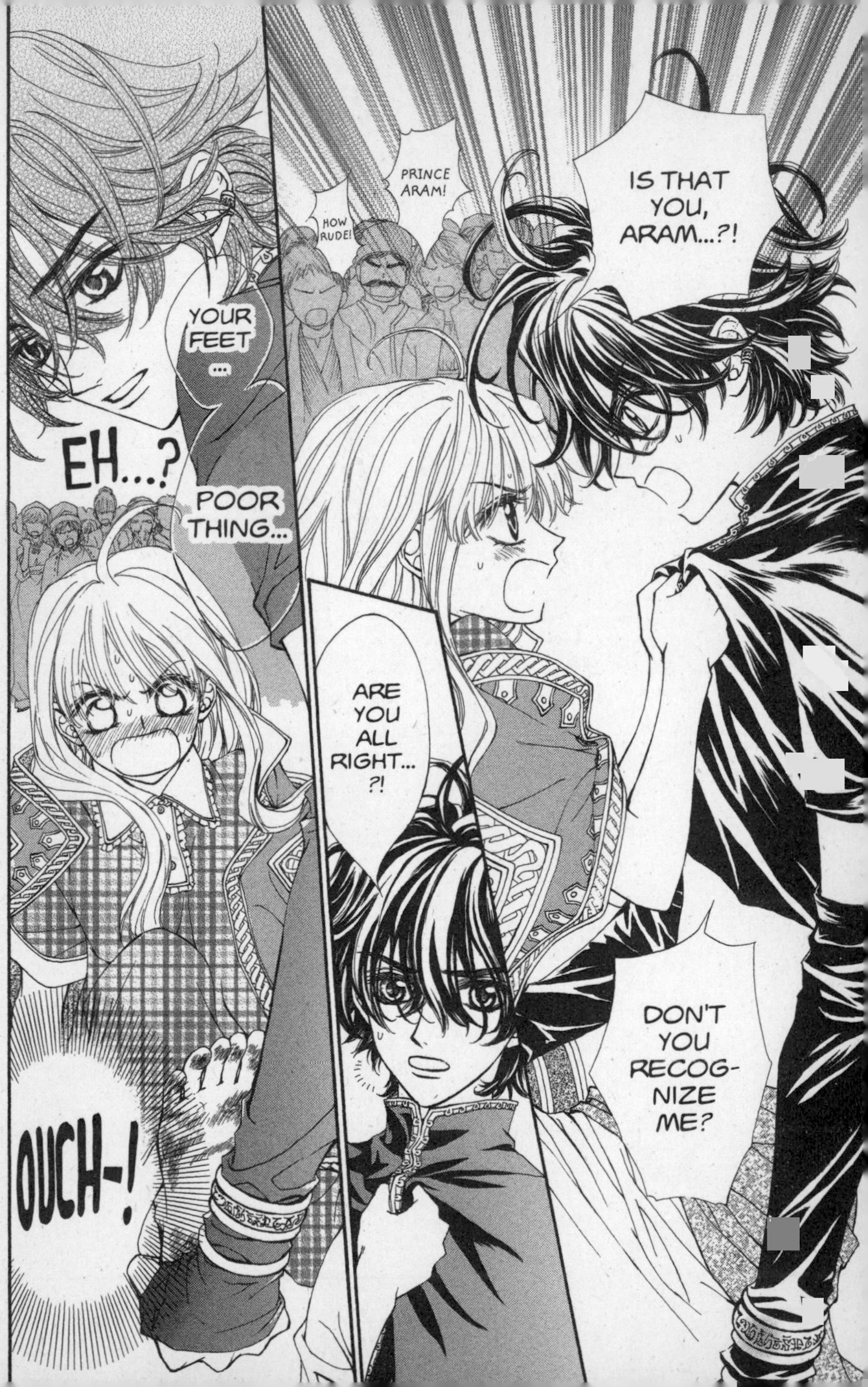
IS THAT YOU, ARAM...?!
DON'T YOU RECOG-NIZE ME?
PRINCE ARAM!
HOW RUDE!
ARE YOU ALL RIGHT...?!
YOUR FEET ...
EH...?
POOR THING...
OUCH-!

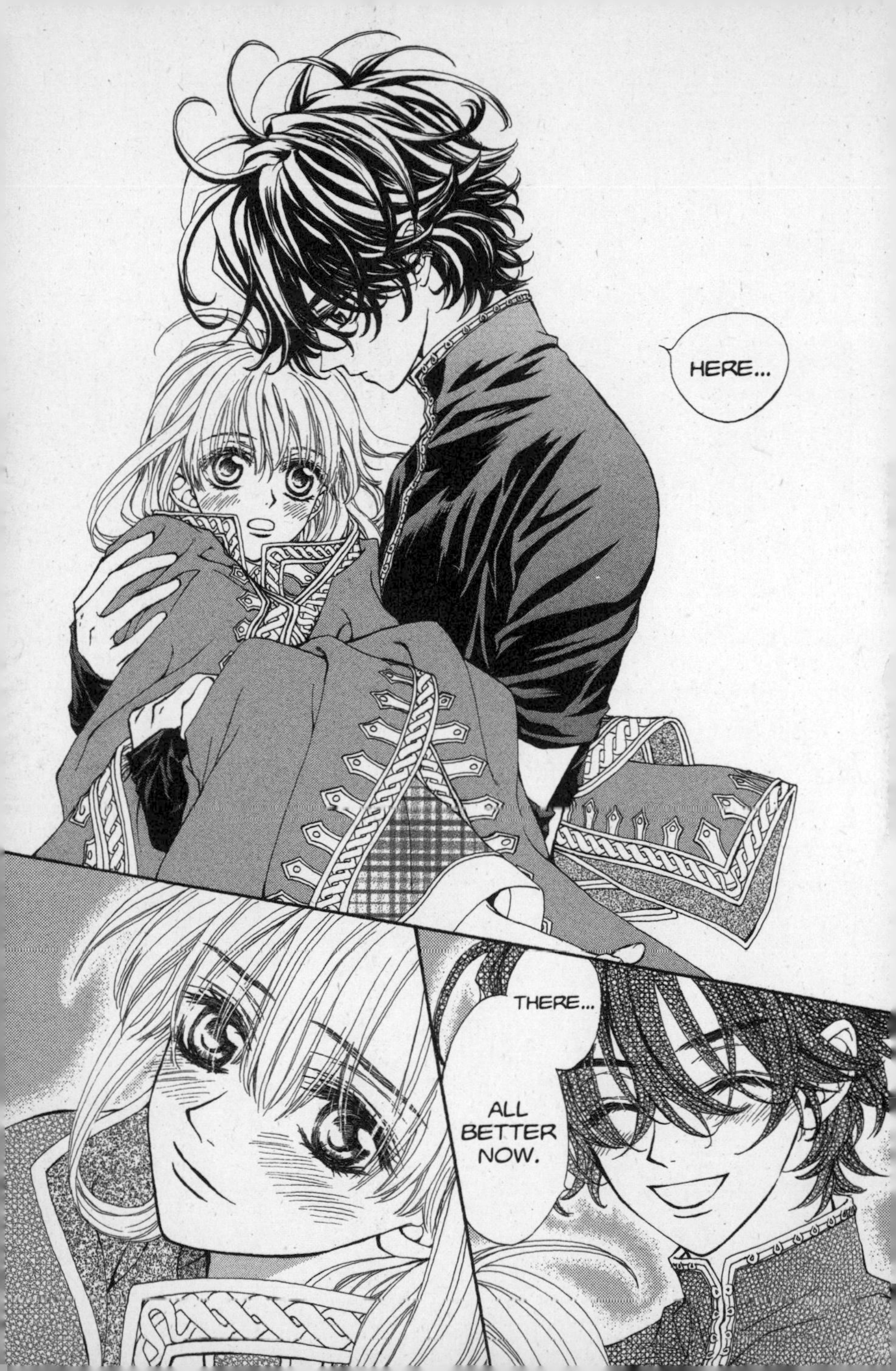
HERE...
THERE...
ALL BETTER NOW.

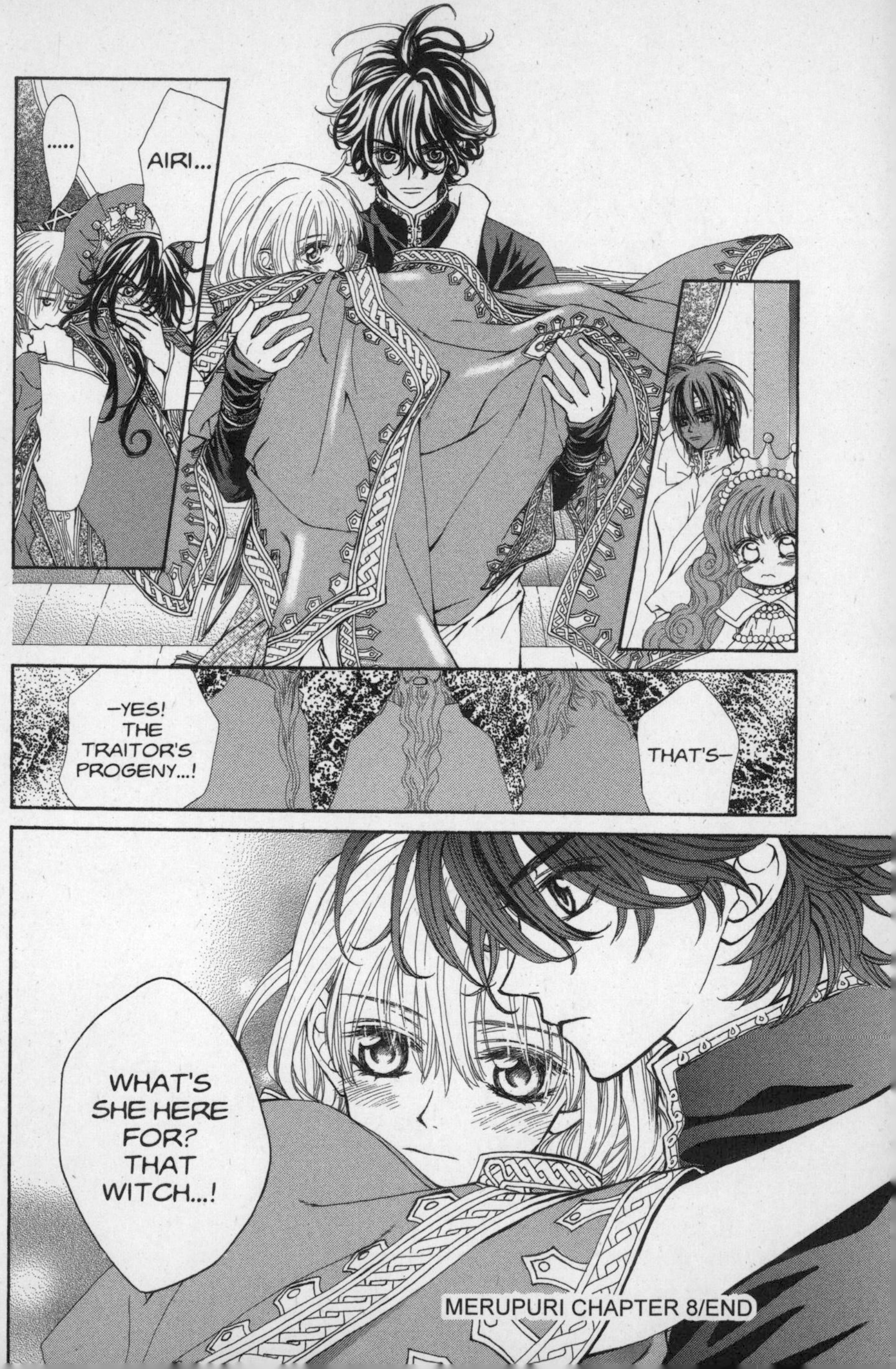
AIRI...
.....
THAT'S—
—YES! THE TRAITOR'S PROGENY...!
WHAT'S SHE HERE FOR? THAT WITCH...!
MERUPURI CHAPTER 8/END

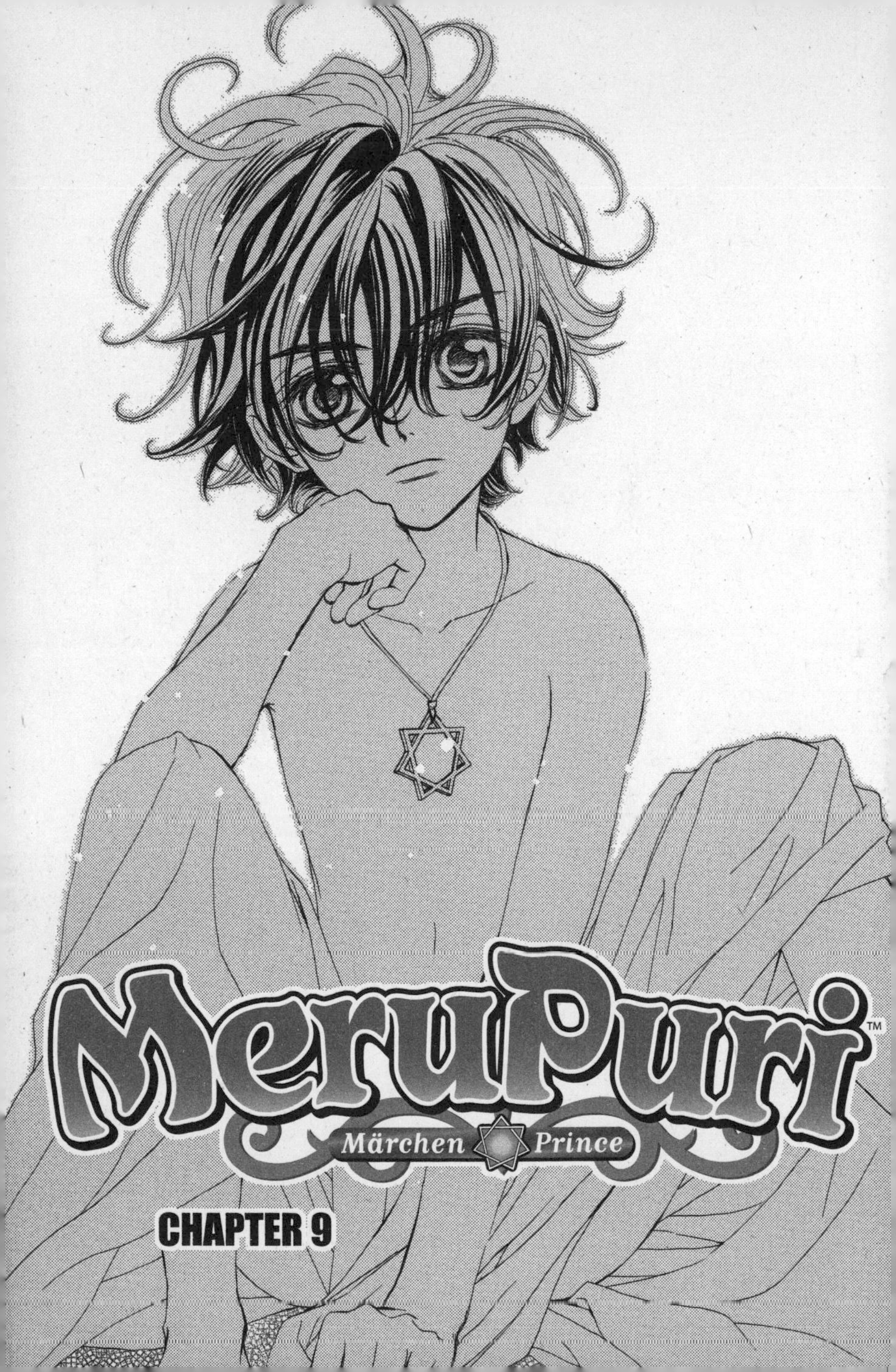
MeruPuri™
Märchen Prince
CHAPTER 9

I CAN'T LET YOU WALK BAREFOOT...

DAZED!

HE REALLY IS A PRINCE...

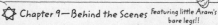

✡ Chapter 9—Behind the Scenes *featuring little Aram's bare legs!!*
I thought the story was plenty erotic already, but my boss thought we should push it further. We had screaming fights over it (eep!), but in the end, the readers supported my boss. I realized I was fighting for something really insignificant, which bruised my fragile ego (ha!). ✤✤ But, hey! I'm the one who has to draw it!
(Between this and Chapter 8, I think it's safe to say that Aram's a boob guy. No wonder he likes Airi! She's about a D cup. Aram must sleep well.)

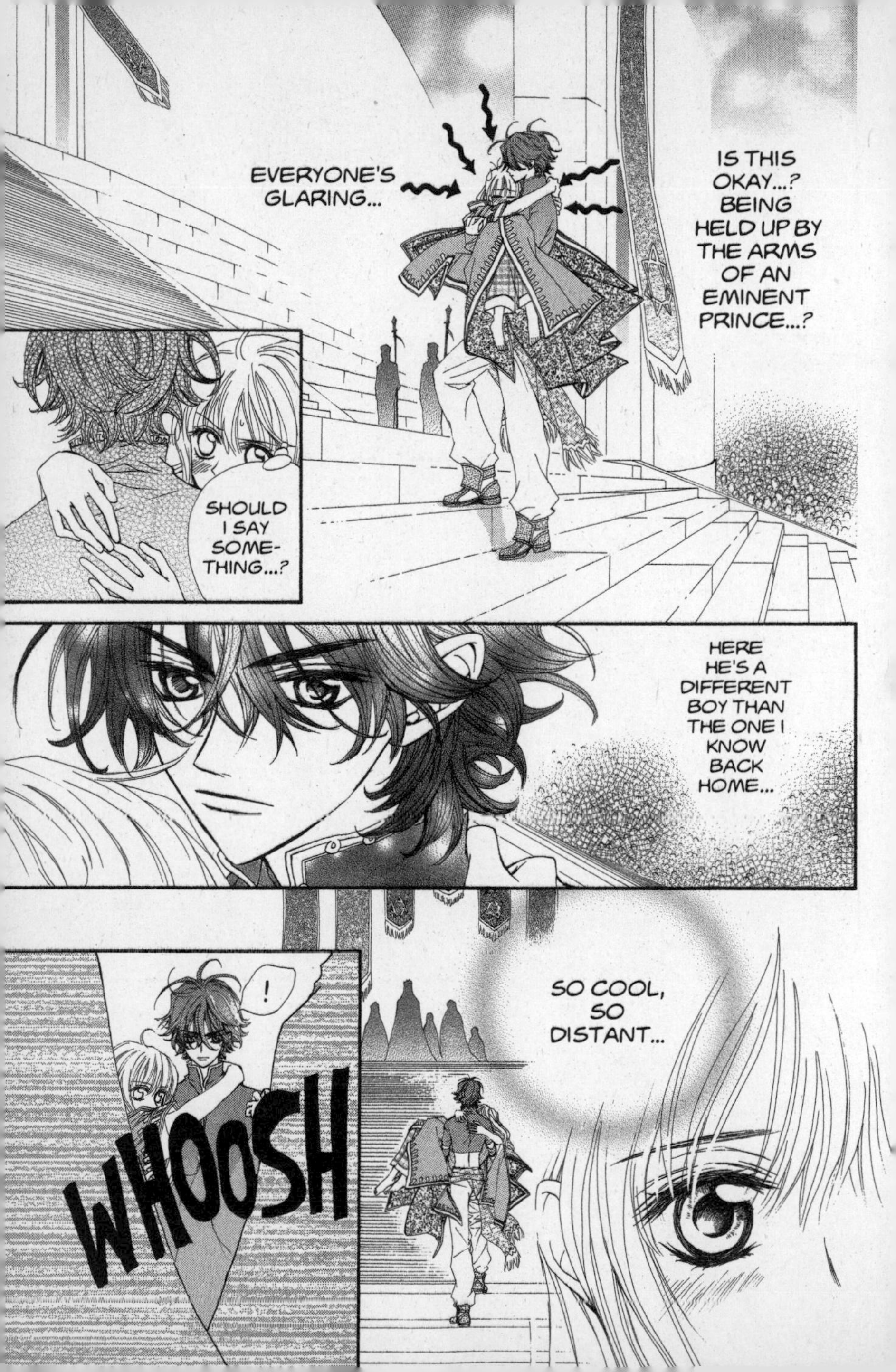
IS THIS OKAY...? BEING HELD UP BY THE ARMS OF AN EMINENT PRINCE...?
EVERYONE'S GLARING...
SHOULD I SAY SOME-THING...?
HERE HE'S A DIFFERENT BOY THAN THE ONE I KNOW BACK HOME...
SO COOL, SO DISTANT...
!
WHOOSH

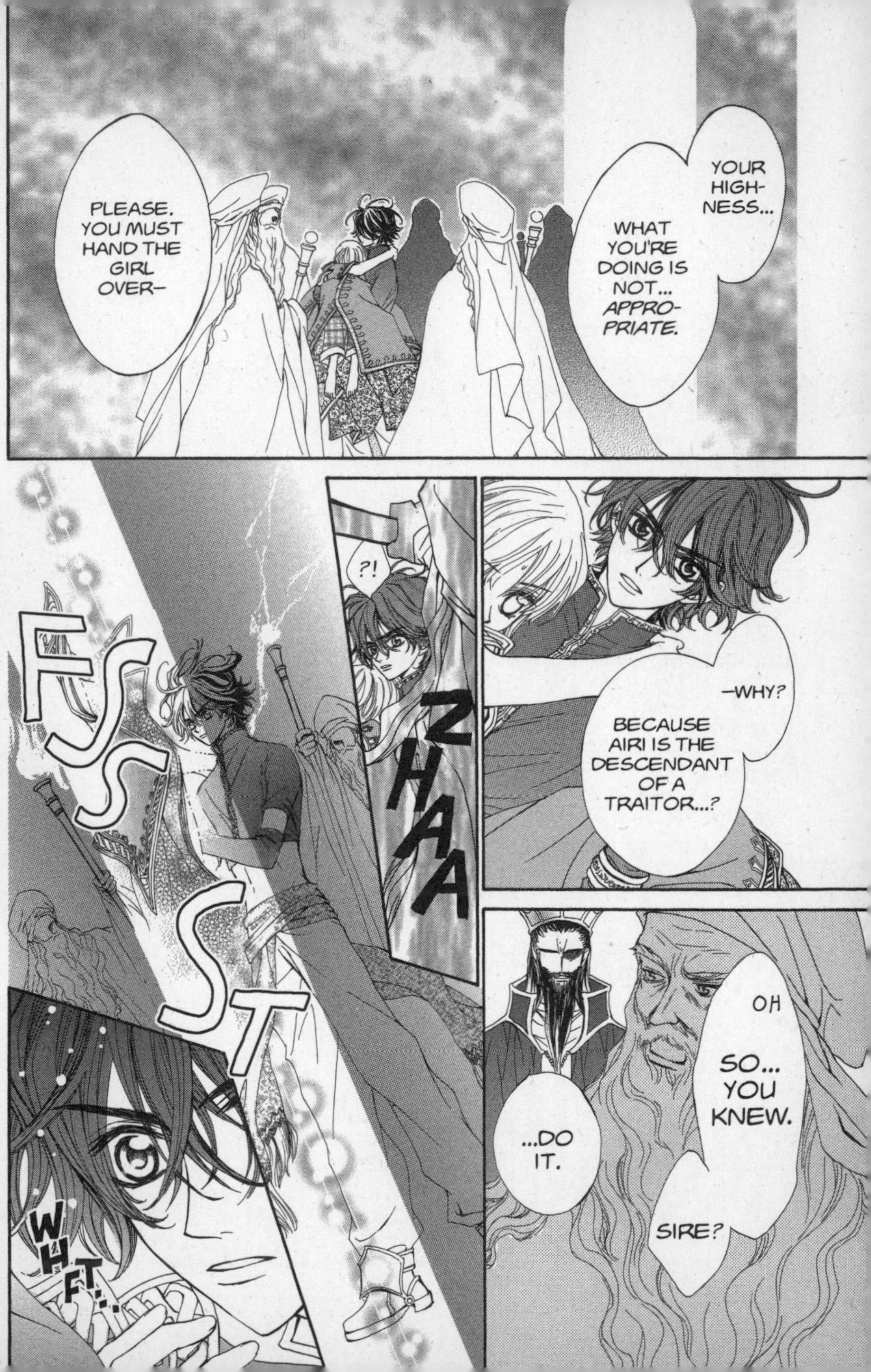
YOUR HIGHNESS...
WHAT YOU'RE DOING IS NOT... APPROPRIATE.
PLEASE. YOU MUST HAND THE GIRL OVER—
—WHY?
BECAUSE AIRI IS THE DESCENDANT OF A TRAITOR...?
OH
SO... YOU KNEW.
SIRE?
...DO IT.
?!
ZHAA
FSSST
WHFT...

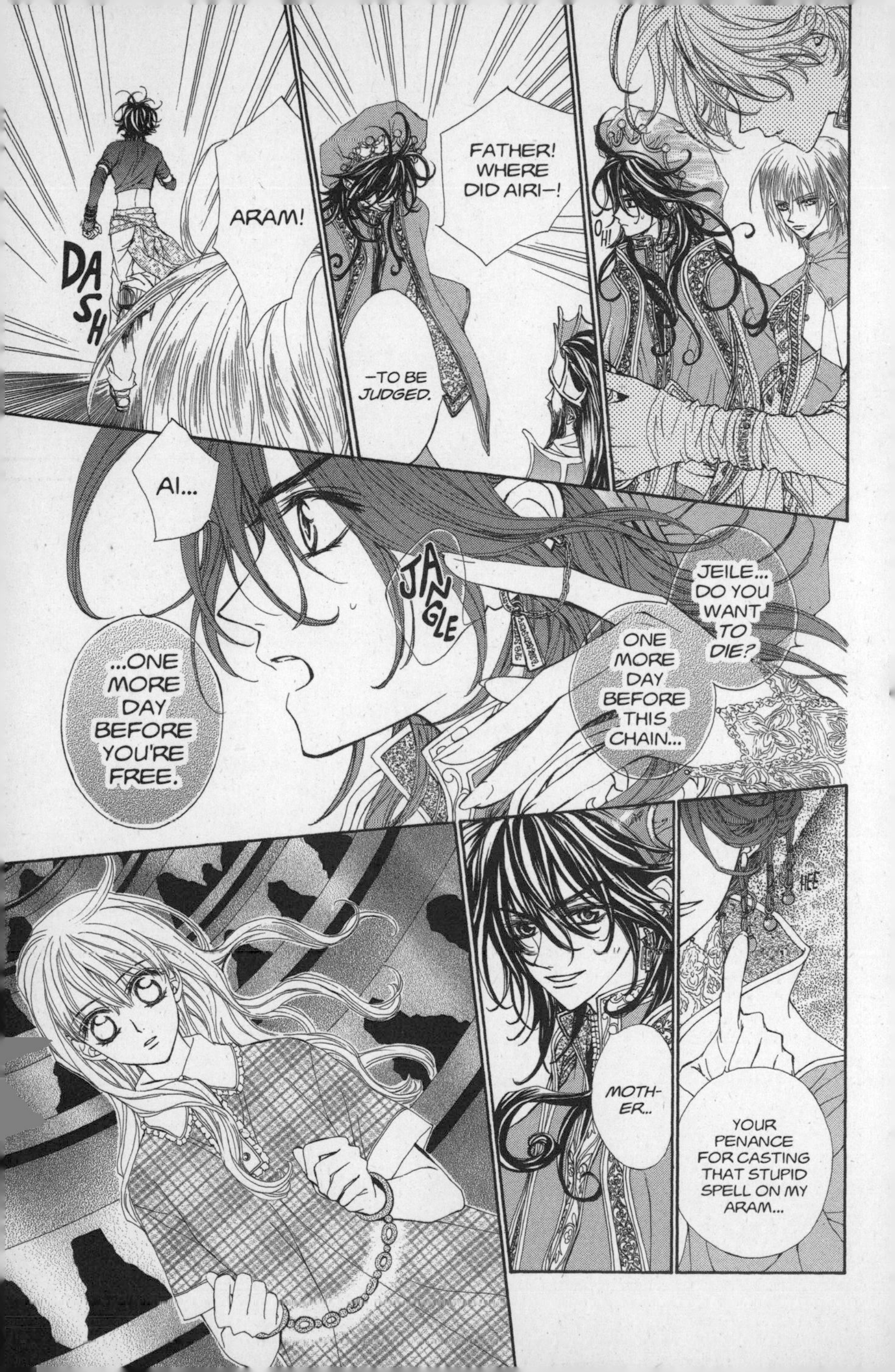
OH!
FATHER! WHERE DID AIRI—!
—TO BE JUDGED.
ARAM!
DASH
JEILE... DO YOU WANT TO DIE?
ONE MORE DAY BEFORE THIS CHAIN...
JANGLE
AI...
...ONE MORE DAY BEFORE YOU'RE FREE.
HEE
YOUR PENANCE FOR CASTING THAT STUPID SPELL ON MY ARAM...
MOTHER-ER...

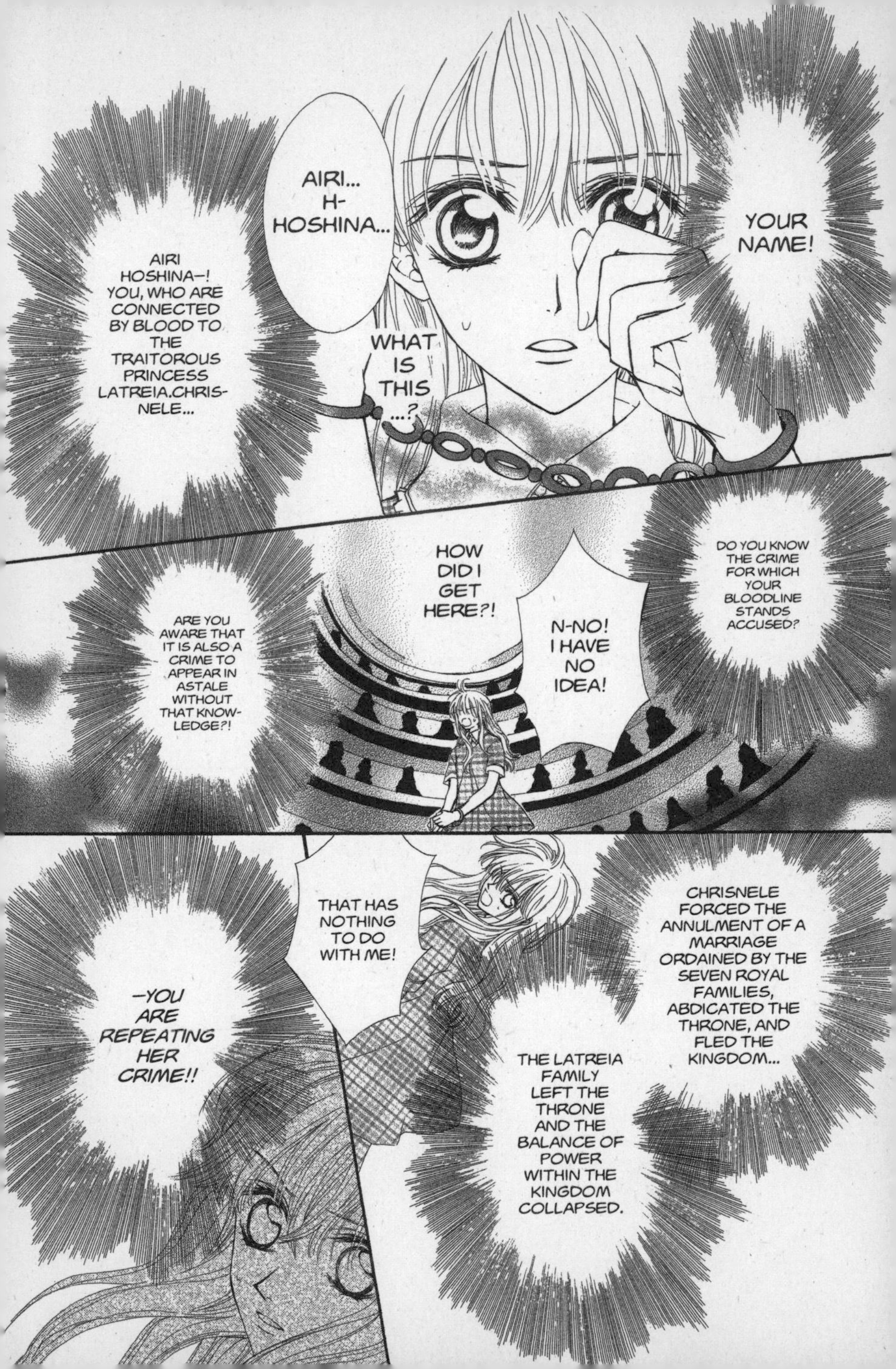
YOUR NAME!
AIRI... H-HOSHINA...
WHAT IS THIS ...?
AIRI HOSHINA—! YOU, WHO ARE CONNECTED BY BLOOD TO THE TRAITOROUS PRINCESS LATREIA.CHRIS-NELE...
DO YOU KNOW THE CRIME FOR WHICH YOUR BLOODLINE STANDS ACCUSED?
N-NO! I HAVE NO IDEA!
HOW DID I GET HERE?!
ARE YOU AWARE THAT IT IS ALSO A CRIME TO APPEAR IN ASTALE WITHOUT THAT KNOW-LEDGE?!
CHRISNELE FORCED THE ANNULMENT OF A MARRIAGE ORDAINED BY THE SEVEN ROYAL FAMILIES, ABDICATED THE THRONE, AND FLED THE KINGDOM...
THE LATREIA FAMILY LEFT THE THRONE AND THE BALANCE OF POWER WITHIN THE KINGDOM COLLAPSED.
THAT HAS NOTHING TO DO WITH ME!
—YOU ARE REPEATING HER CRIME!!

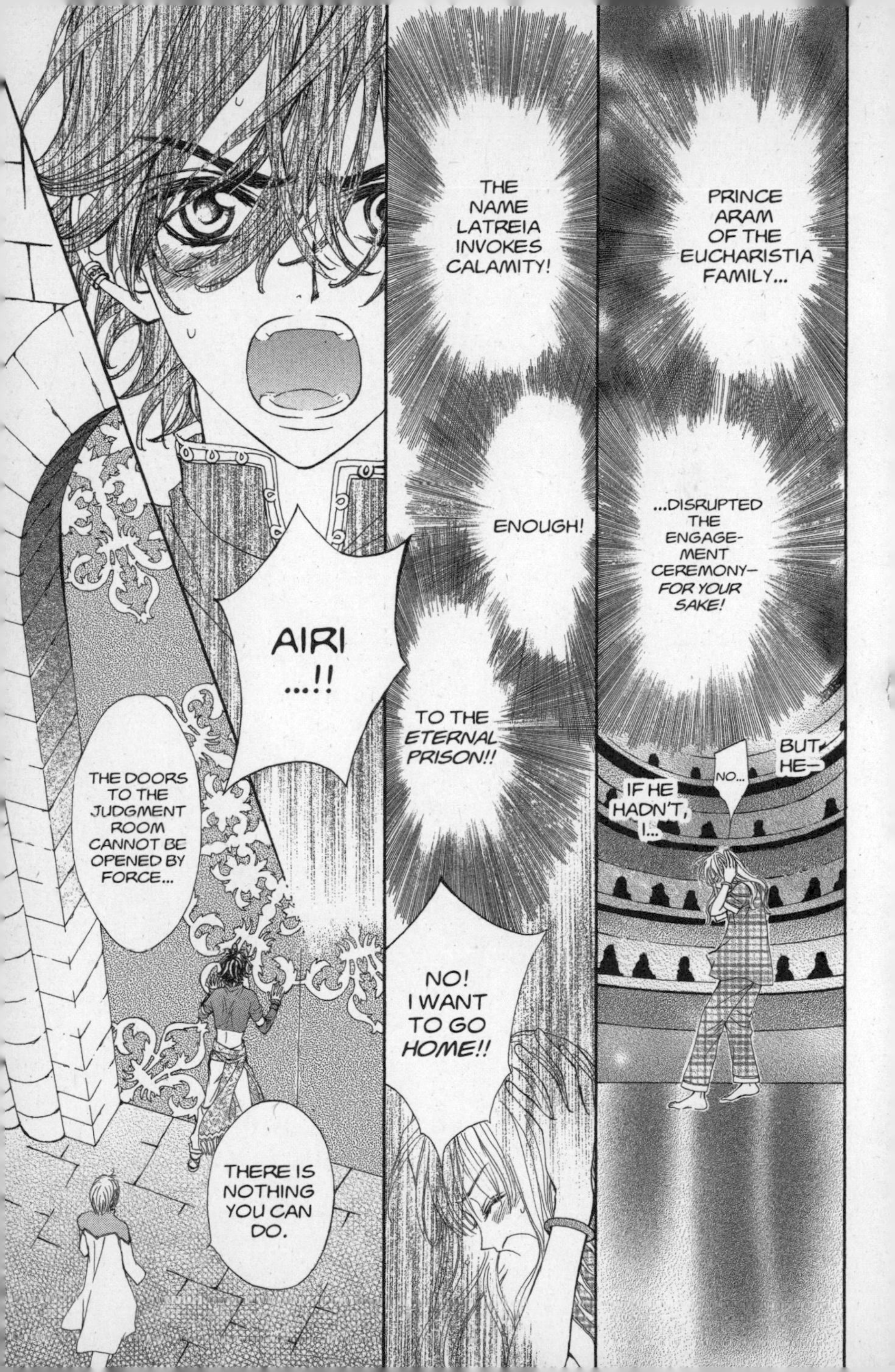

PRINCE ARAM OF THE EUCHARISTIA FAMILY...
...DISRUPTED THE ENGAGEMENT CEREMONY—FOR YOUR SAKE!
BUT HE—
NO...
IF HE HADN'T, I...
THE NAME LATREIA INVOKES CALAMITY!
ENOUGH!
TO THE *ETERNAL PRISON*!!
NO! I WANT TO GO *HOME*!!
AIRI ...!!
THE DOORS TO THE JUDGMENT ROOM CANNOT BE OPENED BY FORCE...
THERE IS NOTHING YOU CAN DO.

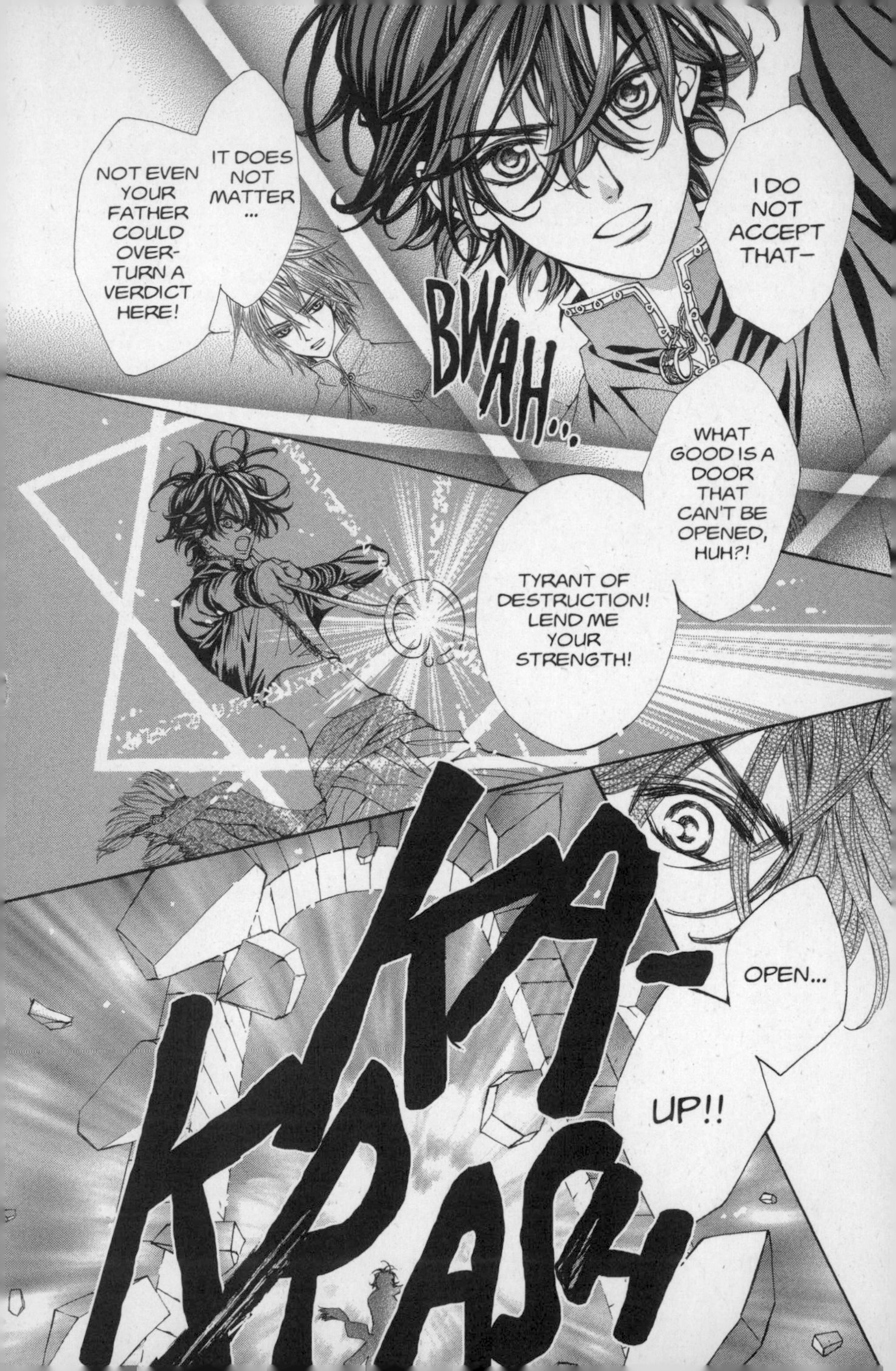

I DO NOT ACCEPT THAT—
BWAH...
IT DOES NOT MATTER...
NOT EVEN YOUR FATHER COULD OVER-TURN A VERDICT HERE!
WHAT GOOD IS A DOOR THAT CAN'T BE OPENED, HUH?!
TYRANT OF DESTRUCTION! LEND ME YOUR STRENGTH!
OPEN...
UP!!
KA-KRASH

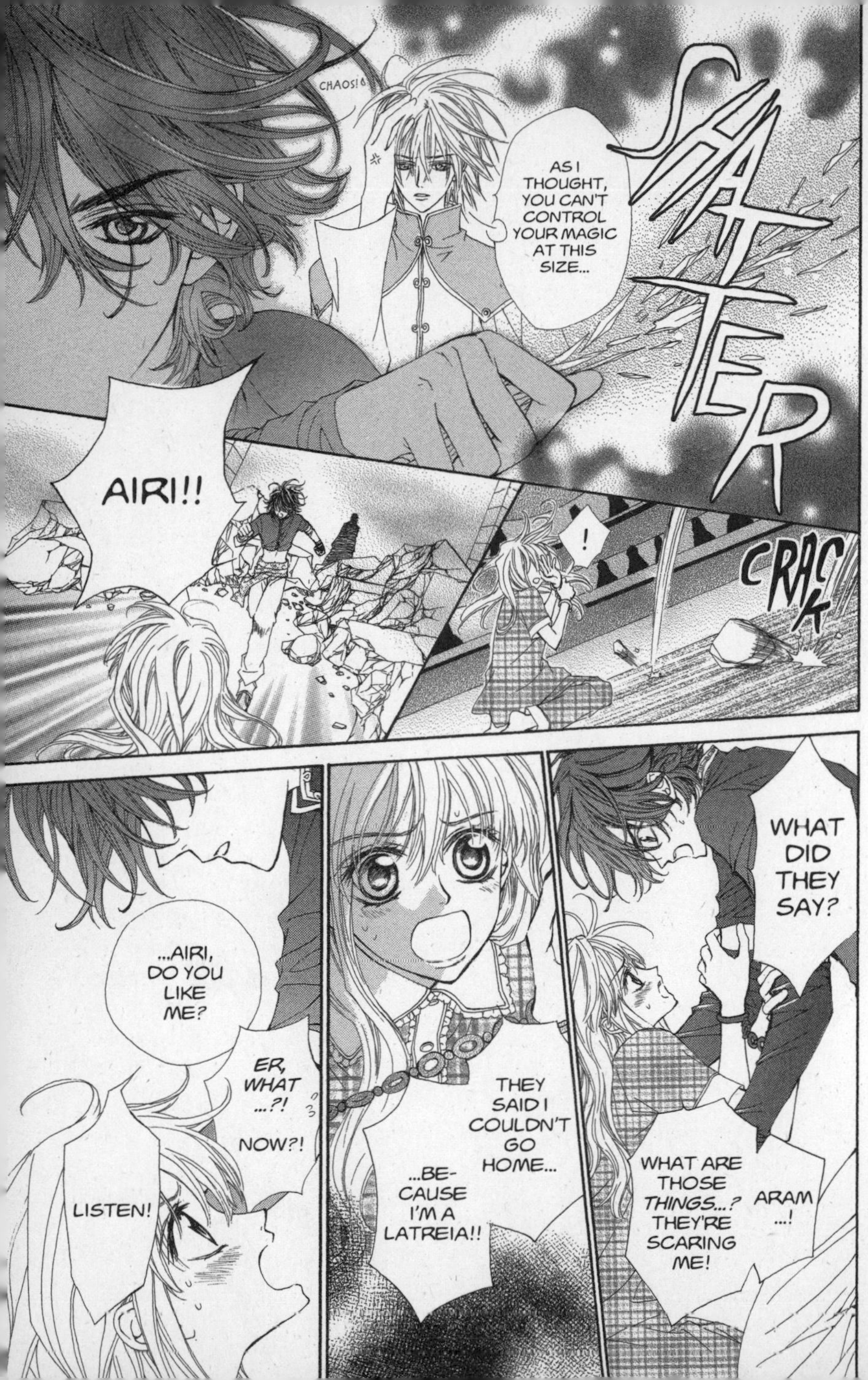
SHATTER
AS I THOUGHT, YOU CAN'T CONTROL YOUR MAGIC AT THIS SIZE...
CHAOS!
CRACK
!
AIRI!!
WHAT DID THEY SAY?
ARAM ...!
WHAT ARE THOSE THINGS...? THEY'RE SCARING ME!
THEY SAID I COULDN'T GO HOME...
...BE-CAUSE I'M A LATREIA!!
...AIRI, DO YOU LIKE ME?
ER, WHAT ...?!
NOW?!
LISTEN!

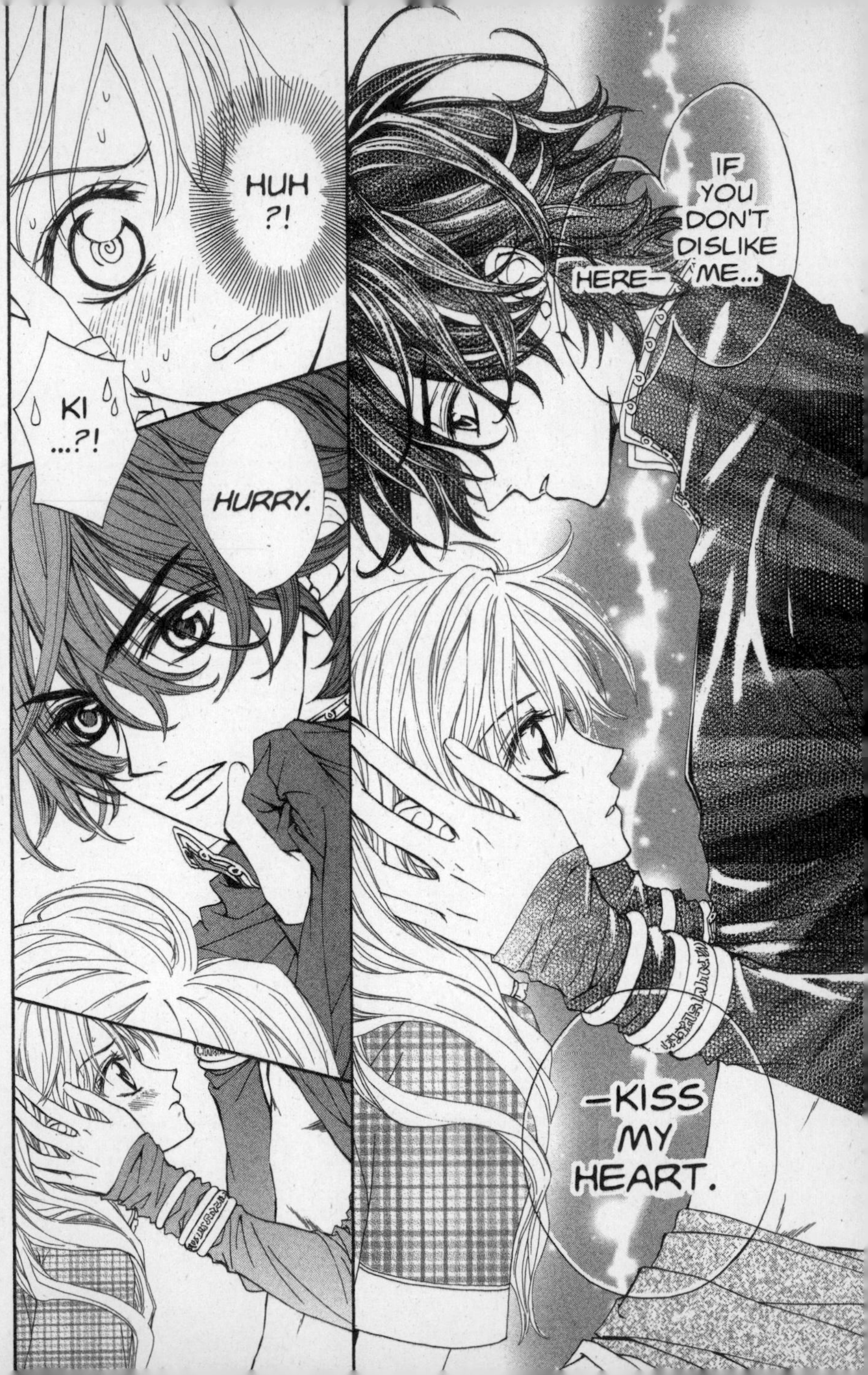
IF YOU DON'T DISLIKE ME...
HERE—
—KISS MY HEART.
HUH ?!
KI ...?!
HURRY.

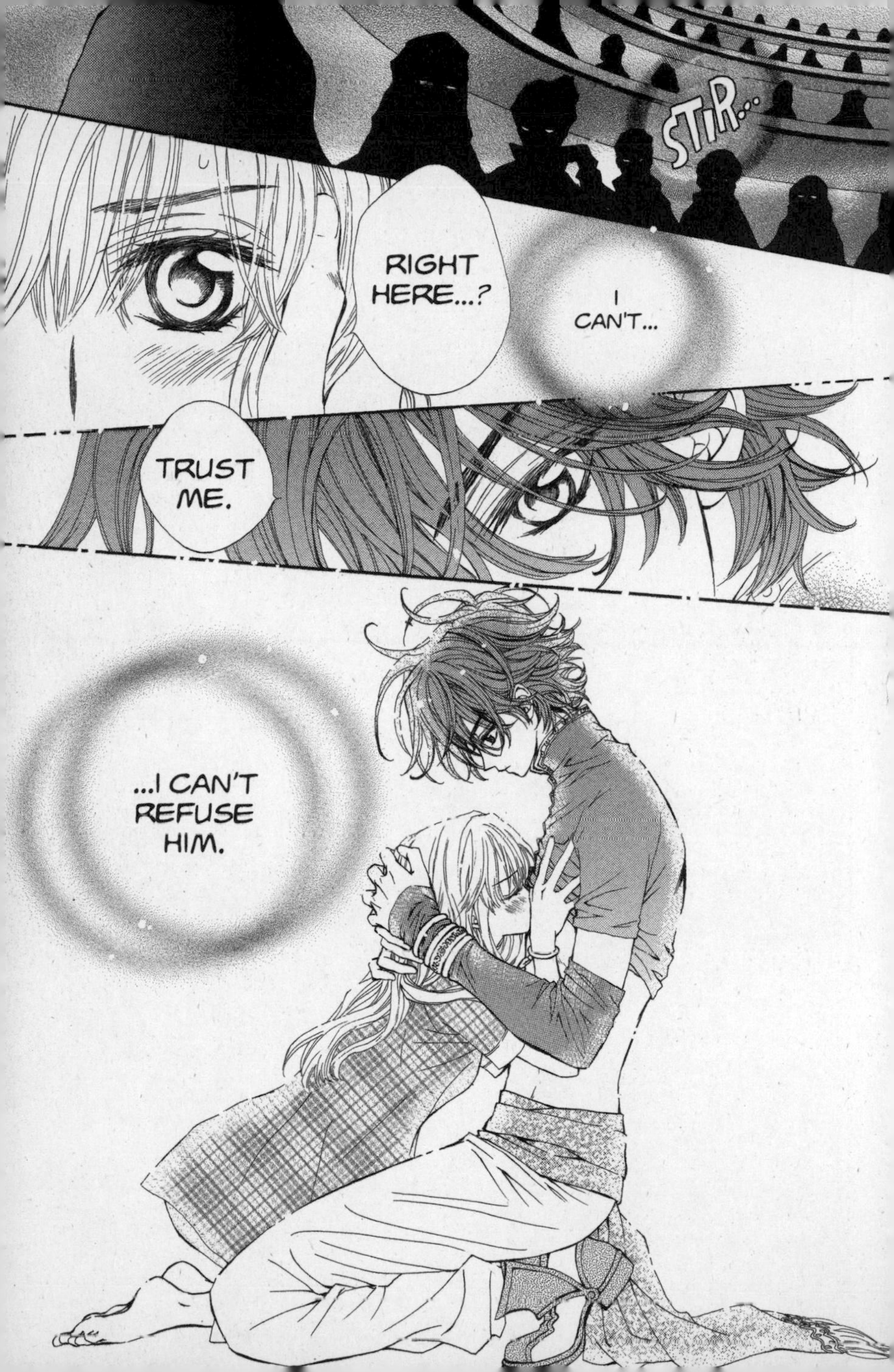
STIR...
I CAN'T...
RIGHT HERE...?
TRUST ME.
...I CAN'T REFUSE HIM.

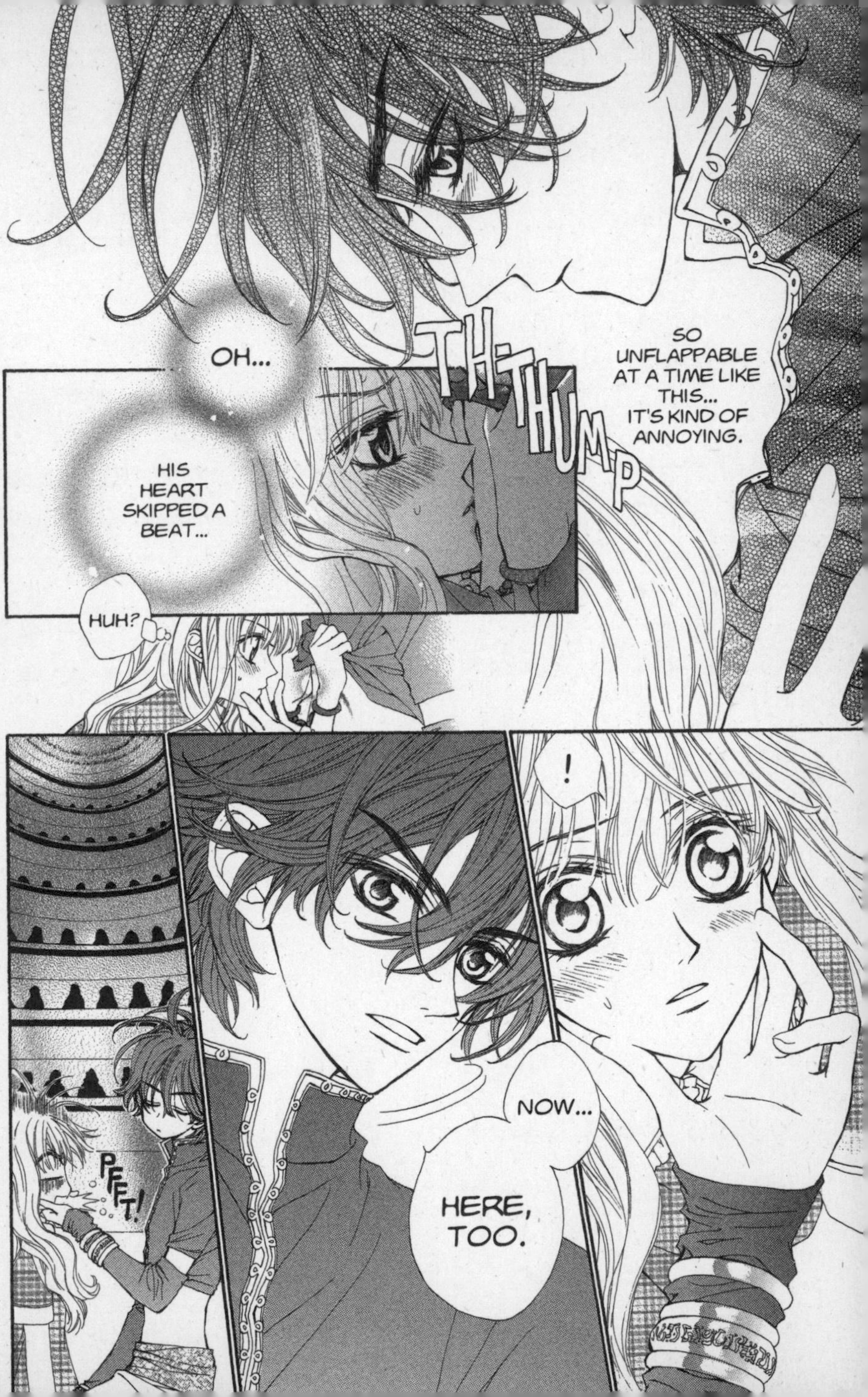
SO UNFLAPPABLE AT A TIME LIKE THIS... IT'S KIND OF ANNOYING.
TH-THUMP
OH...
HIS HEART SKIPPED A BEAT...
HUH?
!
NOW...
HERE, TOO.
PFFT!

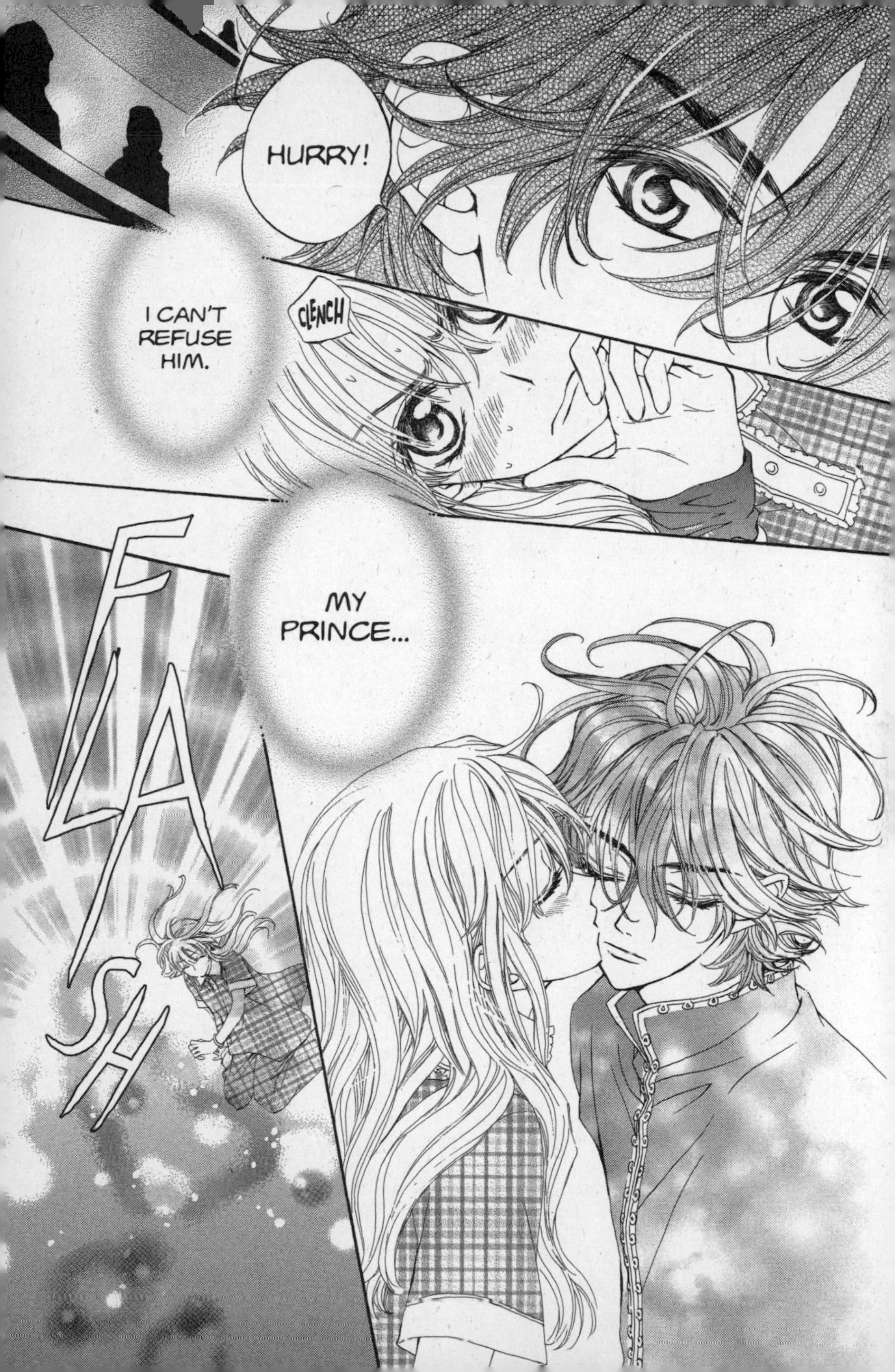
HURRY!
CLENCH
I CAN'T REFUSE HIM.
MY PRINCE...
FLASH

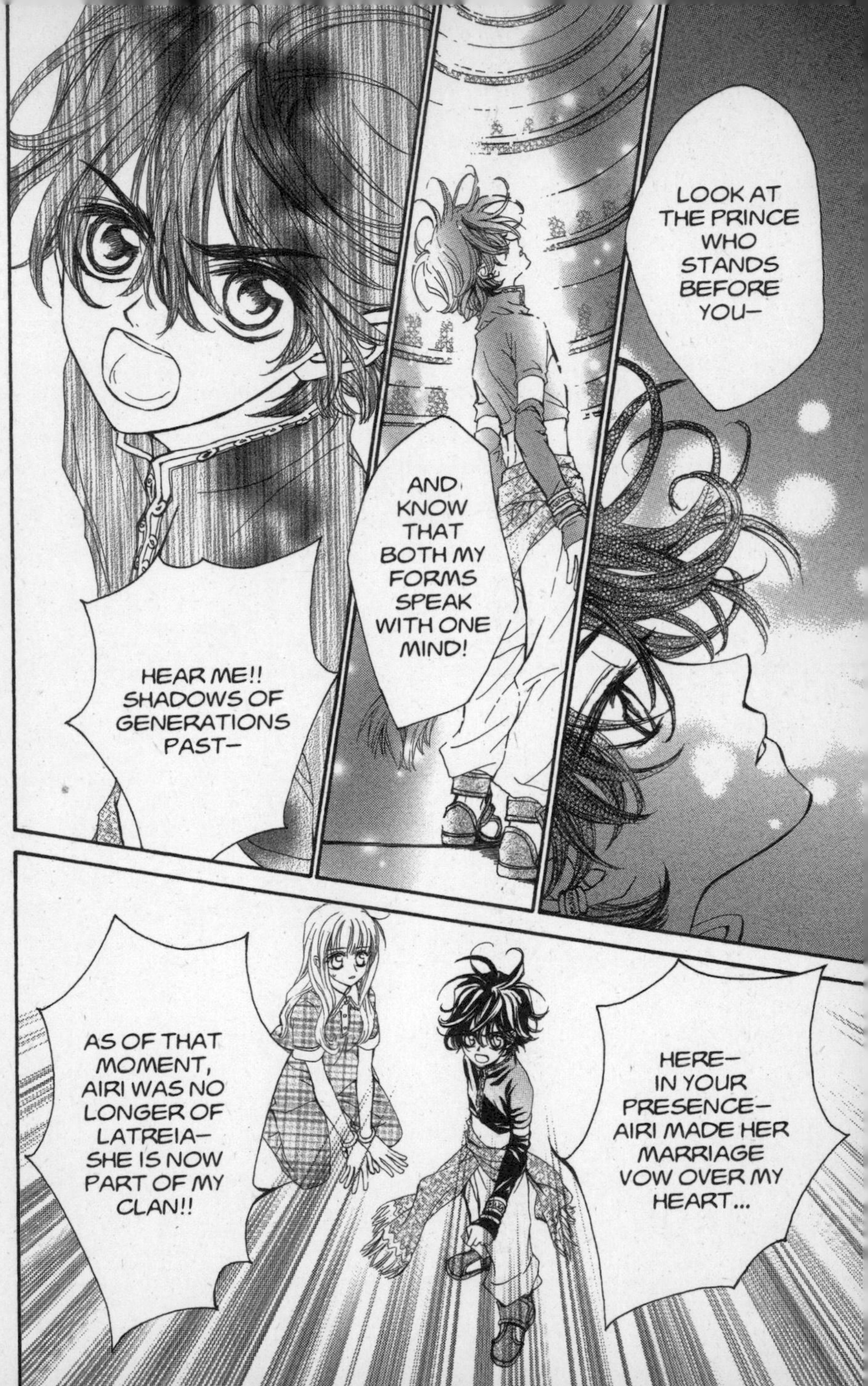
LOOK AT THE PRINCE WHO STANDS BEFORE YOU—
AND KNOW THAT BOTH MY FORMS SPEAK WITH ONE MIND!
HEAR ME!! SHADOWS OF GENERATIONS PAST—
HERE— IN YOUR PRESENCE— AIRI MADE HER MARRIAGE VOW OVER MY HEART...
AS OF THAT MOMENT, AIRI WAS NO LONGER OF LATREIA— SHE IS NOW PART OF MY CLAN!!

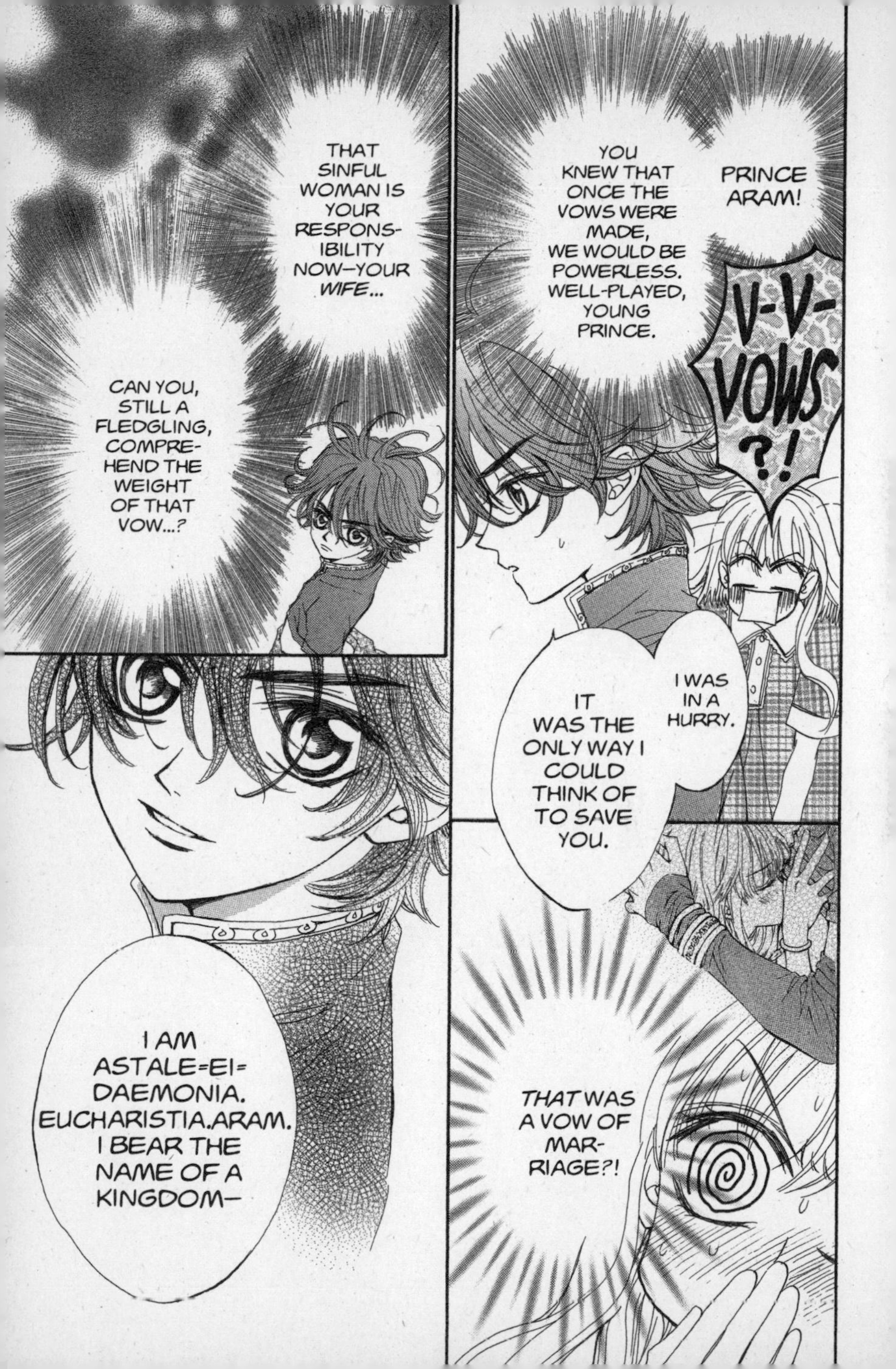
PRINCE ARAM!
V-V-VOWS?!
YOU KNEW THAT ONCE THE VOWS WERE MADE, WE WOULD BE POWERLESS. WELL-PLAYED, YOUNG PRINCE.
THAT SINFUL WOMAN IS YOUR RESPONSIBILITY NOW—YOUR *WIFE*...
CAN YOU, STILL A FLEDGLING, COMPREHEND THE WEIGHT OF THAT VOW...?
I WAS IN A HURRY.
IT WAS THE ONLY WAY I COULD THINK OF TO SAVE YOU.
I AM ASTALE=EI=DAEMONIA. EUCHARISTIA.ARAM. I BEAR THE NAME OF A KINGDOM—
THAT WAS A VOW OF MARRIAGE?!

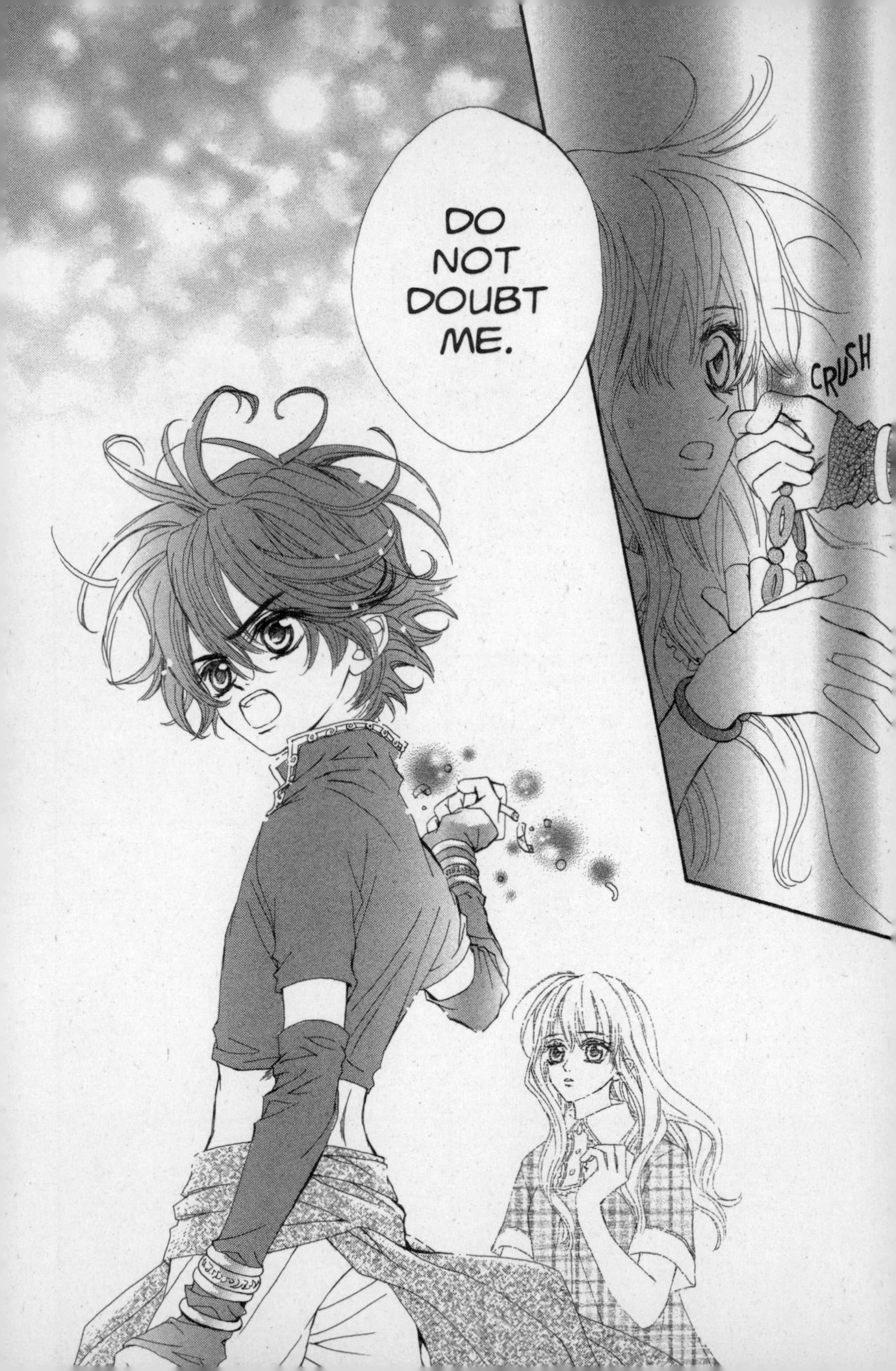
DO NOT DOUBT ME.
CRUSH

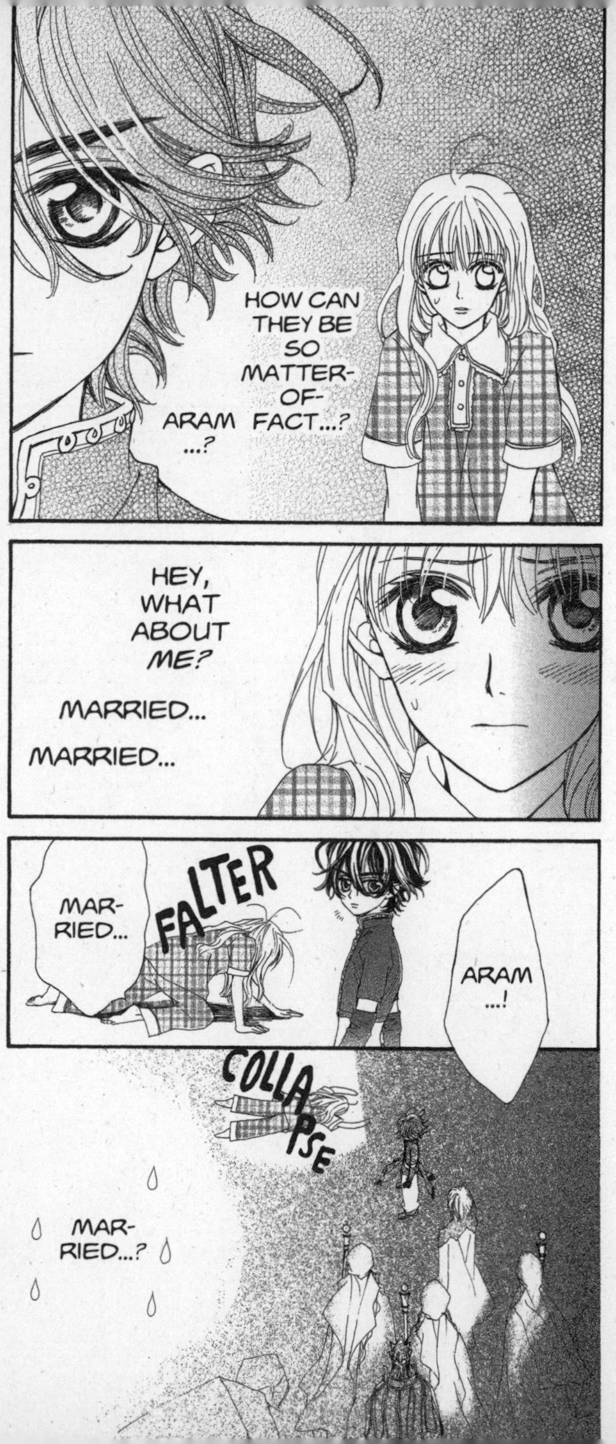
HOW CAN THEY BE SO MATTER-OF-FACT...?
ARAM ...?
HEY, WHAT ABOUT ME?
MARRIED...
MARRIED...
ARAM ...!
FALTER
MAR-RIED...
COLLAPSE
MAR-RIED...?

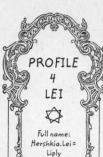

PROFILE 4 LEI

Full name: Hershkia.Lei= Liply

If there's blood flowing in his veins, then it's likely type AB. And he's probably a Capricorn. (And if there are 13 constellations, then he's the Serpent Bearer...) He's the same age as Jeile, and their fates are intertwined. (A supplemental story in the third volume will reveal all!)

Height: 187cm (6'2")
Skin: Ivory
Hair: Honey
Eyes: The Pale Blue of Moonlight
Personality Color: Violet

Because of his position, he knows just about everything there is to know about Aram and Jeile. Consequently, he often plays an expository role in our story...

However, it would be a mistake to think that was his *only* role...

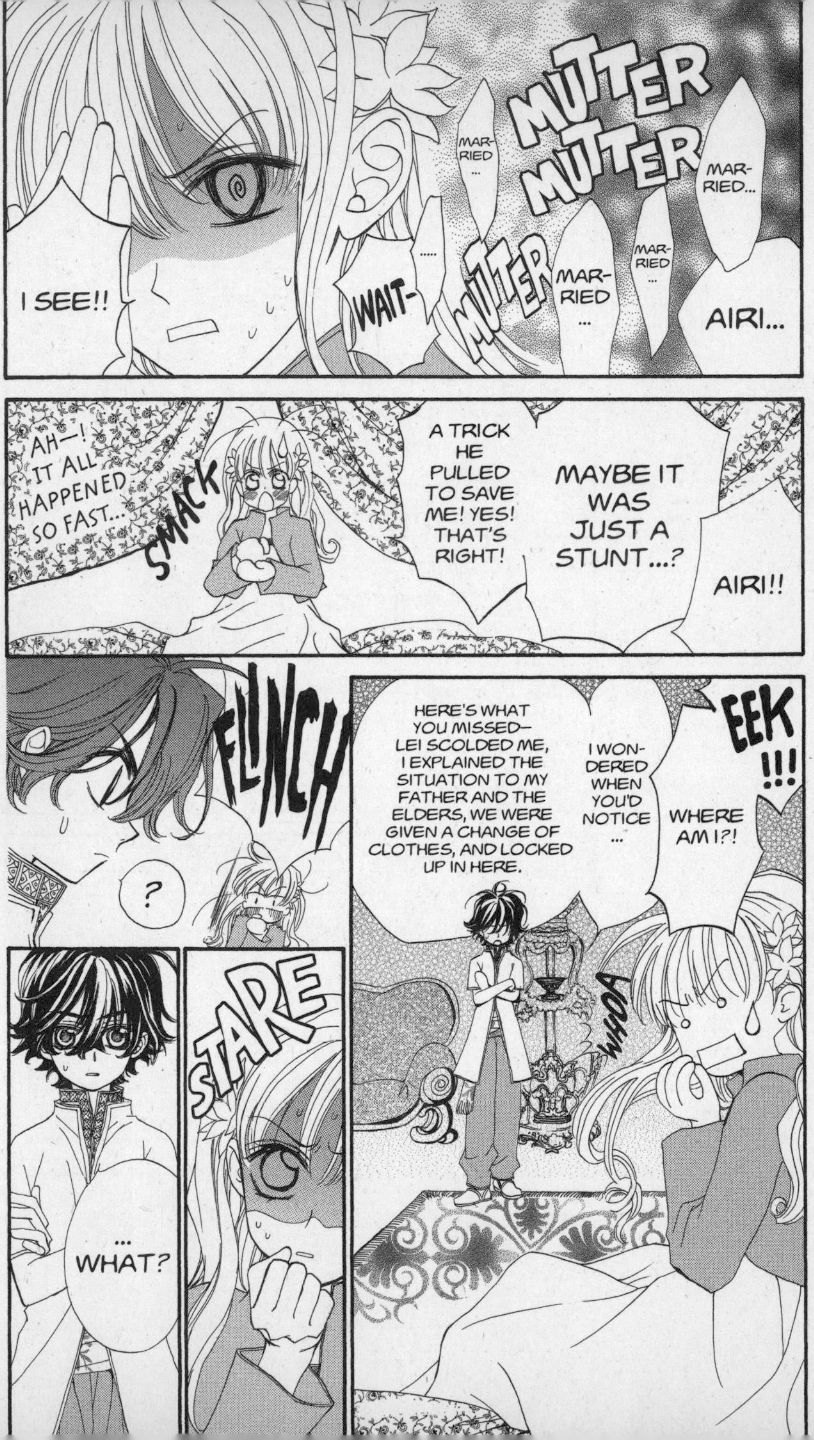
AIRI...
MAR-RIED...
MAR-RIED ...
MAR-RIED ...
MUTTER MUTTER
MUTTER
MAR-RIED ...
......
WAIT-
I SEE!!
AIRI!!
MAYBE IT WAS JUST A STUNT...?
A TRICK HE PULLED TO SAVE ME! YES! THAT'S RIGHT!
SMACK
AH—! IT ALL HAPPENED SO FAST...
EEK !!!
WHERE AM I?!
I WON-DERED WHEN YOU'D NOTICE ...
HERE'S WHAT YOU MISSED— LEI SCOLDED ME, I EXPLAINED THE SITUATION TO MY FATHER AND THE ELDERS, WE WERE GIVEN A CHANGE OF CLOTHES, AND LOCKED UP IN HERE.
WHOA
FLINCH
?
STARE
... WHAT?

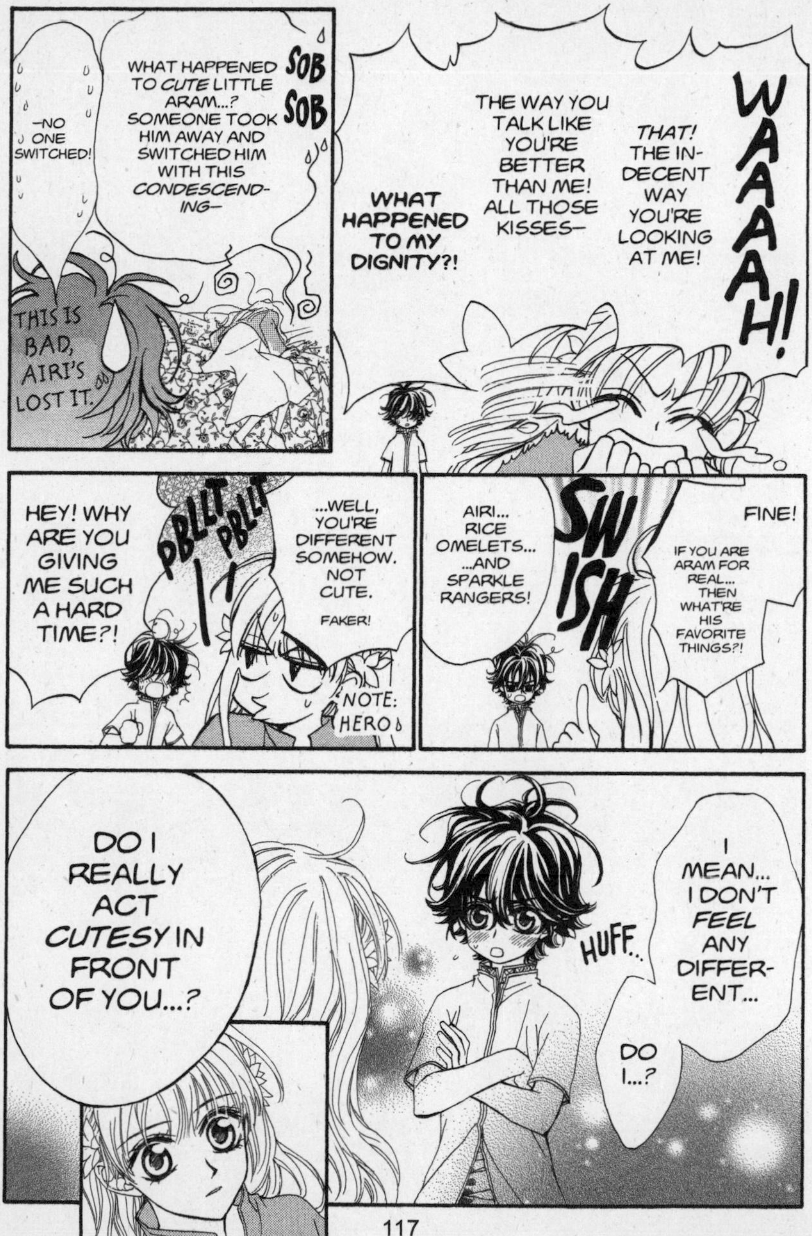
WAAAAH!
THAT! THE INDECENT WAY YOU'RE LOOKING AT ME!
THE WAY YOU TALK LIKE YOU'RE BETTER THAN ME! ALL THOSE KISSES—
WHAT HAPPENED TO MY DIGNITY?!
SOB SOB
WHAT HAPPENED TO *CUTE* LITTLE ARAM...? SOMEONE TOOK HIM AWAY AND SWITCHED HIM WITH THIS *CONDESCENDING*—
—NO ONE SWITCHED!
THIS IS BAD, AIRI'S LOST IT.
FINE!
IF YOU ARE ARAM FOR REAL... THEN WHAT'RE HIS FAVORITE THINGS?!
SWISH
AIRI... RICE OMELETS... ...AND SPARKLE RANGERS!
...WELL, YOU'RE DIFFERENT SOMEHOW. NOT CUTE.
FAKER!
PBLLT PBLLT
HEY! WHY ARE YOU GIVING ME SUCH A HARD TIME?!
NOTE: HERO
I MEAN... I DON'T *FEEL* ANY DIFFERENT...
HUFF...
DO I...?
DO I REALLY ACT *CUTESY* IN FRONT OF YOU...?

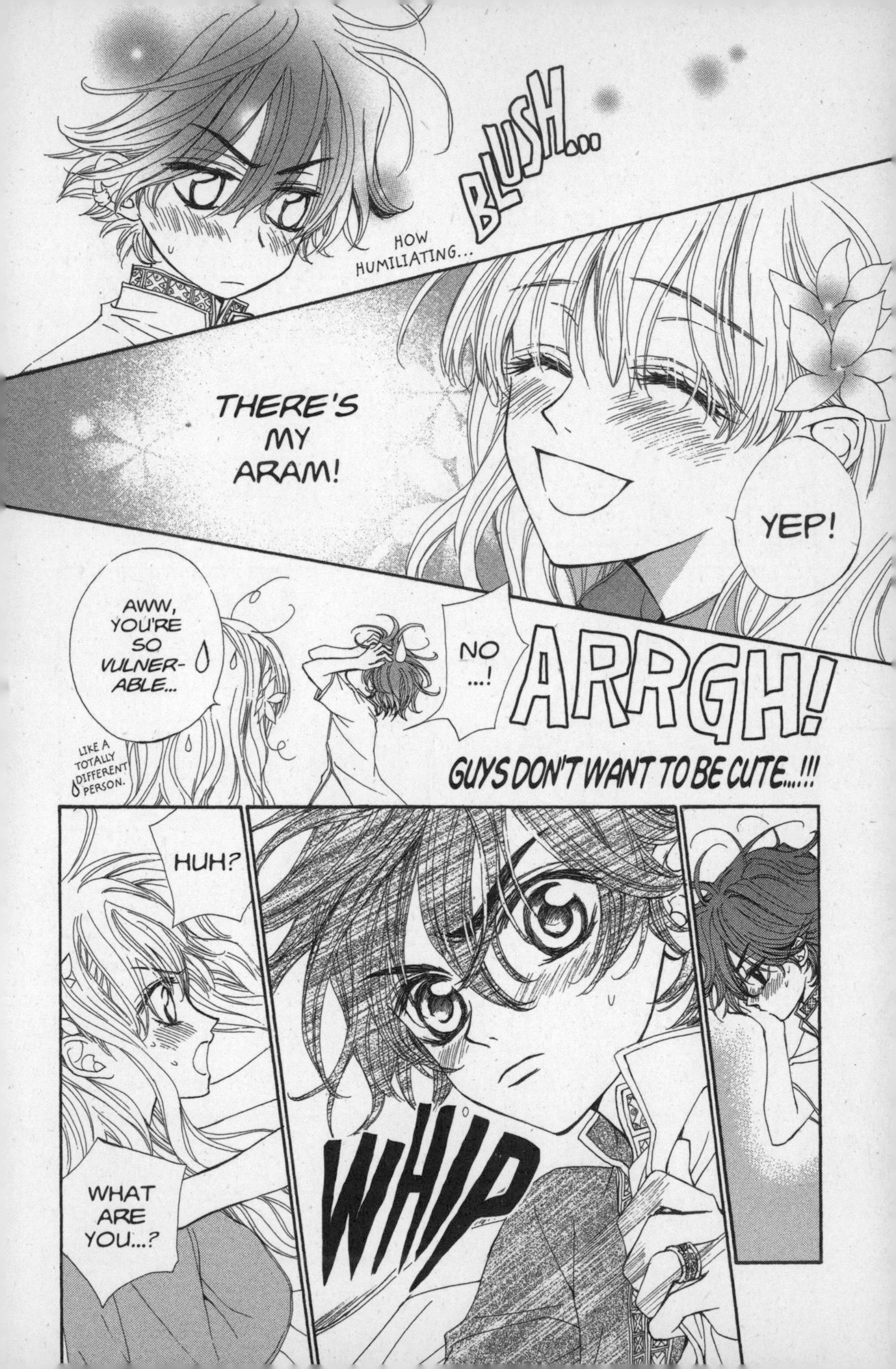

BLUSH...
HOW HUMILIATING...
YEP!
THERE'S MY ARAM!
ARRGH!
GUYS DON'T WANT TO BE CUTE...!!!
NO ...!
AWW, YOU'RE SO VULNER-ABLE...
LIKE A TOTALLY DIFFERENT PERSON.
WHIP
HUH?
WHAT ARE YOU...?

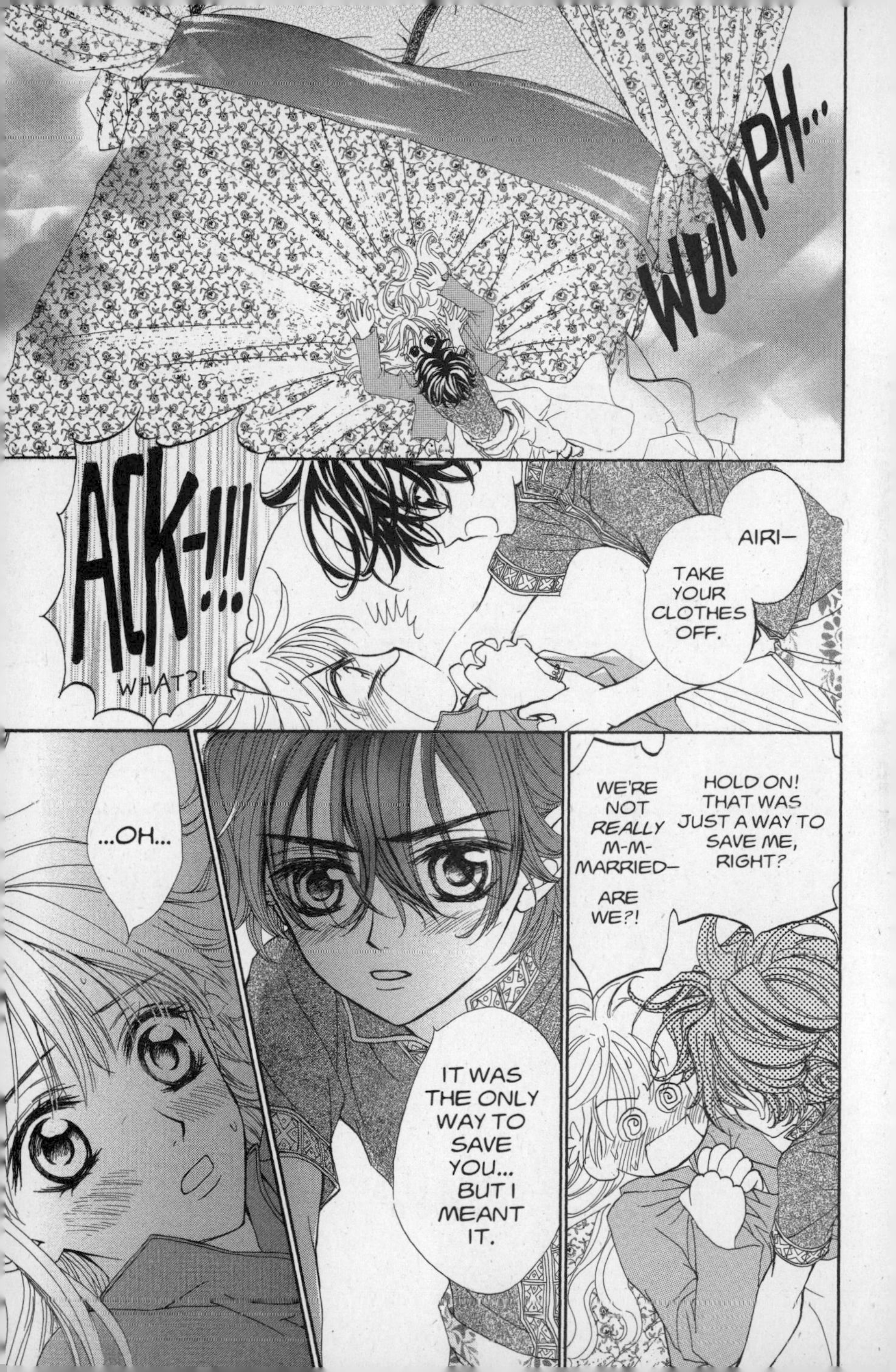
WUMPH...
AIRI—
TAKE YOUR CLOTHES OFF.
ACK-!!!
WHAT?!
HOLD ON! THAT WAS JUST A WAY TO SAVE ME, RIGHT?
WE'RE NOT *REALLY* M-M-MARRIED—
ARE WE?!
IT WAS THE ONLY WAY TO SAVE YOU...
BUT I MEANT IT.
...OH...

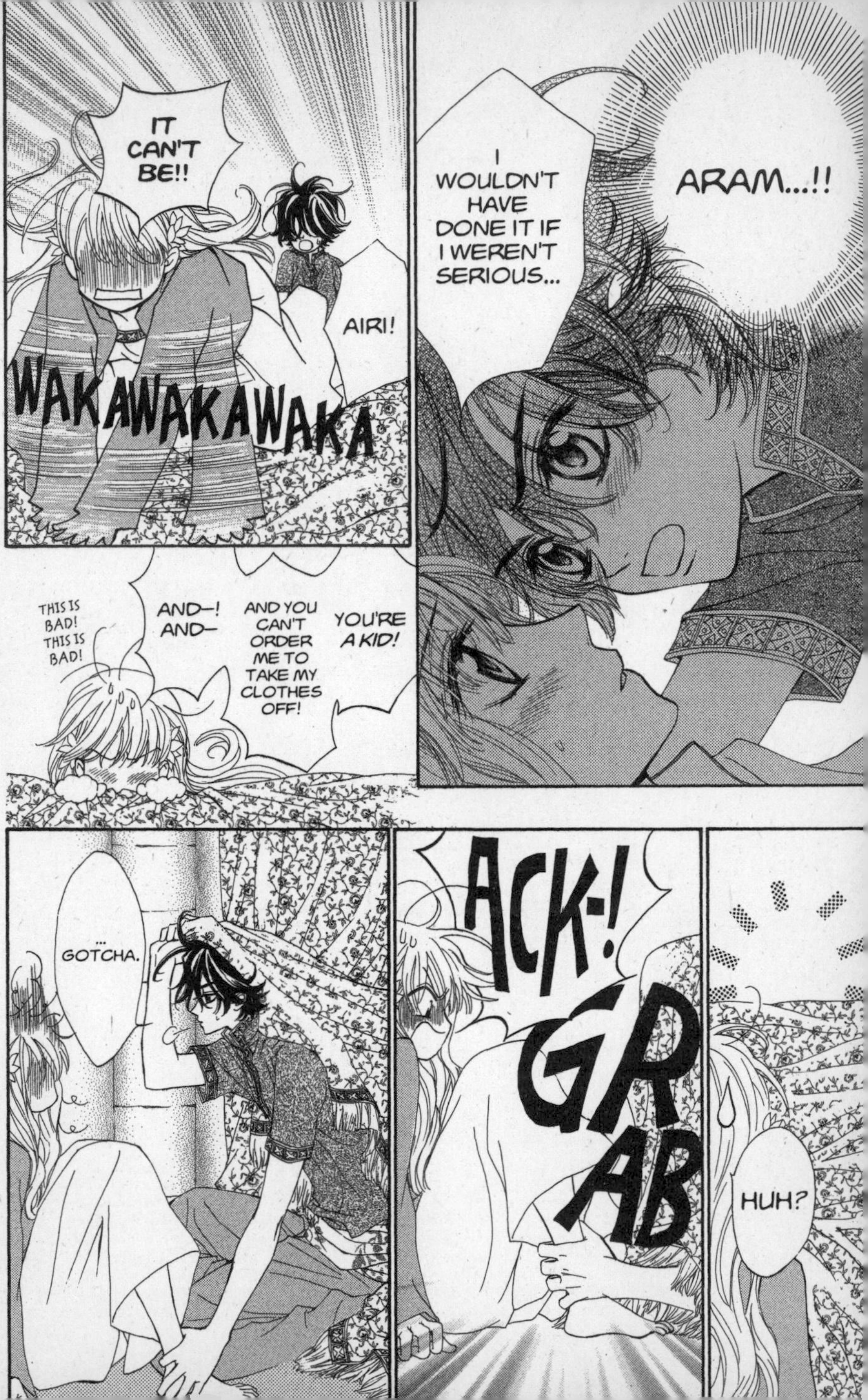
ARAM...!!
I WOULDN'T HAVE DONE IT IF I WEREN'T SERIOUS...
IT CAN'T BE!!
AIRI!
WAKAWAKAWAKA
YOU'RE A KID!
AND YOU CAN'T ORDER ME TO TAKE MY CLOTHES OFF!
AND—! AND—
THIS IS BAD! THIS IS BAD!
HUH?
ACK-!
GRAB
... GOTCHA.

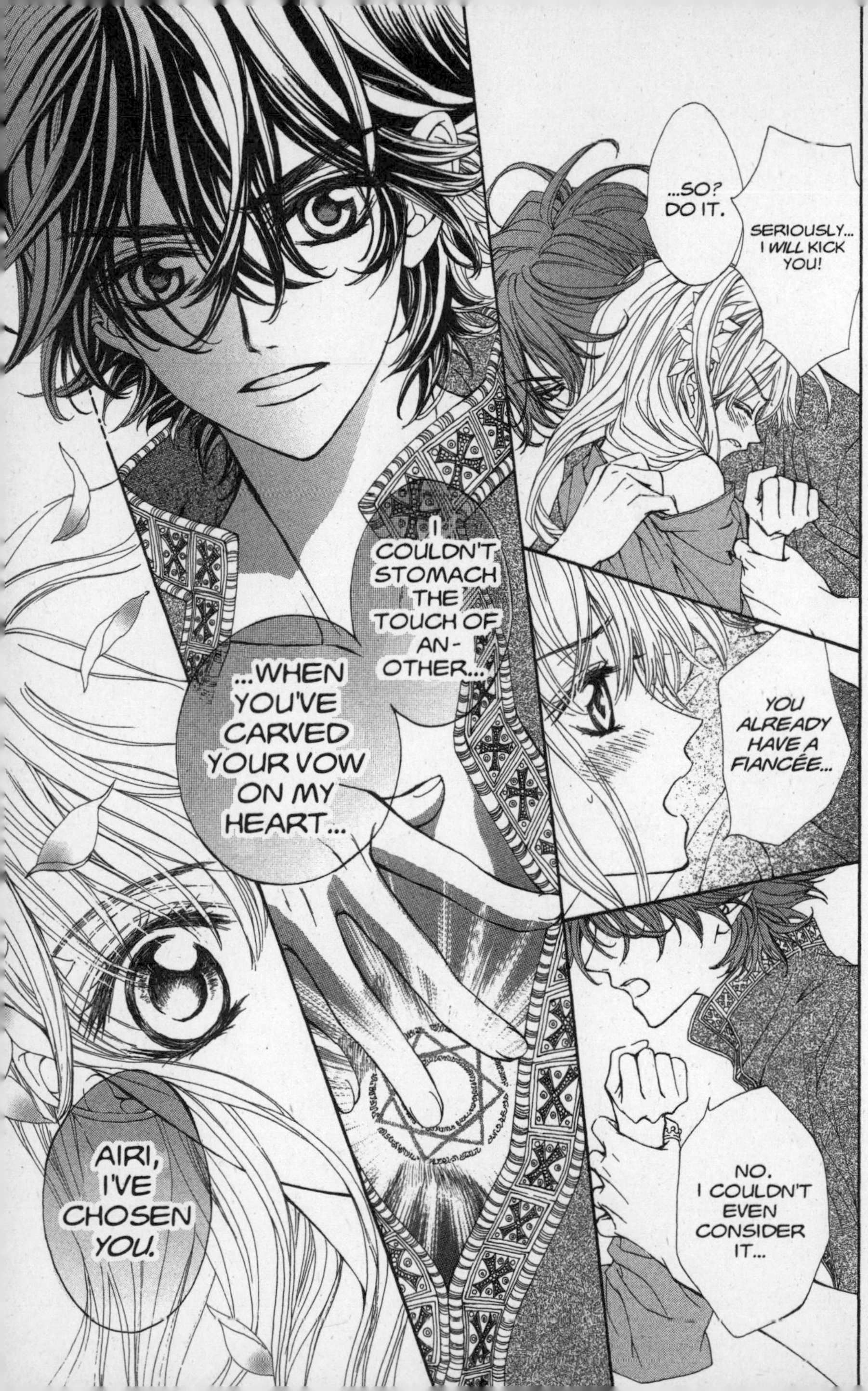
SERIOUSLY... I WILL KICK YOU!
...SO? DO IT.
YOU ALREADY HAVE A FIANCÉE...
NO. I COULDN'T EVEN CONSIDER IT...
I COULDN'T STOMACH THE TOUCH OF AN-OTHER...
...WHEN YOU'VE CARVED YOUR VOW ON MY HEART...
AIRI, I'VE CHOSEN YOU.

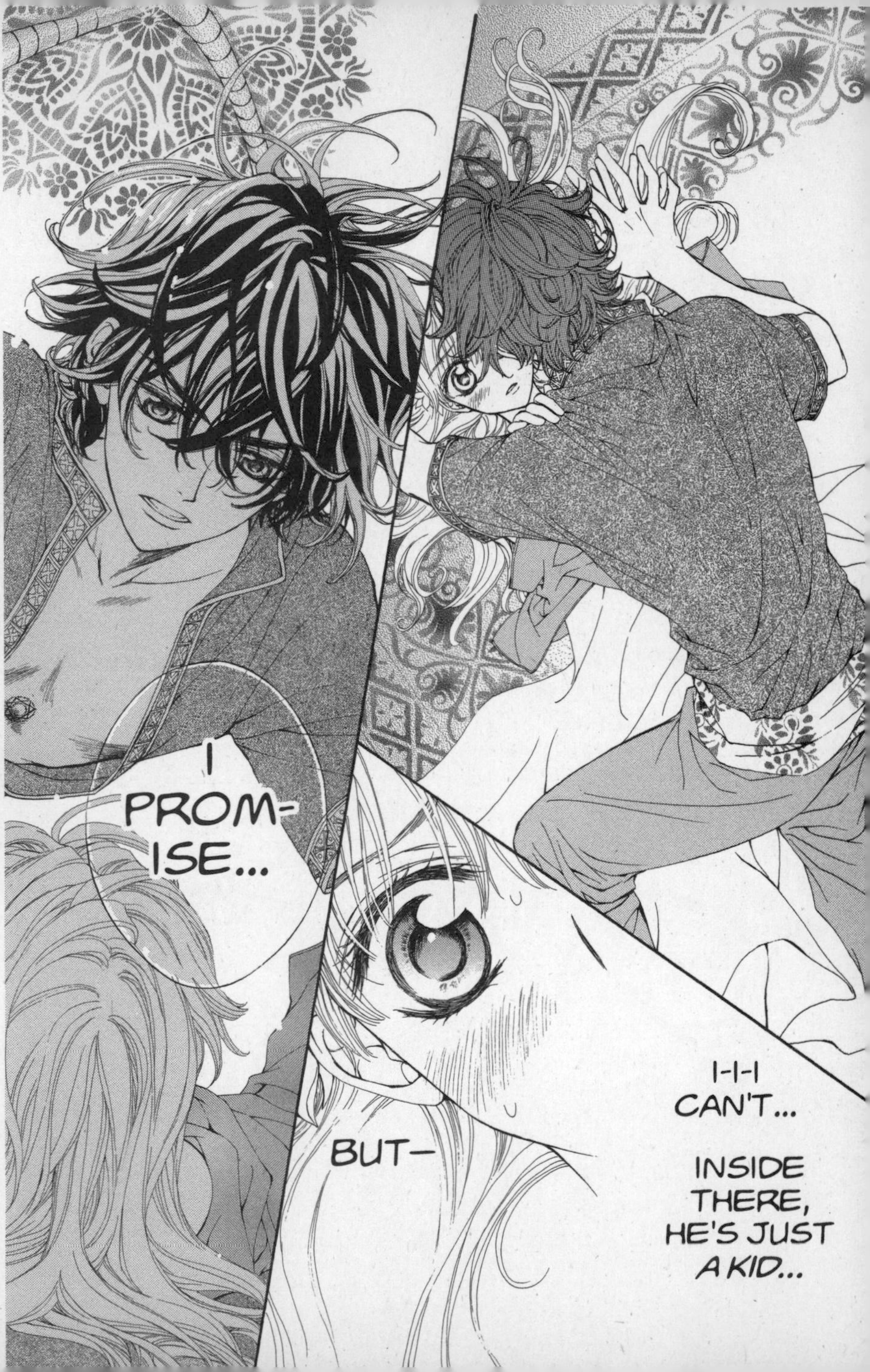
I PROMISE...
I-I-I CAN'T...
BUT—
INSIDE THERE, HE'S JUST A KID...

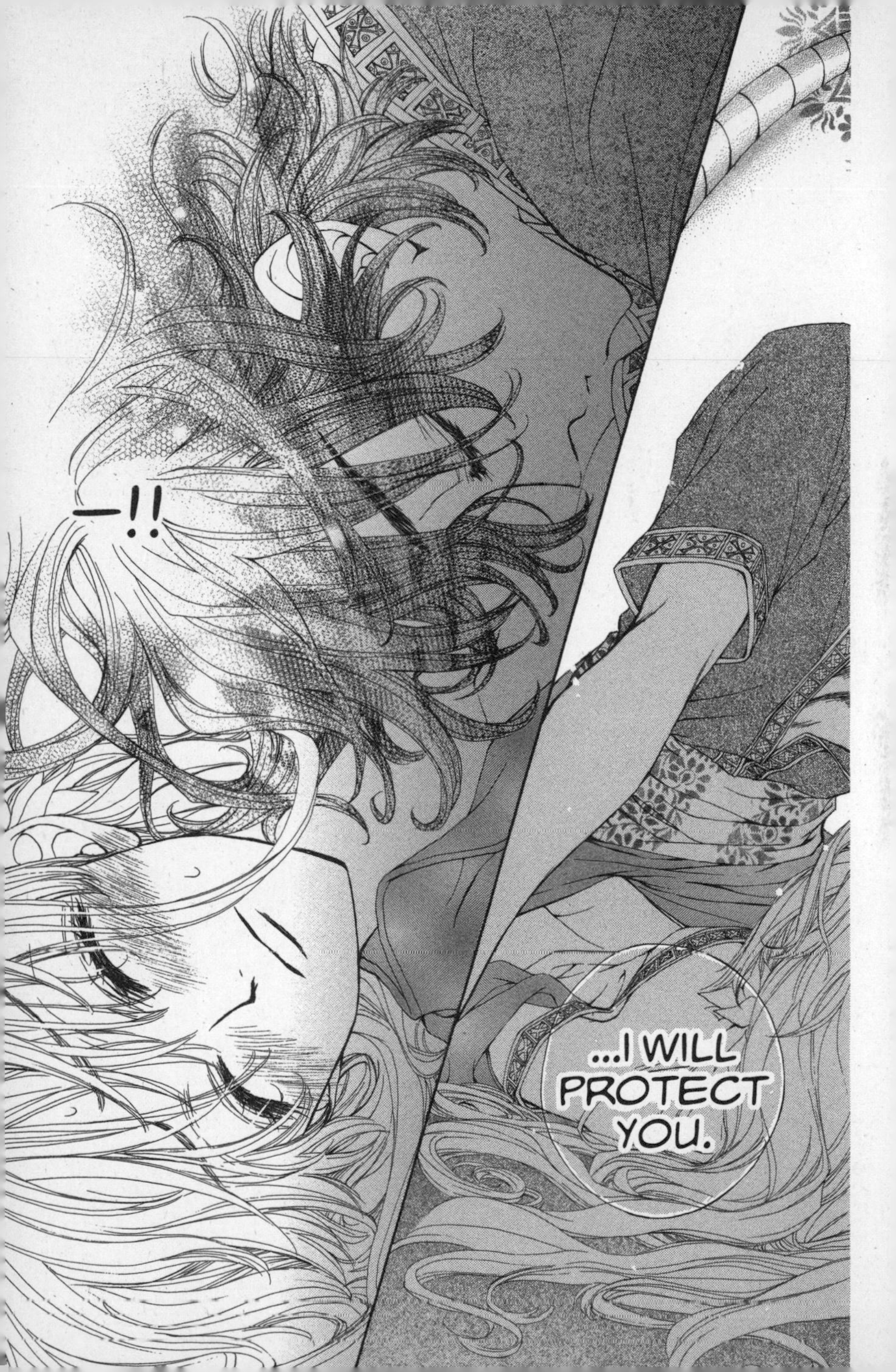
—!!
...I WILL PROTECT YOU.

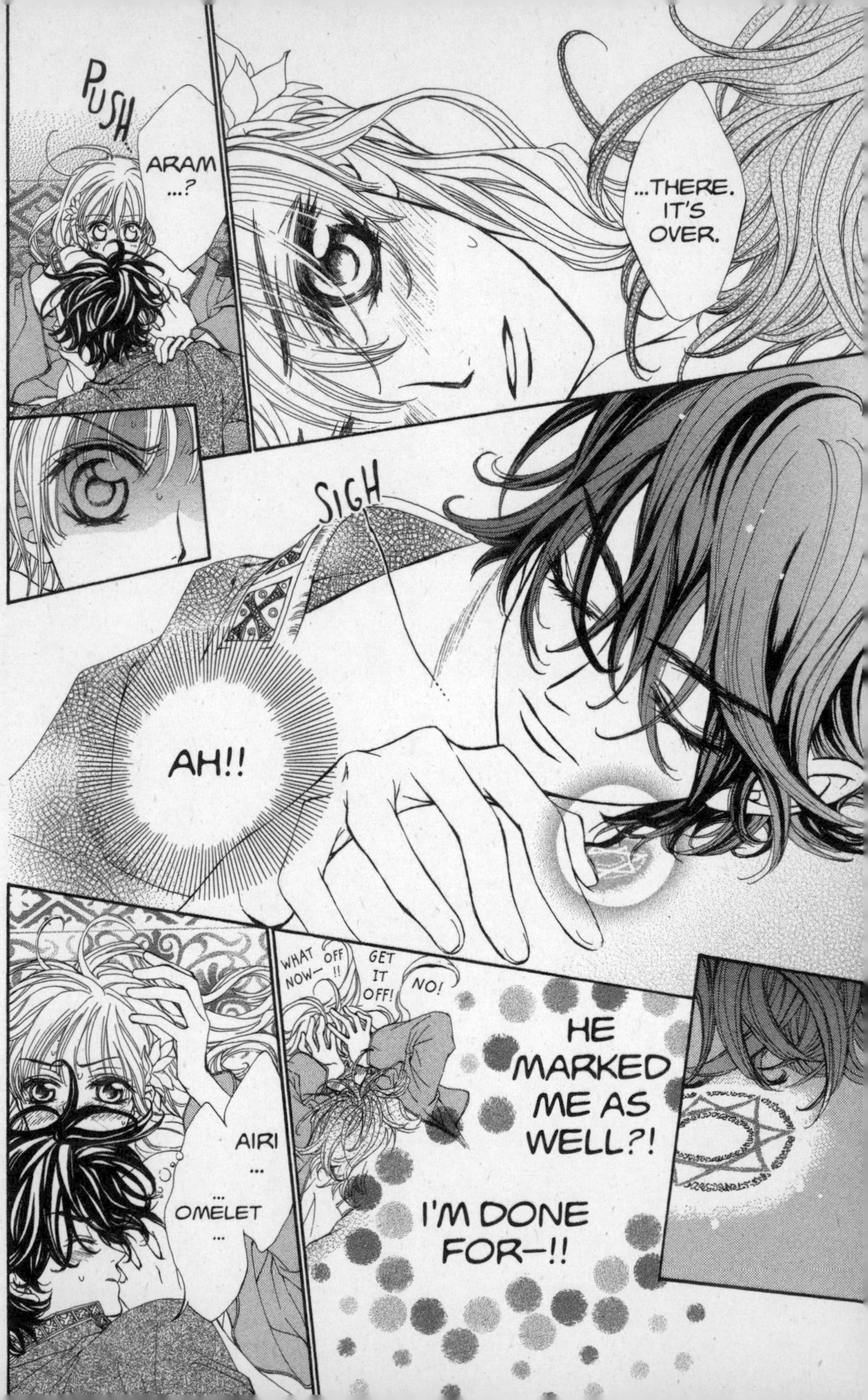
...THERE. IT'S OVER.
PUSH
ARAM ...?
SIGH
AH!!
NO!
GET IT OFF!
OFF !!
WHAT NOW—
HE MARKED ME AS WELL?!
I'M DONE FOR—!!
AIRI ...
... OMELET ...

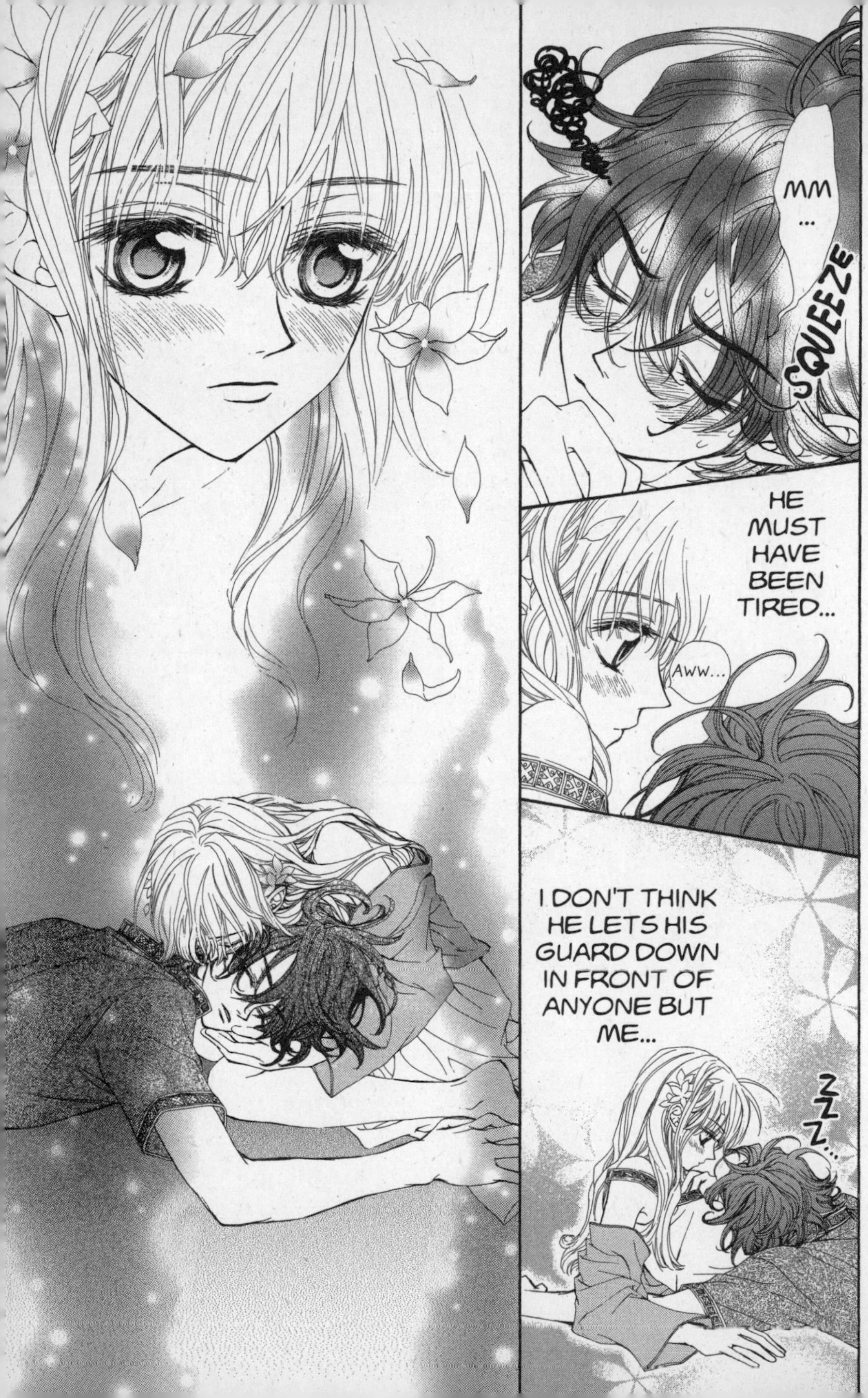
MM ...
SQUEEZE
HE MUST HAVE BEEN TIRED...
AWW...
I DON'T THINK HE LETS HIS GUARD DOWN IN FRONT OF ANYONE BUT ME...
ZZZ...

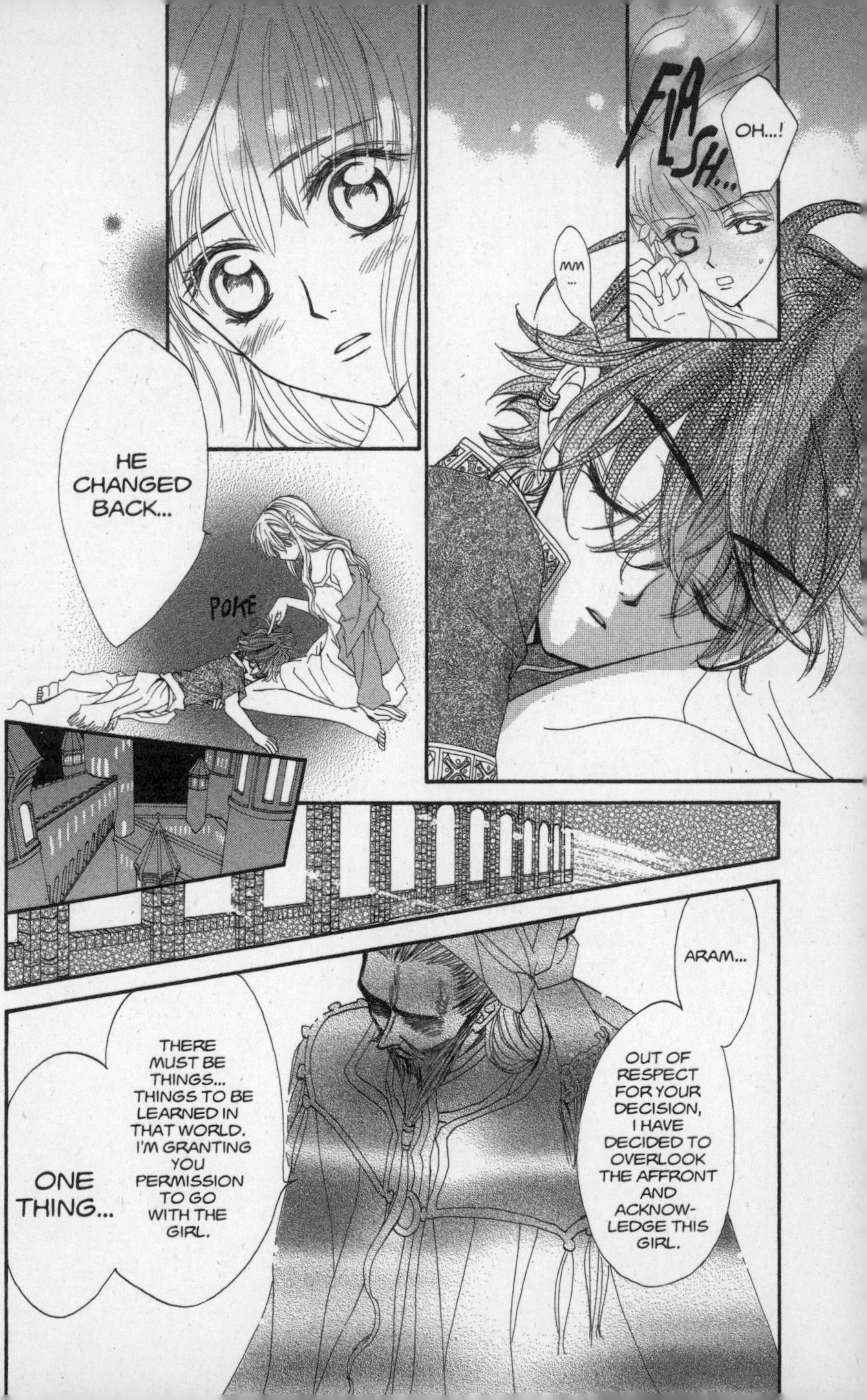
FLASH...
OH...!
MM...
HE CHANGED BACK...
POKE
ARAM...
OUT OF RESPECT FOR YOUR DECISION, I HAVE DECIDED TO OVERLOOK THE AFFRONT AND ACKNOW-LEDGE THIS GIRL.
THERE MUST BE THINGS... THINGS TO BE LEARNED IN THAT WORLD. I'M GRANTING YOU PERMISSION TO GO WITH THE GIRL.
ONE THING...

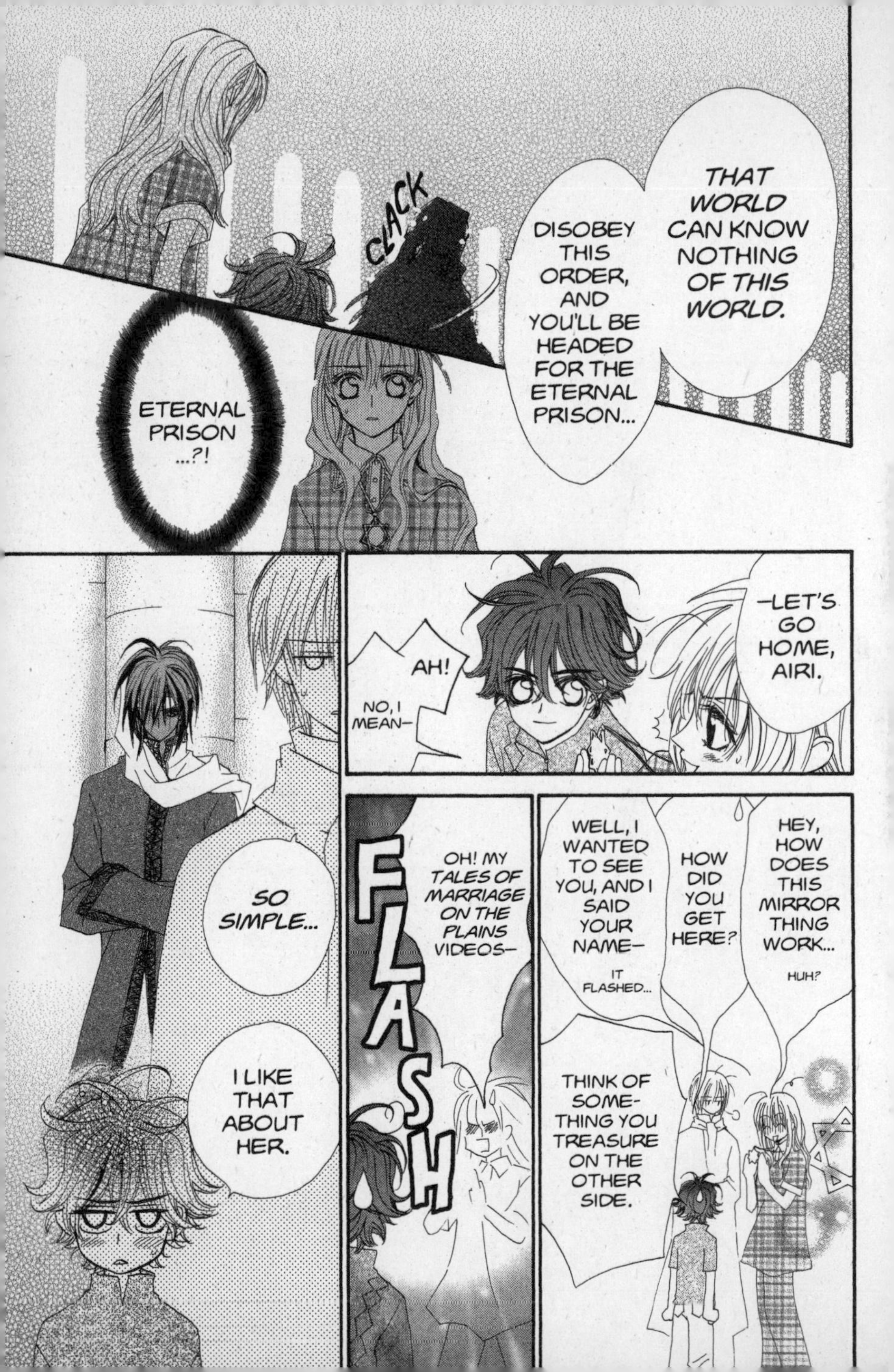
THAT WORLD CAN KNOW NOTHING OF THIS WORLD.
DISOBEY THIS ORDER, AND YOU'LL BE HEADED FOR THE ETERNAL PRISON...
CLACK
ETERNAL PRISON ...?!
—LET'S GO HOME, AIRI.
AH!
NO, I MEAN—
HEY, HOW DOES THIS MIRROR THING WORK...
HUH?
HOW DID YOU GET HERE?
WELL, I WANTED TO SEE YOU, AND I SAID YOUR NAME—
IT FLASHED...
THINK OF SOME-THING YOU TREASURE ON THE OTHER SIDE.
OH! MY TALES OF MARRIAGE ON THE PLAINS VIDEOS—
FLASH
SO SIMPLE...
I LIKE THAT ABOUT HER.

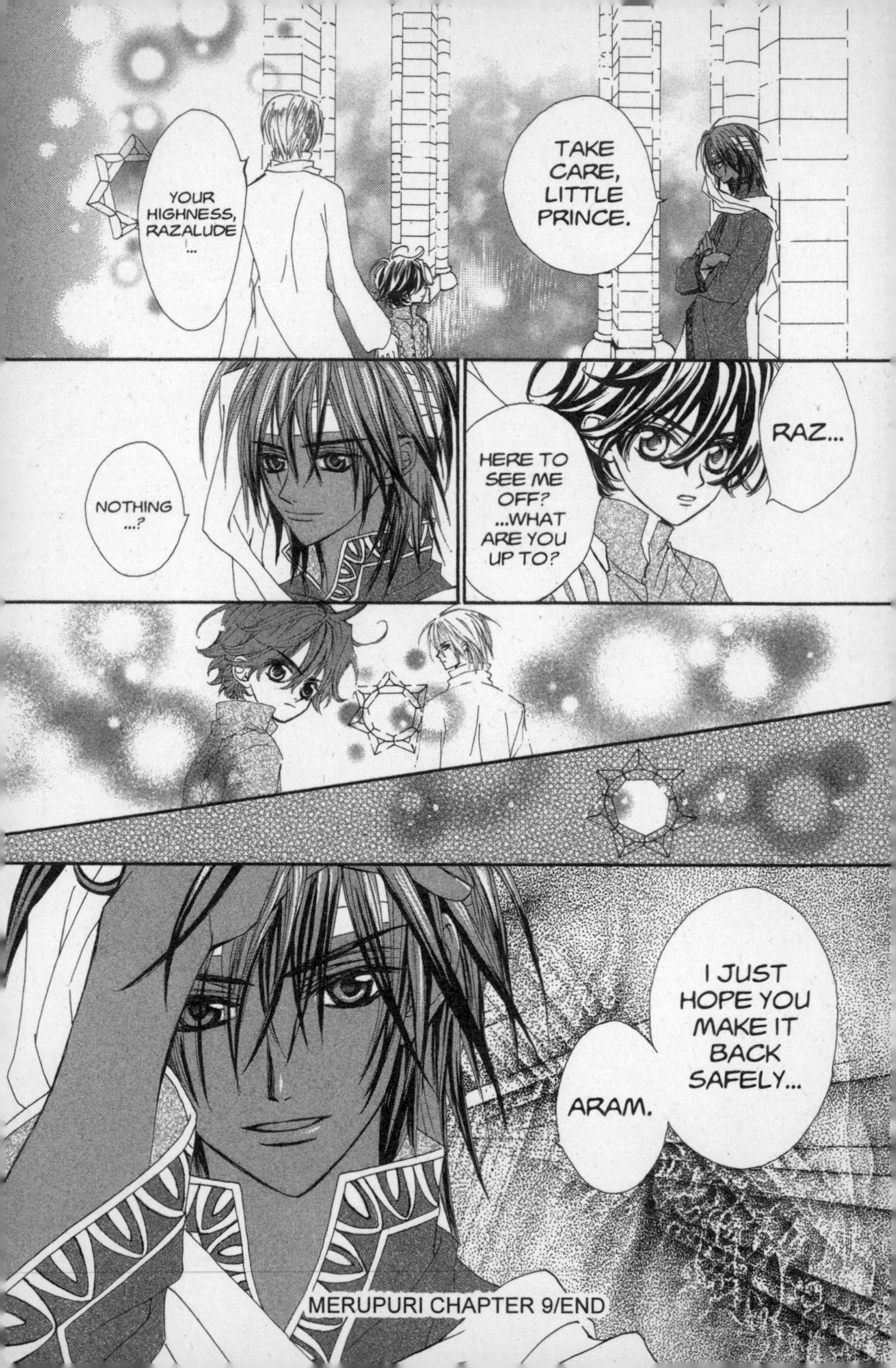
TAKE CARE, LITTLE PRINCE.
YOUR HIGHNESS, RAZALUDE ...
RAZ...
HERE TO SEE ME OFF? ...WHAT ARE YOU UP TO?
NOTHING ...?
I JUST HOPE YOU MAKE IT BACK SAFELY...
ARAM.
MERUPURI CHAPTER 9/END

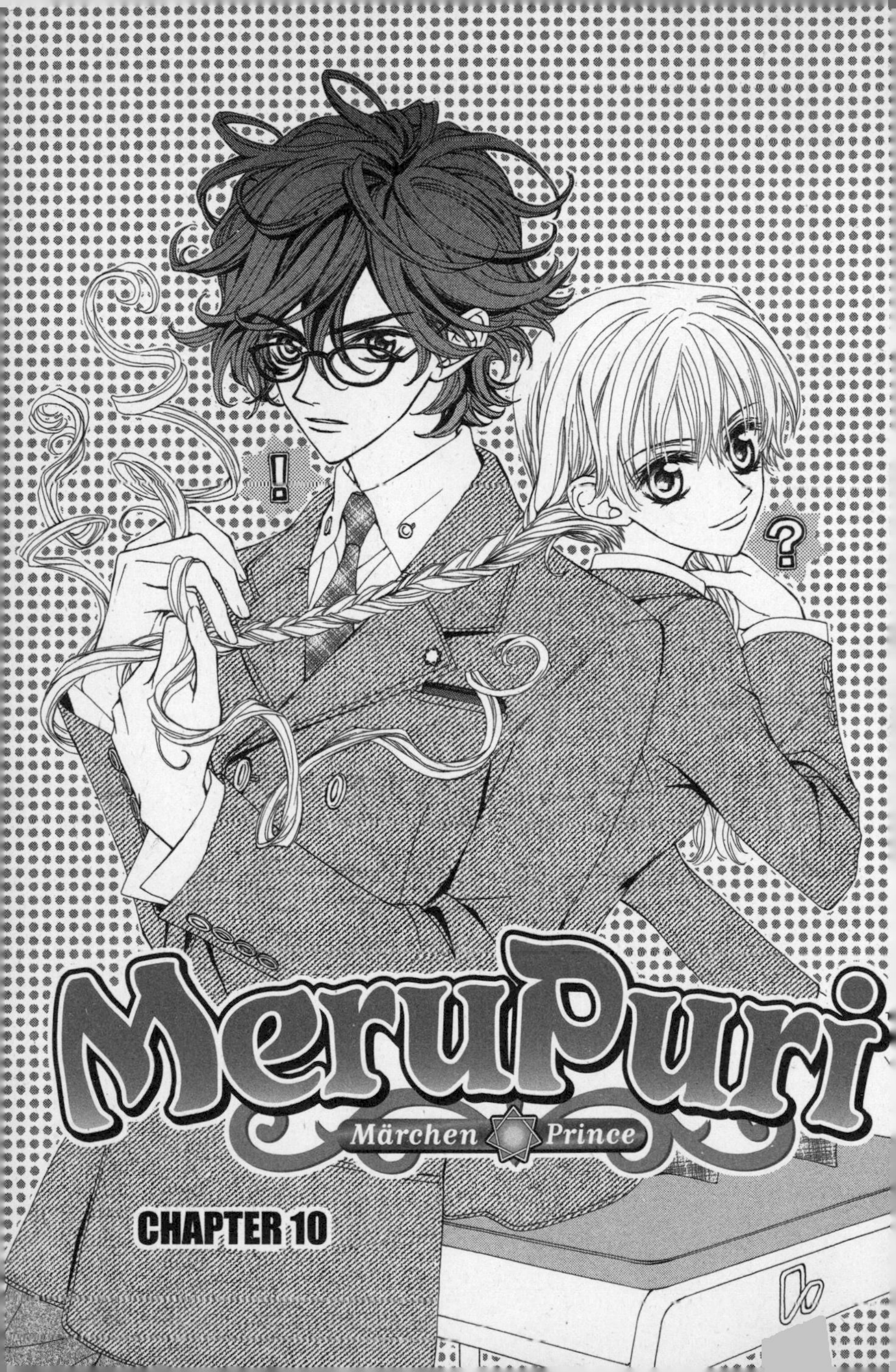
!
?
MeruPuri
Märchen Prince
CHAPTER 10

RIING
RIING

SWOOP

SO NICE...
SAME AS
ALWAYS...

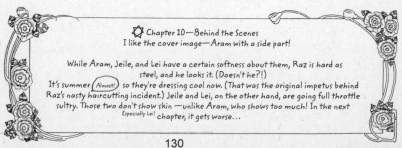

⭐ Chapter 10—Behind the Scenes
I like the cover image—Aram with a side part!

While Aram, Jeile, and Lei have a certain softness about them, Raz is hard as steel, and he looks it. (Doesn't he?!)
It's summer (Almost!) so they're dressing cool now. (That was the original impetus behind Raz's nasty haircutting incident.) Jeile and Lei, on the other hand, are going full throttle sultry. Those two don't show skin —unlike Aram, who shows too much! In the next Especially Lei! chapter, it gets worse...

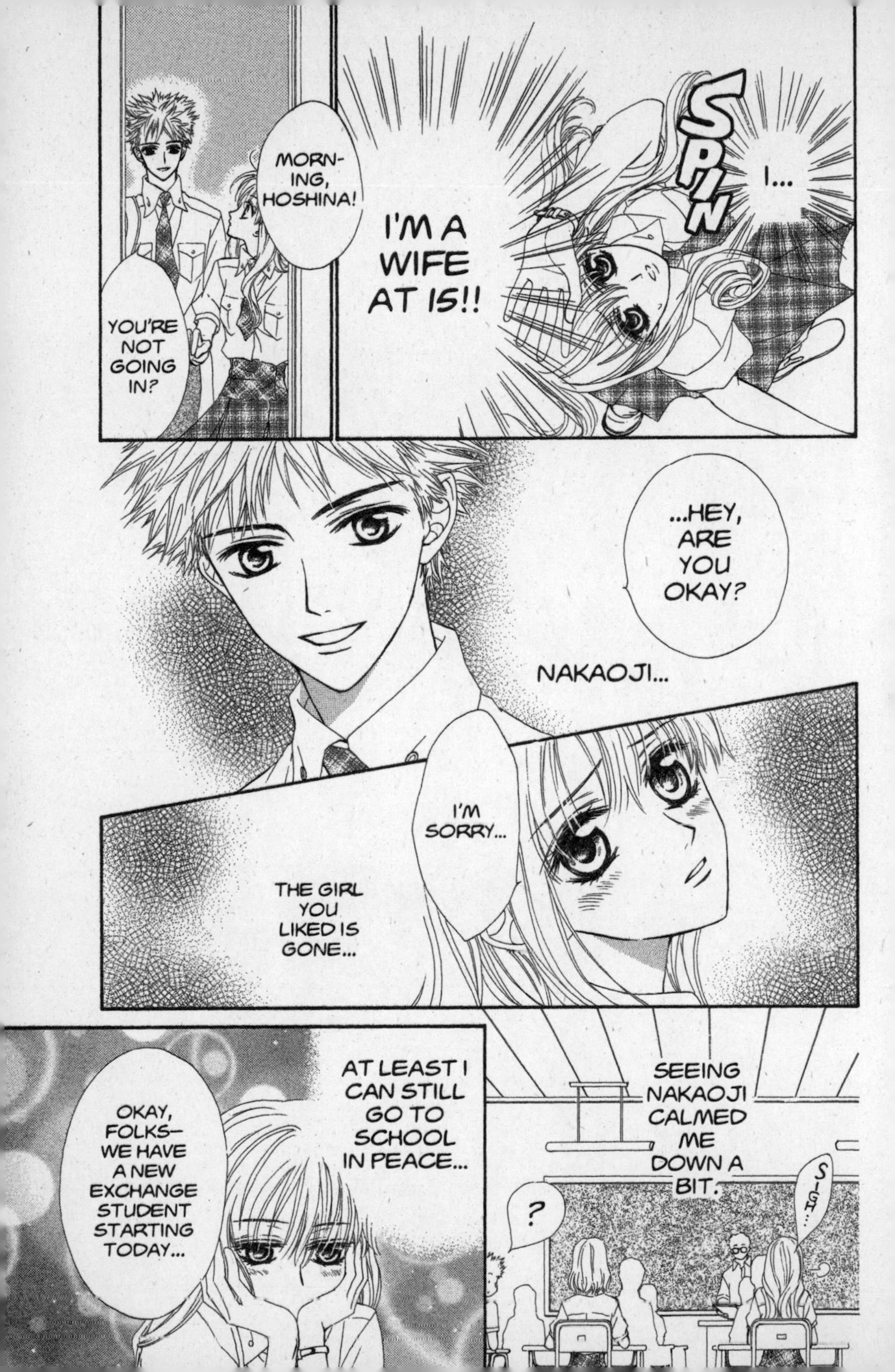
I...
SPIN
I'M A WIFE AT 15!!
MORNING, HOSHINA!
YOU'RE NOT GOING IN?
...HEY, ARE YOU OKAY?
NAKAOJI...
I'M SORRY...
THE GIRL YOU LIKED IS GONE...
SEEING NAKAOJI CALMED ME DOWN A BIT.
SIGH...
?
AT LEAST I CAN STILL GO TO SCHOOL IN PEACE...
OKAY, FOLKS—WE HAVE A NEW EXCHANGE STUDENT STARTING TODAY...

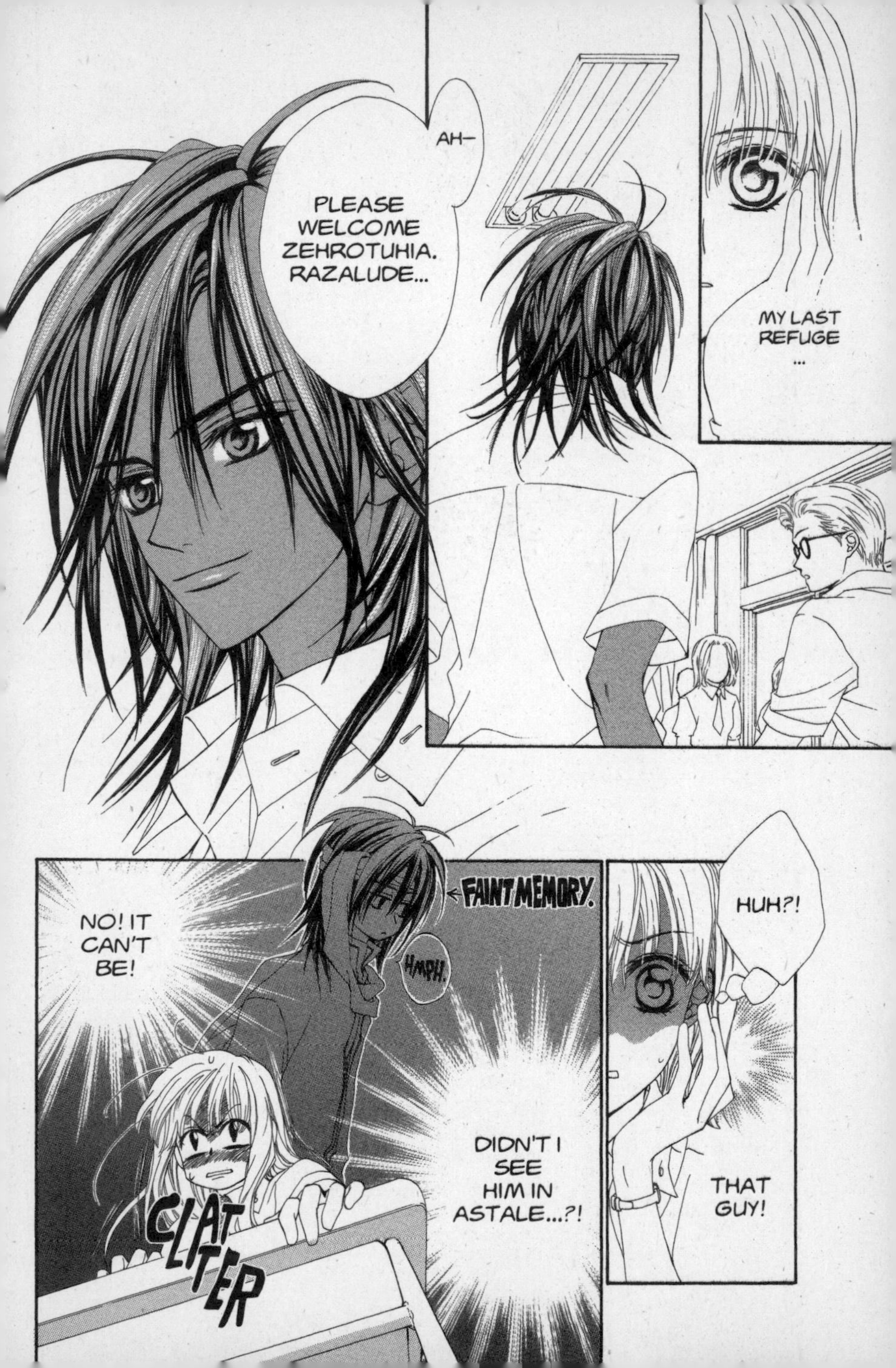
MY LAST REFUGE ...
AH—
PLEASE WELCOME ZEHROTUHIA. RAZALUDE...
HUH?!
THAT GUY!
NO! IT CAN'T BE!
FAINT MEMORY.
HMPH.
DIDN'T I SEE HIM IN ASTALE...?!
CLATTER

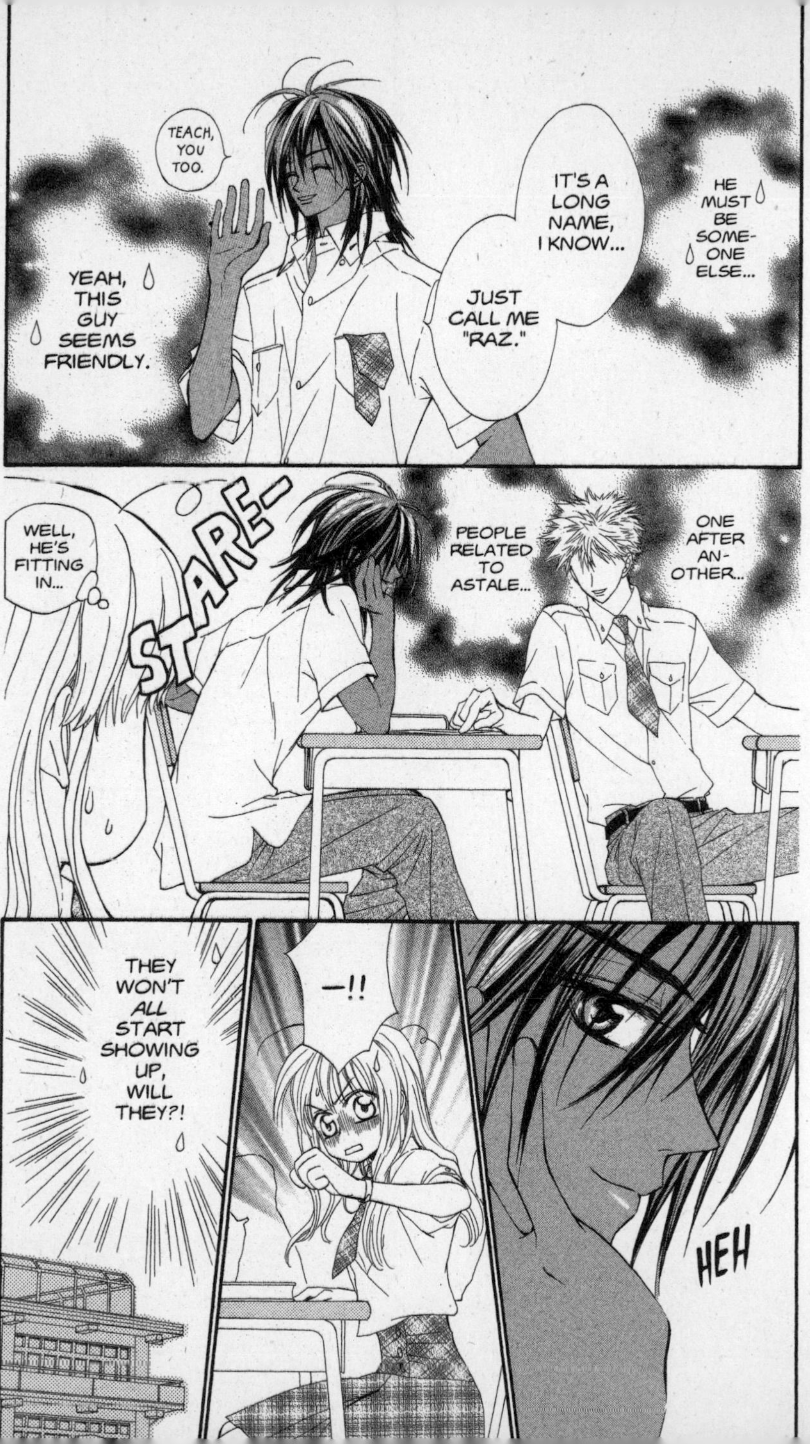
HE MUST BE SOME-ONE ELSE...
IT'S A LONG NAME, I KNOW...
JUST CALL ME "RAZ."
TEACH, YOU TOO.
YEAH, THIS GUY SEEMS FRIENDLY.
ONE AFTER AN-OTHER...
PEOPLE RELATED TO ASTALE...
STARE-
WELL, HE'S FITTING IN...
HEH
—!!
THEY WON'T *ALL* START SHOWING UP, WILL THEY?!

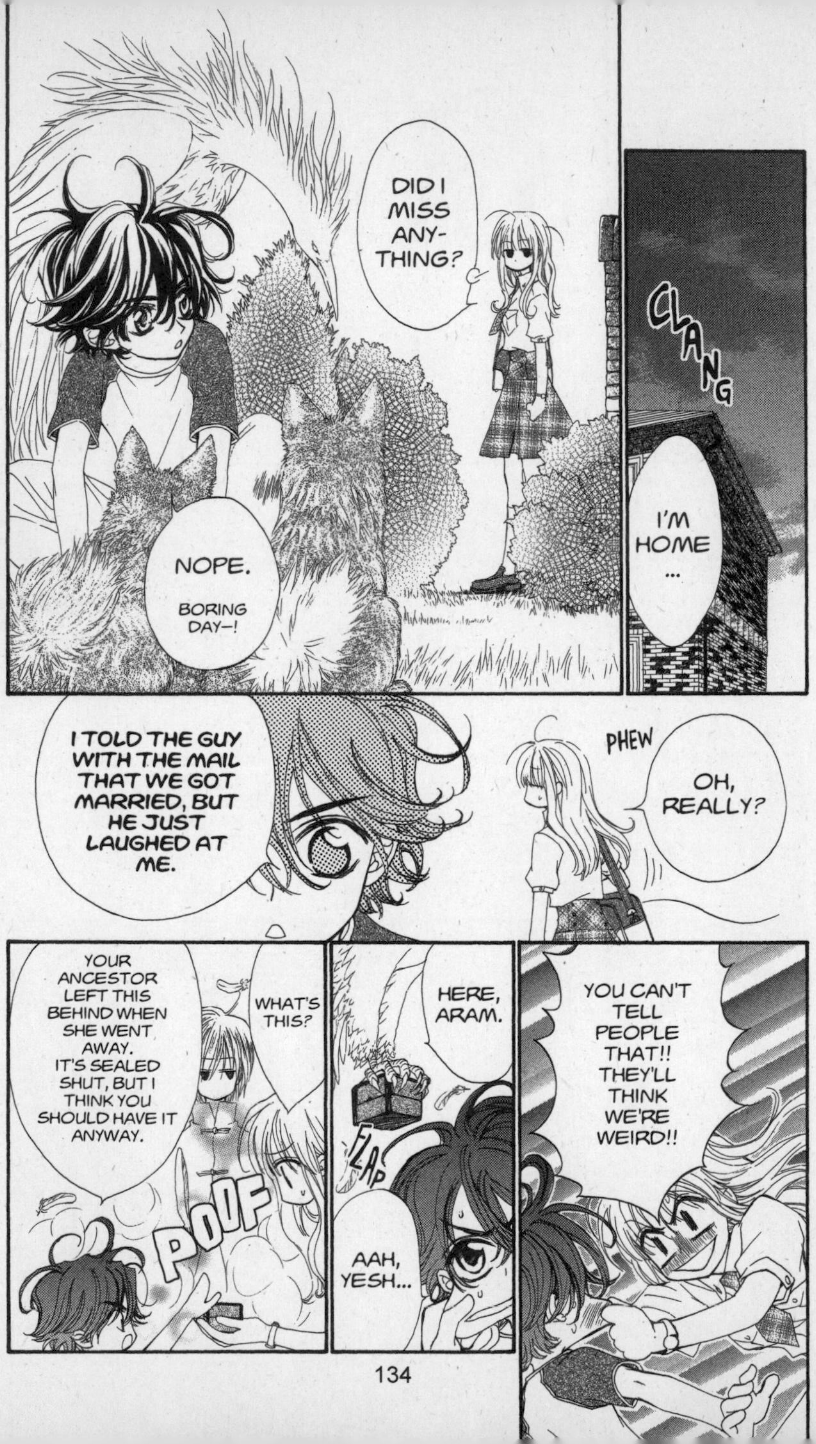
CLANG
I'M HOME ...
DID I MISS ANY-THING?
NOPE.
BORING DAY–!
PHEW
OH, REALLY?
I TOLD THE GUY WITH THE MAIL THAT WE GOT MARRIED, BUT HE JUST LAUGHED AT ME.
YOU CAN'T TELL PEOPLE THAT!! THEY'LL THINK WE'RE WEIRD!!
HERE, ARAM.
FLAP
AAH, YESH...
WHAT'S THIS?
YOUR ANCESTOR LEFT THIS BEHIND WHEN SHE WENT AWAY. IT'S SEALED SHUT, BUT I THINK YOU SHOULD HAVE IT ANYWAY.
POOF

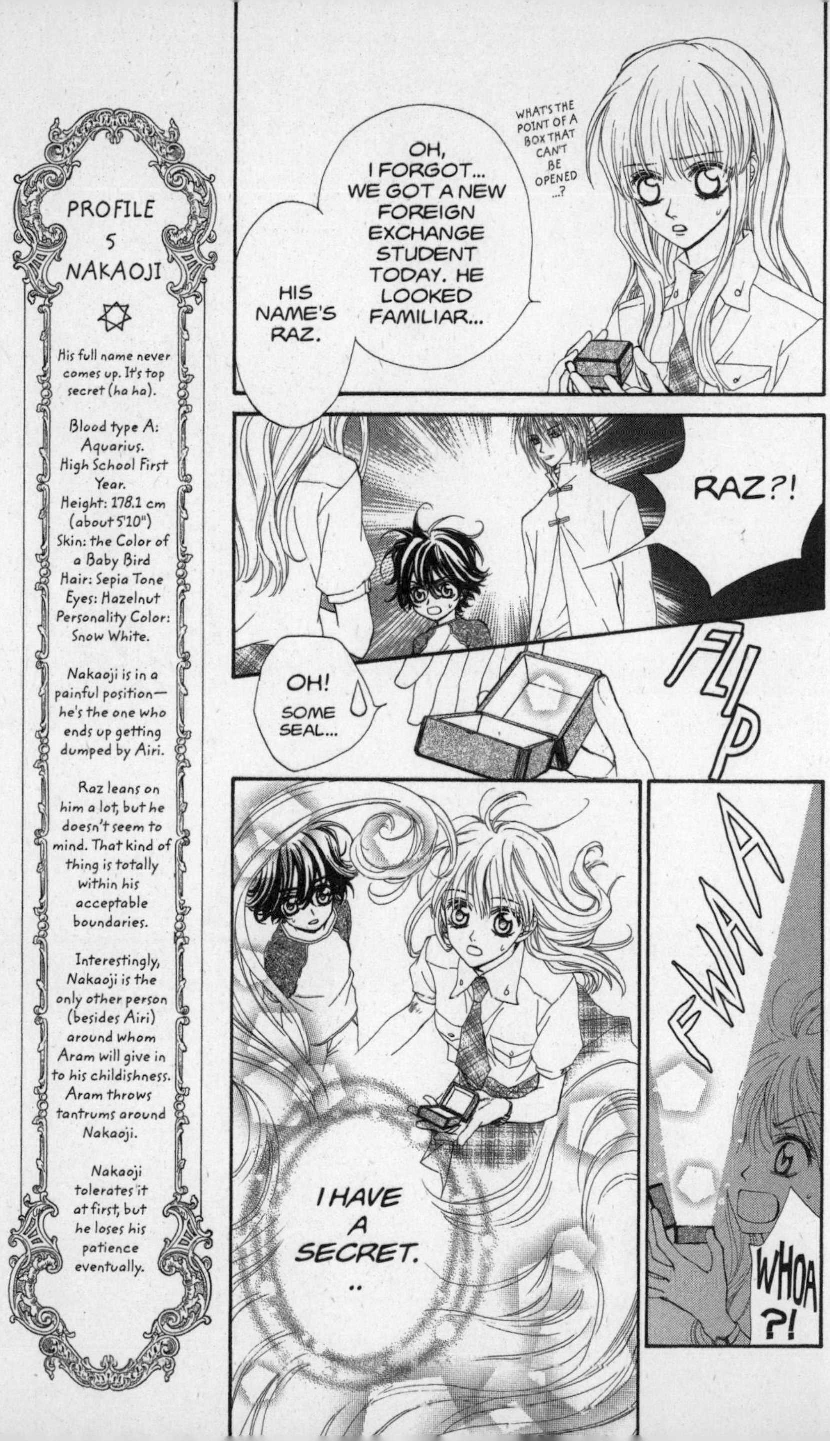
WHAT'S THE POINT OF A BOX THAT CAN'T BE OPENED ...?
OH, I FORGOT... WE GOT A NEW FOREIGN EXCHANGE STUDENT TODAY. HE LOOKED FAMILIAR...
HIS NAME'S RAZ.
RAZ?!
FLIP
OH! SOME SEAL...
FWA A
WHOA ?!
I HAVE A SECRET. ..

PROFILE 5 NAKAOJI

His full name never comes up. It's top secret (ha ha).

Blood type A: Aquarius.
High School First Year.
Height: 178.1 cm (about 5'10")
Skin: the Color of a Baby Bird
Hair: Sepia Tone
Eyes: Hazelnut
Personality Color: Snow White.

Nakaoji is in a painful position—he's the one who ends up getting dumped by Airi.

Raz leans on him a lot, but he doesn't seem to mind. That kind of thing is totally within his acceptable boundaries.

Interestingly, Nakaoji is the only other person (besides Airi) around whom Aram will give in to his childishness. Aram throws tantrums around Nakaoji.

Nakaoji tolerates it at first, but he loses his patience eventually.

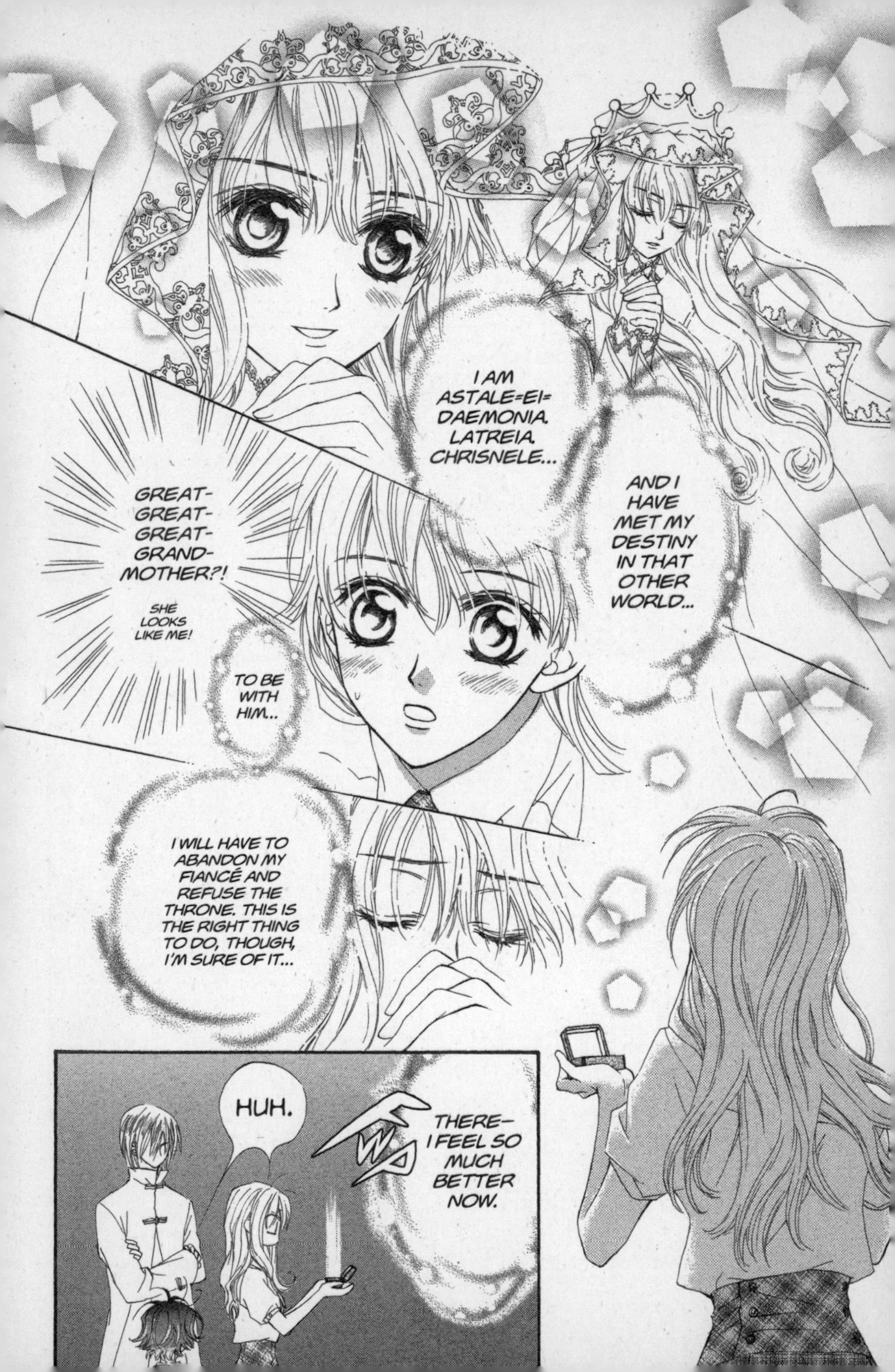
I AM ASTALE=EI=DAEMONIA. LATREIA. CHRISNELE...
AND I HAVE MET MY DESTINY IN THAT OTHER WORLD...
TO BE WITH HIM...
GREAT-GREAT-GREAT-GRAND-MOTHER?!
SHE LOOKS LIKE ME!
I WILL HAVE TO ABANDON MY FIANCÉ AND REFUSE THE THRONE. THIS IS THE RIGHT THING TO DO, THOUGH, I'M SURE OF IT...
THERE-I FEEL SO MUCH BETTER NOW.
HUH.

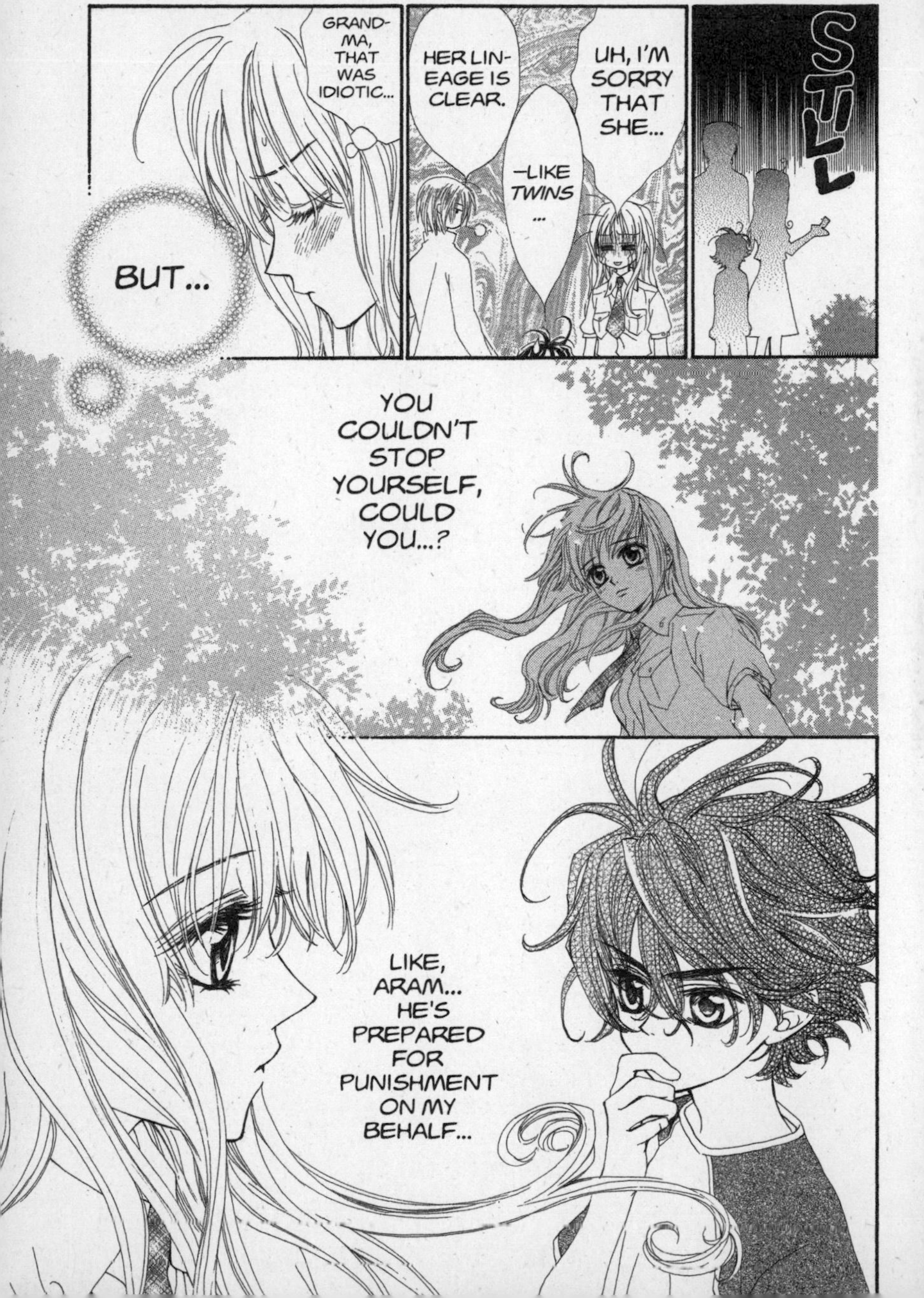
STILL
UH, I'M SORRY THAT SHE...
HER LIN-EAGE IS CLEAR.
—LIKE TWINS ...
GRAND-MA, THAT WAS IDIOTIC...
BUT...
YOU COULDN'T STOP YOURSELF, COULD YOU...?
LIKE, ARAM... HE'S PREPARED FOR PUNISHMENT ON MY BEHALF...

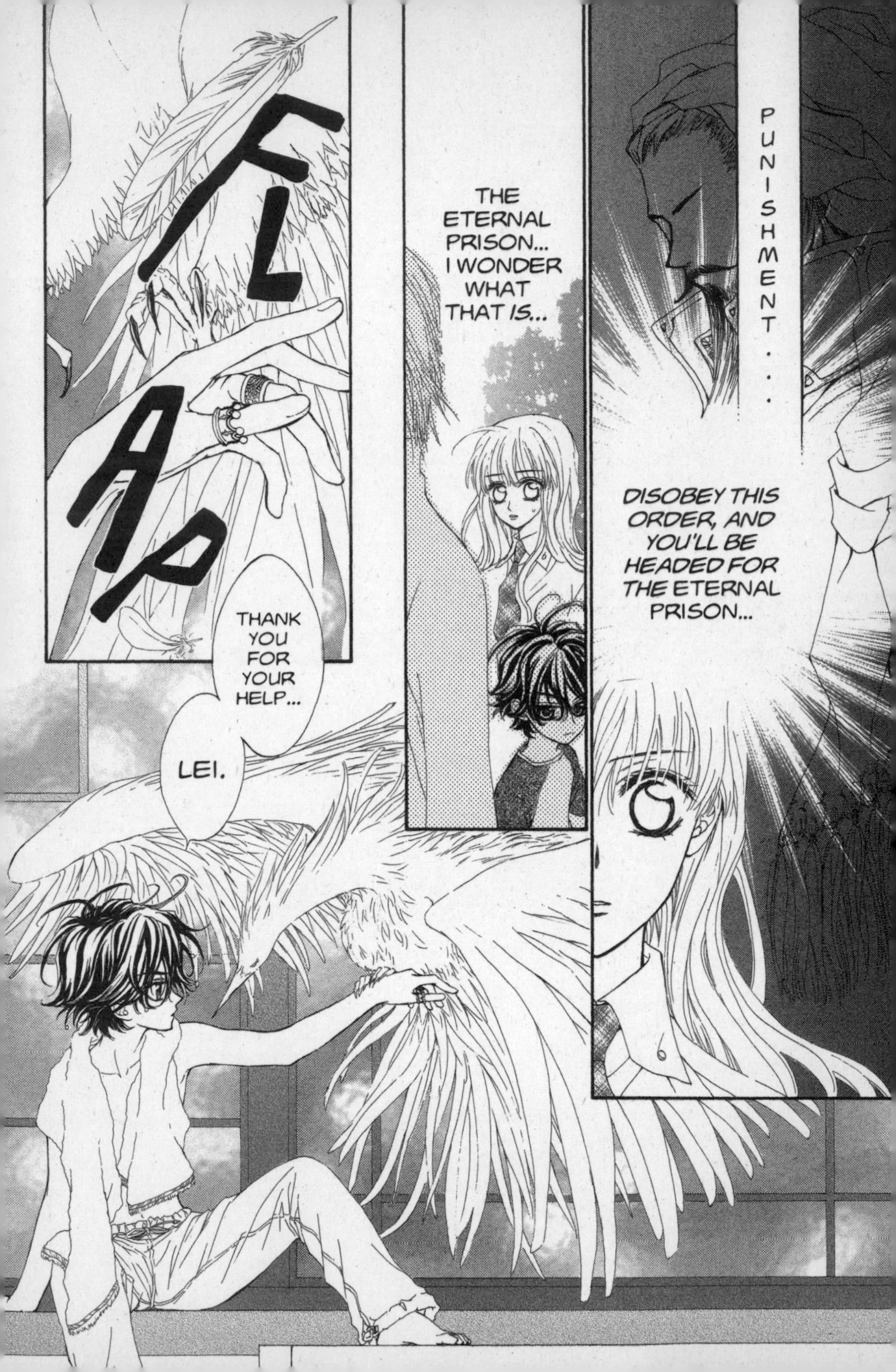
PUNISHMENT...
DISOBEY THIS ORDER, AND YOU'LL BE HEADED FOR THE ETERNAL PRISON...
THE ETERNAL PRISON... I WONDER WHAT THAT IS...
FLAP
THANK YOU FOR YOUR HELP...
LEI.

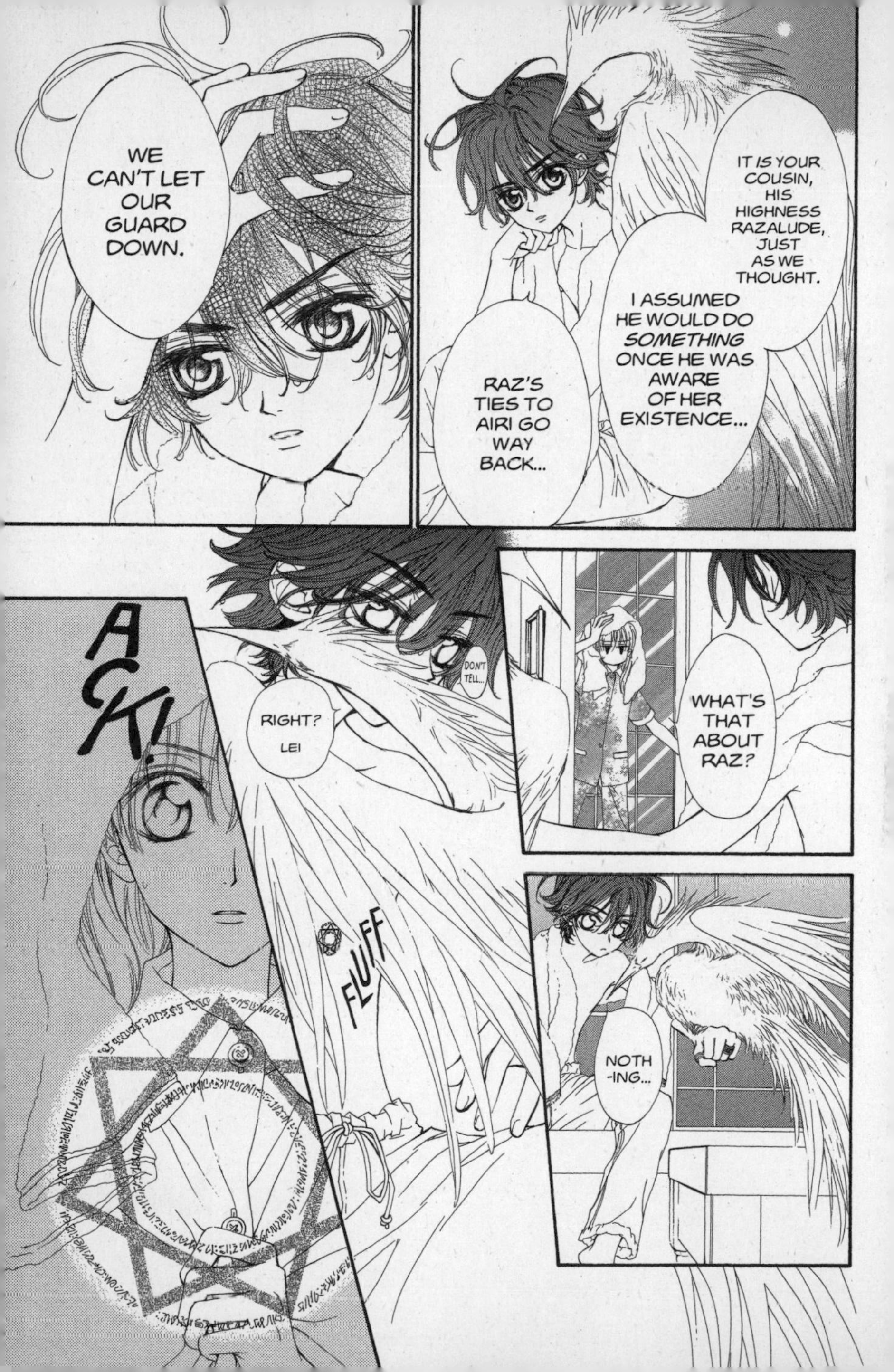
IT *IS* YOUR COUSIN, HIS HIGHNESS RAZALUDE, JUST AS WE THOUGHT.
I ASSUMED HE WOULD DO *SOMETHING* ONCE HE WAS AWARE OF HER EXISTENCE...
RAZ'S TIES TO AIRI GO WAY BACK...
WE CAN'T LET OUR GUARD DOWN.
WHAT'S THAT ABOUT RAZ?
NOTH-ING...
DON'T TELL...
RIGHT? LEI
ACK!
FLUFF

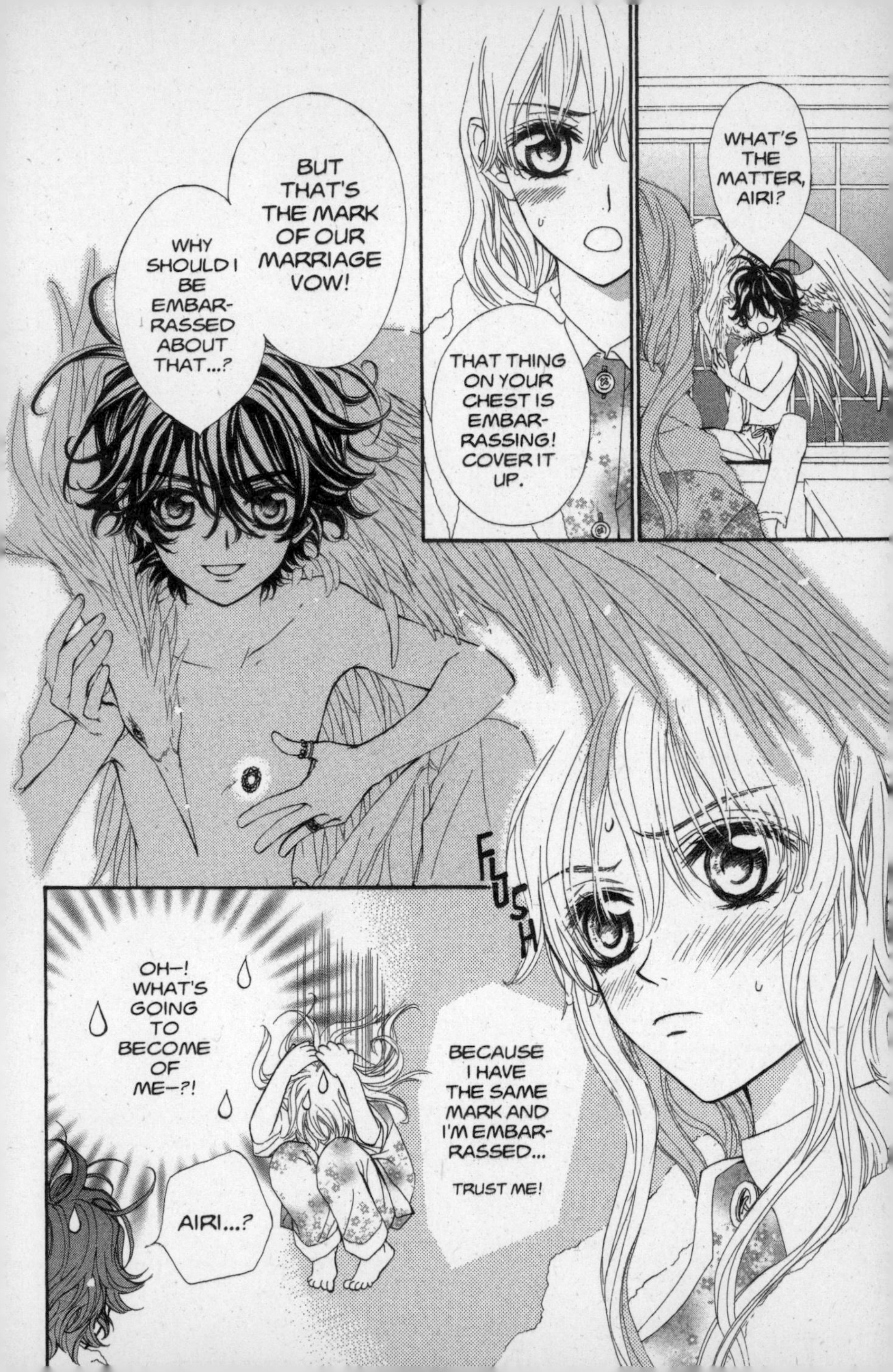
WHAT'S THE MATTER, AIRI?
THAT THING ON YOUR CHEST IS EMBARRASSING! COVER IT UP.
BUT THAT'S THE MARK OF OUR MARRIAGE VOW!
WHY SHOULD I BE EMBARRASSED ABOUT THAT...?
FLUSH
BECAUSE I HAVE THE SAME MARK AND I'M EMBARRASSED...
TRUST ME!
OH--! WHAT'S GOING TO BECOME OF ME--?!
AIRI...?

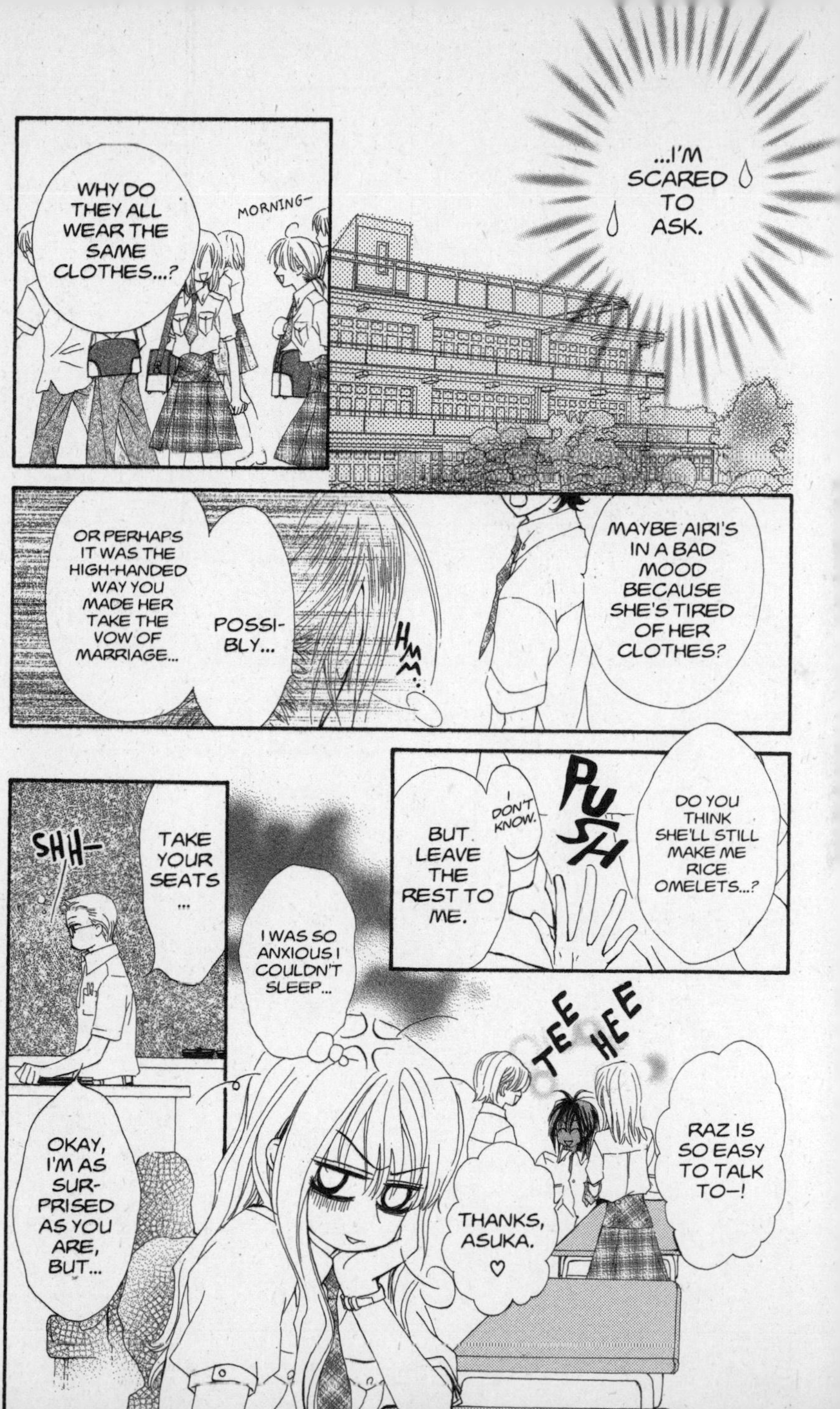
...I'M SCARED TO ASK.
MORNING—
WHY DO THEY ALL WEAR THE SAME CLOTHES...?
MAYBE AIRI'S IN A BAD MOOD BECAUSE SHE'S TIRED OF HER CLOTHES?
HMM
POSSI-BLY...
OR PERHAPS IT WAS THE HIGH-HANDED WAY YOU MADE HER TAKE THE VOW OF MARRIAGE...
DO YOU THINK SHE'LL STILL MAKE ME RICE OMELETS...?
PUSH
I DON'T KNOW.
BUT LEAVE THE REST TO ME.
TAKE YOUR SEATS...
SHH—
RAZ IS SO EASY TO TALK TO—!
TEE HEE
THANKS, ASUKA. ♡
I WAS SO ANXIOUS I COULDN'T SLEEP...
OKAY, I'M AS SUR-PRISED AS YOU ARE, BUT...

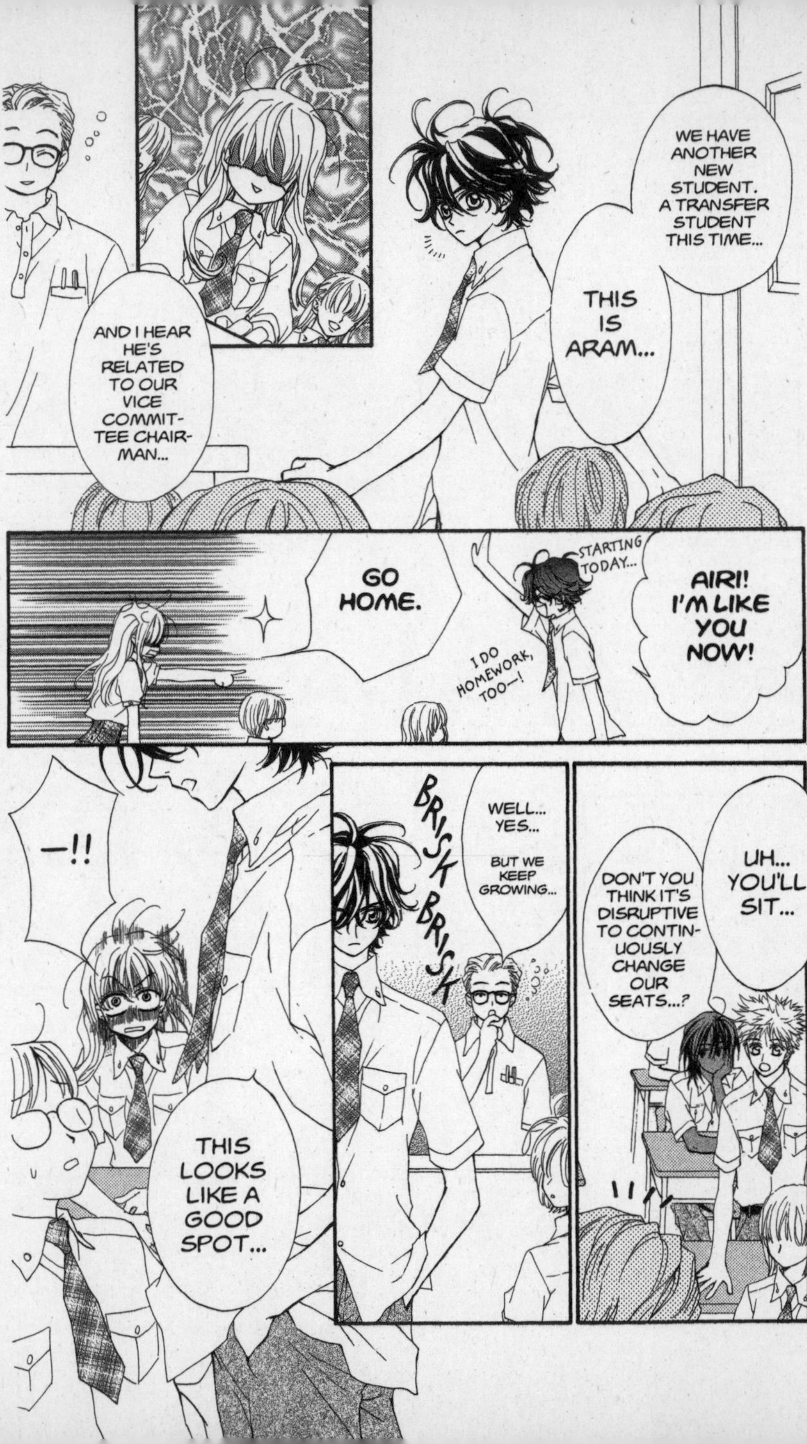
WE HAVE ANOTHER NEW STUDENT. A TRANSFER STUDENT THIS TIME...
THIS IS ARAM...
AND I HEAR HE'S RELATED TO OUR VICE COMMITTEE CHAIRMAN...
AIRI! I'M LIKE YOU NOW!
STARTING TODAY...
I DO HOMEWORK, TOO—!
GO HOME.
UH... YOU'LL SIT...
DON'T YOU THINK IT'S DISRUPTIVE TO CONTINUOUSLY CHANGE OUR SEATS...?
WELL... YES...
BUT WE KEEP GROWING...
BRISK BRISK
—!!
THIS LOOKS LIKE A GOOD SPOT...

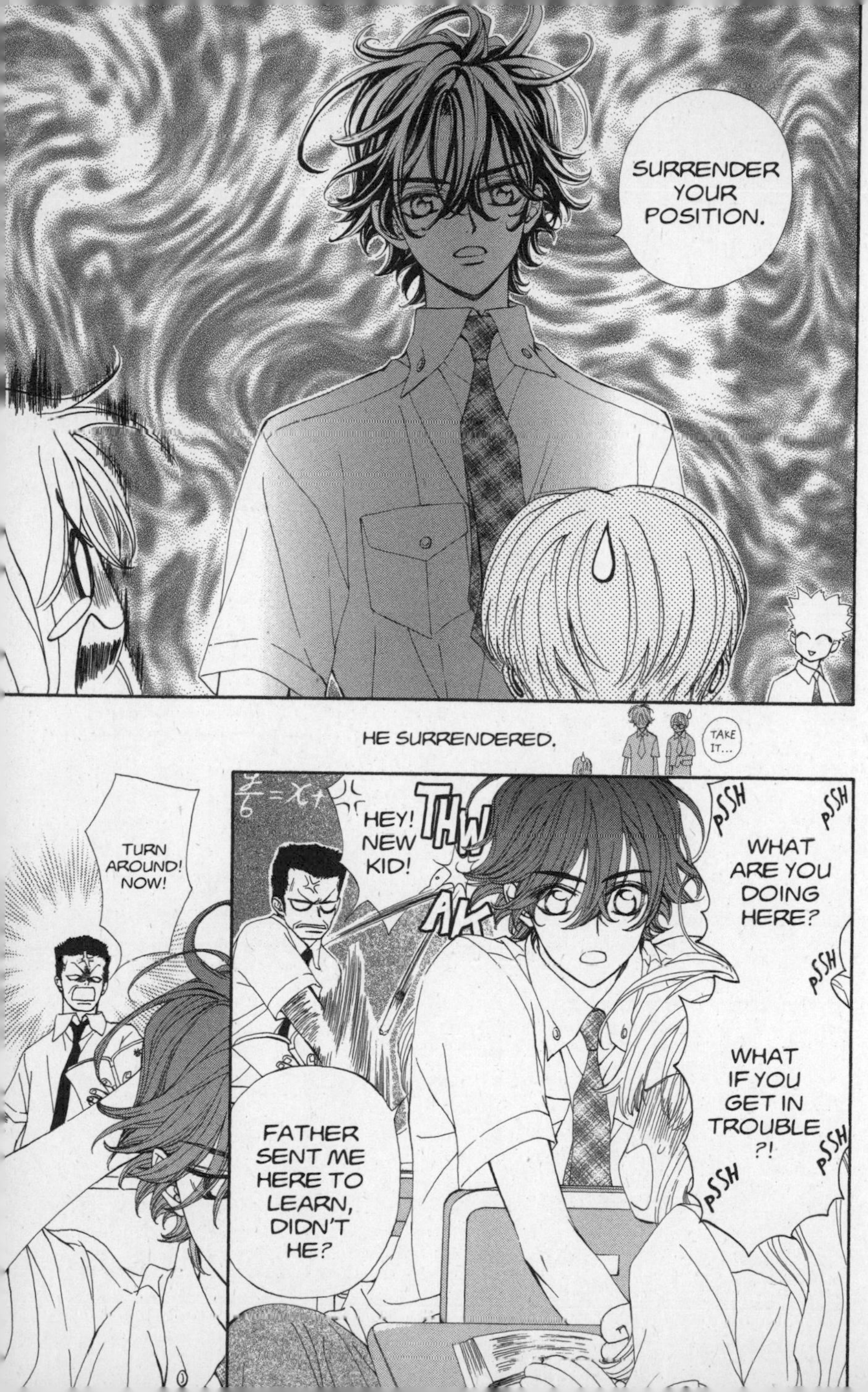
SURRENDER YOUR POSITION.
TAKE IT...
HE SURRENDERED.
PSSH
PSSH
WHAT ARE YOU DOING HERE?
HEY! NEW KID!
THWAK
PSSH
WHAT IF YOU GET IN TROUBLE?!
PSSH
PSSH
FATHER SENT ME HERE TO LEARN, DIDN'T HE?
TURN AROUND! NOW!

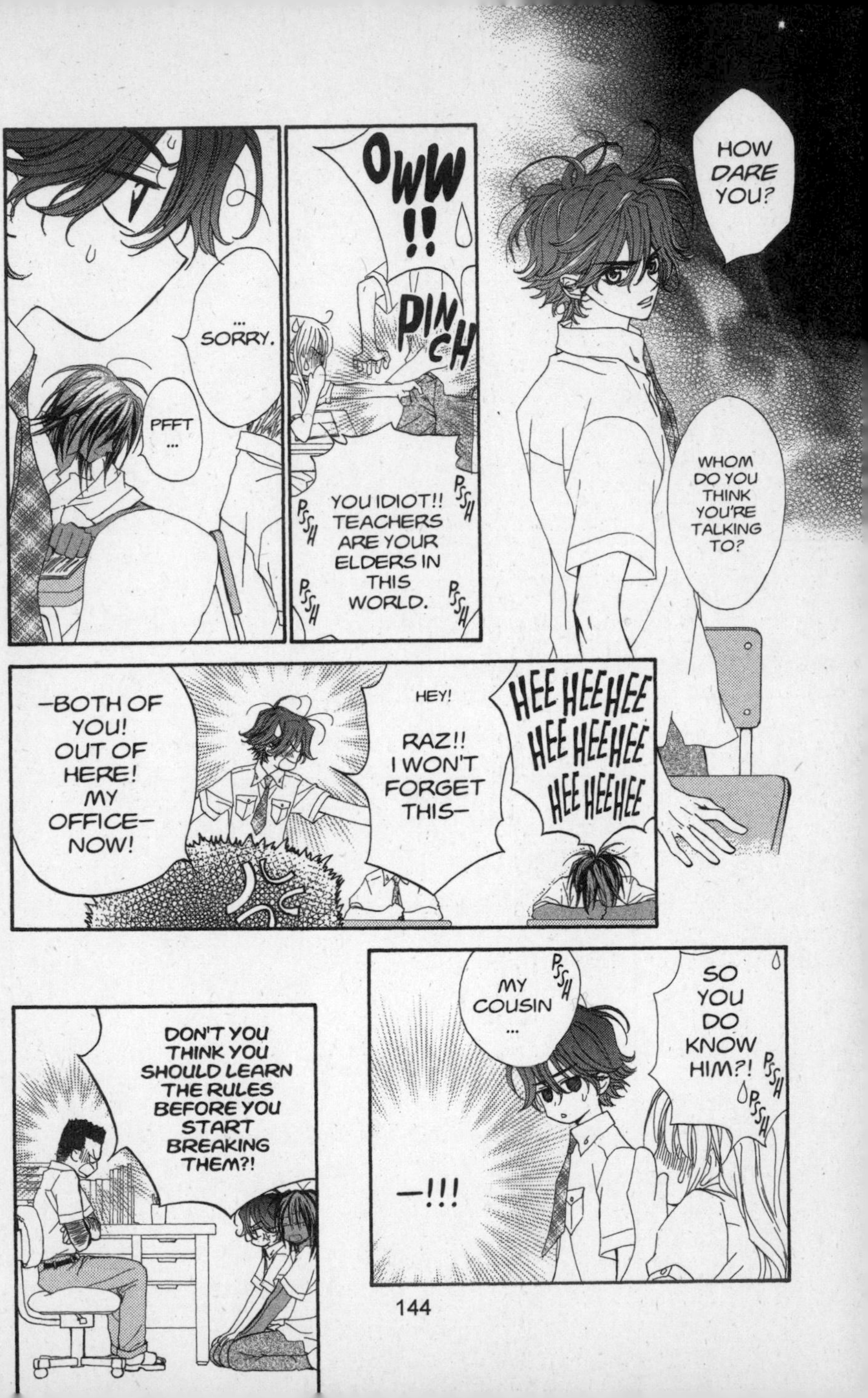
HOW DARE YOU?
WHOM DO YOU THINK YOU'RE TALKING TO?
OWW!!
PINCH
YOU IDIOT!! TEACHERS ARE YOUR ELDERS IN THIS WORLD.
PSSH
PSSH
PSSH
PSSH
... SORRY.
PFFT ...
HEE HEEHEE HEE HEEHEE HEE HEEHEE
HEY!
RAZ!! I WON'T FORGET THIS—
—BOTH OF YOU! OUT OF HERE! MY OFFICE— NOW!
SO YOU DO KNOW HIM?!
PSSH
PSSH
MY COUSIN ...
PSSH
—!!!
DON'T YOU THINK YOU SHOULD LEARN THE RULES BEFORE YOU START BREAKING THEM?!

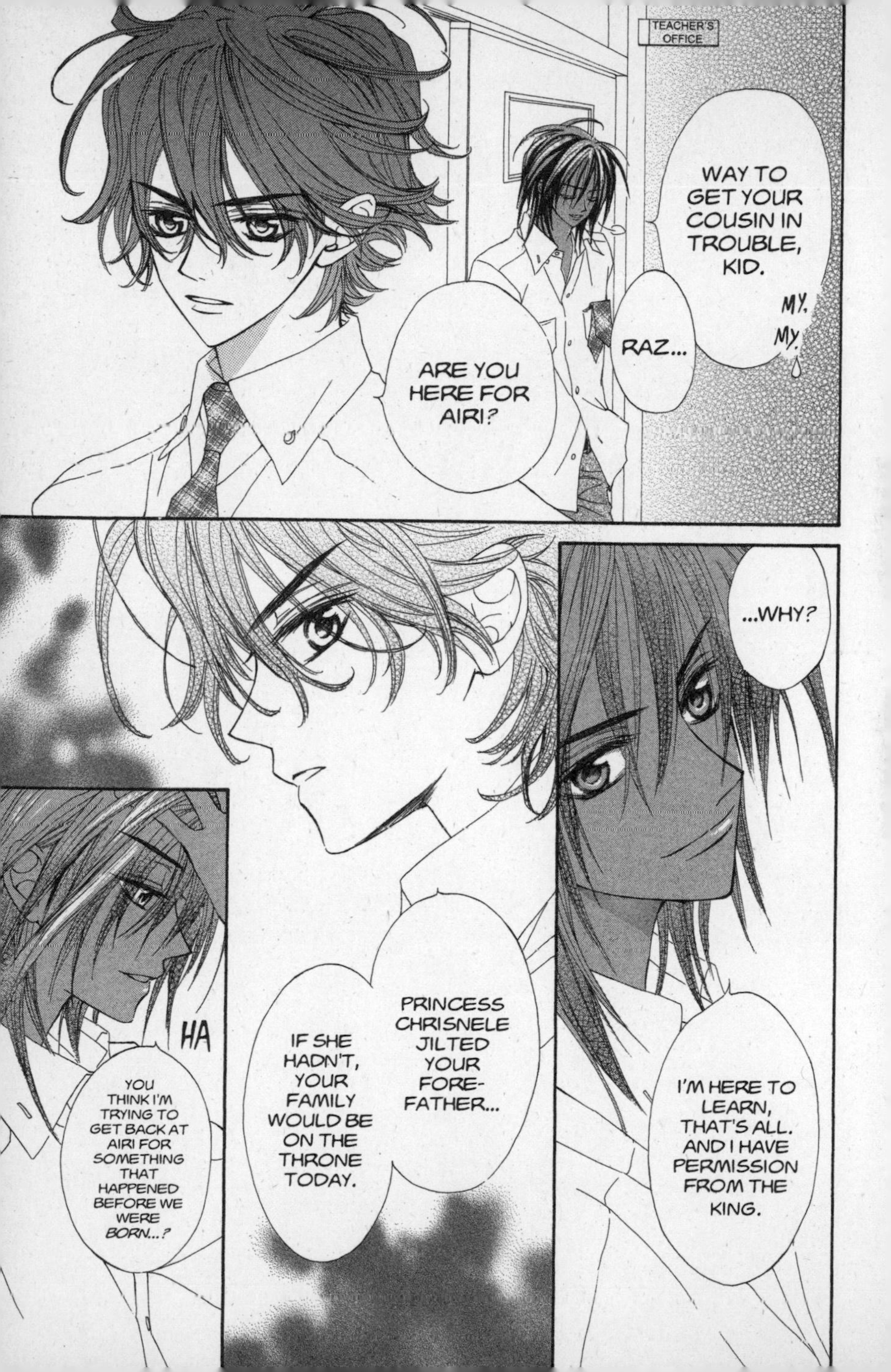
TEACHER'S OFFICE
WAY TO GET YOUR COUSIN IN TROUBLE, KID.
MY, MY.
RAZ...
ARE YOU HERE FOR AIRI?
...WHY?
I'M HERE TO LEARN, THAT'S ALL. AND I HAVE PERMISSION FROM THE KING.
PRINCESS CHRISNELE JILTED YOUR FORE-FATHER...
IF SHE HADN'T, YOUR FAMILY WOULD BE ON THE THRONE TODAY.
HA
YOU THINK I'M TRYING TO GET BACK AT AIRI FOR SOMETHING THAT HAPPENED BEFORE WE WERE *BORN*...?

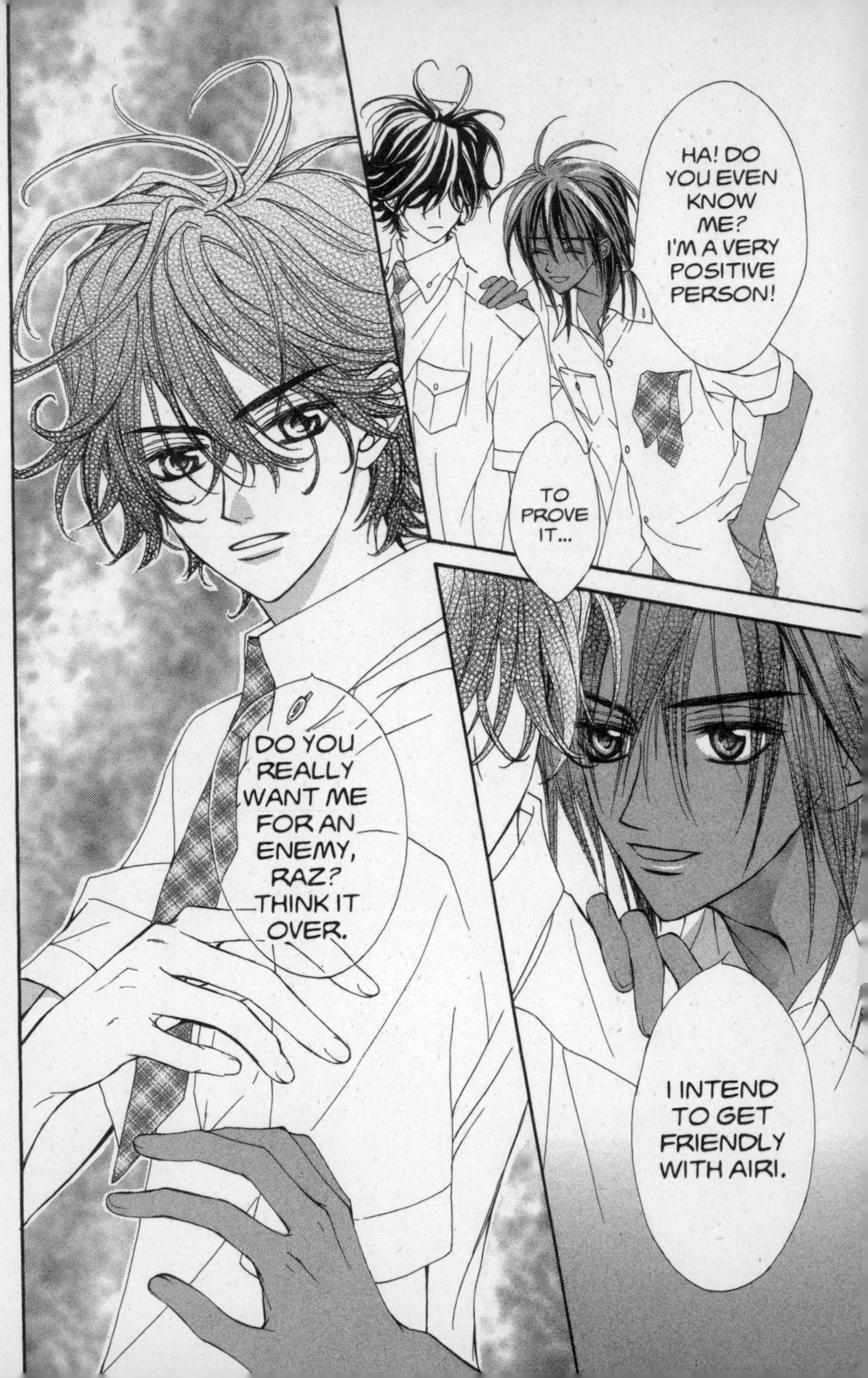
HA! DO YOU EVEN KNOW ME? I'M A VERY POSITIVE PERSON!
TO PROVE IT...
I INTEND TO GET FRIENDLY WITH AIRI.
DO YOU REALLY WANT ME FOR AN ENEMY, RAZ? THINK IT OVER.

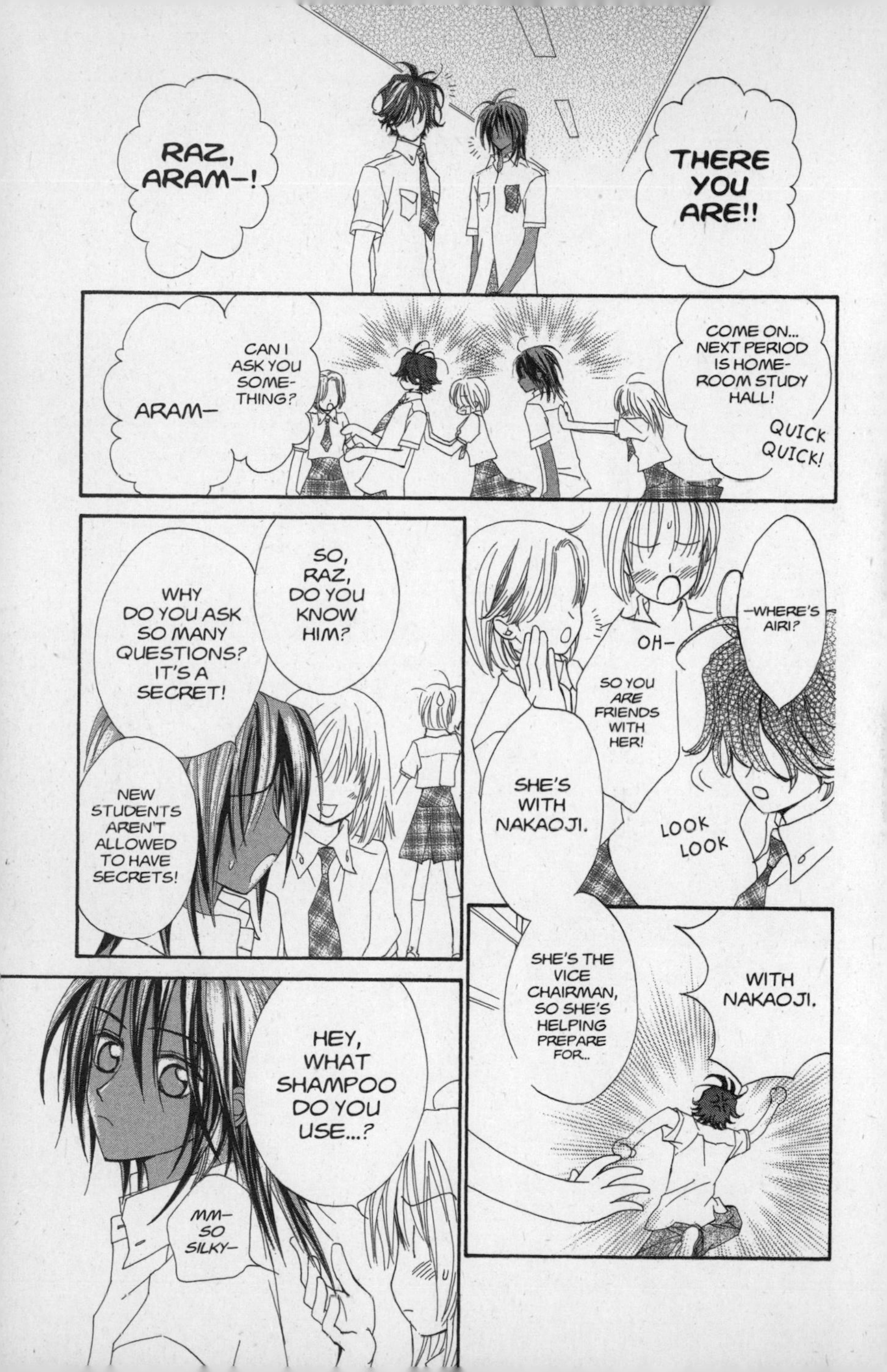
THERE YOU ARE!!
RAZ, ARAM—!
COME ON... NEXT PERIOD IS HOME-ROOM STUDY HALL!
QUICK QUICK!
CAN I ASK YOU SOME-THING?
ARAM—
—WHERE'S AIRI?
OH—
SO YOU ARE FRIENDS WITH HER!
SHE'S WITH NAKAOJI.
LOOK LOOK
SO, RAZ, DO YOU KNOW HIM?
WHY DO YOU ASK SO MANY QUESTIONS? IT'S A SECRET!
NEW STUDENTS AREN'T ALLOWED TO HAVE SECRETS!
WITH NAKAOJI.
SHE'S THE VICE CHAIRMAN, SO SHE'S HELPING PREPARE FOR..
HEY, WHAT SHAMPOO DO YOU USE...?
MM— SO SILKY—

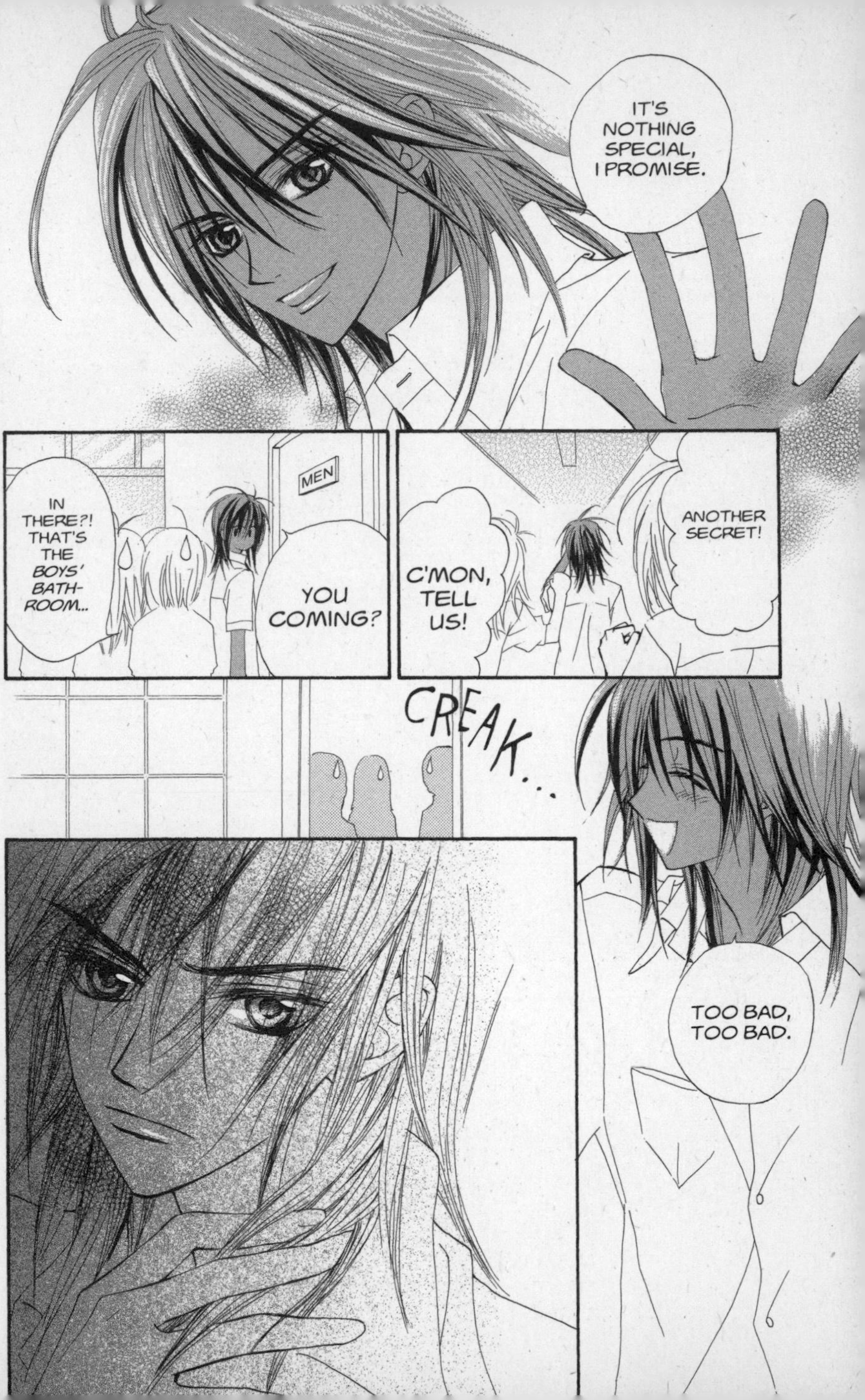
IT'S NOTHING SPECIAL, I PROMISE.
ANOTHER SECRET!
C'MON, TELL US!
YOU COMING?
IN THERE?! THAT'S THE *BOYS'* BATHROOM...
CREAK...
TOO BAD, TOO BAD.

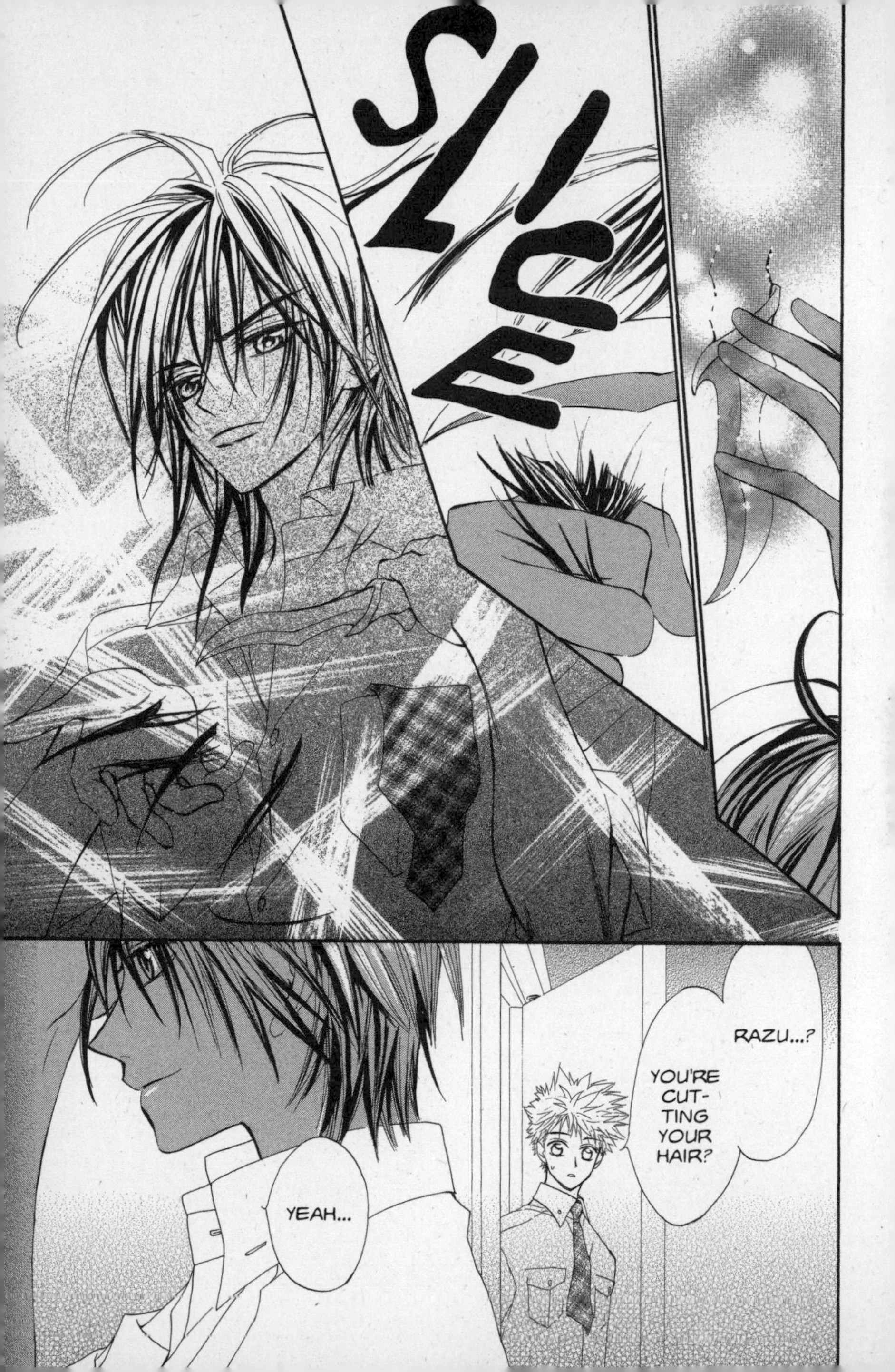
SLICE
RAZU...?
YOU'RE CUT-TING YOUR HAIR?
YEAH...

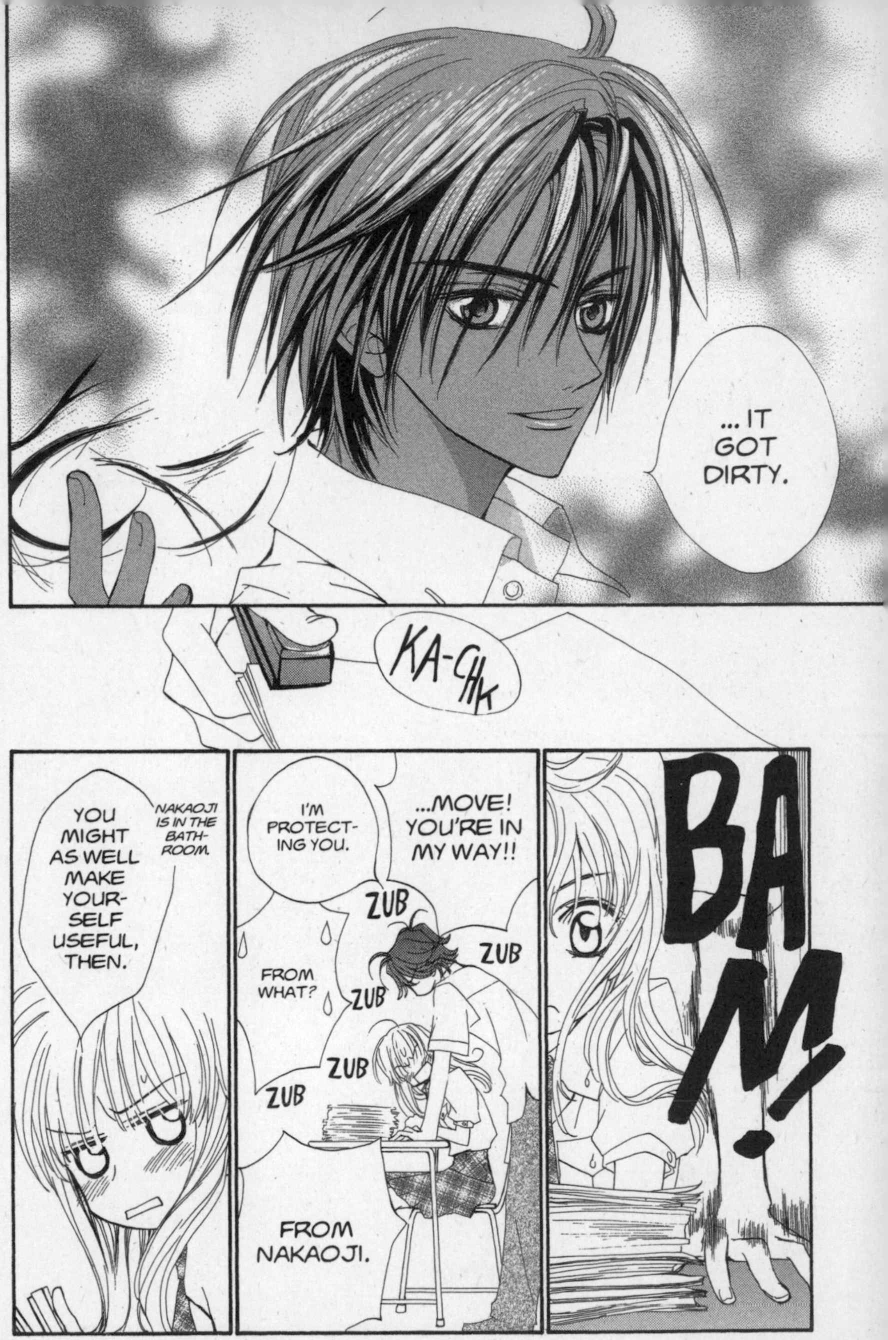
...IT GOT DIRTY.
KA-CHK
BAM!!
...MOVE! YOU'RE IN MY WAY!!
I'M PROTECT-ING YOU.
ZUB
ZUB
ZUB
FROM WHAT?
ZUB
ZUB
FROM NAKAOJI.
NAKAOJI IS IN THE BATH-ROOM.
YOU MIGHT AS WELL MAKE YOUR-SELF USEFUL, THEN.

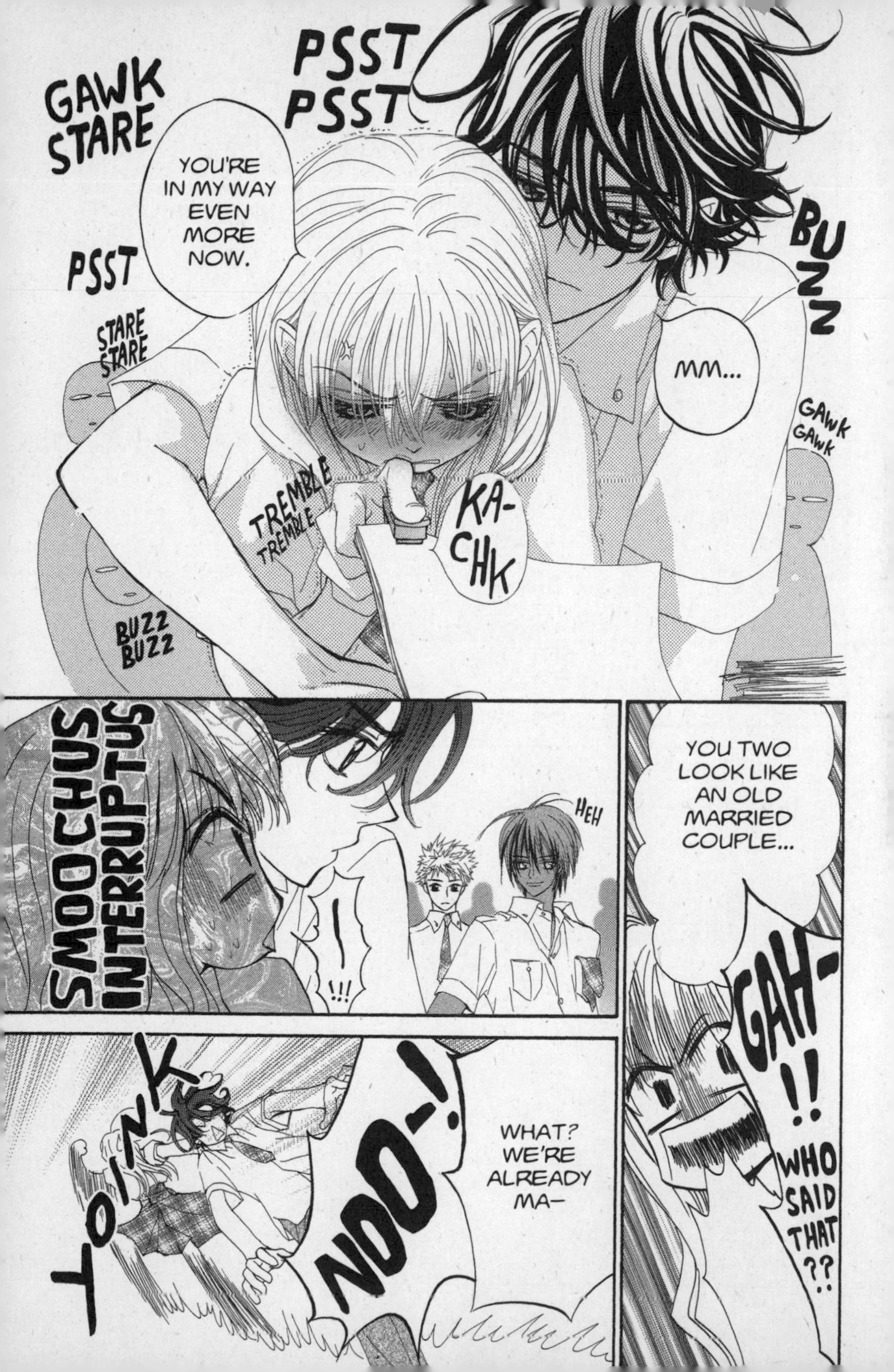
PSST PSST
BUZZ
GAWK STARE
YOU'RE IN MY WAY EVEN MORE NOW.
MM...
PSST
STARE STARE
GAWK GAWK
KA-CHK
TREMBLE TREMBLE
BUZZ BUZZ
YOU TWO LOOK LIKE AN OLD MARRIED COUPLE...
HEH
SMOOCHUS INTERRUPTUS
!!!
GAH-!!
WHO SAID THAT??
WHAT? WE'RE ALREADY MA-
NOO-!
TOINK

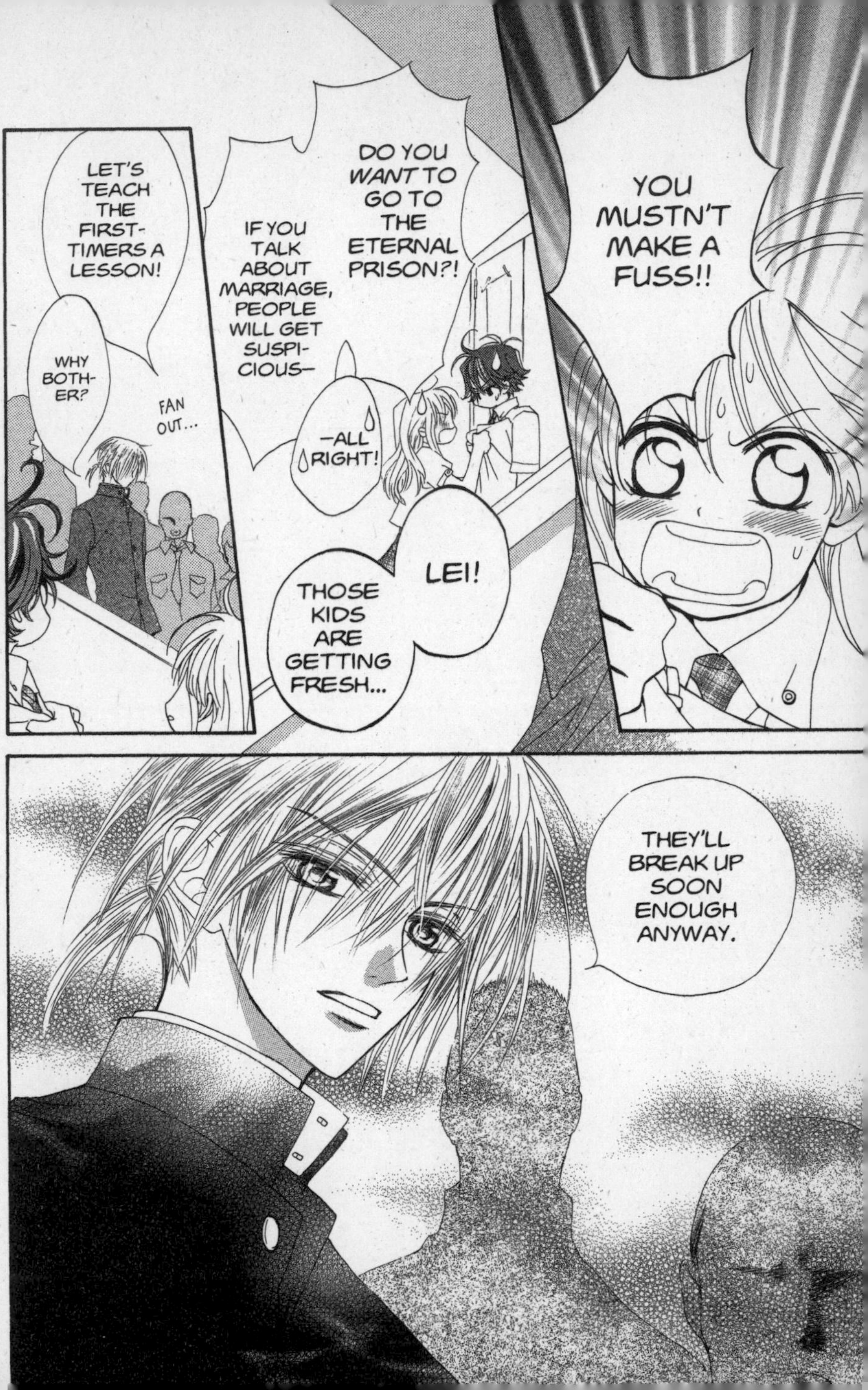
YOU MUSTN'T MAKE A FUSS!!
DO YOU WANT TO GO TO THE ETERNAL PRISON?!
IF YOU TALK ABOUT MARRIAGE, PEOPLE WILL GET SUSPICIOUS—
—ALL RIGHT!
LEI!
THOSE KIDS ARE GETTING FRESH...
LET'S TEACH THE FIRST-TIMERS A LESSON!
WHY BOTHER?
FAN OUT...
THEY'LL BREAK UP SOON ENOUGH ANYWAY.

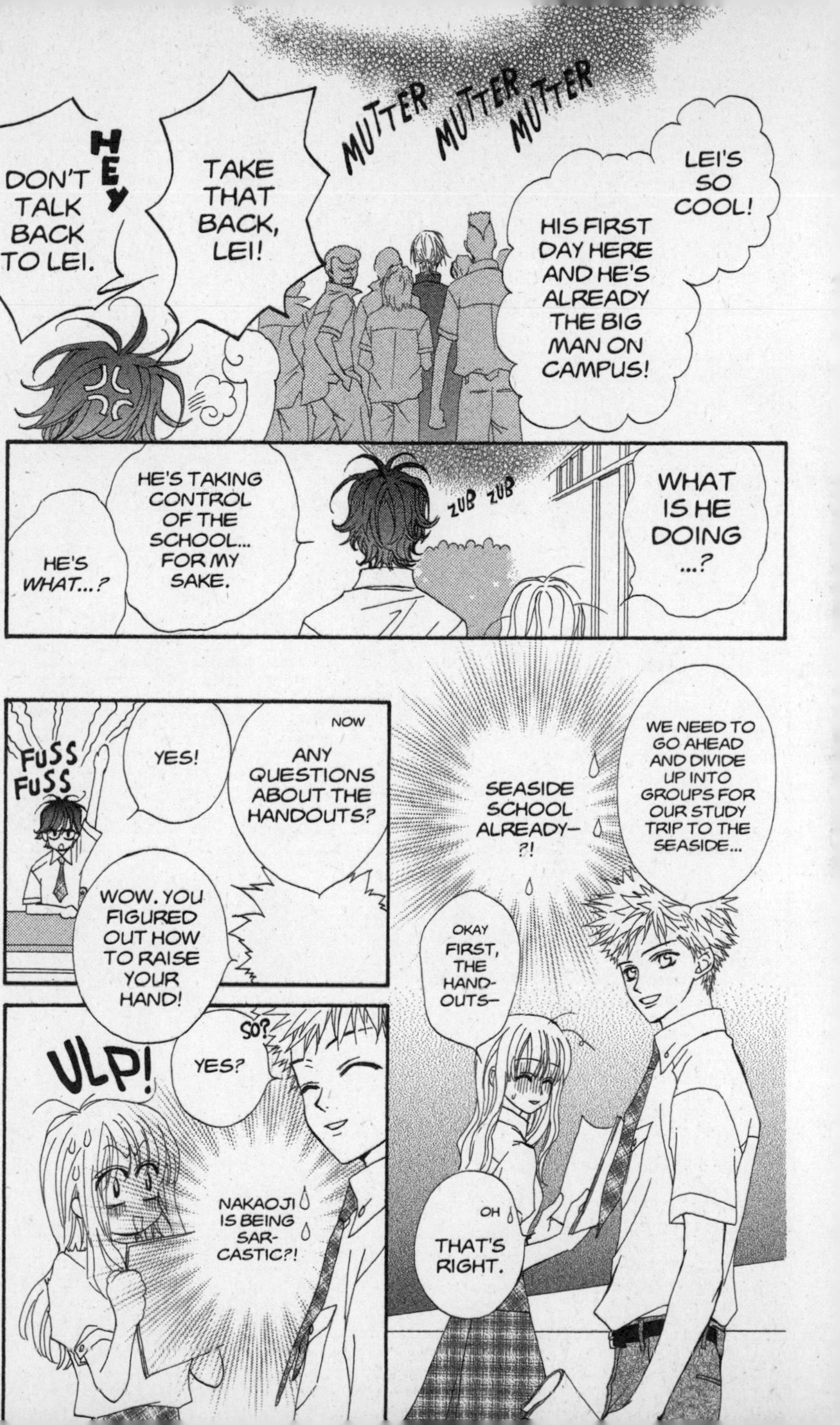
MUTTER MUTTER MUTTER
LEI'S SO COOL!
HIS FIRST DAY HERE AND HE'S ALREADY THE BIG MAN ON CAMPUS!
TAKE THAT BACK, LEI!
HEY
DON'T TALK BACK TO LEI.
WHAT IS HE DOING ...?
ZUB ZUB
HE'S TAKING CONTROL OF THE SCHOOL... FOR MY SAKE.
HE'S WHAT...?
WE NEED TO GO AHEAD AND DIVIDE UP INTO GROUPS FOR OUR STUDY TRIP TO THE SEASIDE...
SEASIDE SCHOOL ALREADY—?!
OKAY FIRST, THE HAND-OUTS—
OH THAT'S RIGHT.
NOW ANY QUESTIONS ABOUT THE HANDOUTS?
YES!
FUSS FUSS
WOW. YOU FIGURED OUT HOW TO RAISE YOUR HAND!
SO?
YES?
ULP!
NAKAOJI IS BEING SAR-CASTIC?!

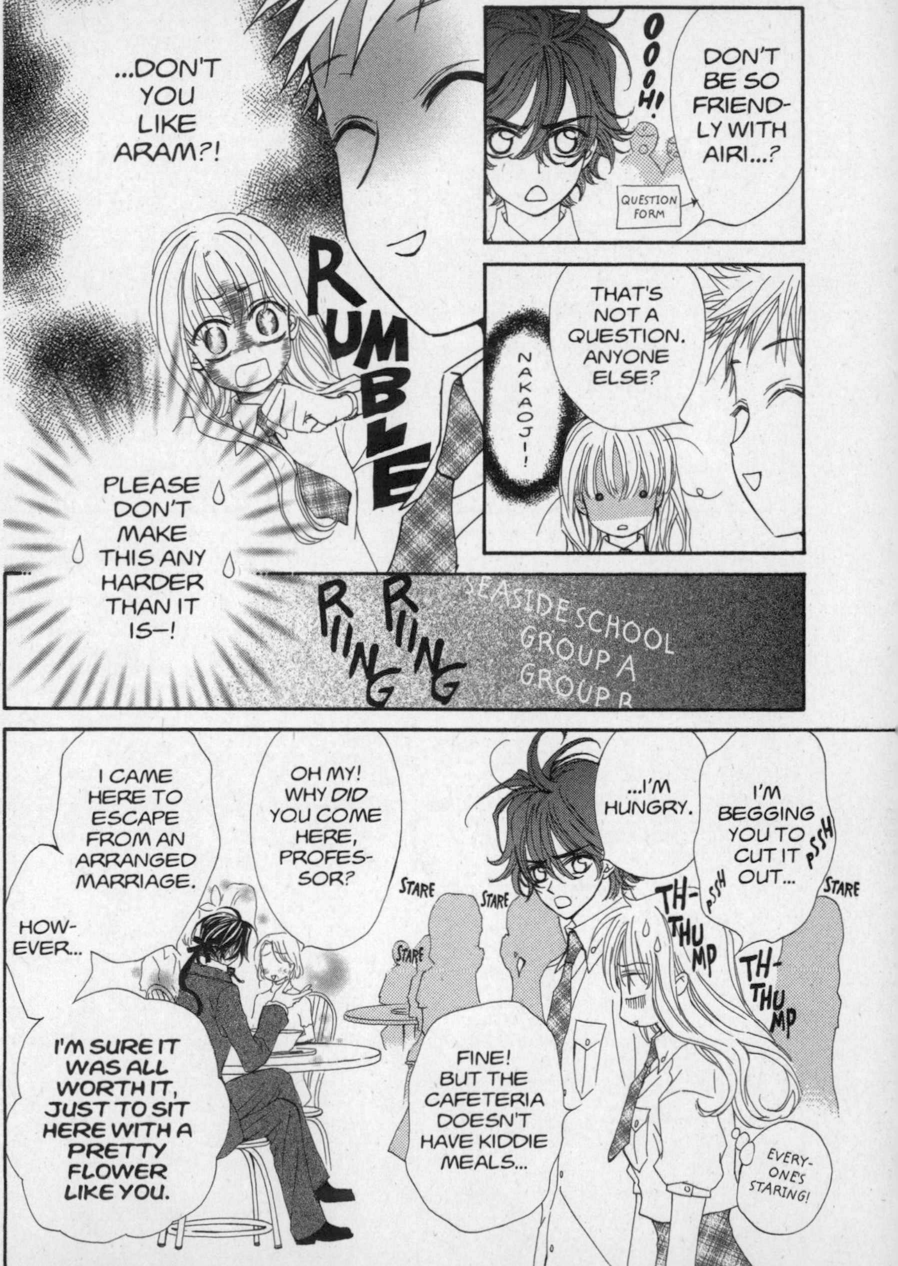
DON'T BE SO FRIENDLY WITH AIRI...?
OOOOH!
QUESTION FORM
THAT'S NOT A QUESTION. ANYONE ELSE?
NAKAOJI!
...DON'T YOU LIKE ARAM?!
RUMBLE
PLEASE DON'T MAKE THIS ANY HARDER THAN IT IS—!
RIIING RIIING
SEASIDE SCHOOL
GROUP A
GROUP B
I'M BEGGING YOU TO CUT IT OUT...
PSSH PSSH
...I'M HUNGRY.
STARE
TH-THUMP TH-THUMP
STARE STARE STARE
FINE! BUT THE CAFETERIA DOESN'T HAVE KIDDIE MEALS...
EVERYONE'S STARING!
OH MY! WHY DID YOU COME HERE, PROFESSOR?
I CAME HERE TO ESCAPE FROM AN ARRANGED MARRIAGE.
HOWEVER...
I'M SURE IT WAS ALL WORTH IT, JUST TO SIT HERE WITH A PRETTY FLOWER LIKE YOU.

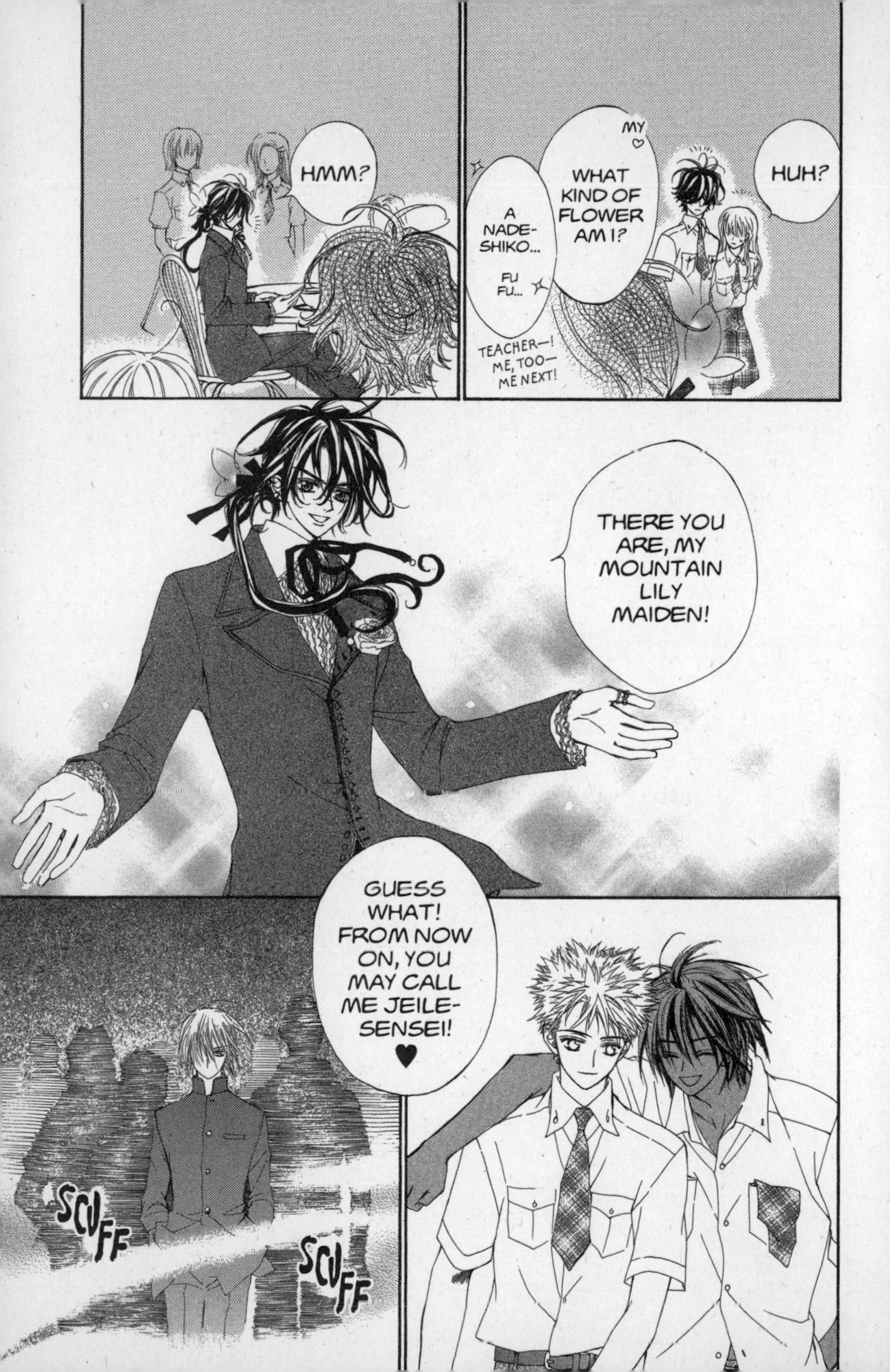
HUH?
MY ♥ WHAT KIND OF FLOWER AM I?
A NADE-SHIKO...
FU FU...
TEACHER—! ME, TOO— ME NEXT!
HMM?
THERE YOU ARE, MY MOUNTAIN LILY MAIDEN!
GUESS WHAT! FROM NOW ON, YOU MAY CALL ME JEILE-SENSEI! ♥
SCUFF
SCUFF

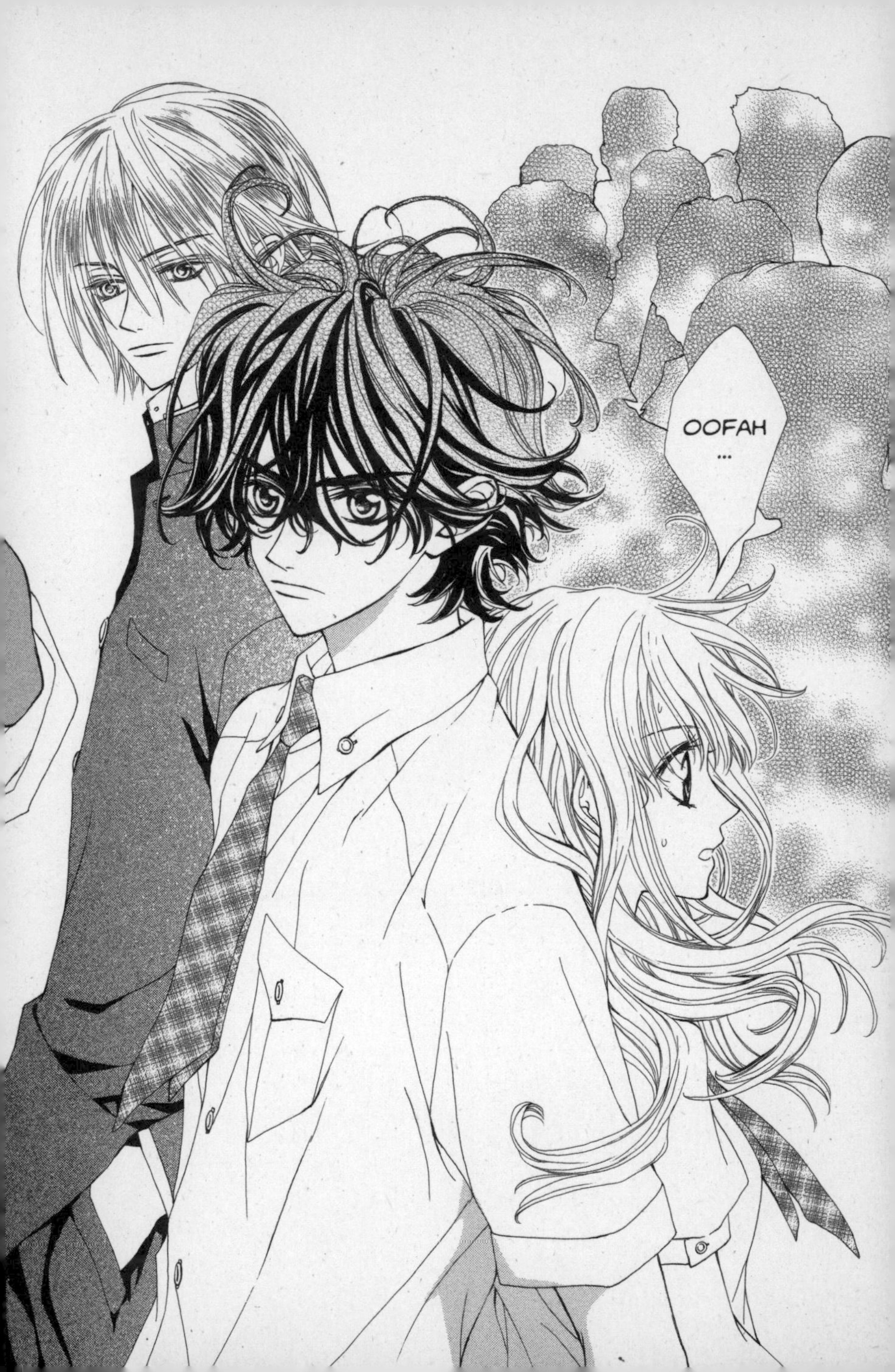
OOFAH
...

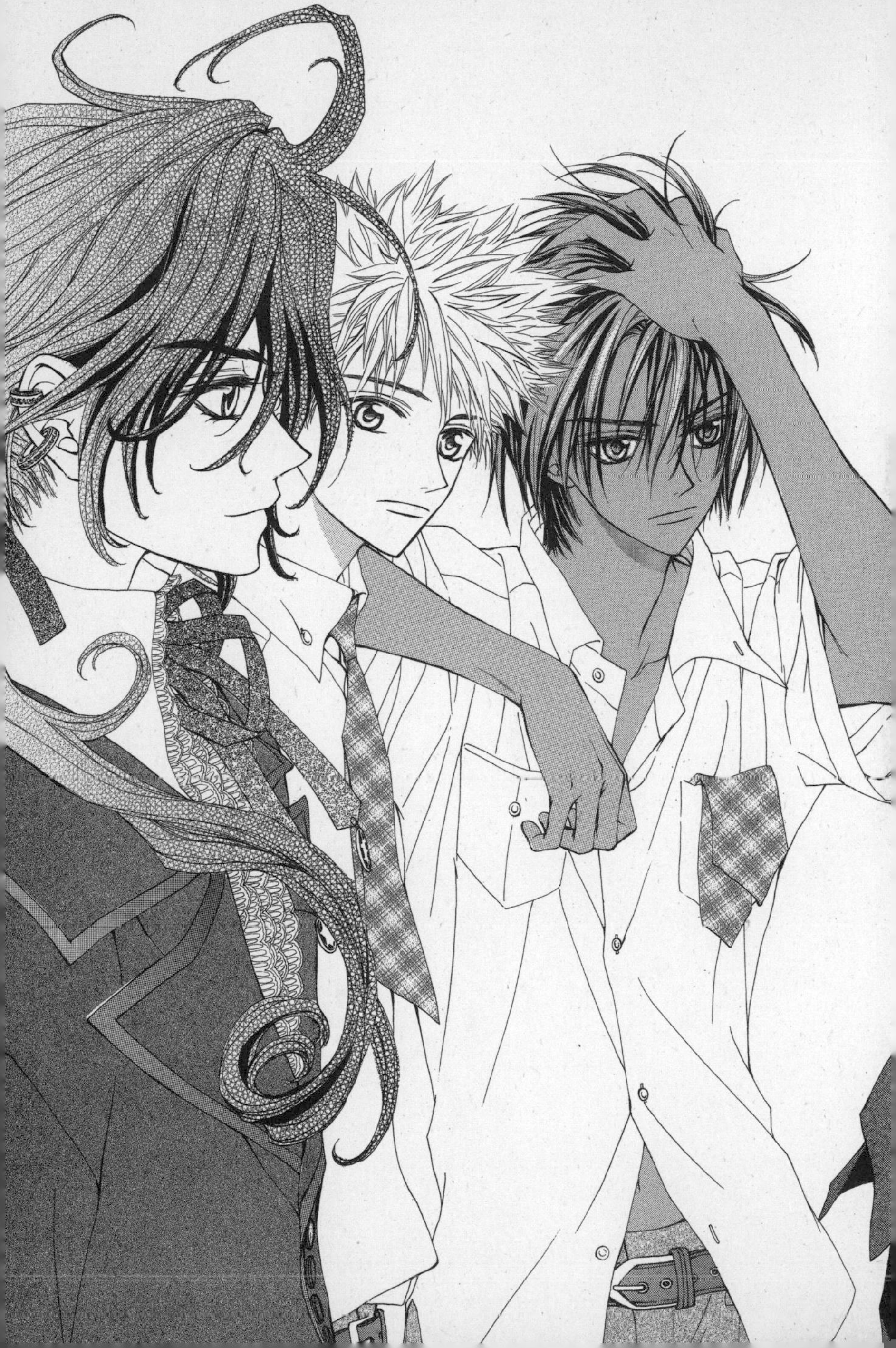

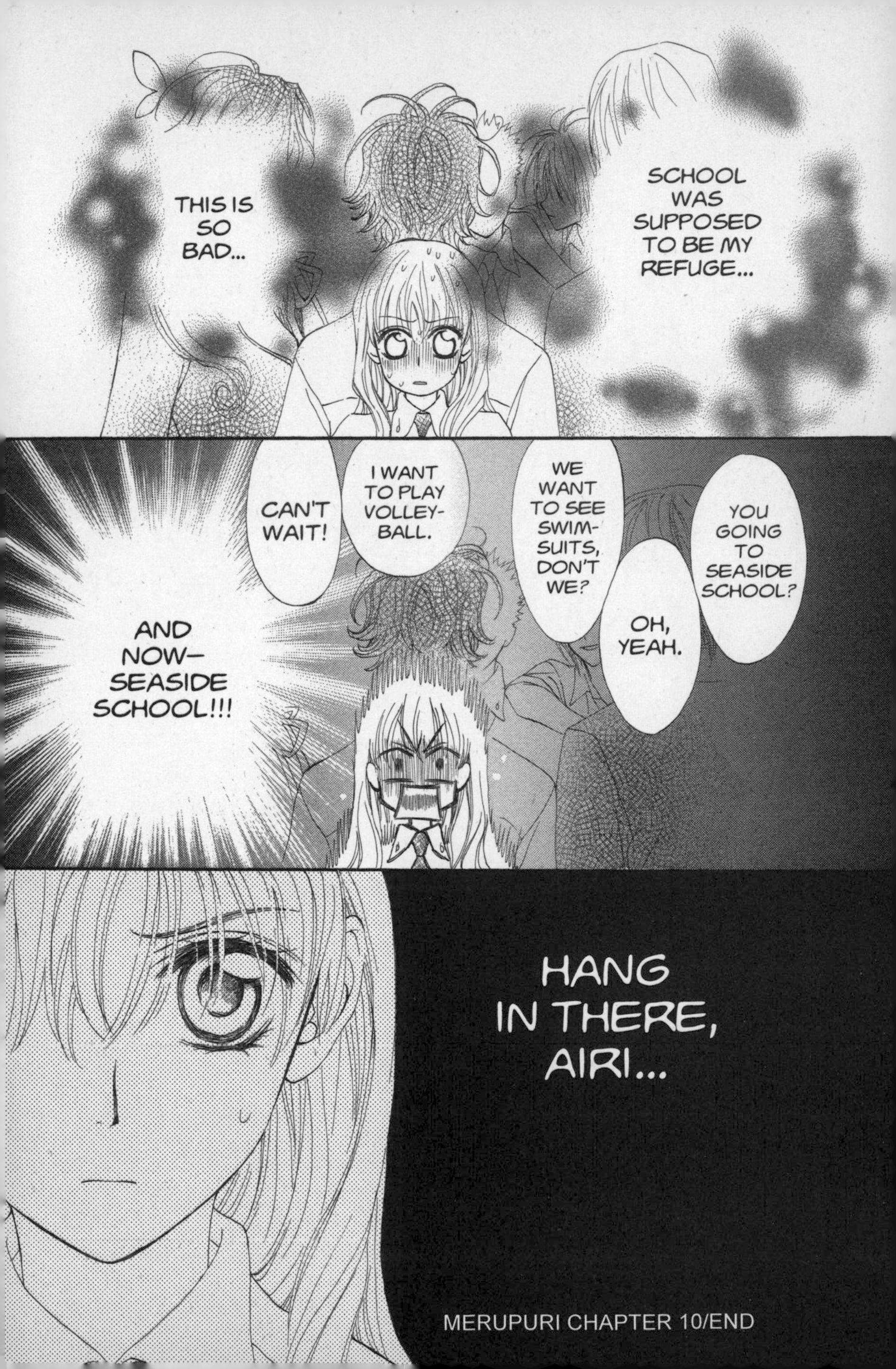
SCHOOL WAS SUPPOSED TO BE MY REFUGE...
THIS IS SO BAD...
YOU GOING TO SEASIDE SCHOOL?
OH, YEAH.
WE WANT TO SEE SWIM-SUITS, DON'T WE?
I WANT TO PLAY VOLLEY-BALL.
CAN'T WAIT!
AND NOW—SEASIDE SCHOOL!!!
HANG IN THERE, AIRI...
MERUPURI CHAPTER 10/END

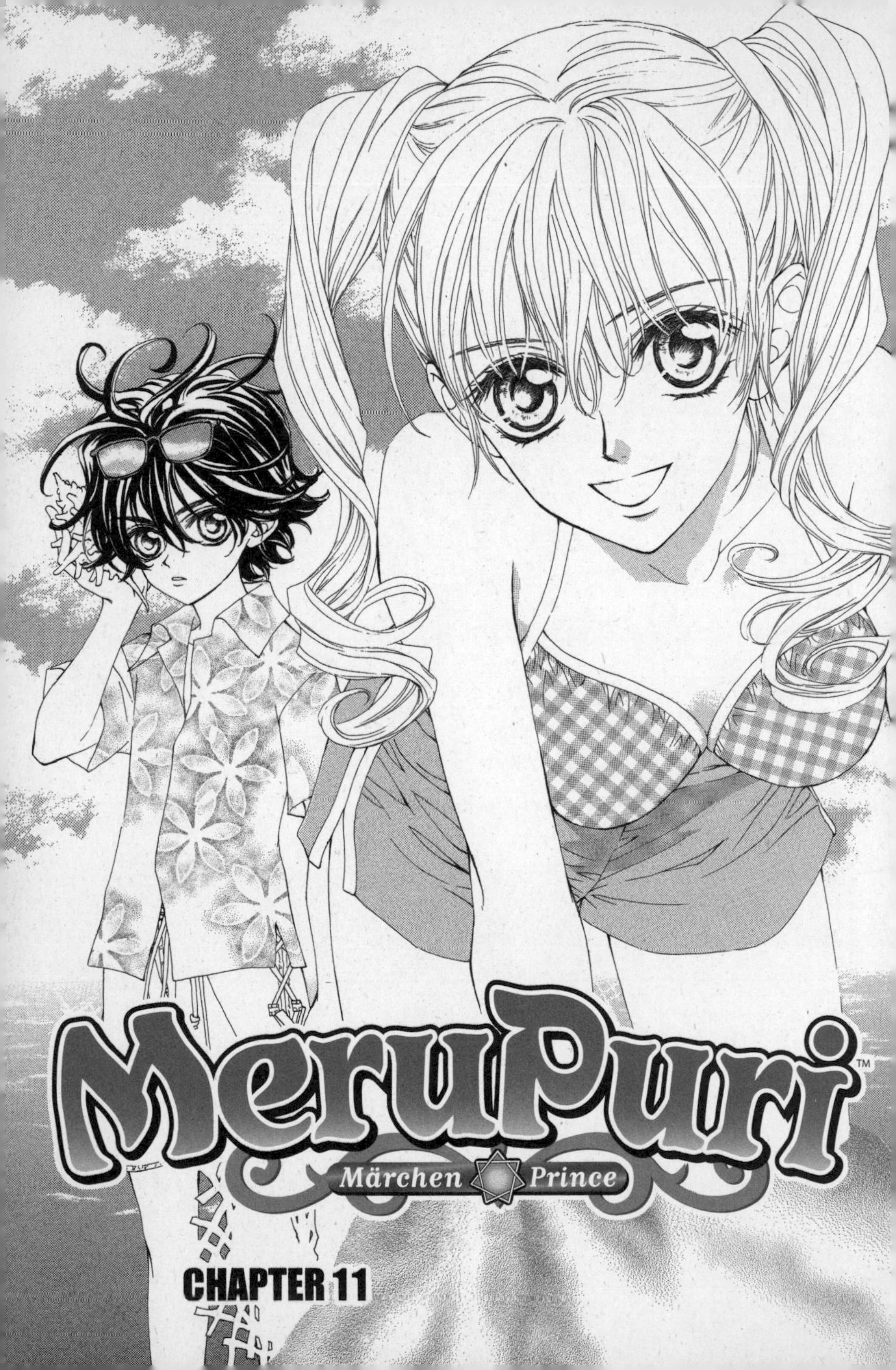
MeruPuri™
Märchen Prince
CHAPTER 11

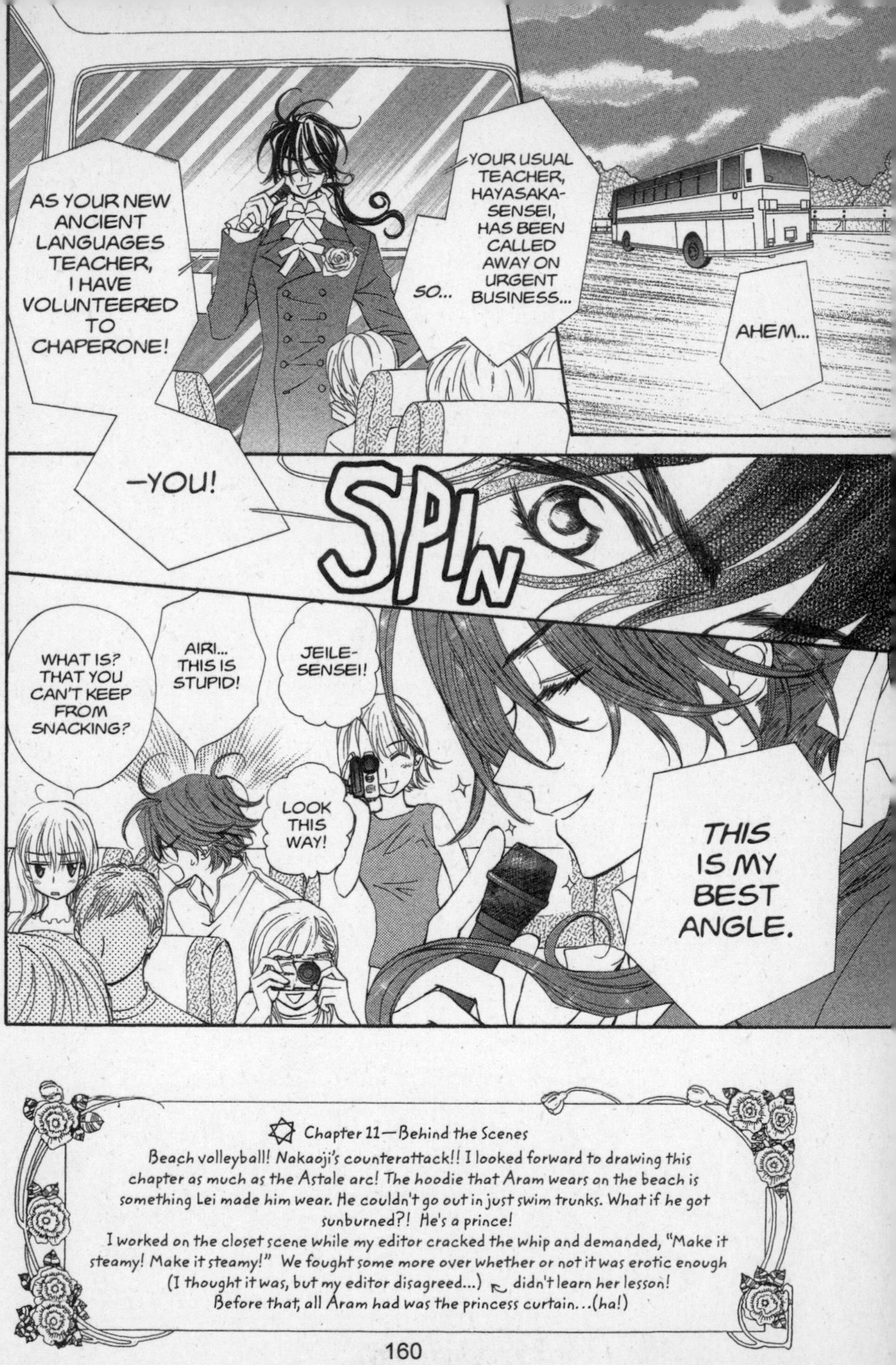
AHEM...
YOUR USUAL TEACHER, HAYASAKA-SENSEI, HAS BEEN CALLED AWAY ON URGENT BUSINESS...
SO...
AS YOUR NEW ANCIENT LANGUAGES TEACHER, I HAVE VOLUNTEERED TO CHAPERONE!
—YOU!
SPIN
THIS IS MY BEST ANGLE.
JEILE-SENSEI!
LOOK THIS WAY!
AIRI... THIS IS STUPID!
WHAT IS? THAT YOU CAN'T KEEP FROM SNACKING?

Chapter 11—Behind the Scenes

Beach volleyball! Nakaoji's counterattack!! I looked forward to drawing this chapter as much as the Astale arc! The hoodie that Aram wears on the beach is something Lei made him wear. He couldn't go out in just swim trunks. What if he got sunburned?! He's a prince!

I worked on the closet scene while my editor cracked the whip and demanded, "Make it steamy! Make it steamy!" We fought some more over whether or not it was erotic enough (I thought it was, but my editor disagreed...) ← didn't learn her lesson! Before that, all Aram had was the princess curtain...(ha!)

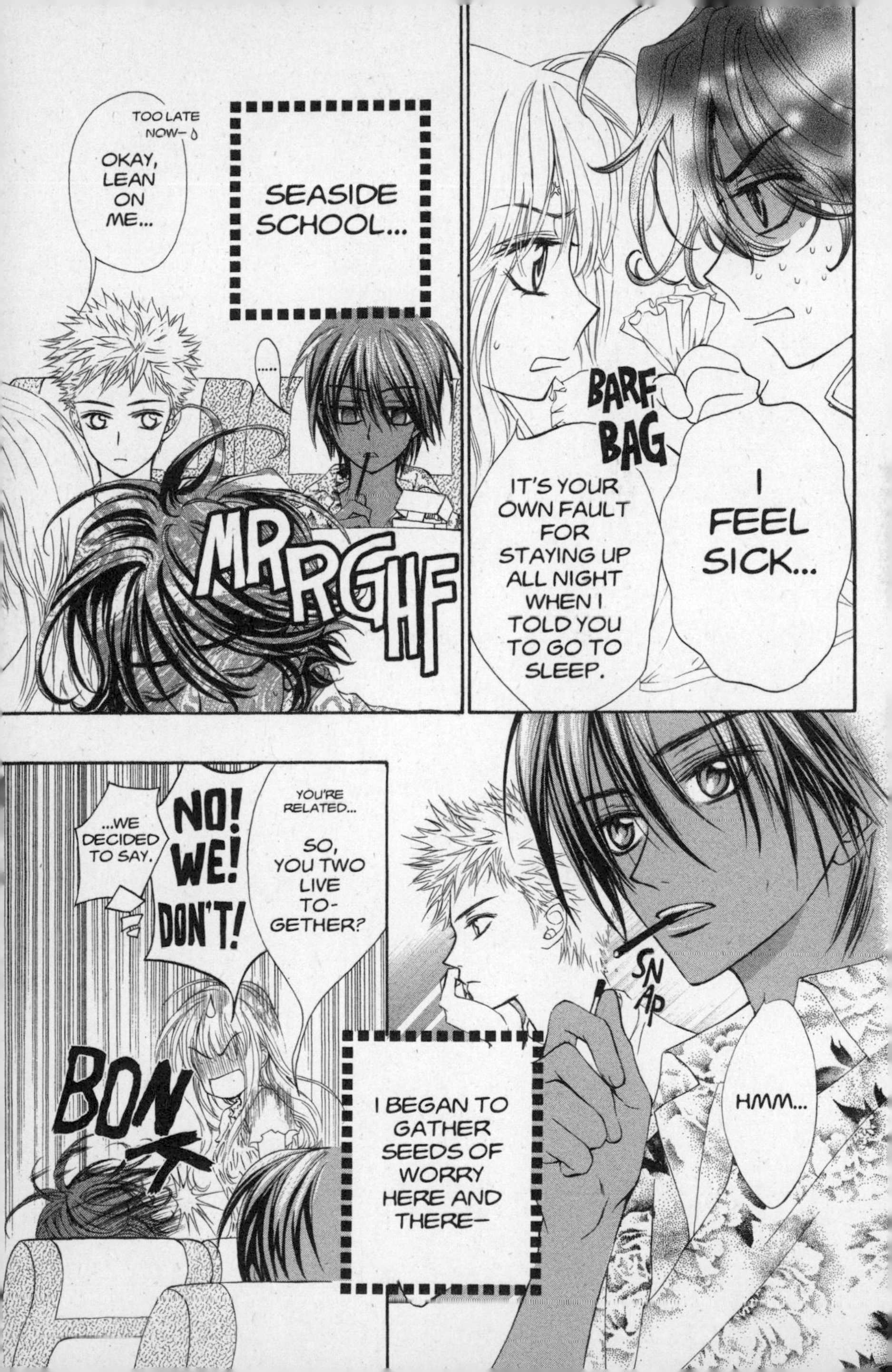
BARF BAG
I FEEL SICK...
IT'S YOUR OWN FAULT FOR STAYING UP ALL NIGHT WHEN I TOLD YOU TO GO TO SLEEP.
SEASIDE SCHOOL...
TOO LATE NOW–
OKAY, LEAN ON ME...
.....
MRRGHF
HMM...
SNAP
I BEGAN TO GATHER SEEDS OF WORRY HERE AND THERE–
YOU'RE RELATED...
SO, YOU TWO LIVE TO-GETHER?
NO! WE! DON'T!
...WE DECIDED TO SAY.
BON

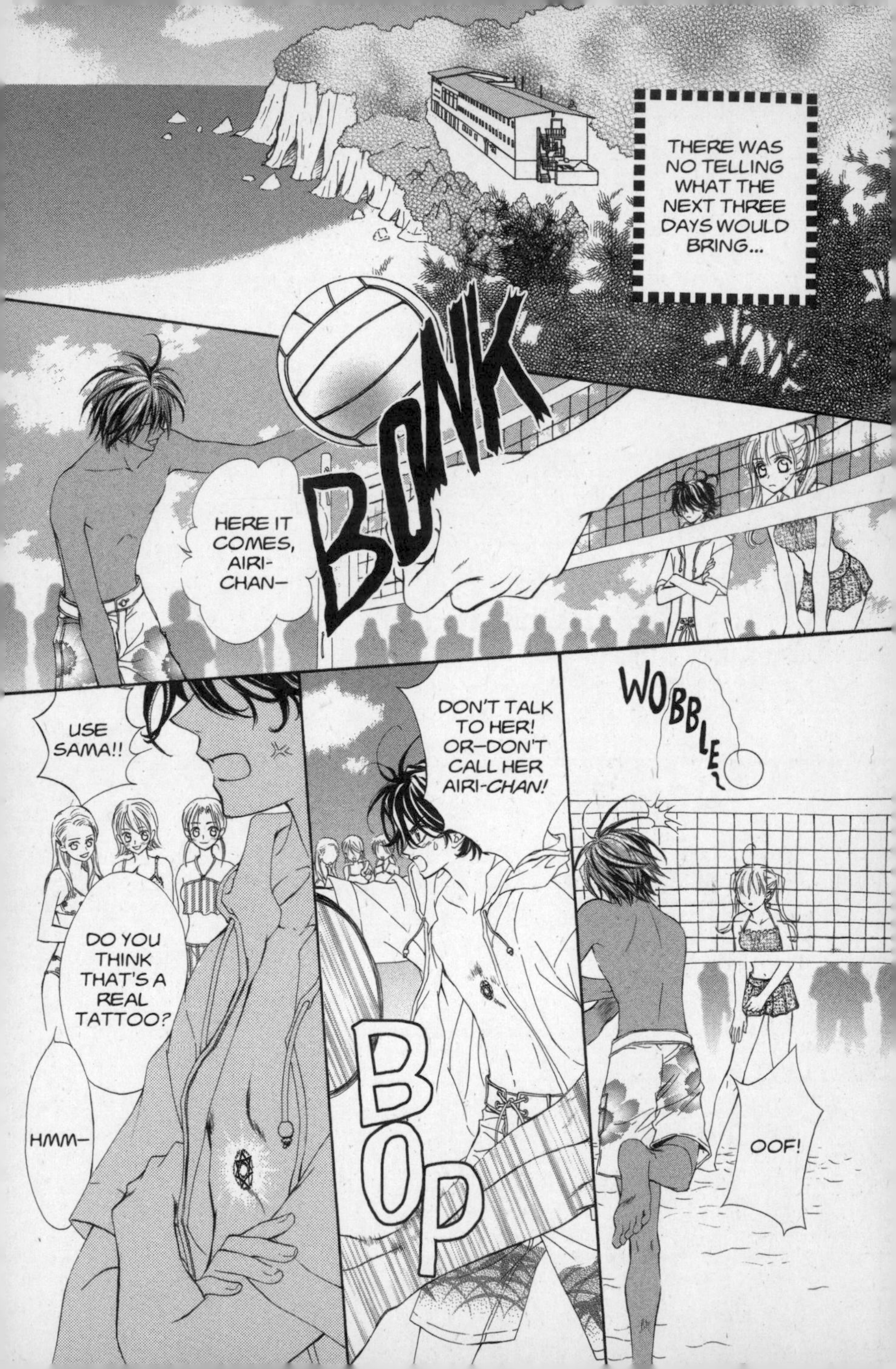
THERE WAS NO TELLING WHAT THE NEXT THREE DAYS WOULD BRING...
HERE IT COMES, AIRI-CHAN—
BONK
WOBBLE
OOF!
DON'T TALK TO HER! OR—DON'T CALL HER AIRI-*CHAN*!
BOP
USE SAMA!!
DO YOU THINK THAT'S A REAL TATTOO?
HMM—

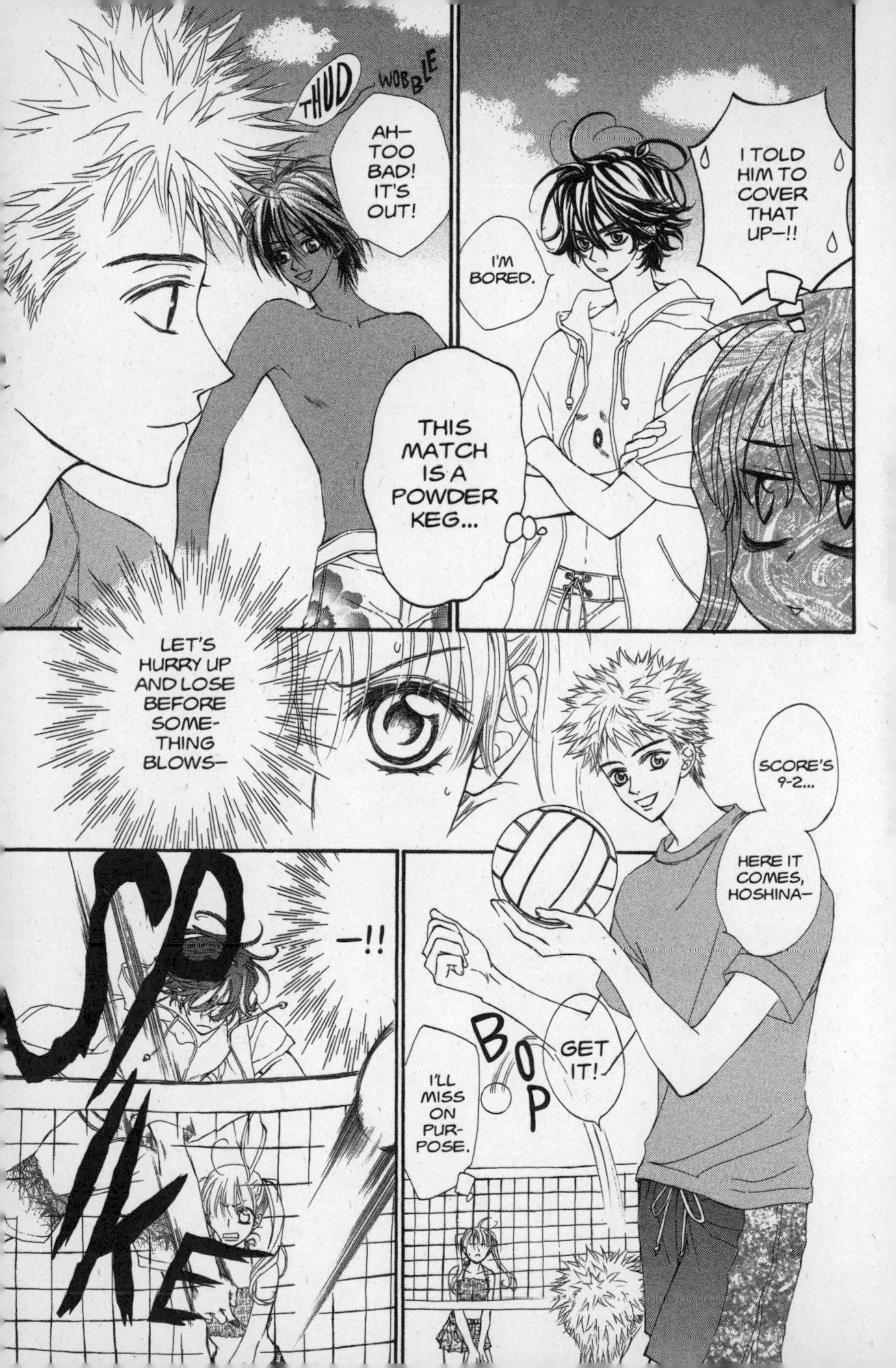
I TOLD HIM TO COVER THAT UP—!!
I'M BORED.
THIS MATCH IS A POWDER KEG...
THUD
WOBBLE
AH— TOO BAD! IT'S OUT!
LET'S HURRY UP AND LOSE BEFORE SOMETHING BLOWS—
SCORE'S 9-2...
HERE IT COMES, HOSHINA—
GET IT!
BOP
I'LL MISS ON PURPOSE.
—!!
SPIKE

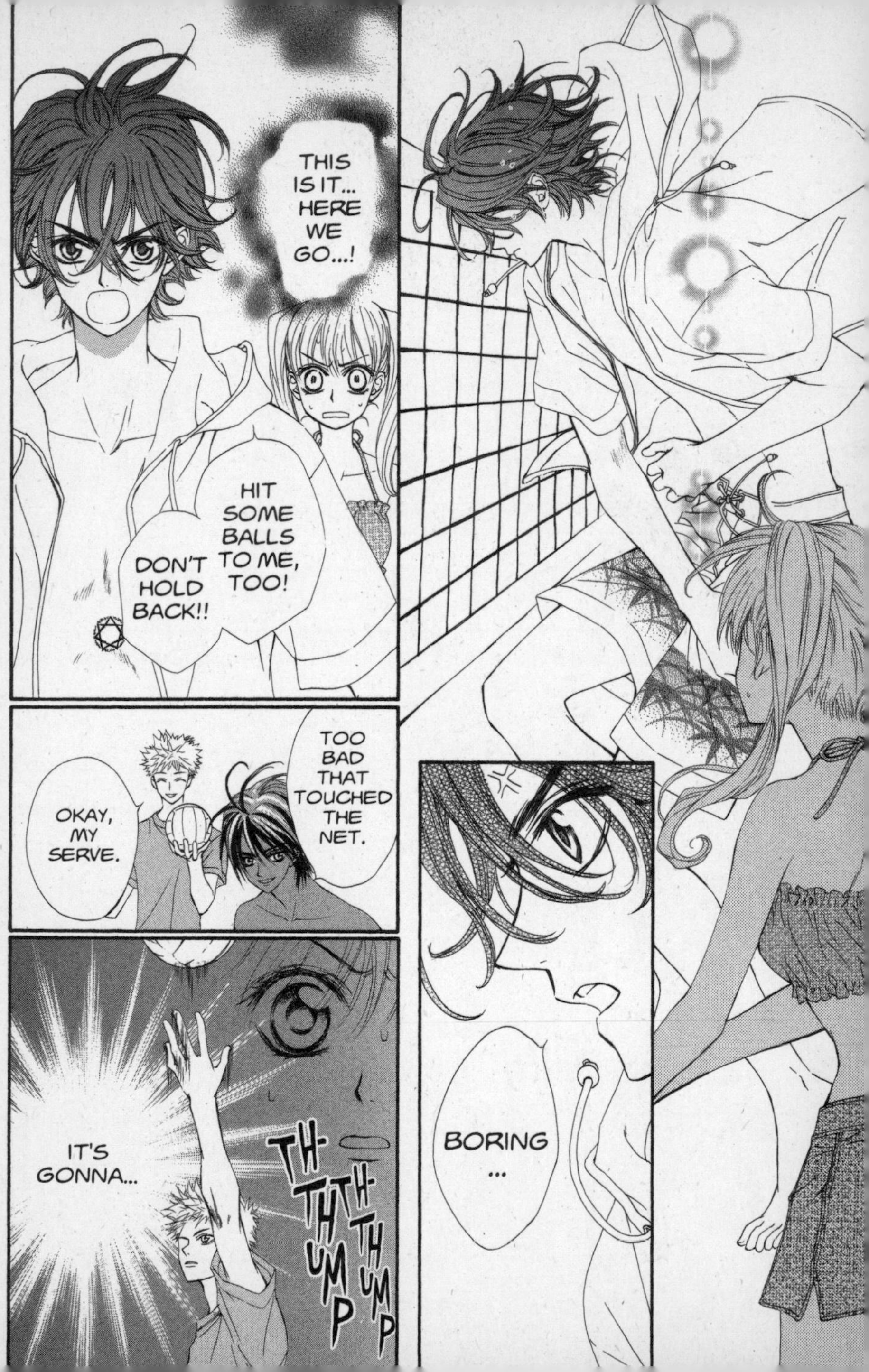
BORING ...
THIS IS IT... HERE WE GO...!
HIT SOME BALLS TO ME, TOO!
DON'T HOLD BACK!!
TOO BAD THAT TOUCHED THE NET.
OKAY, MY SERVE.
IT'S GONNA...
THTHTHUMP THTHTHUMP

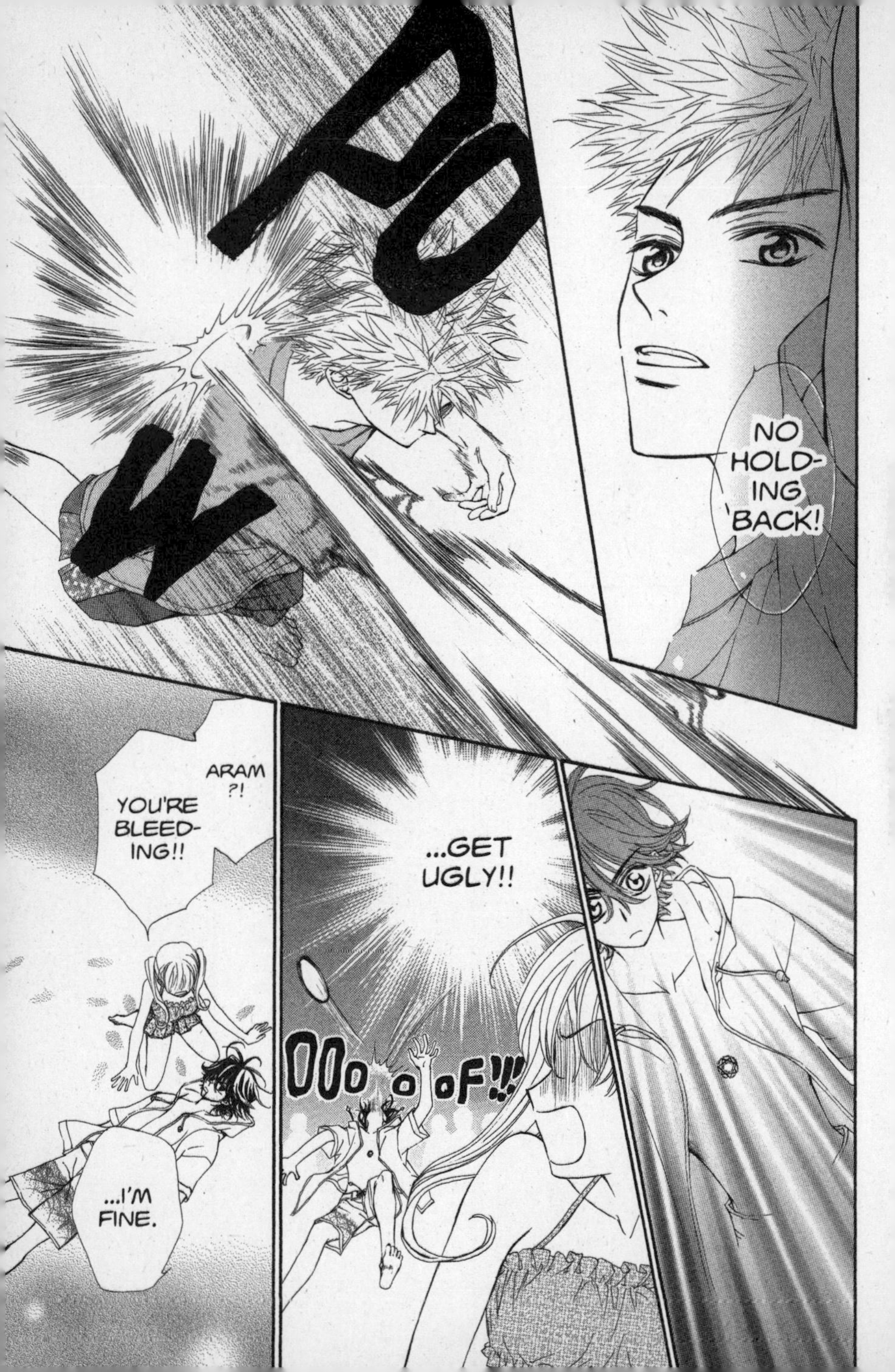
NO HOLDING-ING BACK!
POW
...GET UGLY!!
OOOOOF!!!
ARAM ?!
YOU'RE BLEEDING!!
...I'M FINE.

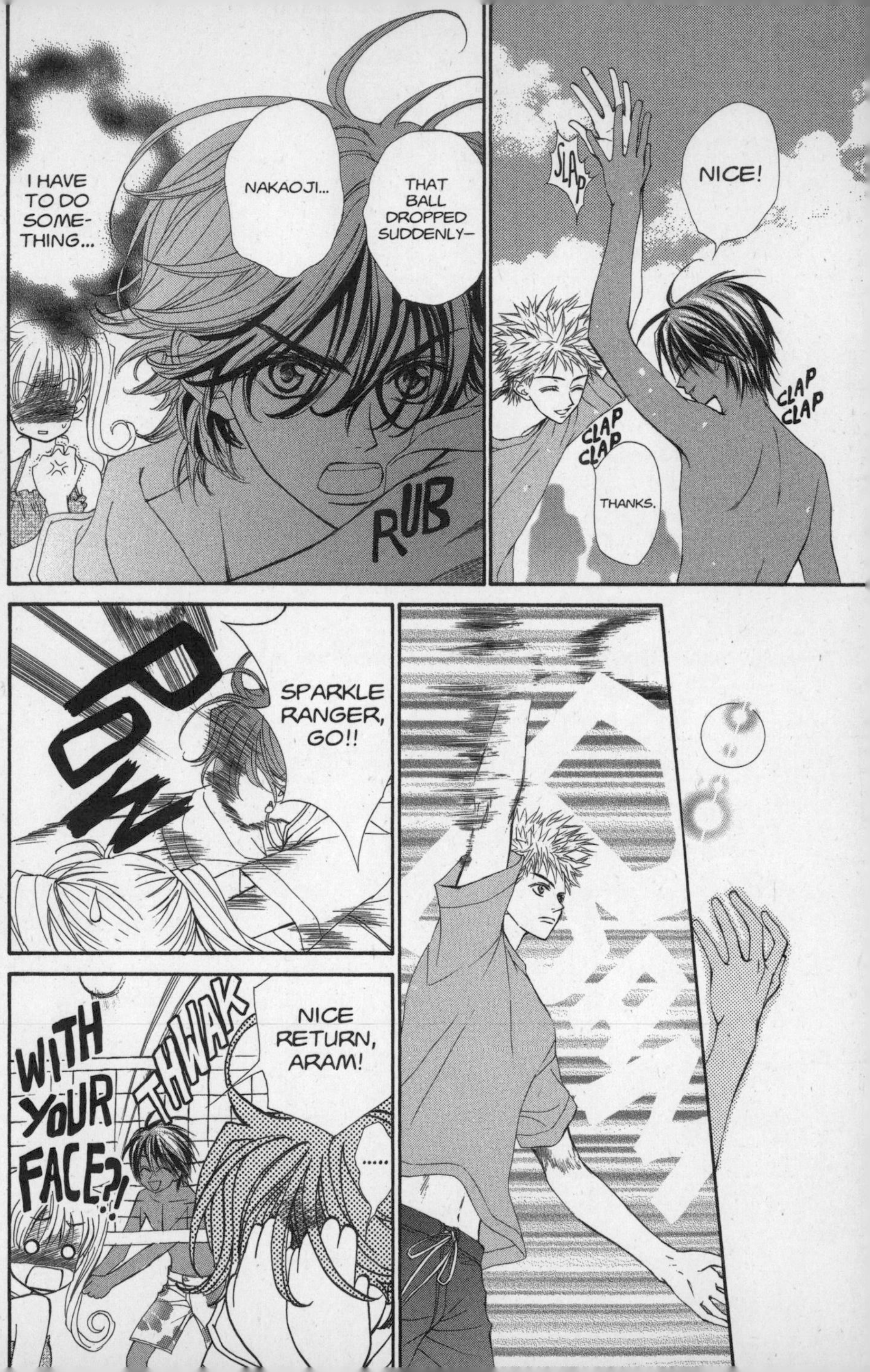
SLAP
NICE!
CLAP CLAP
CLAP CLAP
THANKS.
NAKAOJI...
THAT BALL DROPPED SUDDENLY—
I HAVE TO DO SOME-THING...
RUB
SPARKLE RANGER, GO!!
POW
NICE RETURN, ARAM!
THWAK
WITH YOUR FACE?!
......

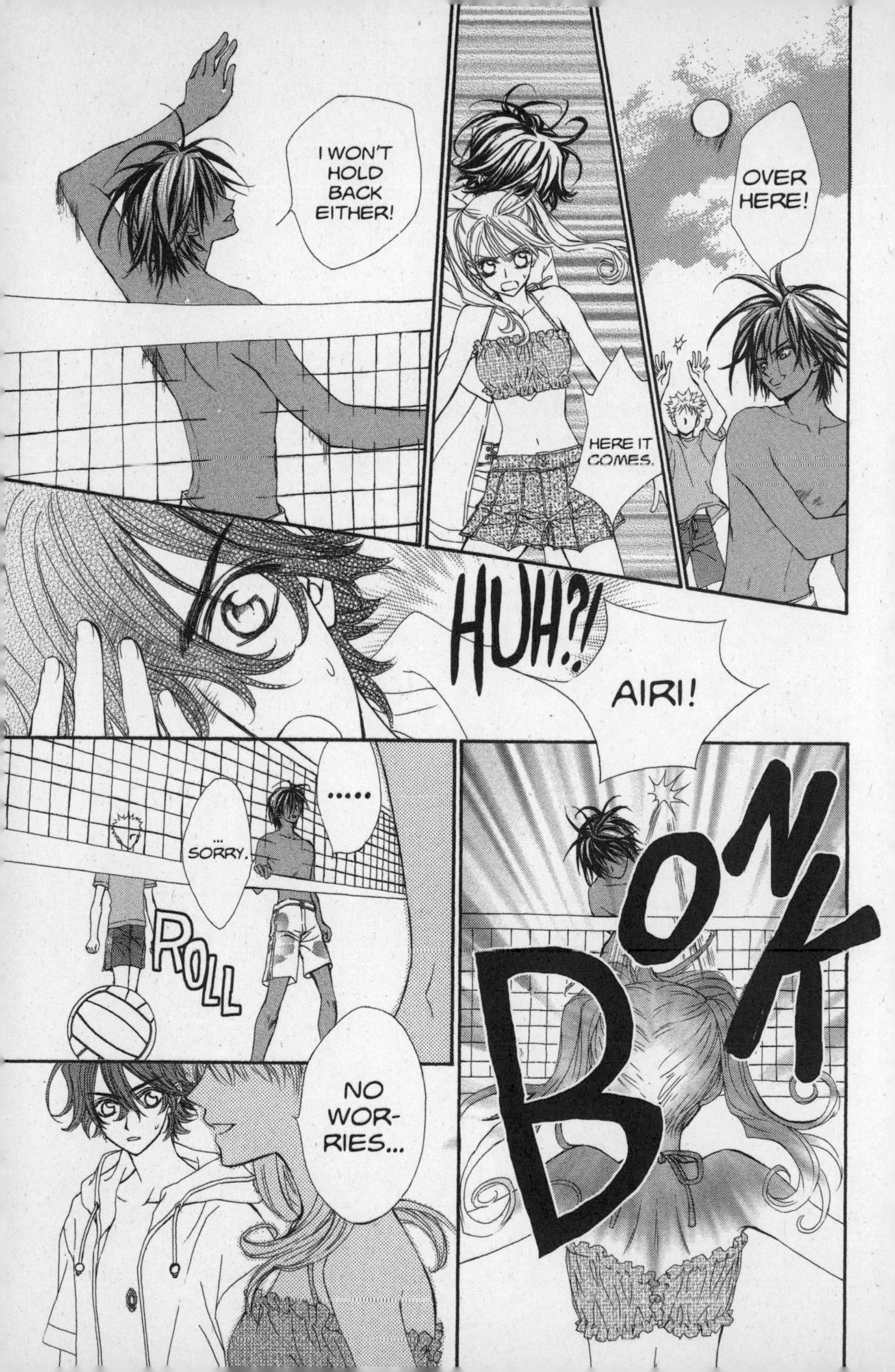
OVER HERE!
HERE IT COMES.
I WON'T HOLD BACK EITHER!
HUH?!
AIRI!
BONK
.....
...SORRY.
ROLL
NO WORRIES...

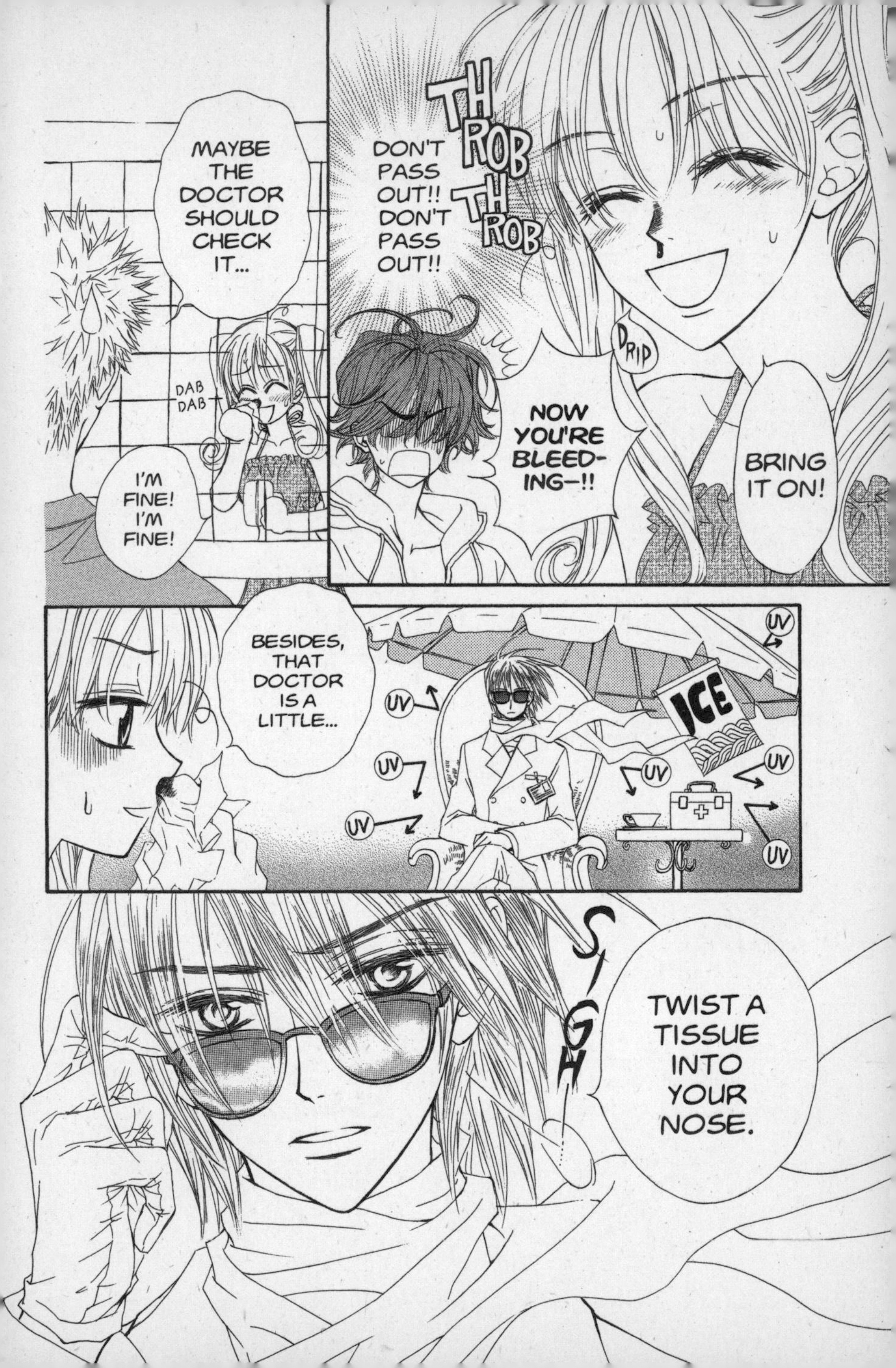
THROB THROB
DON'T PASS OUT!! DON'T PASS OUT!!
DRIP
BRING IT ON!
NOW YOU'RE BLEEDING–!!
MAYBE THE DOCTOR SHOULD CHECK IT...
DAB DAB
I'M FINE! I'M FINE!
UV
ICE
BESIDES, THAT DOCTOR IS A LITTLE...
SIGH
TWIST A TISSUE INTO YOUR NOSE.

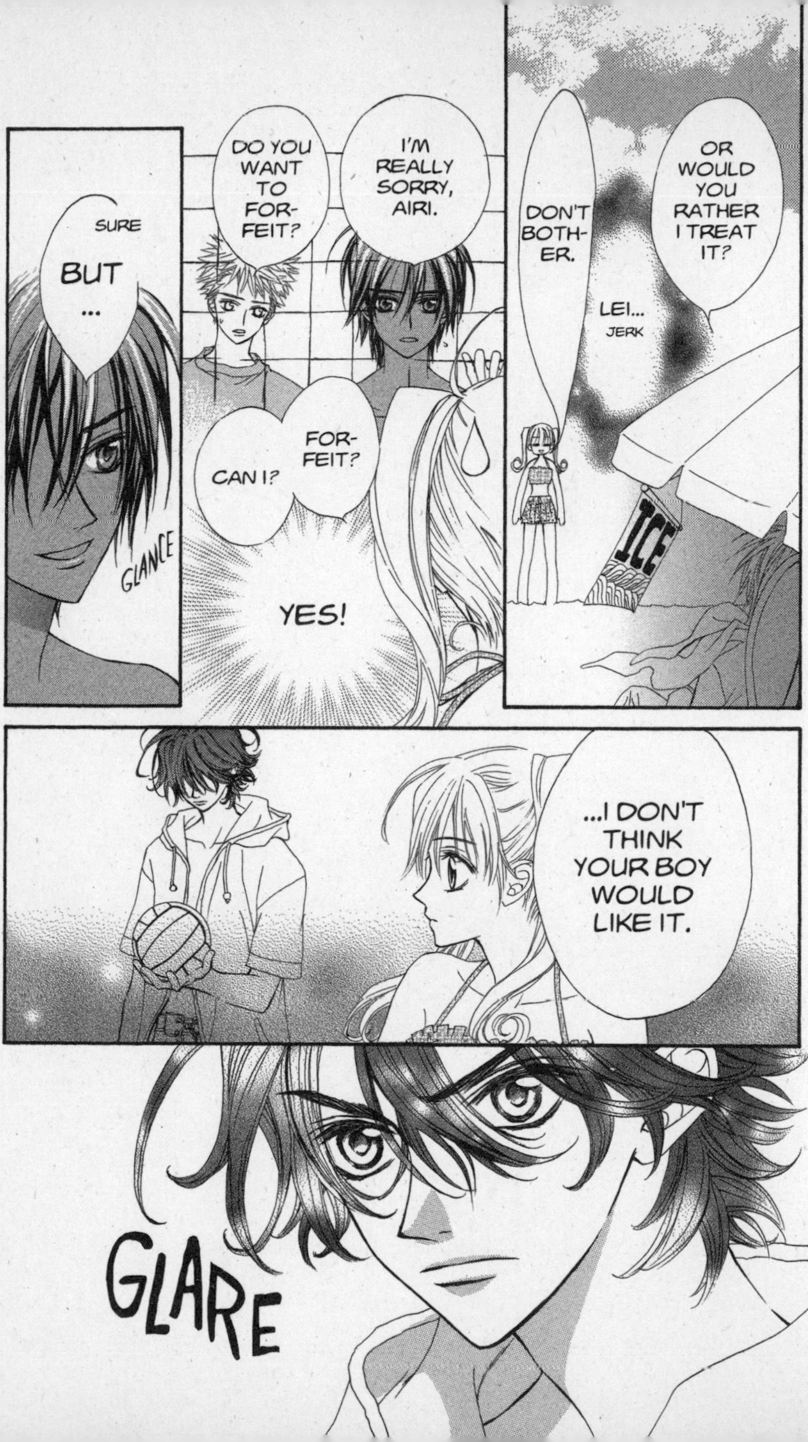
OR WOULD YOU RATHER I TREAT IT?
DON'T BOTH-ER.
LEI... JERK
I'M REALLY SORRY, AIRI.
DO YOU WANT TO FOR-FEIT?
FOR-FEIT?
CAN I?
YES!
SURE BUT ...
GLANCE
...I DON'T THINK YOUR BOY WOULD LIKE IT.
GLARE

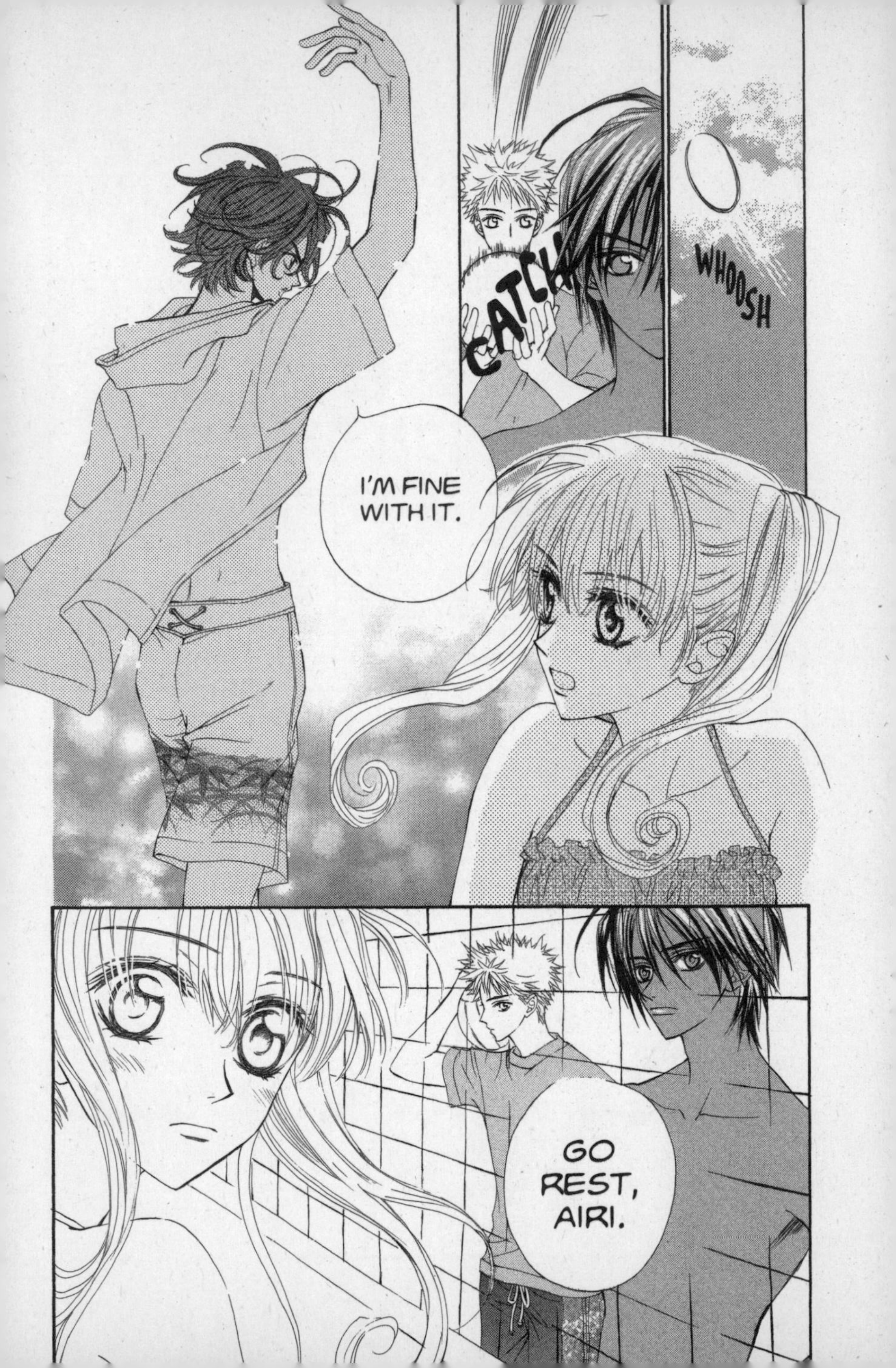
WHOOSH
CATCH
I'M FINE WITH IT.
GO REST, AIRI.

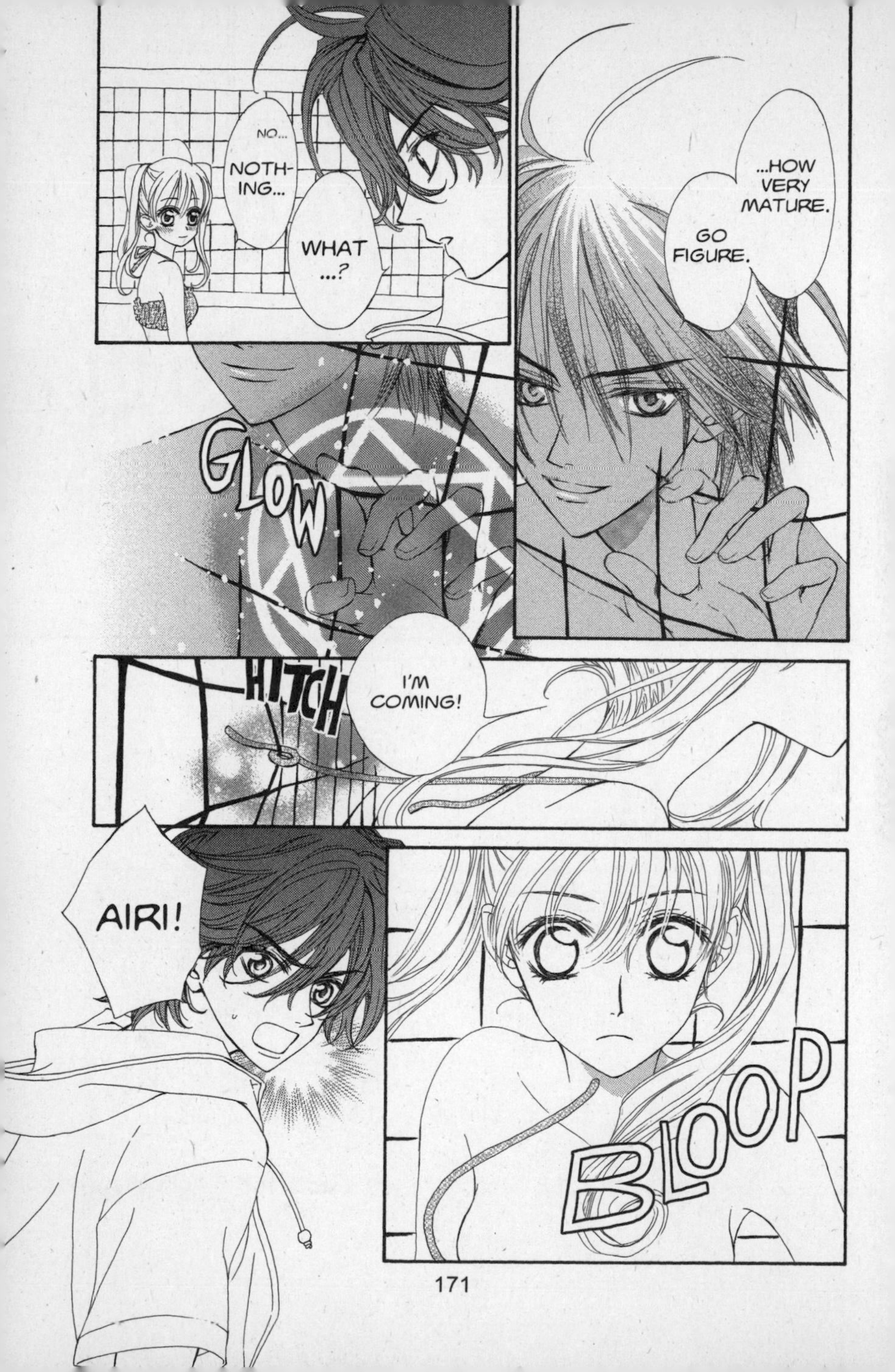
...HOW VERY MATURE.
GO FIGURE.
WHAT ...?
NO... NOTHING...
GLOW
I'M COMING!
HITCH
BLOOP
AIRI!

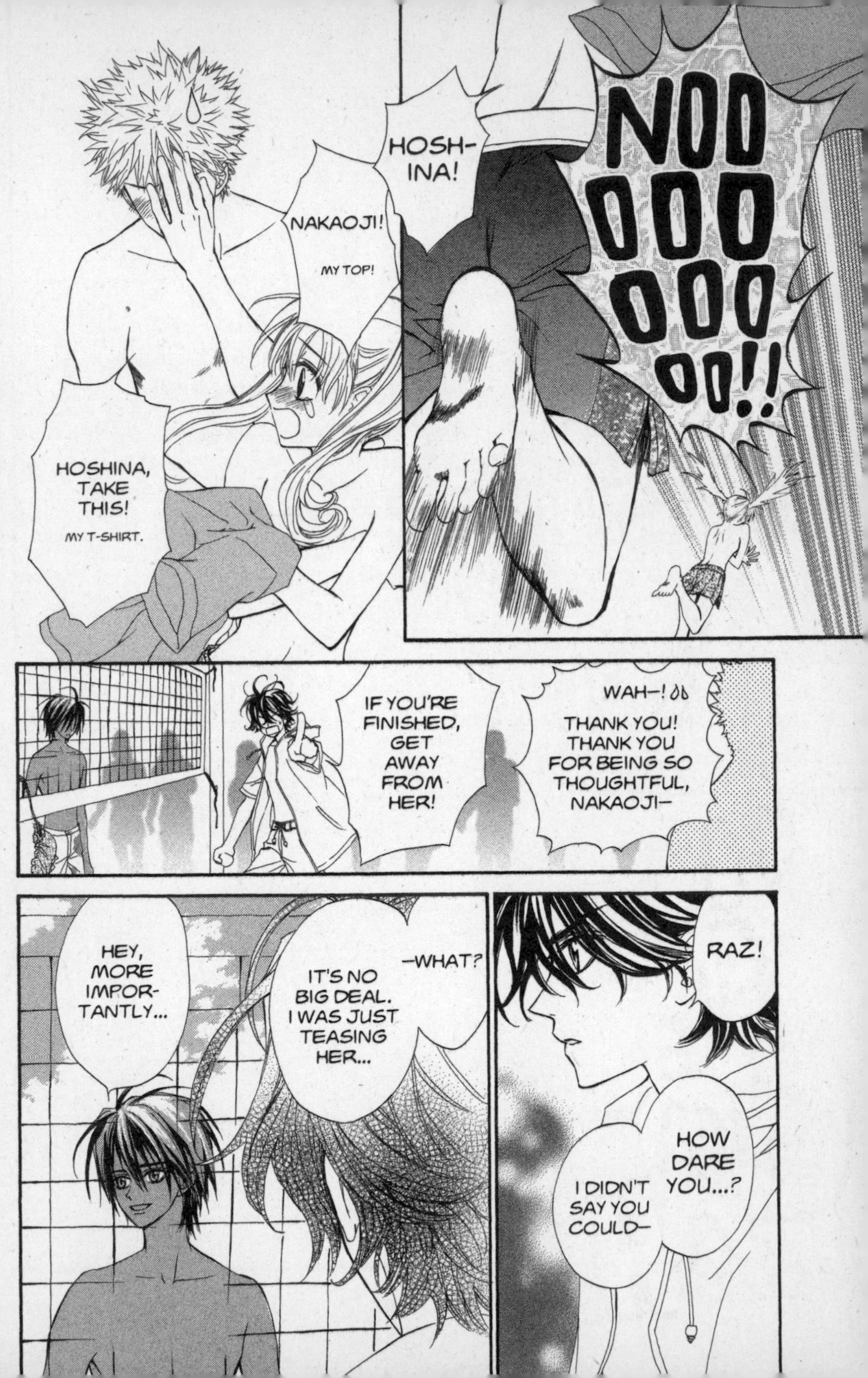
NOOOOOOOOOOOOOO!!
HOSH-INA!
NAKAOJI!
MY TOP!
HOSHINA, TAKE THIS!
MY T-SHIRT.
WAH-!
THANK YOU! THANK YOU FOR BEING SO THOUGHTFUL, NAKAOJI-
IF YOU'RE FINISHED, GET AWAY FROM HER!
RAZ!
HOW DARE YOU...?
I DIDN'T SAY YOU COULD-
-WHAT?
IT'S NO BIG DEAL. I WAS JUST TEASING HER...
HEY, MORE IMPOR-TANTLY...

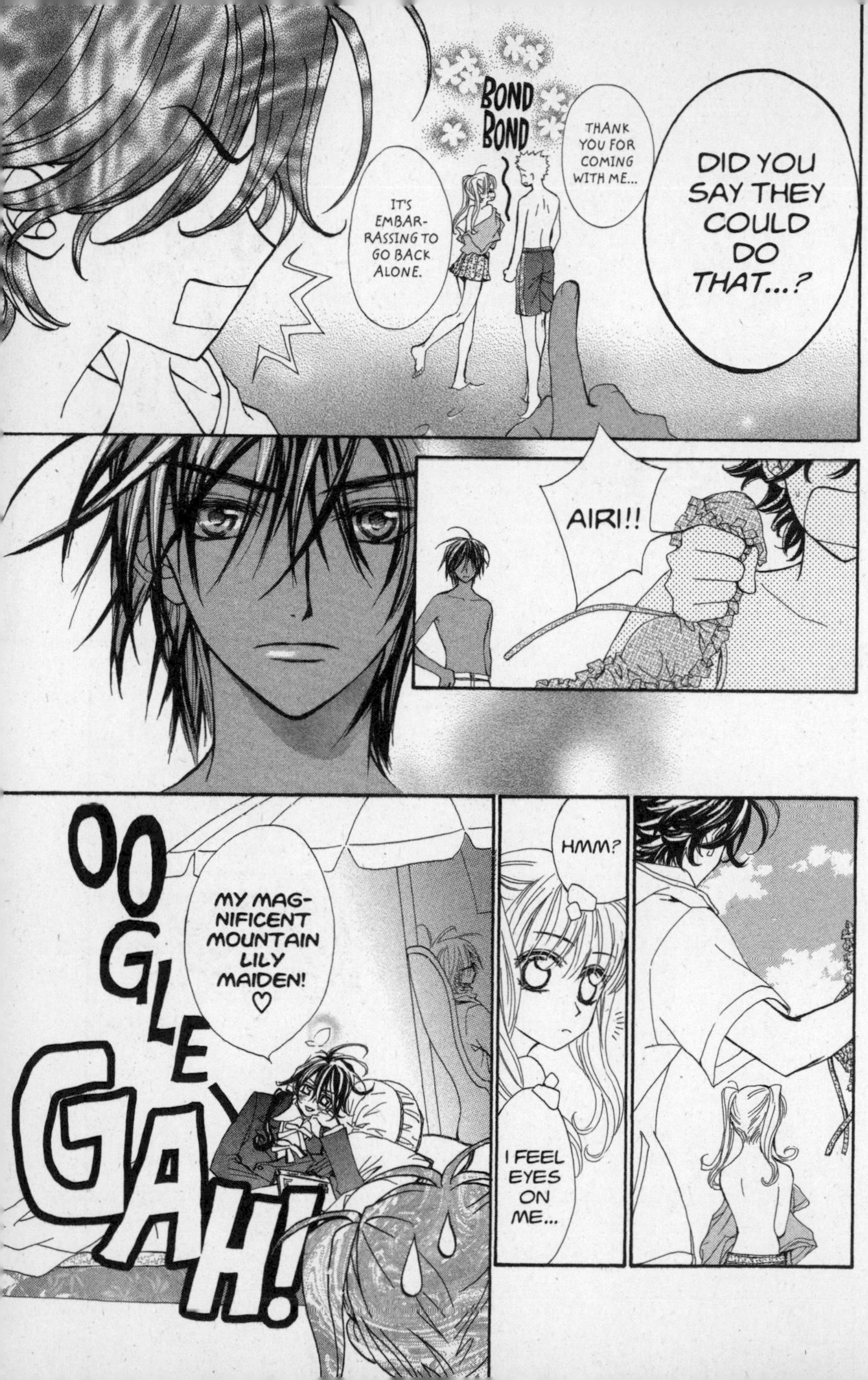
DID YOU SAY THEY COULD DO THAT...?
THANK YOU FOR COMING WITH ME...
BOND BOND
IT'S EMBAR-RASSING TO GO BACK ALONE.
AIRI!!
HMM?
I FEEL EYES ON ME...
MY MAG-NIFICENT MOUNTAIN LILY MAIDEN! ♡
OOGLEY GAH!

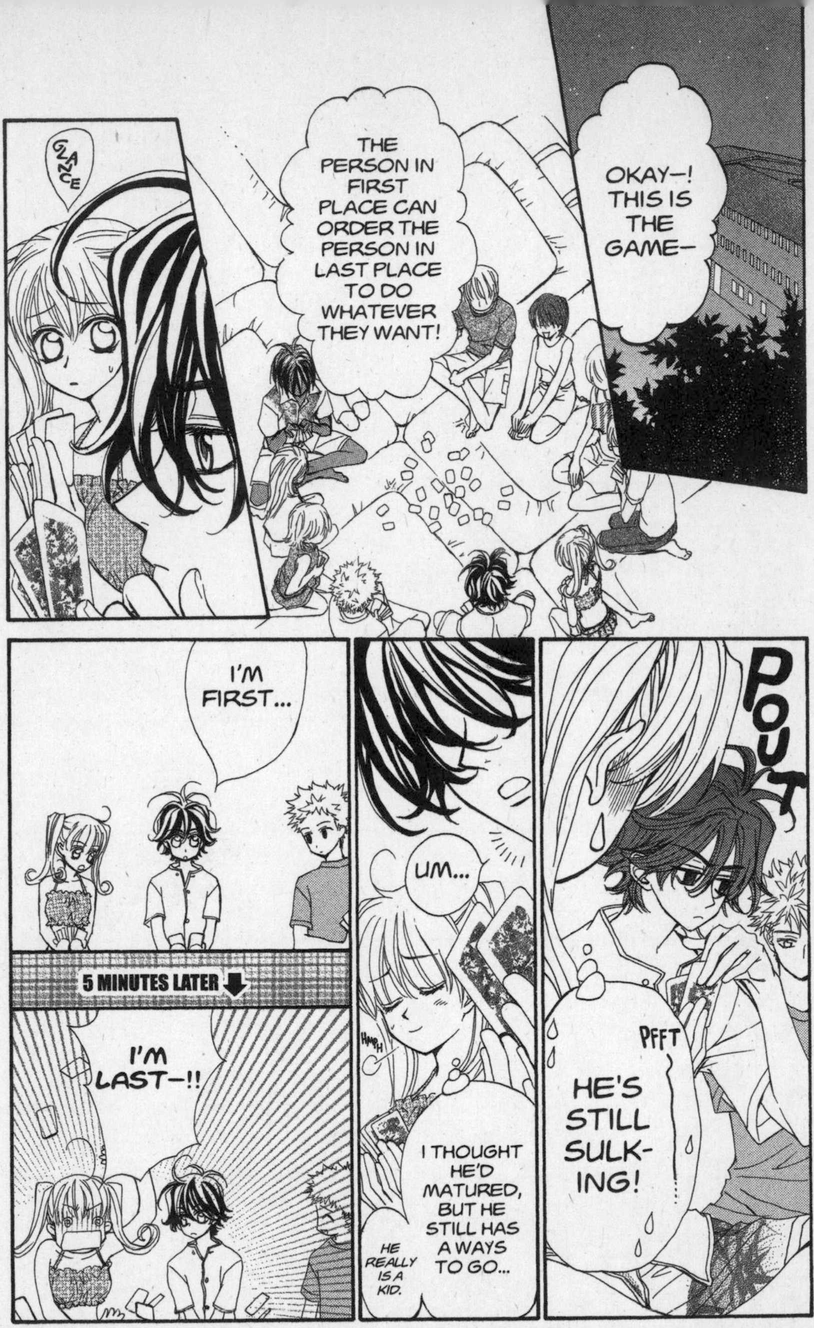
OKAY—! THIS IS THE GAME—
THE PERSON IN FIRST PLACE CAN ORDER THE PERSON IN LAST PLACE TO DO WHATEVER THEY WANT!
GLANCE
POUT
PFFT
HE'S STILL SULKING!
UM...
HMPH
I THOUGHT HE'D MATURED, BUT HE STILL HAS A WAYS TO GO...
HE REALLY IS A KID.
I'M FIRST...
5 MINUTES LATER
I'M LAST—!!

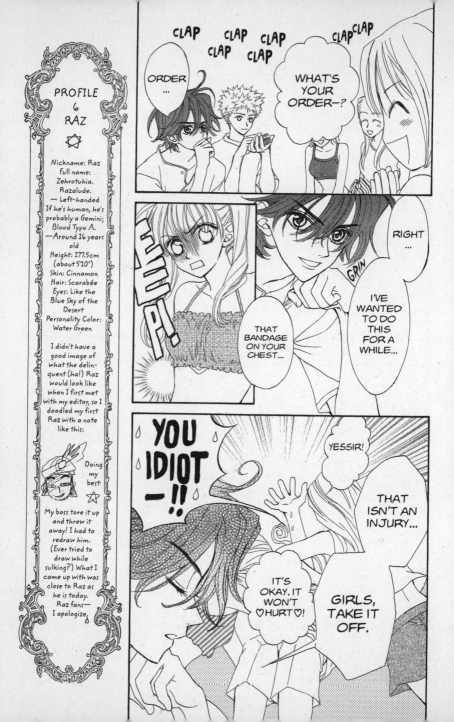

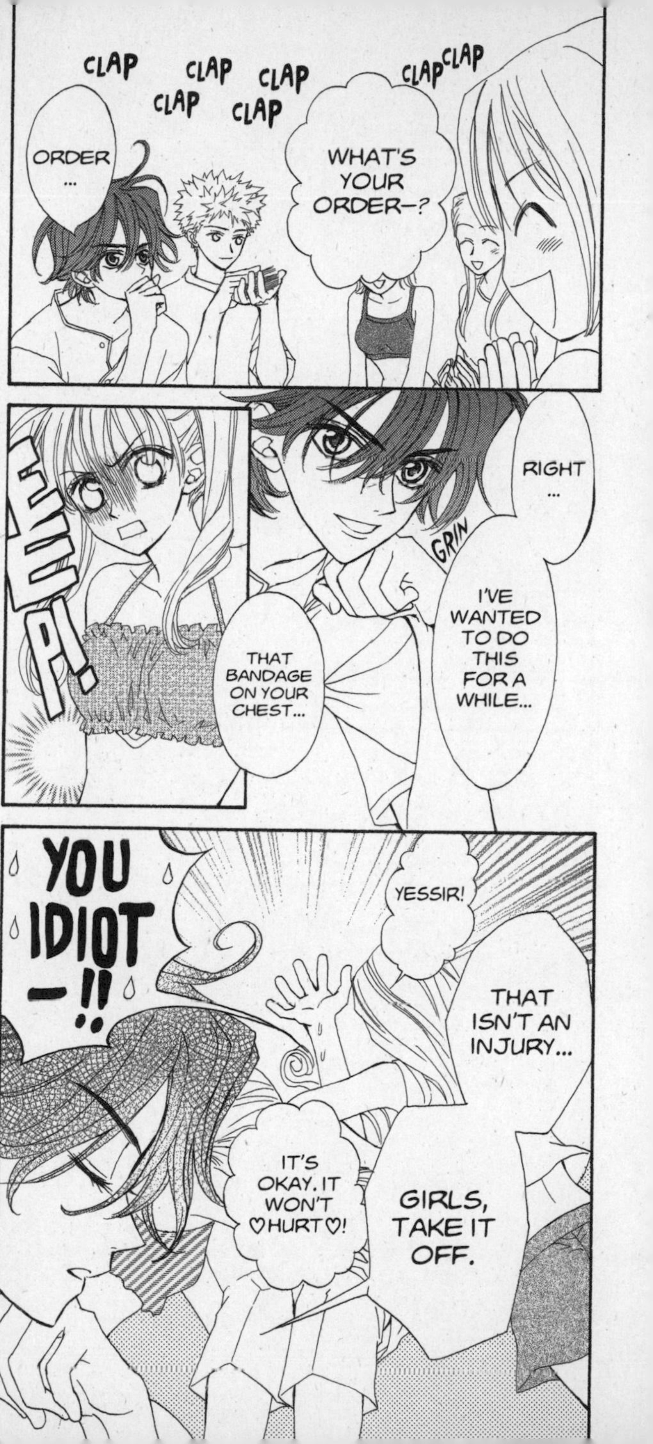
CLAP CLAP
WHAT'S YOUR ORDER—?
CLAP CLAP
CLAP CLAP
ORDER ...
RIGHT ...
GRIN
I'VE WANTED TO DO THIS FOR A WHILE...
THAT BANDAGE ON YOUR CHEST...
FLIP!
YESSIR!
THAT ISN'T AN INJURY...
GIRLS, TAKE IT OFF.
IT'S OKAY. IT WON'T ♡HURT♡!
YOU IDIOT—!!

PROFILE 6 RAZ

☆

Nickname: Raz
Full name: Zehrotuhia. Razalude.
— Left-handed
If he's human, he's probably a Gemini; Blood Type A.
—Around 16 years old
Height: 177.5cm (about 5'10")
Skin: Cinnamon
Hair: Scarabée
Eyes: Like the Blue Sky of the Desert
Personality Color: Water Green

I didn't have a good image of what the delinquent (ha!) Raz would look like when I first met with my editor, so I doodled my first Raz with a note like this:

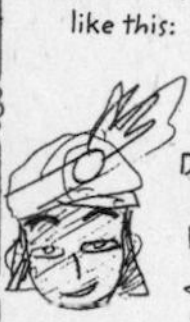
Doing my best

My boss tore it up and threw it away! I had to redraw him. (Ever tried to draw while sulking?) What I came up with was close to Raz as he is today. Raz fans— I apologize.

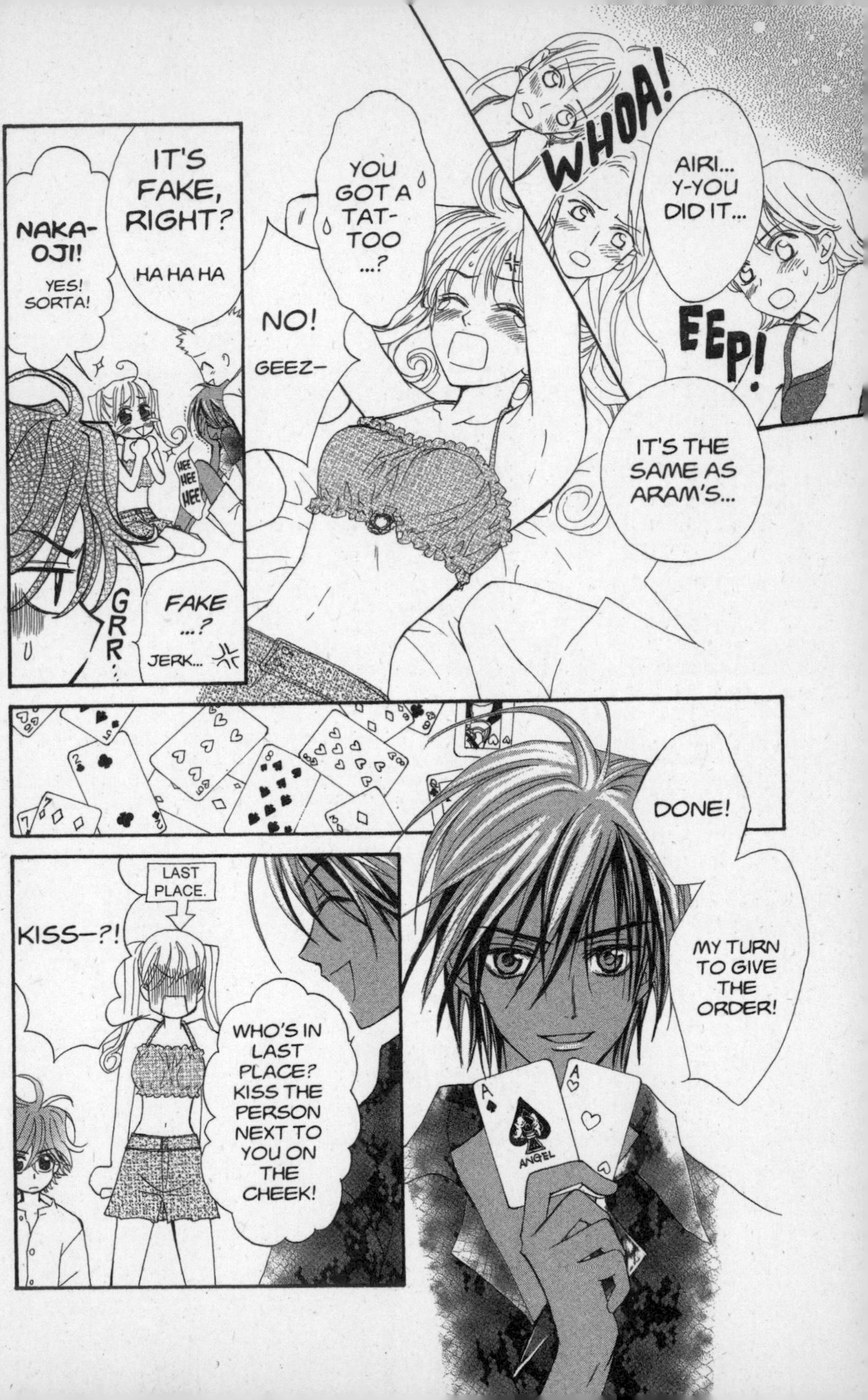
WHOA!
AIRI... Y-YOU DID IT...
EEP!
IT'S THE SAME AS ARAM'S...
YOU GOT A TAT-TOO ...?
NO!
GEEZ–
IT'S FAKE, RIGHT?
HA HA HA
NAKA-OJI!
YES! SORTA!
HEE HEE HEE
FAKE ...?
JERK...
GRR...
DONE!
MY TURN TO GIVE THE ORDER!
WHO'S IN LAST PLACE? KISS THE PERSON NEXT TO YOU ON THE CHEEK!
LAST PLACE.
KISS–?!

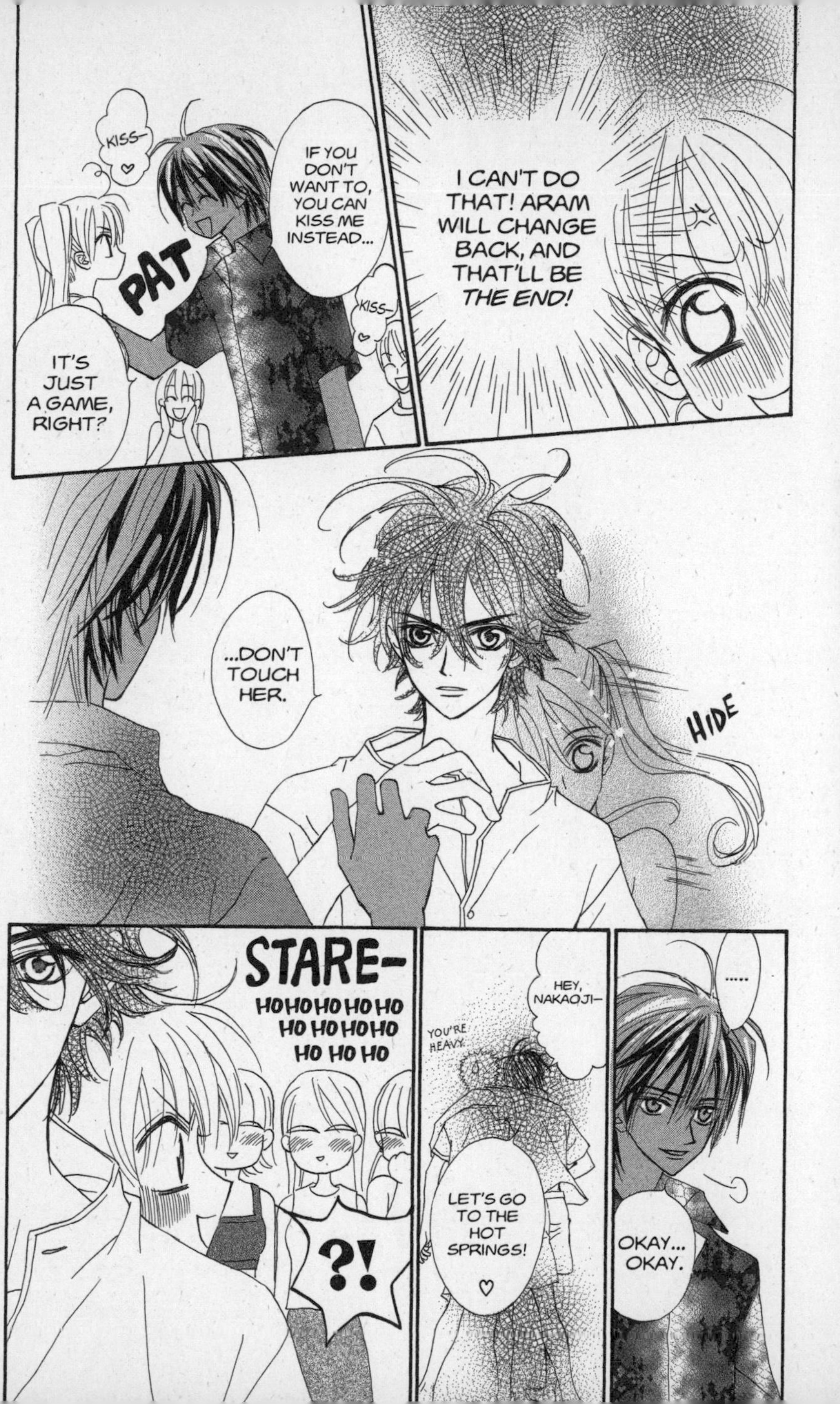
I CAN'T DO THAT! ARAM WILL CHANGE BACK, AND THAT'LL BE THE END!
IF YOU DON'T WANT TO, YOU CAN KISS ME INSTEAD...
KISS– ♡
PAT
KISS– ♡
IT'S JUST A GAME, RIGHT?
...DON'T TOUCH HER.
HIDE
......
OKAY... OKAY.
HEY, NAKAOJI–
YOU'RE HEAVY.
LET'S GO TO THE HOT SPRINGS! ♡
STARE–
HO HO HO HO HO HO HO HO HO HO HO HO HO
?!

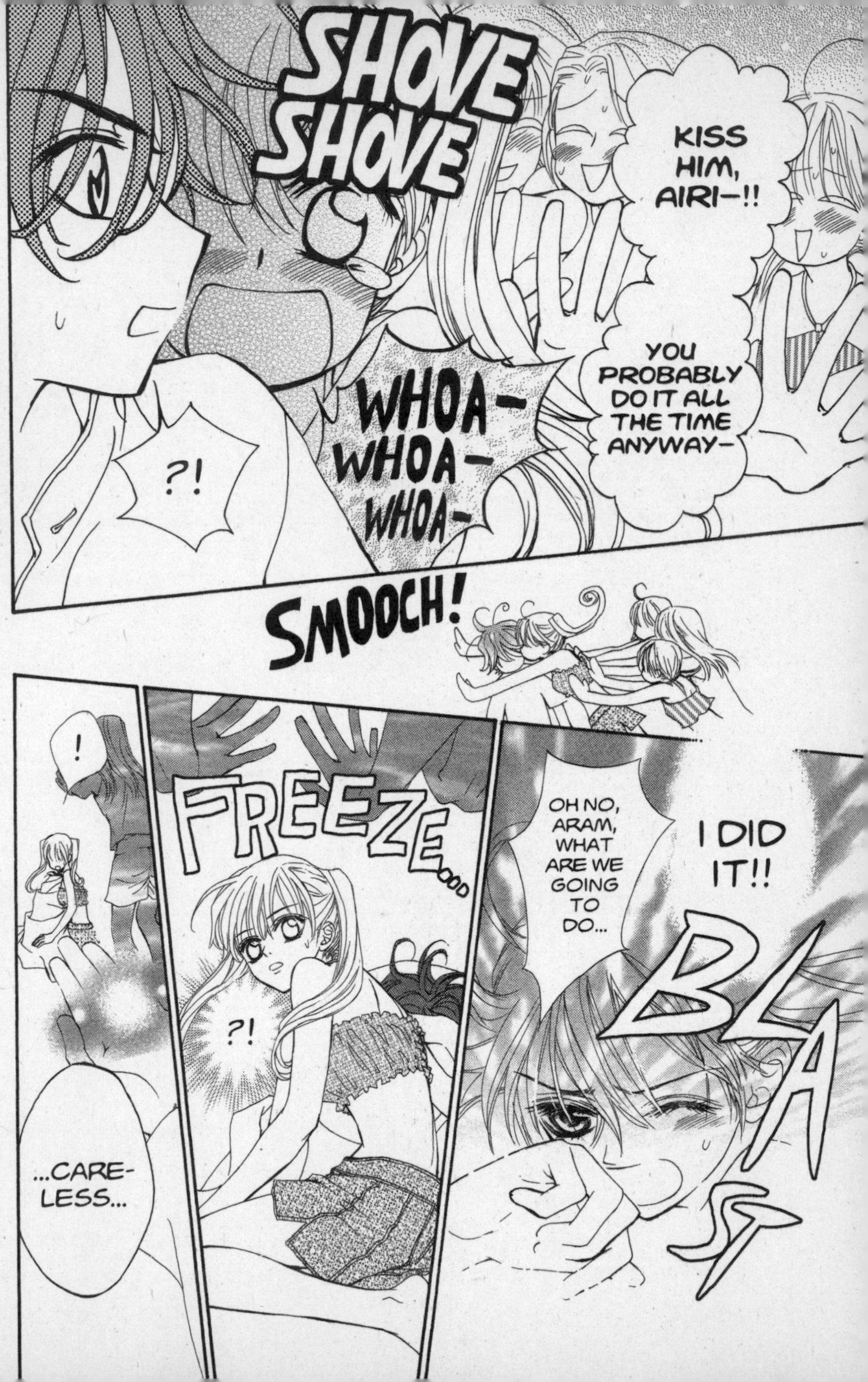
KISS HIM, AIRI—!!
YOU PROBABLY DO IT ALL THE TIME ANYWAY—
SHOVE SHOVE
WHOA- WHOA- WHOA-
?!
SMOOCH!
OH NO, ARAM, WHAT ARE WE GOING TO DO...
I DID IT!!
BLAST
FREEZE
?!
!
...CARE-LESS...

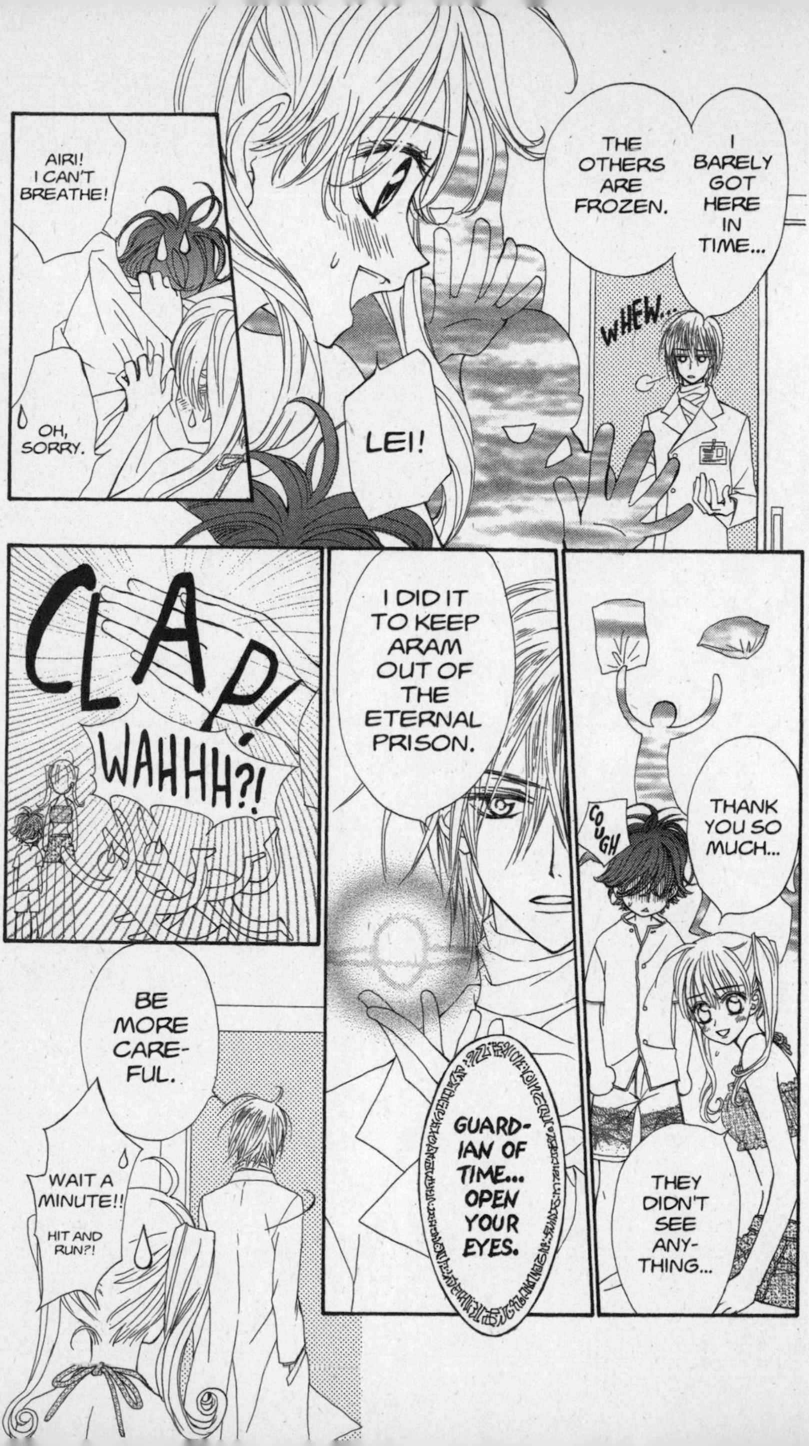
WHEW...
I BARELY GOT HERE IN TIME...
THE OTHERS ARE FROZEN.
LEI!
AIRI! I CAN'T BREATHE!
OH, SORRY.
THANK YOU SO MUCH...
COUGH
THEY DIDN'T SEE ANY-THING...
I DID IT TO KEEP ARAM OUT OF THE ETERNAL PRISON.
GUARD-IAN OF TIME... OPEN YOUR EYES.
CLAP!
WAHHH?!
BE MORE CARE-FUL.
WAIT A MINUTE!!
HIT AND RUN?!

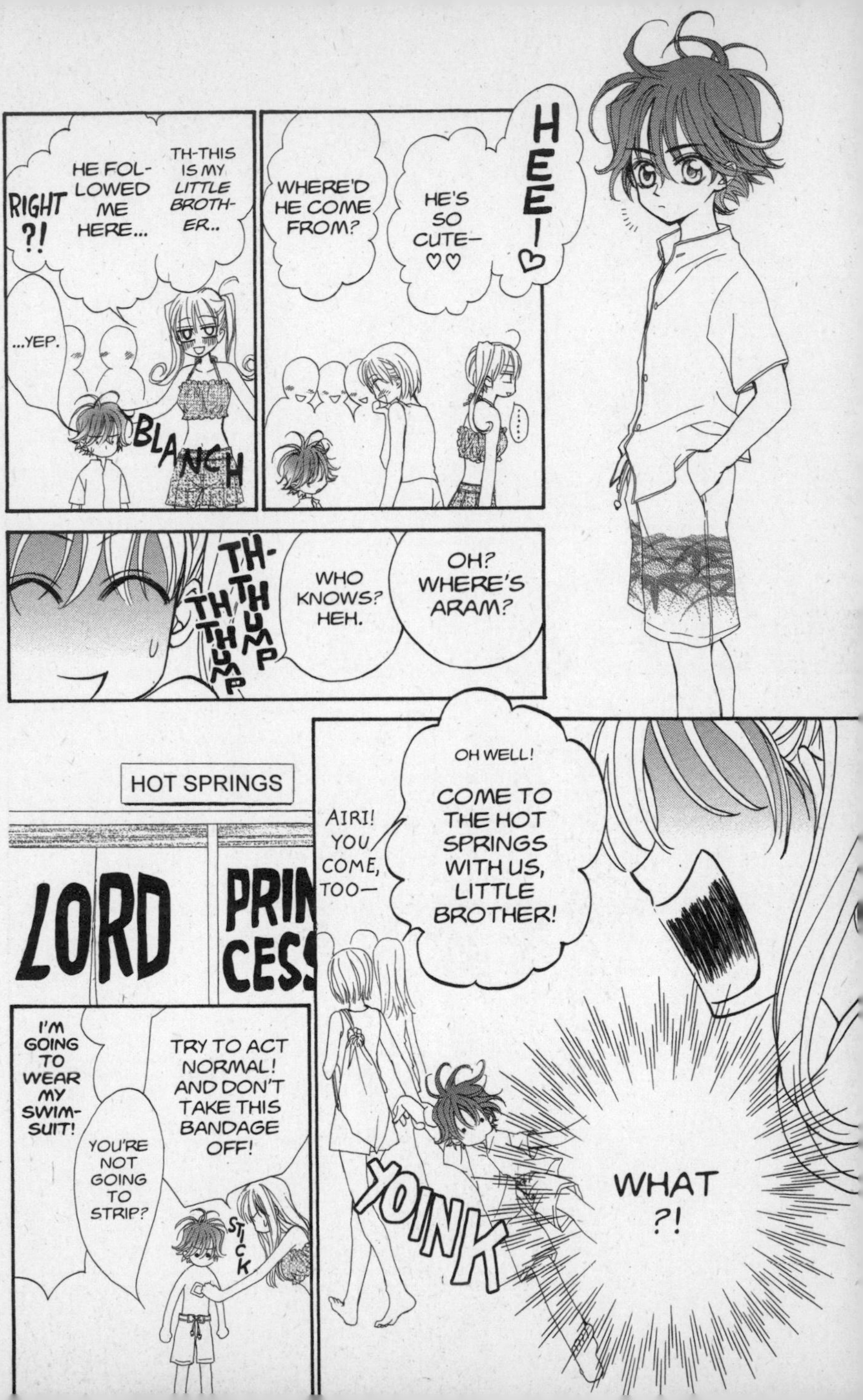
HEE!♡
HE'S SO CUTE-♡♡
WHERE'D HE COME FROM?
TH-THIS IS MY LITTLE BROTHER...
HE FOL-LOWED ME HERE...
RIGHT?!
...YEP.
BLANCH
OH? WHERE'S ARAM?
WHO KNOWS? HEH.
TH-THUMP
TH-THUMP
OH WELL!
COME TO THE HOT SPRINGS WITH US, LITTLE BROTHER!
AIRI! YOU COME, TOO—
WHAT?!
YOINK
HOT SPRINGS
LORD
PRINCESS
TRY TO ACT NORMAL! AND DON'T TAKE THIS BANDAGE OFF!
I'M GOING TO WEAR MY SWIM-SUIT!
YOU'RE NOT GOING TO STRIP?
STICK

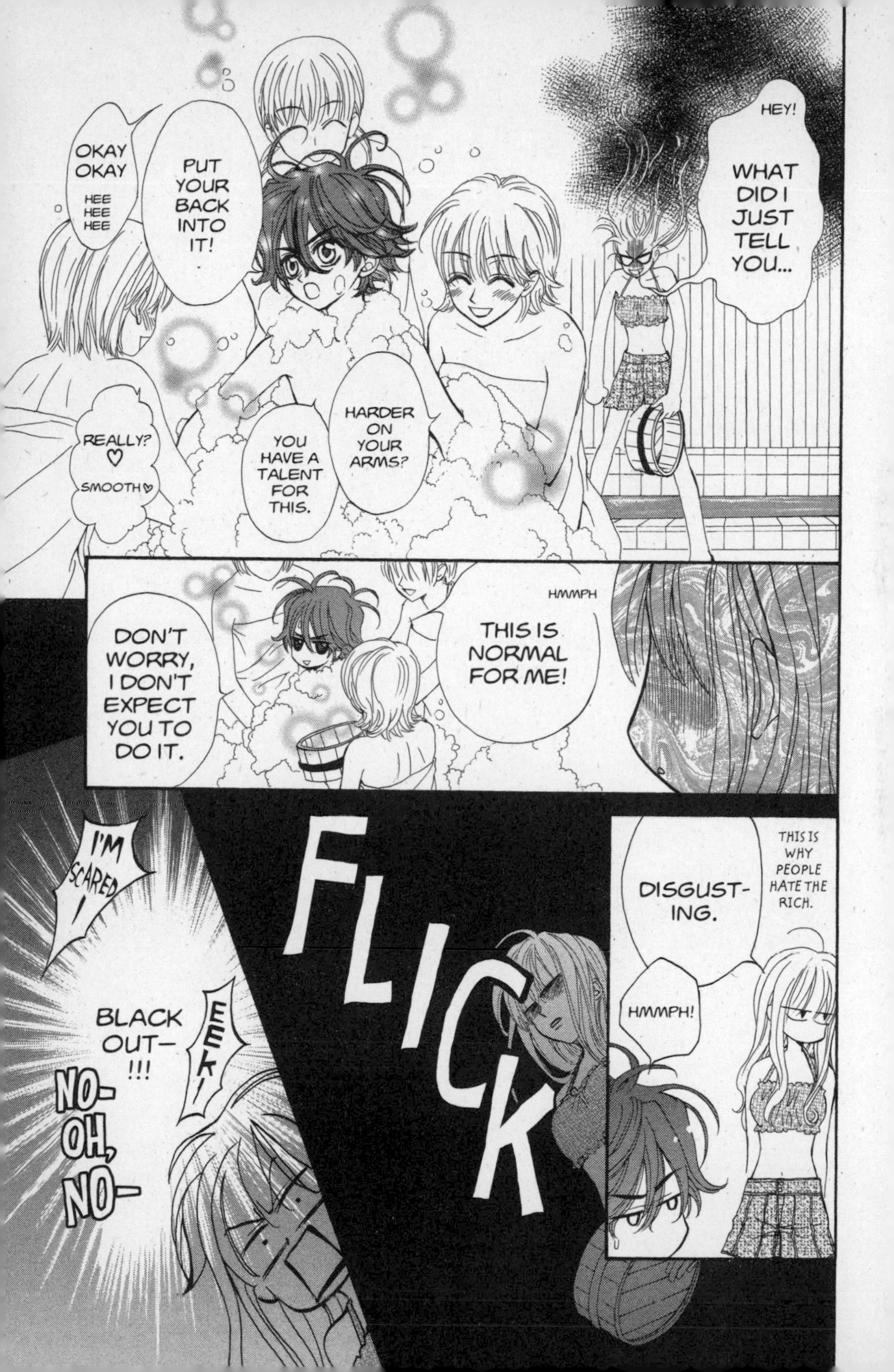
HEY!
WHAT DID I JUST TELL YOU...
PUT YOUR BACK INTO IT!
OKAY OKAY HEE HEE HEE
HARDER ON YOUR ARMS?
YOU HAVE A TALENT FOR THIS.
REALLY? ♥ SMOOTH♥
HMMPH
THIS IS NORMAL FOR ME!
DON'T WORRY, I DON'T EXPECT YOU TO DO IT.
THIS IS WHY PEOPLE HATE THE RICH.
DISGUST-ING.
HMMPH!
FLICK
I'M SCARED!
EEK!
BLACK OUT—!!!
NO-OH, NO-

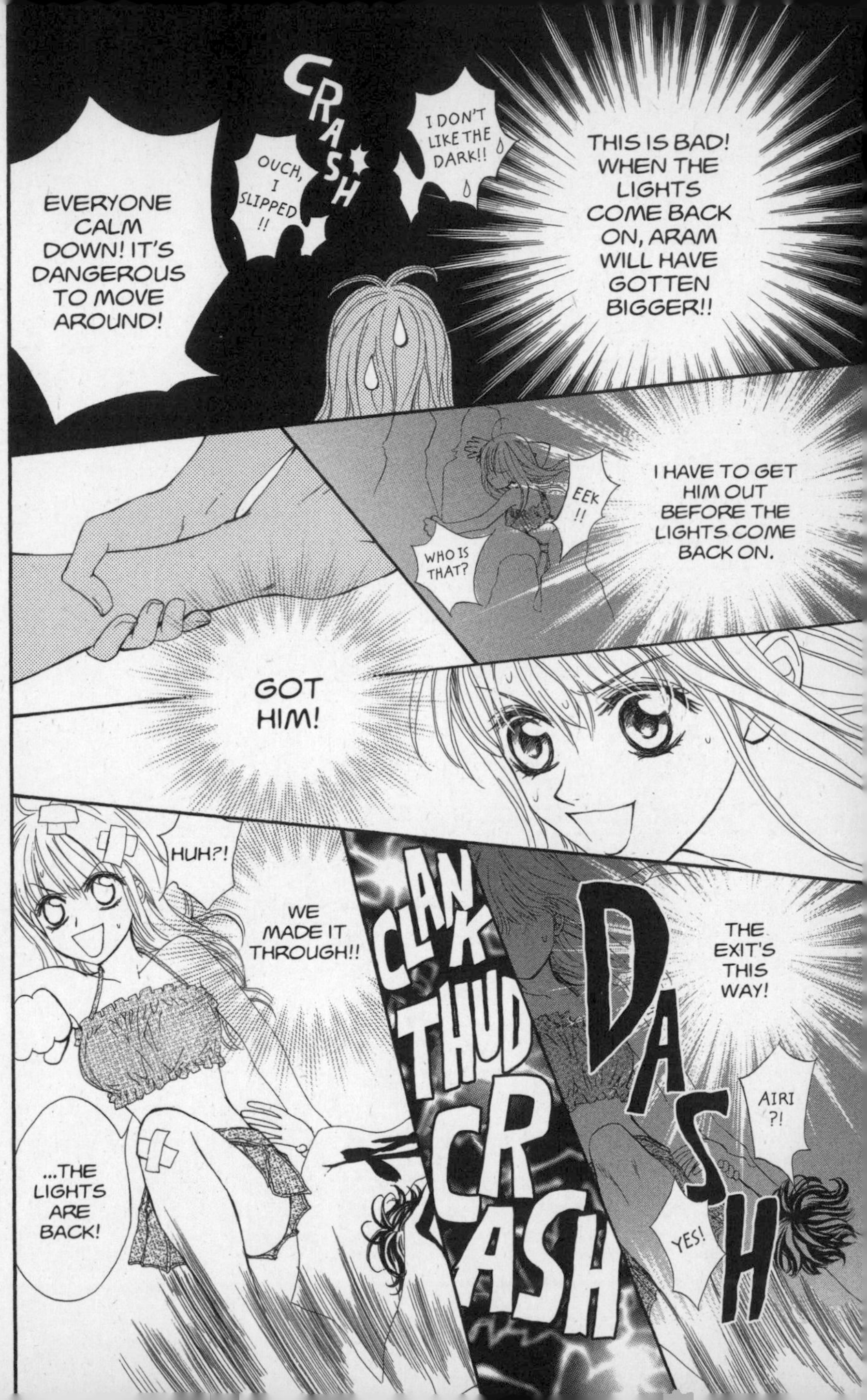
THIS IS BAD! WHEN THE LIGHTS COME BACK ON, ARAM WILL HAVE GOTTEN BIGGER!!
I DON'T LIKE THE DARK!!
CRASH
OUCH, I SLIPPED!!
EVERYONE CALM DOWN! IT'S DANGEROUS TO MOVE AROUND!
I HAVE TO GET HIM OUT BEFORE THE LIGHTS COME BACK ON.
EEK!!
WHO IS THAT?
GOT HIM!
THE EXIT'S THIS WAY!
DASH
AIRI?!
YES!
CLANK
THUD
CRASH
HUH?!
WE MADE IT THROUGH!!
...THE LIGHTS ARE BACK!

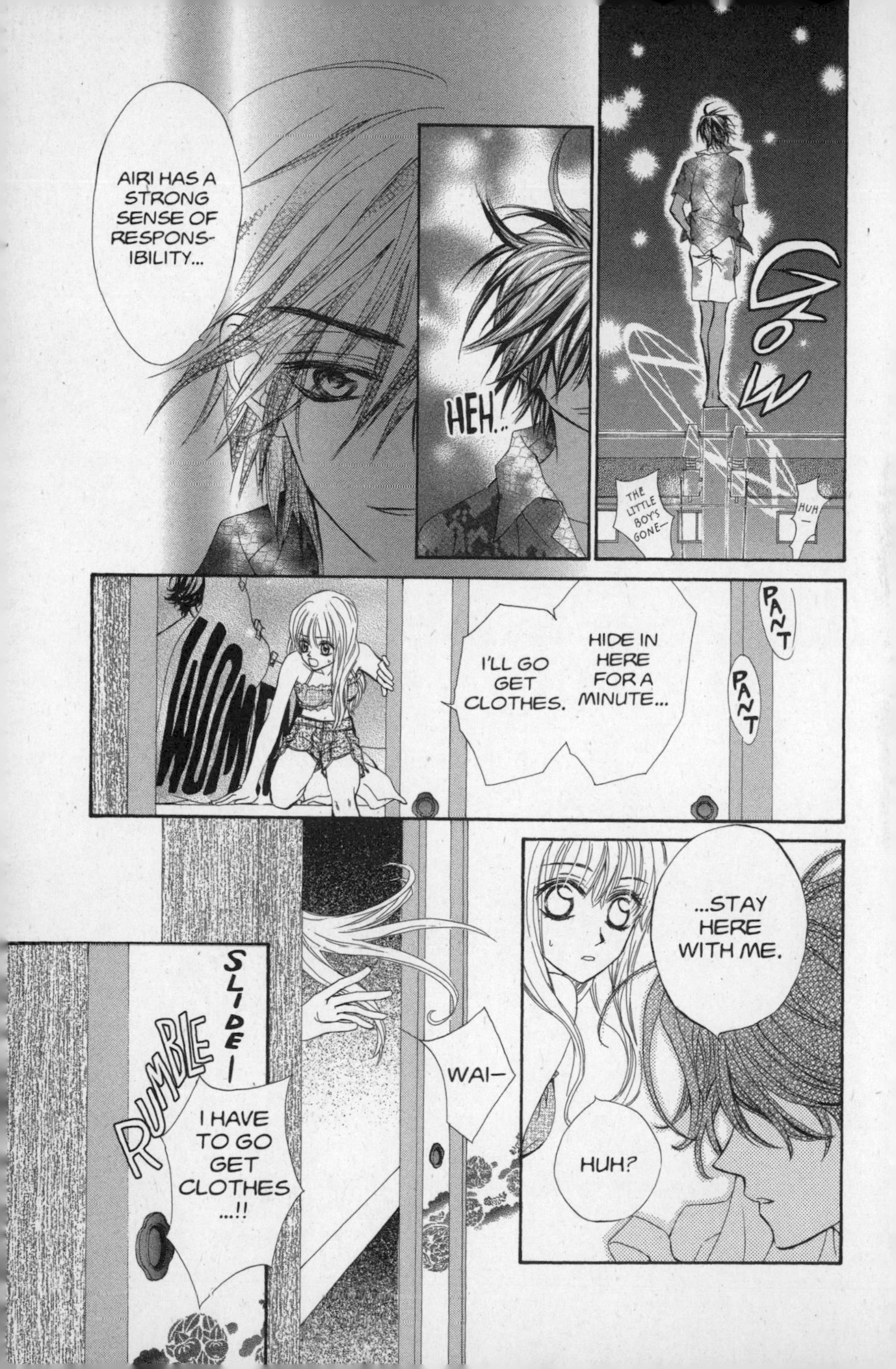
GLOW
HUH—
THE LITTLE BOY'S GONE—
HEH...
AIRI HAS A STRONG SENSE OF RESPONSIBILITY...
PANT
PANT
HIDE IN HERE FOR A MINUTE...
I'LL GO GET CLOTHES.
...STAY HERE WITH ME.
HUH?
WAI—
SLIDE
RUMBLE
I HAVE TO GO GET CLOTHES ...!!

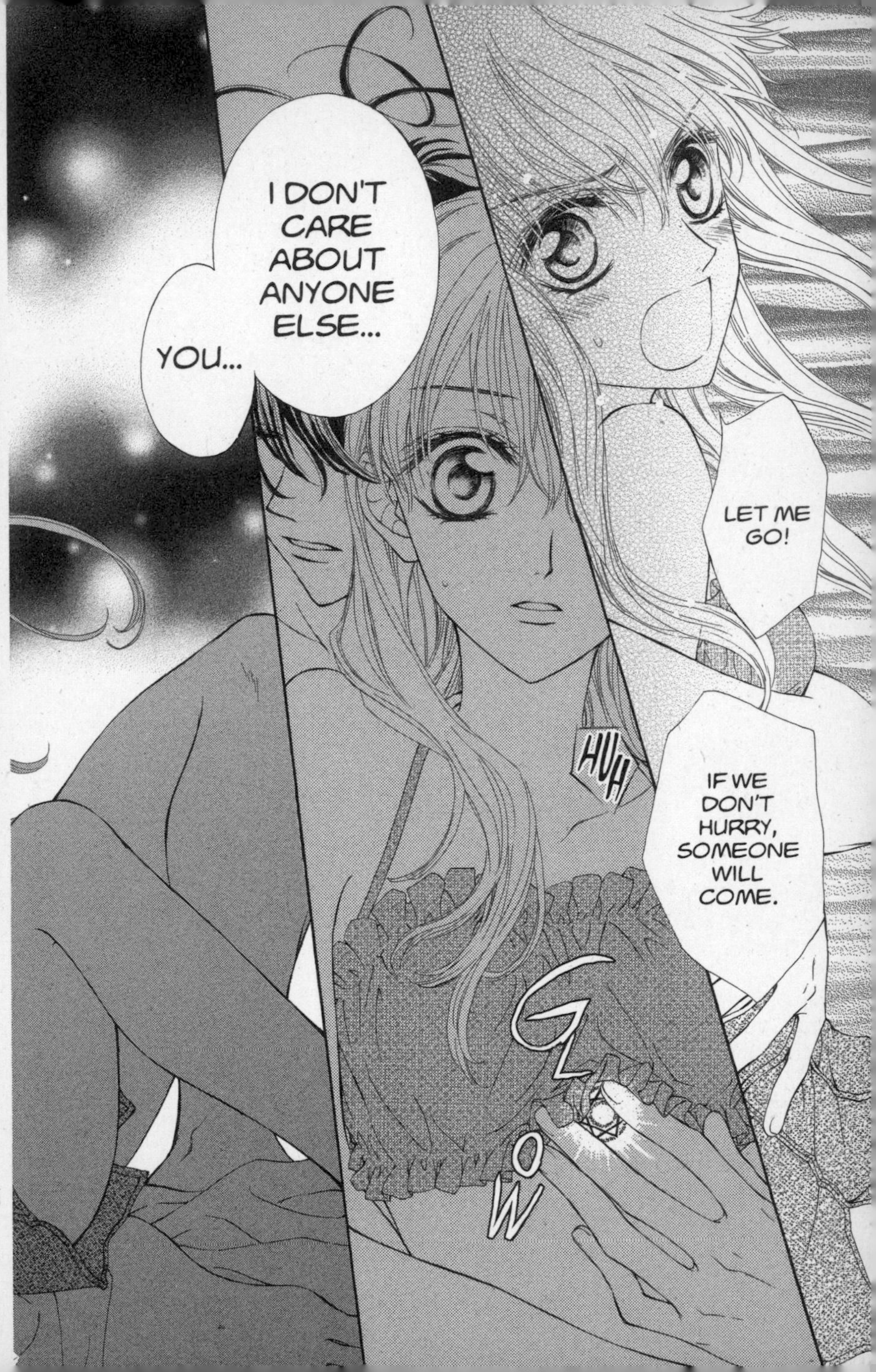
LET ME GO!
IF WE DON'T HURRY, SOMEONE WILL COME.
HUH
GLOW
I DON'T CARE ABOUT ANYONE ELSE...
YOU...

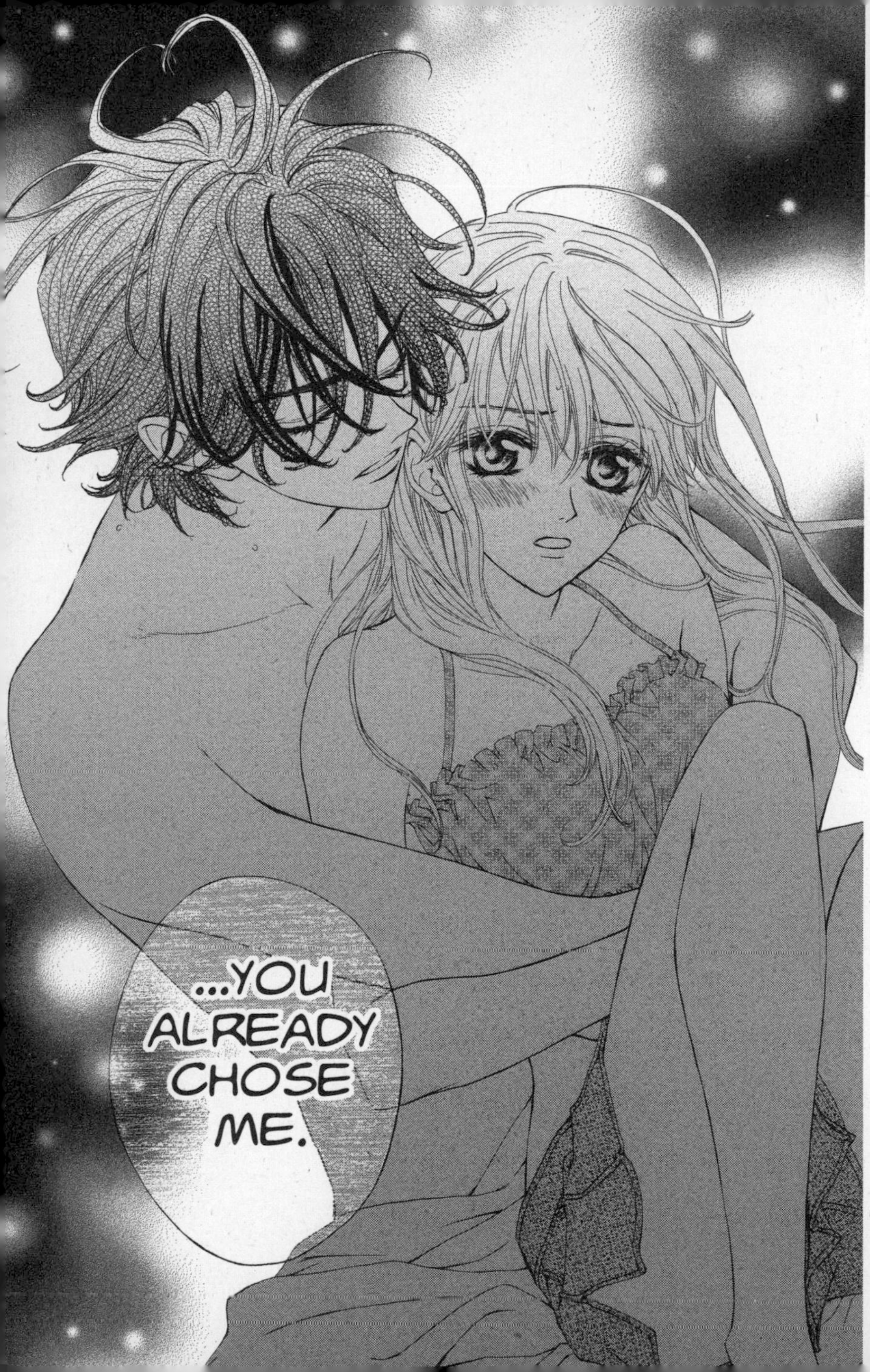
...YOU ALREADY CHOSE ME.

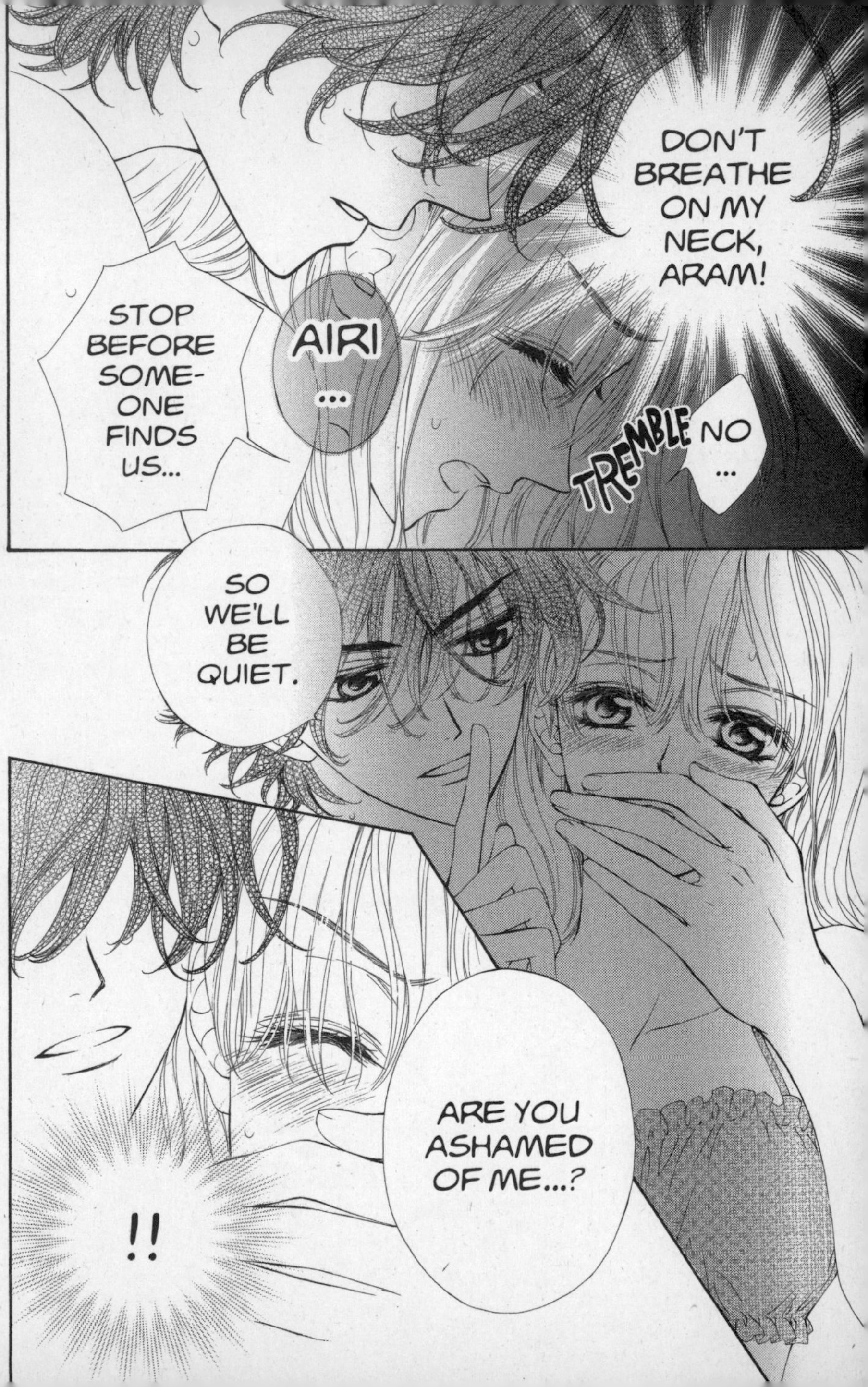
DON'T BREATHE ON MY NECK, ARAM!
TREMBLE
NO ...
AIRI ...
STOP BEFORE SOME-ONE FINDS US...
SO WE'LL BE QUIET.
ARE YOU ASHAMED OF ME...?
!!

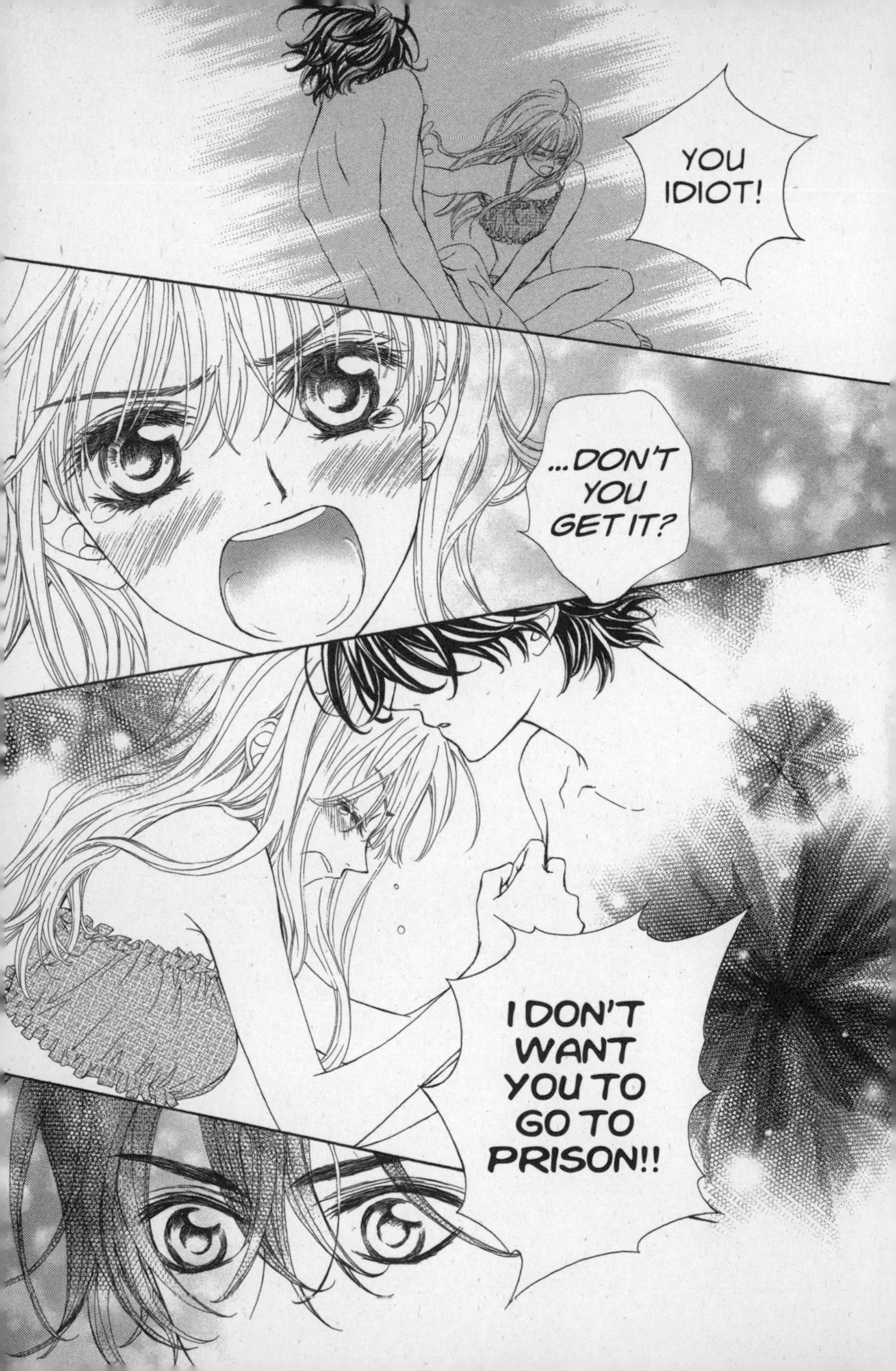
YOU IDIOT!
...DON'T YOU GET IT?
I DON'T WANT YOU TO GO TO PRISON!!

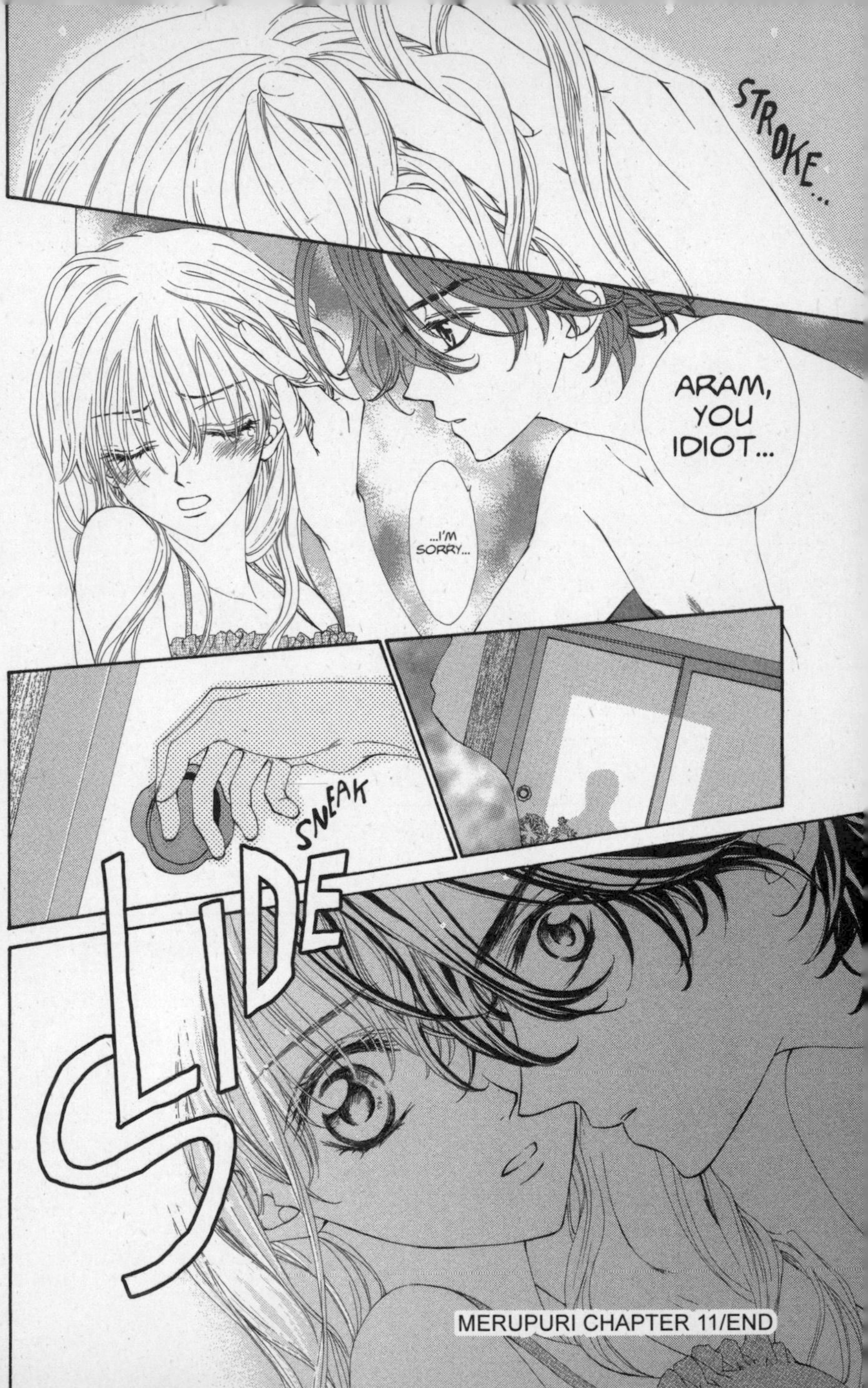
STROKE...
ARAM, YOU IDIOT...
...I'M SORRY...
SNEAK
SLIDE
MERUPURI CHAPTER 11/END

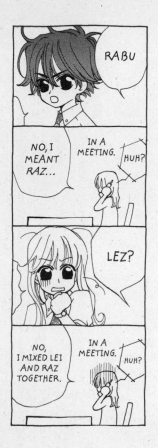

BONUS MANGA

3

THE SAY-THE-NAMES-WRONG CONTEST

RABU
HUH?
IN A MEETING.
NO, I MEANT RAZ...
LEZ?
HUH?
IN A MEETING.
NO, I MIXED LEI AND RAZ TOGETHER.

SIDE STORY
IN A MEETING.
THESE TWO ALWAYS GET MIXED UP.
WHEN ARAM KISSES HER, AIRI REVERTS TO HER SMALL FORM...

(➡)Such a cruel spot to end, isn't it?! Right now, I'm challenging myself to explore both little and big Aram in one chapter! I also want to include a two-page spread in every chapter from now on! I wonder how long I can keep this up...

Volume 1 moved too slowly, so I aimed for a rich, rapid development in Volume 2. I plan to keep up this pace now that we've hit it.

I also want to explore Airi as a heroine! And I want Aram to remain as pure as possible... Ha ha! Well, I don't want to disappoint the readers of MeruPuri either, so I'll do my best!

Thank you very much for your letters! Your letters are the root of my energy and inspiration—the core of MeruPuri's vigor—and I always receive them eagerly. I'll make an effort to reply to as many as possible!! Thank you!!

This has been Hino Matsuri—.

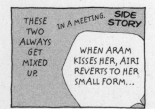

A former bookstore shopkeeper, **Matsuri Hino** burst onto the manga scene with her title *Kono Yume ga Sametara (When This Dream Is Over)*, which was published in *LaLa DX* magazine. Hino was a manga artist a mere nine months after she decided to become one.

With the success of her popular series *Toraware no Minoue (Captive Hearts)*, and *MeruPuri*, Hino has established herself as a major player in the world of shojo manga. Her new title, *Vampire Knight*, currently runs in *Monthly LaLa* magazine.

Hino enjoys creative activities and has commented that she would have been either an architect or an apprentice to traditional Japanese craft masters if she did not become a manga artist.

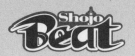

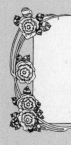

MERUPURI: MÄRCHEN PRINCE, VOLUME 2
The Shojo Beat Manga Edition

STORY AND ART BY
MATSURI HINO

English Adaptation/Kelly Sue DeConnick
Translation/Priscilla Yim
Touch-up Art & Lettering/Andy Ristaino
Design/Courtney Utt
Editor/Michelle Pangilinan

VP, Production/Alvin Lu
VP, Sales & Product Marketing/Gonzalo Ferreyra
VP, Creative/Linda Espinosa
Publisher/Hyoe Narita

A CIP catalogue record for this book is available from the British Library.

Printed in the U.S.A.

Published by VIZ Media, LLC
P.O. Box 77010
San Francisco, CA 94107

Shojo Beat Manga Edition
10 9 8 7 6 5 4
First printing, September 2005
Fourth printing, August 2009

Tell us what you think about Shojo Beat Manga!

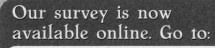

Our survey is now available online. Go to:

shojobeat.com/mangasurvey

Help us make our product offerings better!